I0188053

The Philosophy of Inequality

Letters to my Contemners, Concerning Social Philosophy

(1923)

****

Spirits of the Russian Revolution:

Gogol/Dostoevsky/L. Tolstoy

(1918)

Nicholas Berdyaev

Translated by Fr. S. Janos

The Philosophy of Inequality

ISBN: 978-0-9963992-0-3

Library of Congress Control Number: 2015941845

Printed in the United States of America

Printed on acid-free paper.

For information address:

frsj Publications
Fr. Stephen J. Janos
P.O. Box 210
Mohrsville, PA 19541

Contents

The Philosophy of Inequality

***

Spirits of the Russian Revolution

The Philosophy of Inequality

Letters to my Contemners, Concerning Social Philosophy

(1923, Berlin, Obelisk)

Klepinina # 20.

First Letter

Concerning the Russian Revolution

These letters, in which I want to sum up all my thoughts on social philosophy, I address directly to my despisers, people hostile to me in spirit, against me in the feel of life, alien in thought to me. I have many a non-friend, endlessly moreso, than friends, and they are quite varied, surrounding me round about on every which side. The very foremost of my non-friends -- these are the despisers of my faith, apostates from Christ in their spirit, betraying Him and rising up against Him in the name of earthly idols and gods. The world is entering upon such an arduous and answerable time, in which religiously there has to be exposed everything duplicitous, twofold, hypocritical and unenduring. It is not peace, but the sword that Christ has brought. And by the spiritual sword has to be a cleaving apart of the world into those standing for Christ and those standing against Christ. But this basic division cannot mechanically and externalistically be applied to the infinite complexity of life. In the Gospel is not that extent of revealedness and fullness, such as might allow unmediated an application of Gospel criteria to all vital values. Every vital value presents the human spirit a creative task. In the Gospel is given only the leavening for new life, only the seed of grain, from which will sprout forth the higher life of spirit, but it is impossible to see in it merely a collection of rules and commands. In the New Testament there is no positive revelation of a Christian societal structure. The problem of the relationship of Christianity and of societal structure -- is a complex creative problem, set facing the free human spirit; it does not permit of a simplistic and one-sided resolution. The problem of a Christian societal structuring always has been a great temptation both for true Christians, and for the enemies of Christianity. Bad use has been made of Christ and the Gospel for quite contrary ends. Those of the most extreme reactionism and the most extreme revolutionism are alike ready to justify themself as

Christian. It is quite indeed apparent, that the absoluteness of the Christian spirit cannot be so easily transformed into the relative aspect of the historical world. Always there remains the incommensurable. Alike mistaken are both those, who regard Christianity as felicitous to an absolute Caesarism, and those, who regard it as felicitous to anarchism. Christianity is not reactionary, just the same also as it is not revolutionary, and it is impossible to derive any sort of advantages for this world from it.

At present there triumph in the world those, who have desired to either completely overthrow Christianity, or to draw from it revolutionary advantages, advantages socialistic and anarchistic. Against these foes first of all my book is directed. I want to expose them, since in them is the coming danger and the approaching evil. The evil of the past, which is gone, dead or dying is less dangerous. The Anti-Christ is manifest in what is coming, his temptations -- are the coming temptations of mankind. In the old evil there was not this acutely ambiguous sense of temptation and twofold images of what approaches. There is not in the world a people, so subjected to these temptations of the ambiguous and twofold images of what is coming, as is my people, the Russian people. There is in the world no land, which could be so readily rendered the hearth and home of those temptations, as is my land -- Russia. You, who having poisoned the soul of the Russian people with a terrible poison, you, who have laid waste to Russia, it is to you that my letters are dedicated. Many of you, you -- a majority, you long ago have begun your work, gnawing at the spiritual foundations of the life of the Russian people, as the oppressed, with an innocent and exalted preaching of humane and progressive ideas. But soon began to be shown your true spirit, the spirit of non-being, and soon ye were transformed into oppressors. At first you were spiritual oppressors, you took dominion over the weak souls of the Russian intelligentsia, you became persecutors of all the higher spiritual life and declared boycott against all, who believed in the higher spiritual realities and spiritual values, who admitted the religious meaning of life and the religious value of life. You justified your persecution by that oppressed position, in which you were situated under the blundering politics of the old powers. But the hour ensued, when ultimately your nature shew itself, -- ye received the possibility to become material oppressors and ye created an unprecedented tyranny, threatening ultimately to annihilate the human image. Ye were always haters of freedom, always ye were quenchers of the human spirit, destroyers of the Divine. Always ye sold out man's birthright primacy for the lentil soup of transitory goods and temporal interests. Ye -- are exterminators of eternity, ye desired as though to rip out from the human heart the sense of eternity and the anguish for eternity. Through you this is a time, bringing death, waging a struggle against eternity. I long since already sensed this, long since already have contended against you in the measure of my strength. Now begin to recognise you even those, who earlier were tempted by your spirit, al those enlighteners, those progressivists and humanists, flitting about at the surface of life, not knowing evil, those pretty-souled ones innocently dreaming about the welfare of the people and about happiness on earth. We long since already have cautioned, long since already have disclosed, to what would lead out those paths, along which went the intelligentsia Russian society and upon which the Russian people have thrust. We have spoken about that terrible responsibility, which falls upon those holding power, upon the ruling classes, for doing almost nothing for the creative averting of this fateful collapse of Russia and the Russian people into the abyss. Let them now think back on the "Vekhi" anthology and appreciate it now more impartially.

The plan of this book was conceived within the elements of the Russian revolution. And I began to write it on the anniversary day of the revolution. Least of all did I intend to write some system of social philosophy. The time for such systems has already passed. I want to ascertain the spiritual foundations of societal thought, to provide that, what might be called an ontological psychology or phenomenology of the societal. The Russian revolution provides the inner impulses and inducements for such a work of thought. The revolution provides the vast setting and brings into sharp focus all the basic problems of social philosophy. It is not the revolution itself that sharpens and deepens thought. On the contrary, those making the revolution and swept up in its rush, thrown off onto the surface aspect, they likewise lose all capacity for distinctions and deep evaluations. These people are torn off from the depths, from all the wellsprings of spiritual life and are nowise capable of perception. But in the spiritual reaction against the revolution, of its inner signification thought becomes sharpened, perception becomes deepened and much now is discerned. There are those, who think, that revolution -- is something religious, and that the Russian revolution -- is religious predominantly, that in it is born the new man, and a new consciousness revealed. Such a playing at juxtaposition of revolution and religion, such a veiling over of the revolutionary element with the pompous attire of a religious phraseology, such a mystical idealisation of it, is spiritual a profligacy. The judgemental prosaicness of the genuine revolutionaries, those making the revolution, and not those poeticising and mystifying it from the sidelines, is a thousand times both better and worse. When the romantic, the lyrical poet began to sing hymns to the ragings of the revolution and to write verses, justifying all its wicked deeds, he laid bare merely the dissolution within his own soul, having lost every distinction between truth and falsehood, between realities and apparitions, and has committed a betrayal of the Spirit. You, the people of spirit and spiritual creativity, called to be "preservers of mystery and faith", when you passively and impotently yield to the prevailing elements, when ye connive with the raging blackness, threatening the greatest sanctities and values, when ye find not a single strong word in defense of eternity and the higher life of spirit, ye make of yourselves a pitiful and wanton spectacle. In such a terrible and responsible hour of life's tribulations, when there is manifest the specific gravity of all human thoughts and words, of all human beliefs and hopes, ye shew yourselves spiritually incapable and desolate, having lost all criteria of spirit, of you is not manifest words of your own, gained from the spiritual experience of a communing with eternity. Ye have conversed with foreign words, and the noise of the streets and squares is felt in your sayings and articles. Ye have not proven of knightly fidelity and chivalrant nobility, you prove to be but plebians of spirit. Ye have forgotten the eternal distinction between the knights of spirit and the rabble. In you was never the strength of spirit, ye never gained yourself the gifts of spirit. Ye -- are weak, bereft of will, duplicitous people, incapable of total choosing of an object of love, of its truth, its rightness and beauty. If your beauty, your rightness, your truth should depend upon the wafting of the winds, upon the raging of the elements, upon the noise and din of the streets, of the squares and roadways, then with you there is no beauty, there is no rightness and no truth, ye are but beggars unarmed in the hour of battle, unprepared for war. Yet some of you have loved to say, that a man ought to forge himself armour of bronze, get cuirass and helmet, and take up shield and spear. Where indeed have ye displayed knightly arms in the hour of battle, in the terrible hour of the fateful dueling of contrary spirits? Ye have proven weak and wavering, like unto a reed, unarmed and defenseless. From out of a meanness of spirit ye have begun to plot together a justification of your weakness afront the dark powers, of your caving in to the spirits of darkness. But ye have deceived no one. Ye have but disgraced the dignity of the Russian writer, the Russian poet, the Russian thinker. Your names I shall not name, what interests me at present is the aspects of spirit, and not individual people with their weaknesses, with their riddled fate. revolutions never have been and never can be religious. Revolution, every revolution, is by its nature anti-religious, and vile are all its religious justifications. But revolution on the large scale can have a religious significance, in it one can see signs of the Providence of God, of the "fated sentence pronounced by God". This significance and these signs I see also in the most anti-religious of all revolutions, in the Russian Revolution.

The revolution is a chastisement sent down from above for the sins of the past, the fateful consequences of the old evil. Thus too having tended to look at the French Revolution are those, who the more deeply have penetrated into its meaning, getting beyond the surface aspects of it. For J. de Maistre [1753-1821] the revolution was a mystical fact, he regarded it as providential, sent down from above for the sins of the past. Carlyle [1795-1881], having written the finest history of the revolution, saw in it the consequences of non-belief, the loss of the organic centre of life, the punishment for sins. Revolution -- is the end of the old life, and not the beginning of a new life, the payback for prolonged a going off the path. In revolution are expiated the sins of the past. Revolution always tells of this, that those possessing power have not fulfilled their destiny. And the culpability for revolution of the governing levels of society is this, that they have brought about the revolution, they have permitted its possibility. Within society have been sickness and rot, which too have made revolution inevitable. This is true also in regard to the old regime, preceeding the Russian revolution. At the top there did not transpire creative developement, there shone no light, and therefore the darkness burst through from below. Thus it always occurs. This -- is a law of life. What preceeds revolutions is a process of dissolution, the collapse of faith, the loss within society and the people of an unifying spiritual centre to life. It is not constructive and creative processes that lead to revolutions, but rather processes of rot and decay. The sense of love, bursts of creativity and acts constructive, never lead to revolutions. Upon every revolution lies the mark of a lack of grace, of God-forsakenness and a curse. The people, having fallen under the grip of the revolutionary element, loses its spiritual freedom, becomes subject to a fateful law, it undergoes a sickness, running its irreversible course, and becomes obsessed and demonic. It is already no longer people that think and act, but beyond them and in them it is someone and something that thinks and acts. It seems to the people, that it becomes free in revolutions, but this -- is a terrible delusion. It -- is the slave of dark elements, it is led about by inhuman elemental spirits. In revolution there is not and cannot become freedom, revolution is always hostile to the spirit of freedom. In the element of revolution dark urges overwhelm a man. In the element of revolution there is no place for person, for individuality, in it always prevail impersonal principles. By revolution man is not rendered as the image and likeness of God, revolution is wrought upon man, it happens with a man, like a sickness happens, or a misfortune, an elemental woe, like a conflagration or flood happens. In revolution the popular mass element becomes a phenomenon of nature, like thunderstorms, floods and fires, and not a manifestation of the human spirit. The image of man always becomes muddled in revolution, submerged by the surges of the elemental darkness underlying being. That luminous circle, which with such tremendous effort takes form in the process of history and becomes ascendant over the inimical darkness, in the element of revolution becomes inundated by the bad infinity of an unrestrainable darkness. The Dionysian element overthrows every Apollonian principle, every form and boundary, every face and image, connected with form and limit. It is naive to think, that a people, having fallen under the grip of the law of the revolutionary element, having entered into the magic circle of revolution, can be guided by the more reasonable, the enlightened and moderate currents, the Girondists or Cadets. No, in revolutions it is invariably the domain of the Jacobins or Bolsheviks. The sickness has to run its course, the poison has to eradicate itself. To guide revolutions is impossible. And it is in vain for you, making the revolution and glorifying in it, it is vain for you to think, that you are guiding it, that you are directing and constructing it. O, how naive, how dismal and impotent ye are, in thinking that ye are free, that the spirit of freedom acts within you, that you are active, that you are mighty. No, ye are -- mere powerless and passive slaves, slaves of dark passions, mere tools of the dark elements. You, the Bolsheviks, the maximalists, anarchists etc., -- you -- are the most passive of people, spiritually stagnant, incapable of resistance to the elements, incapable of intensity of soul, in the grip of energies, situated outside you. Your face is not visible and ye have no visage. Ye -- are but a medium of faceless elements, in you speak strange voices, and in these voices it is impossible to distinguish the human voice, and heard only is the noise and the roar of the elemental natural forces. In vain do you, ye people of the revolution, think, that you -- represent new souls, that within you is born the new man. Ye -- represent the old souls, in you ends the old man with his old sins and inabilities. All your negative feelings -- malice, resentment, rage -- fetter you to the old life and make you slaves of the past. Ye -- represent a passive reflex to the evil of the past, and ye cannot free yourself of it. But ye have no memory of the good of the past, about the imperishable truth and beauty in it, ye lack memory of the creative and resusciative.

Was Robespierre a new soul, a new man? No, he was to the depths of his being the old man, a man of the old regime, full of the old violent instincts. The French Revolution was made by people of the old soul, and they carried over into it all the old sins and passions. The new soul was born later, after the deep spiritual reaction against the revolution, when Chateaubriand wrote his "Rene" and "The Genius of Christianity". Then began a new era, inwardly distinct from the two preceeding centuries. The new man was born in the Catholic and romantic reaction. This is vouched for in the most positively credible of histories. In vain do you, the makers of the revolution, in the grip of its demons, in vain do ye think, that ye -- are creative people and that your deeds -- are creative deeds. In vain ye do think, that epochs of revolution -- are creative epochs within the life of mankind. Ye are people, completely bereft of creative spirit, cut off from it, hating and destroying creativity. Because indeed creativity -- is something aristocratic, it is a deed of the finest, it does not tolerate the grip of the worst, the rule of the mob, whom ye serve. Is there creative a spirit in Robespierre or in Lenin? Have they not exterminated every creative impulse? Creativity does not endure equality, it demands inequality, an uplift, it does not permit of glancing about at neighbours, so as not to outpace them. The spirit of revolution, the spirit of the people of the revolution hates and eradicates genius and the sacred, it is in the grip of black envy towards the great and towards the sublime, it is intolerant of qualities and always thirsts to drown them in the quantitative. Never within an epoch of revolution did there blossom forth spiritual creativity, nor happen a religious and cultural rebirth, nor happen the flourishing of "science and the arts". The measure of revolution -- is flatness, and not depth. In revolutions there is no genuine inward motion. Revolution signifies the remaining remnant of inward motion. Revolution represents merely external dynamics, whereas inwardly it is static. Revolutions have no appreciation for people of spiritual stirring and spiritual creativity; they make outcasts of these people, often they hate them and always regard them as unnecessary for their doings. Your stormy outward motions, ye people of revolution, ought not to lead you into delusion. In these motions is but an inescapable vicious circle. Within this circle play out wanton passions. The movement of a revolution always tends to destroy itself, it does not lead to new life. This is not a movement into the depths, this is merely movement along the superficial surface. And along the surface it spreads about, like a flame. Go into the depths, ye people of revolution, and all your furious motions, all your cruelties and all your fabricated noise will cease. Then will begin also in you, ye people of the surface aspect of life, true movement, then, perhaps, for you also will open up the possibility of creativity. The principle of inward movement, the principle of creativity, of a spiritual deepening signifies an end to revolution, a beginning of reaction. The kettle of revolution boils away. And there becomes apparent the need of deeply thinking over the experiment of revolution, to conceive of the tragic contradictions of life.

Revolution by its nature is non-spiritual. Revolution is born of the decrease, the waning of spiritual life, and not of its upsurge, not of its inward growth. The faces of people, caught up in the revolution, tell about the downfall of spiritual life. the expressions of these faces is frightfully non-spiritual, and it is already rendered a judgement against revolution. Your faces express malice and obsession, upon them it is impossible to detect any profound thoughts, or noble feelings. Your visages lack for any spiritual inspiration, and in them is sensed a falling to the very bottom of the material world. Revolution denies the significance of spiritual life. The ideology of revolution takes its lead from the external and material and defines everything by it, and not from the inward and spiritual. And therefore never can people of spirit approve of your revolutions, they have their own sort of revolutions unknowable to you. Revolution of spirit has nothing in common with your outwardly material, political and social revolutions. Marx was never a revolutionary of spirit. The revolutionary of spirit was Nietzsche. But what does he have in common with your external outward revolutions? He had contempt for them as a mere plebian uprising. In Dostoevsky there was a revolutionary of spirit. But ye always regarded him s a conservative and reactionary. And what do the prophetic insights of Vl. Solov'ev have to do with you, what has he to do with you? Everything, which was spiritually significant within the history of Russian thought and Russian creativity in the XX Century, was not with you, was against you. The greatest phenomenon of Russian culture -- Pushkin -- was not yours. Ye mocked and denounced him, ye compared him to an open pot and boots. Even L. Tolstoy had no love for you and condemned your doings. With you have been merely people second or third rate, not one thought of genius has been born in your midst, nor emerged from you, from your giftless grey spirit. Ye -- the people of revolution -- are people of the spiritual average and mediocrity, people of mediocre, grey, mass-popular thoughts. And your rage -- is the rage of the grey masses, envious in soul of everything grand, everything of glory, everything of genius. Dostoevsky with genius grasped your nature and prophetically predicted, to what you would arrive. Only in a condition of complete blindness and obsession could one compare and confuse your revolutions with revolutions of spirit. Revolution of spirit is born of a deep inner reaction against your revolutions, against your denial of everything of spirit. Ye -- the quenchers of spirit, ye -- are the blackest of reactionaries in the deepest meaning of this word. Ye always were quenchers of thought, and the inertia of your thought is terrible, it gives the impression of a stone-like immobility. Always ye have persecuted religion, philosophy, poetry, the aesthetics of life. Your revolutions make not for the better, but for the worse, while grasping at revolution and attempting to gain from them are all those considering themself unfortunate and downtrodden, all the angry ones, all the stepsons of God, and not the sons of God. Revolutions are born not from the noble consciousness of guilt by the sons of God, but rather from the ignoble consciousness of outrage by the sons of dust.

All revolutions end by reactions. This -- is inevitable. This -- is a law. And howsoever the more furious and raging have been the revolutions, stronger then become the reactions. In the alternate turns of revolution and reaction there is something of a vicious circle. Much of the murky happens in reactions, -- in them is the same rage and vindictiveness, as is also in revolutions. And you, ye people of pure reaction, ye are not capable of rising above the flat-plane movement left and right, above the contrary opposites of revolution and reaction, and ye are likewise incapable to see the truth more fully, more at a distance. Often ye become quite the converse side in likeness to revolutionaries. But after the raging shock of the revolution the reaction is inevitable, there is in it its own truth, distended in the dark human element. Ye, the people of a banal and stale revolutionary consciousness, have become accustomed to employ the word "reaction" within the superficial meaning of the word, exclusively in the negative sense. Ye contrast "reaction" against everything progressive, creative, everything of growth and movement. For you reaction is a standing still or movement backwards, a return to that which was before the revolution. This -- is incorrect. In reactions there is a different depth. Reaction can be also creative, in it can be also a genuine inner movement towards new life, towards new values. And sometimes reaction is not a return simply to the old life. In every spiritual reaction to revolution is revealed something new, unknown to the old world, creative thoughts are begotten. There is begotten a third something, distinct both from that which was in the revolution, and from that which was before the revolution. In this third thing there is discerned something new, hitherto non-existent. In experiencing the clash of two worlds the awareness is sharpened, thought is quickened, providing a new feel to life. This is shown by the spiritual reaction in the France of the early XIX Century against the revolution. I advise you also, ye ideologues of the revolution, to study this spiritual movement and carefully consider its instructive meaning. The chief significance, perhaps, of the French revolution mustneeds be seen in this, that at the beginning XIX Century it provoked both the Catholic movement and the Romantic movement, thus making the thought of the XIX Century all the more fruitful. The appearance of J. de Maistre was most remarkable a result of the French revolution, more remarkable than the appearance of Marat and Robespierre within the revolution. The "progressive", the creative significance of the ideas of J. de Maistre have begun to be acknowledged by the most positive and objective histories of the thought of the XIX Century. In the depths of his spirit he underwent the terrible experience of the revolution, and from this occurred the deepening of the whole of Catholic thought. J. de Maistre was already the new sort of man, a man from-revolution, and not pre-revolutionary. He condemned the French emigrants and their external restoration intents. And all the whole of the French Catholicism of the XIX Century was a new, a from-revolution Catholicism, much deepened in comparison to the Catholicism of the XVII and XVIII Centuries. The "reactionary" J. de Maistre went so far, that he even allowed for the possibility of a new revelation, a revelation of the Holy Spirit. There was likewise a new, a from-revolution phenomenon in also the Christian romanticism of Chateaubriand. The reorientation of the "reactionaries" of the beginning XIX Century back towards the past and the searching out of its roots in the Middle Ages was a creative reorientation and a creative searching. The rationalistic Enlightenment, having undermined the spiritual foundations of the life of the French people and having infected also the whole of Catholicism, was defeated in the creative spiritual reaction of the early XIX Century. And after this creative victory any return to the rationalistic Enlightenment would have to be reconsidered, as reaction-thought in the most negative sense of the word. The Catholics and the romantics of the era of the spiritual reaction against the French revolution and against the negative enlightenmentism -- are our spiritual grandfathers. Since that time our thought our manner of thought has become all the more alert, more complex and enriched by new experiences, but in spirit they are nigh close to us, while foreign to us are those, who trace their geneology from Voltaire or from Diderot. It is with joy that I should repeat the words of Montalembert: "We are grandsons of the crusaders and we yield not to the seeds of Voltaire". But ye however, ye people of the revolution of the present day, ye have no forebears, ye are people without lineage, since descent from Robespierre or from Marx shews not a creditable lineage. The revolutionary ideology cannot be termed profound, it does not know its ancient sources, and it is doomed to be superficial. Nowise profound within the ideology of revolution is that rationalistic denial of the evil, lodged within the nature of man and in the nature of the world, nowise profound is that optimistic outlook on the future. The revolutionary rift between the future and the past can only be a splitting away of the surface aspect from the depths, a departing the spiritual centre of life. Revolutionism is always a splitting apart between the sons and their fathers as regards hypostasis, a denying of paternity, i.e. an affirmation of death and decay in place of eternal life. Within your outwardly external revolutions is violated the eternal hierarchical principle, the principle of organic connection, i.e. a denial of the Divine world-order.

The Russian revolution possesses the typical fateful features, characteristic to all revolutions. within it are evident those same elements, which are revealed in all revolutions, and over it rules the fate, ruling over all revolutions. All the major revolutions have had their own inevitable coursing, all had their ragings, hatreds and revenges, in all the revolutions prevailed the extreme currents, in all the revolutions freedom was negated and the image of man distorted. Naive and blind among you have been those, who created for themselves illusions about the revolution and presented it as idyllic. Revolutions are not idyllic, never have there been revolutions pretty and fine, never have there triumphed in them the best sides of human nature. All revolutions have aroused the dark and evil element in man, the ancient chaos. Never have there been revolutions based upon reason. Never have they brought joy nor have they provided that liberation, about which prior generations dreamt. Never within history has there come about, what they had dreamt to expect. And in the Russian revolution, as also in every historical event, there are unrepeatably individual particularities. This involves a particularity of a people, unlike any other one people in the world, and the particularity of historical settings, unlike any other settings formerly before the revolution. The Russian revolution is an event resulting from the world war. It is an episode of the world war. And this revolution involves first of all one sad and humiliating fact for the Russian people: the Russian people did not hold up under the great tribulation of the war. All the nations took part in the world war with such whatever spiritual and material baggage, which they had accumulated over the course of their long history. The Russian people has proven bankrupt. It has proven to have a weakly developed sense of honour. But it is not the masses of the people that is at fault in this, the blame lies deeper. And it is not about the connection of the revolution with the war that I want to speak about now. I want to speak about the peculiarities of the Russian people and about the effects of these peculiarities upon the Russian revolution. The Russian people is incomprehensible to the Western peoples. Incomprehensible for them is also the Russian revolution. The whole texture of the Russian nature is different from the texture of the Western nature.

The Russian people is not a Western European people, and it -- to a large degree is an Asiatic Eastern people. The soul of the Russian people -- is a complex and tangled soul, within it have clashed and intermixed two currents of world history, the Eastern and the Western. And these two currents in the soul of the Russian people have not been organically reworked into a totally complete character, into a single will and a single reasoning. All of you, having appropriated for yourself the summits of Western thought, yet never having penetrated into its secrets, ye Russian intelligentsia, in which the unenlightened Eastern element is combined with a superficial Western consciousness, ye remain still incapable of an act of self-consciousness, and ye are powerless to grasp the mystery of Russia. Neither the Westernisers nor the Slavophils could comprehend the mystery of the Russian soul. In order to understand this mystery, it is necessary to become something third, it is necessary to rise above the opposition of the two principles Eastern and Western, and the two outlooks -- the Slavophil and the Westerniser, it is necessary to know the East not only as regards the gloomy experiences of the Eastern element, and also the West -- not only as regards the superficial Western consciousness. An acuity of knowledge is engendered by a transition over into a third from the two opposites. Russia is a great and entire East-West as regards God's plan, and it is a failed and mixed-up East-West as regards the fact of its condition, as regards its empirical condition. Ye, as revolutionaries, -- Easterners as regards your element and Westerners as regards teachings, ye have made a mess of God's great design for Russia, ye have impeded the transforming of the two elements and the two principles into an higher fullness, a genuine all-humanity. The mystery of the soul of Russia and the Russian people, the enigma of all our ills and sufferings -- is in the unnecessary, the false correlation of the masculine and feminine principles. In the secret matters of Russia, in the soul of the Russian people has not happened the inner marriage, the marital uniting between the masculine and feminine principles, there has not been realised the androgynous image. The masculine spirit has not united organically with the feminine soul of Russia, has not taken hold inwardly with the element of the people. In Russia there has not occurred that which occurred in England, in Germany, in all the peoples of the West. There to a certain degree of developement in nationally unique form was awakened the masculine spirit and inwardly, organically it gave form to the element of the people. The Russian earth has remained totally feminine, everything was as though betrothed, everything awaited the bridegroom aside. It was swayed by many a man, arriving from the sidelines, but never did there occur from this a true marriage. The Russian people from its own loins never could give birth to a masculine power, it sought it from the sidelines, it invited the Varangians or German dignitaries. The Russian church and the Russian state were organised and maintained with Byzantine principles. The Russian element itself however -- is khlysty-like, pagan-Dionysian and counter-cultural. The collapse of the Byzantine principles has opened up the danger of the collapse also of the whole of Russia. In the construct of the Great Russian state, now shattered and divided, there was something strained, something unhealthy, a non-normal attitude of the people towards power. The people needed to have a power over them and they sensed the foreignness of the ruling power. The people was powerless, anarchistic, and the people upheld and gave sanction to a power autocratic and unbounded. The lack of developement within Russia of societal classes and estates and the quite exceptional developement of the bureaucratic principle was also from a deficient masculinity in the people, of a masculine activeness and self-initiative. The Russian autocracy, a phenomenon original to Russian life, is to be explained by the exclusive femininity of the Russian soul. A manifestation of the masculine in the Russian state was Peter. But Peter was not so much a man, as rather a man of violence. He violated the feminine soul of the Russian people. A legitimate marriage of Russian masculinity and Russian femininity was not accomplished even through him. Part of the people regarded Peter as the Anti-Christ. And then the people meekly submitted to the German bureaucratic principle, introduced by Peter. Peter dragged Russia to the rack, and he called Russia to a great future. But in the feminine Russian soul there remained a dull dissatisfaction to the call of Peter, and it passed over into discontent. For whole centuries the Russian intelligentsia prepared the abolishing and destroying of the deed of Peter. The schism-like split in the soul of Russia remained insurmountable and led to a terrible catastrophe, to the downfall of Russia as a great state. within Russian history there was no chivalrant knighthood, and therefore Russia did not pass through a tempering and discipline of person, through a culture of personal honour.

In Russian spiritual life, in Russian spiritual culture there was always that same strained and sickly correlation between the masculine and the feminine principle, which was also in the life of the Russian state. Spiritually the Russian people became too subject to the Byzantium foreign to it, and this submission distorted much in its soul. The oppressive weight of Byzantinism lay heavily upon Russian life. And under this pressure there awakened, stormed and trembled the Russian khlysty element. Within Russian Orthodoxy itself there was this peculiar inorganic admixture of Byzantinism and khlystyism. Russian Orthodoxy -- is an original phenomenon of the Russian spirit, it is very distinct from the Greek. I speak here not about the Universal Church, having lodged within it one singular truth, I speak about the unique religiosity of the Russian people. The Russian people received a different religious upbringing than the peoples of the West. The Russian people was raised religiously in the cult of the saints and sanctity. The Orthodox Church gave the Russian people the possibility to carry out its grievous historical lot. But the Orthodox religious upbringing did not provide that tempering of the person, that self-discipline of the soul and culture of the soul, which was provided in the West by the Catholic religious upbringing, and the Protestant also in its own way. Catholicism armoured the soul, it provided the soul firm features and clear, crystalline criteria of good and evil. The crystalline clarity of Catholicism fortified the soul, but it also however veiled away the unbounded and infinite perspectives, and rendered it insufficiently sensitive to mystical wisps. The Russian soul has remained in the boundlessness, it did not sense boundaries and it was rendered indistinct. Dark elements beset the Russian soul and dominate it, not meeting resistance. Therefore the Russian soul is receptive to spirits, to which the Western soul is little susceptive. This can be termed an apocalyptic aspect of the Russian soul. But for historical life, for the creation of culture, Orthodoxy did not provide Russian man the upbringing. The Western religious upbringing even after the falling-away from faith retained a strong residue in the form of norms of culture, the virtues of civilisation. The soul of Russian man after a falling-away from faith falls instead under the grip of nihilism. The Frenchman becomes a dogmatist or sceptic; the German -- a mystic or criticist; the Russian -- an apocalyptic or nihilist. The most difficult lot -- is the lot of the Russian soul. It is possible to build a culture whether dogmatic or sceptical, mystical or critical. But apocalypsis and nihilism -- is the end of everything. Neither apocalypsis, nor nihilism admit of a middle realm of culture. And therefore for Russian man it becomes so difficult for a participation in the historical process, and the creativity of culture. He desires that all the sooner everything should come to an end or else become nothing. The Russian popular element alike finds its expression both in the Black Hundredism, and in Bolshevism. the extreme right and the extreme left among us become conjoined, as one and the same dark element, the same jumble of an unconsciousness and distorted apocalypsis with nihilism.

Russia was a dark peasant realm, headed by the tsar. And this immense realm was covered over by a very thin cultural stratum. The idea of the tsar held enormous significance for the discipline of soul of the Russian people. The tsar was the spiritual mortar of the Russian people, he entered organically into the religious upbringing of the people. Without the tsar unthinkable to the people was any sort of state, any sort of law, any sort of order, any sort of submission to the common whole. Without the tsar, for the enormous masses of the Russian people, Russia would collapse and be transformed into an ant-hill. The tsar prevented the atomisation of Russia, he held the anarchy in check. The tsar indeed guarded the cultural segment from the onrush of the people's darkness, which had no need of higher culture. Either the tsar, or total anarchy -- between these poles vacillated the thought of the people. With the tsar was connected also churchly discipline. When the idea of the tsar was brought forth from the soul of the people, the soul let go, there vanished every discipline, every safeguard, for everything seemed sufficient. That which had been created by the long history of the people and which had been bound up deeply with its spiritual life, could not be changed so quickly. Towards all this all tended to relate quite thoughtlessly, not only you, the Russian revolutionaries, socialists, anarchists, nihilists, but also quite many of us. The feminine and passive soul of the Russian people underwent a shock, when became lost from it the disciplinising masculine idea of the tsar. Orthodoxy over the course of many a century had inculcated into the Russian people a religious submissiveness to the tsar. But Orthodoxy did not inculcate the self-initiative and self-discipline of the people. Here is one of the reasons for our tragedy. This mustneeds be admitted irregardless of whatever the political ideal we confess.

You, the intelligentsia Russian little-boys, about whom Dostoevsky so well wrote, feminine in your nature, ye always sought a spiritual marriage from the sidelines. Ye never were able to manifest a masculine spirit from within, from your own depths, ye borrowed it from the West, in Western masculine teachings. In your depths always there stirred the Russian, the Eastern chaos. But with great frenzy ye appropriated for yourself the latest Western teachings and surrendered to them in a sort of rapture. A manly tempering of spirit ye never discovered from this. And most of all ye have sought a fruition of the masculine in the German spirit. The spirit of Marx has wrought over your souls a most terrible compulsion. The masculine German spirit long since already has set itself the task to civilise the feminine Russian earth, it has intruded itself as the man for it. By complex and manifold paths the German has been active: both through Marx, and through Kant, and through Steiner, and through many other teachers, tempting us and weakening the Russian will. The exclusive grip of Germanism in Russia, in our civil and spiritual life, is to be explained by this, that in the soul of the Russian people there has not been consummated the inward marriage, and that the masculine and the feminine principles have remained separate. Upon this basis has been fashioned a metaphysical hysteria in the Russian character, nigh close to obsessiveness. In this must be sought the riddle of many of our misfortunes. When Russian people have been rendered cultured Western people, when they have become pervaded by discipline of spirit, they have not of themself begotten culture, not from their own organic basis, not by their own spirit have they mastered their emotional and corporeal elements, but rather only from the outside have they borrowed culture, from the outside have they grafted to themself a formative spirit. This is a path, contrary to what Fichte led the German people, towards a national self-consciousness. The mature national self-consciousness of a people is also a mysterious uniting within it of the masculine and feminine principles, of the masculine spirit and the feminine soul elements. In each people this occurs in quite original and unique a manner. In Russia up til now this has not occurred. And ye, Russian intelligentsia of the most varied currents, have not helped, but rather have impeded this mature, masculine national self-consciousness, ye have not fulfilled your national duty. A mature national self-consciousness for us would imply the surmounting of both Slavophilism and of Westernism, which were bound up with our immaturity. The Russian can resemble the German in two opposite ways: he can relate to Russia, as the German relates to Russia, or he can relate to Russia, as the German relates to Germany. We ought to resemble the Germans in the second way.

Russian populism has always stood as an hindrance upon the path of our mature national self-consciousness, and in various forms it has governed the minds and hearts of Russian people. There has been with us a populism conservative and a populism revolutionary, a populism religious and a populism materialistic. But always it represented a capitulation on the part of our cultured stratum, called to bear light into the darkness, facing the vast darkness of the peasant realm, and always it was an expression of Russian backwardness, of the Russian extensiveness, always it signified the lack of a spiritual manliness. The populist mindset led to an idol-worship as regards the Russian people, as an empirical fact, as a quantitative mass, always it subordinated spiritual life to the material social medium, always it stifled the creative personal principle, and submerged the person into the collective. This mustneeds be said likewise for Slavophilism, which represents an unique type of religious populism. But Slavophilism stands infinitely higher than that revolutionary and materialistic populism, which dominated the Russian intelligentsia for almost an entire century and led to the catastrophe of the Russian revolution. In Slavophilism there was an one-sidedness, there were illusions, but there was also its own truth. The leftist populism however was quite varied in religious, national and cultural values. God got substituted for by the people, values by particular interests, spiritual realities got replaced by the transitory benefits of social classes. Here was this godless and idolatrous populism, having betrayed all the non-transitory sanctities and values, and it undermined Russia. Over the course of a century it sapped the spiritual foundations of Russia, it contaminated the Russian church, the Russian state, Russian culture, and impeded also the material developement of Russia. This indeed you, ye populists of all stripes, quenchers of spirit in the name of a phantasmic welfare of the people, ye have murdered Russia and brought it down. For you Russia does not exist, as an higher reality, as an integral intent of God, for you there exists only the people, not the people as a nation, not a living being, not an integral organism, existing for a thousand years, and uniting all generations, but rather the people -- peasants and workers with their transitory material interests. In the name of the welfare of the people ye have killed Russia, ye have murdered a great nation with a great destiny before it. In the name of the lowly and least ye have risen up against the great and the greatest. Ye -- are destroyers of everything majestic. Ye could not bear the grandeur of Russia. Under various guises ye were reborn again and again. Ye Russian populists, flesh from flesh and blood from blood of the Russian darkness and the Russian cultural backwardness, have donned upon yourself various Western dresses, and the most dreadful, the most destructive of your doings ye have done in the German garb of the social-democrats. But even in the capacity of the social-democrats ye have remained populists, ye were expressers of an extensive spirit of redistribution, and not the intensive spirit of creativity. This indeed -- is the age-old idea of the Russian intelligentsia, that the social question needs to be decided by redistribution, and not by increase in productivity, not by creative work. Ye Russian social-democrats, having forgotten certain sides of the teaching of your idol Marx, having instead brought into your social-democratism the Russian

Pugachevism and Russian anarchism, have produced an all-Russian pogrom and ruination and have reduced Russia to poverty, have doomed it to a long miserable existence. And thus ye have realised the from of old dreams of the populists about redistribution, about an overall levelling, thus too ye have tumbled Russian culture into the dark abyss. The Russian state and Russian culture were surrendered for rending by the dark masses, within which ye had fired up the most vicious instincts. And thus drowned the Russian state and Russian culture within the vast darkness of the people, to the glory and advantage of our enemies. Here is what ye have accomplished, initially having started out with innocent slogans as lovers of the people, but then ye were transformed into raging beasts. Future generations of the Russia people will not forgive you your evil deeds.

You, Russian populists of all hues, always have been enemies of culture, and ye always set the welfare of the people in opposition to culture. For you nothing ever possessed value of itself, everything was transformed into a mere utilitarian tool. Not religion, not the church, not the state, nor nationality, nor philosophy, nor science and art, nor morality and what is right, -- nothing for you possessed value of itself, nothing was genuine, spiritually real. Everything was subordinated to the welfare of the people, to the interests of people, to accommodate people. And ye dragged down everything into the dark abyss of the interests and instincts of the masses. Ye always regarded culture as bourgeois, since it was created by the governing classes. But you yourselves -- are the lowliest, most doltish, most miserable philistines, the bourgeoise of spirit. You want to transform the world into a preconceived association, ye want all human society to be rendered into a consuming society. Your core ideal -- is an ideal akin to the animal. But regretably for us it mustneeds be admitted, that not only the populist revolutionaries and materialists, but also the populists of the Slavophil type, standing upon religious a ground, likewise displayed an hostile attitude towards culture and its values, they sought truth not in the cultural stratum, not in creative persons, but in the simple people, in the collective. The age-old Russian collectivism always was hostile to culture, always hemmed us in, always hindered us from going out into the light, onto the world stage. This collectivism for us paralysed the sense of personal responsibility and made personal initiative impossible. This collectivism was not new, but rather from our old life, the remnant of a primitive naturalism. But many of us confused it with a spiritual Sobornost', with an higher type of the brotherhood of people. Upon this basis they idealised the Russian peasant commune, the obschina etc, as a phenomenon of Russian life. And with Russian collectivism was bound up also a negative attitude towards truth, a confusion of truth with morals. But the denial of truth, which among Russians has happened both on the right and the left, is a denial of the person, its enslavement to the collective. Truth preserves the person from the enroachment upon it by an evil will. Truth renders the human person free irregardless of the virtues and vices of other people, their moral level, their capriciousness. Truth makes possible the freedom of the person even amidst the existence of evil, amidst the wicked will of people. Russians confuse truth with morals and posit judgement of the person dependent upon the moral consciousness of people, on their virtues. But there is a freedom, which ought to be guaranteed me even amidst people's tendency to vice, even amidst their tendency towards violence. There never was understanding of this in the populist mindset, whether from the right, or the left. Suchlike a denial of freedom is a sign of the debilitation of personal self-consciousness, it is a deficiency of the sense of personal dignity, it is a submersion into an impersonal collective. This trait has proven fatal for Russia.

The Russian revolution is a grievous retribution for the sins and sicknesses of the past, for the heaped-up falsehood, for the non-fulfillment of duty by the Russian ruling power and governing classes, for the century-long path of the Russian intelligentsia, inspired by negative ideals and deceptively false apparitions. The Russian revolution is the ruination of many, of quite many Russian illusions, illusions populist, socialist, anarchist, Tolstoyan, Slavophil, theocratic, imperialistic, etc. The traditional worldview of the Russian intelligentsia has suffered a terrible crash. The lesson for the Russian intelligentsia comes now at dear a price, at dear a price knowledge is gained for it. Russia had to be brought to the extremity of ruin, in order for elemental truths to be learned. It sees the Bolsheviks as myopic and unjust in everything. But ye, the all more moderate Russian socialists and Russian radicals of all shades, Russian enlighteners, all ye, descendant from Belinsky, from the Russian critics, from the Russian populists, all ye ought to put upon yourself the blame. The Bolsheviks merely made the final deduction from your long path, they rendered apparent, to what all your ideas would lead. Many of you became frightened, when the long wished-for by you socialistic revolution, grounded upon your supposedly materialistic basis, began to destroy you and cast you beyond the pale of life. Ye even spoke about the usefulness of religion, which you were always negative to, and began to turn towards the church, which ye always had hated and condemned. But too late did ye turn for help to religion, and your attitude towards religion was too utilitarian. The grace of God descends not upon those, who flee to it out of utilitarian deliberation, out of the need for self-protection. One should think earlier about God and about the spiritual groundings of life. Not altogether still too long ago ye tended to think, that the people could exist without spiritual groundings, without faith in an higher Divine meaning of life, without sanctities, that what sufficed for the life of the people was the material grounds and rationalistic enlightenment. But now ye have seen, what happens with the people, when in its soul the sanctities have fallen, when it becomes bereft of faith in everything, that stands higher than its interests. But for quite long a while ye have wanted, that in the people should fall everything sacred and everything of faith, and for all this ye have been at work. Be mindful indeed of your terrible guilt, reflect all the deeper on the experienced tragedy. Cease with thinking that everything would have been fine, if it had been done with more reasonable and more moderate tactics. At such moments as this it is impossible to remain still with superficialities. Necessary is the awareness, that there has occurred a terrible crash, not outwardly only, but also an inner crash, and that is exposed the falsity of that spirit, to which ye have been in service for nearly a century. Shamefully has fallen your earthly faith, cast down are your earthly idols. There has occurred the terrible collapse of the age-old Russian atheism and materialism, of Russian socialism and anarchism, of all, that ye breathed, ate and lived. The hour of the too easy triumph of your age-old beliefs was also the hour of their terrible collapse, the hour of the fierce exposing of their lie and phantasmic aspect. Never, never yet were ye reborn spiritually, and never will your ideas hold yet their charm. The new generations of Russian people will outgrow them and be raised in hatred and horror towards your ideas and will curse those wicked deeds, to which these ideas have led. And, indeed, they will go quite far in this. Too much was false in your consciousness and in your constructs. False was your attitude towards the state, your attitude towards nationality, your attitude towards economic life and towards the developement of industry. False was your intelligentsia morality, your moralism, conjoined with nihilism, your utilitarianism. False was your attitude towards beauty and your persecution of beauty. False was your disdain for knowledge and your indifference towards truth, which ye always subjected to utilitarian calculations. And very foremost, your most terrible lie was your faithlessness and godlessness, your betrayal of the spiritual principles of life, your rupturing off from the religious wellsprings of life. Your ecstatic thirst for equality was to the destroying of the manner of life and of all its riches and values, was a thirst for the plundering of God's world and the abolishing of everything of grandeur in the world. The spirit of non-being stirs in you, he has inspired in you your egalitarian ideas and passions. The law of entropy, which leads to the death of the universe by way of the proportionate expansion of heat, acts through you in social life. But ye always had no love for freedom and always foreign to you was the sense of brotherhood. Never in the revolutionary spirit did there happen either freedom, or brotherhood. In your domain, within the bounds of your consciousness and your spiritual horizon, any sort of further movement was not possible. The domain of Bolshevism was the limit of movement along your paths, in your spirit. This -- is the end, the limit, the dark abyss of non-being. Ye never had love for creativity, to you it seemed an improper luxury. Creativity -- is aristocratic. Ye long since have conjectured about this. And when the era of creativity ensues, when there begins the hour of genuine renewal, ye will be shunted aside, as unnecessary, as spiritual corpses. Ye long since already have undermined the hierarchical principle of life. And in the Russian revolution has occurred an unprecedented destruction of the hierarchical order, the casting down of every hierarchy of qualities. But the destruction of every hierarchism is likewise a destruction of the person, since person is connected with hierarchism. Only within hierarchy is possible the qualitative differentiations of individuality. Ye however have led everything to the equality inherent of non-being.

The spiritual consequences of the Russian revolution will be enormous. These consequences will be not only negative, but also positive. We are passing over into another dimension of being. All the traditional outlooks have been subjected to doubt. There is occurring a revaluation of all social values. Bismarck once expressed the wish, to come across suchlike a land, where the experiment of the application of socialism had been made, in the hope, that after this there would appear no further wish to repeat this experiment a second time. Suchlike a land has been found, and it has done this experiment on colossal a scale. True, the experiment of the realisation of socialism in Russia is very reminiscent of pillaging and plunder. But a social revolution also cannot but bring to mind pillaging and plunder. This has been ultimately revealed by the Russian revolution. Yet this was apparent already back in the ancient world. The liberal and radical Russian intelligentsia always was inclined to think, that socialism is very exalted a matter, though also perhaps not to be realised at the given time. Always within the depths of your hearts ye Russian radicals have thought, that there is nothing higher than revolutionary socialism, that the revolutionary socialist represents the highest human type, but that you yourself by your weakness and hemmed in by your vital measures, ye cannot stand upon this height and thus go to compromise. Russian radicalism never possessed an idea of its own, it always lived off foreign ideas, diluted down with water. Ye Russian radicals, multifaceted and varied -- are the most unnecessary sort of people, with you there is nothing uniquely your own. The end has beset you. Now already one mustneeds have an idea of one's own. Henceforth it will be impossible still to be delighted by socialism from the sidelines, at a fine distance. Henceforth socialism will have become problematic, will have become a complex problem for the consciousness, and everything in socialism will need to be revalued. Now is not the time for a liberalism lacking in character and bereft of a deep spiritual basis. Your time is past, for all of you, -- socialists, and radicals, and liberals, and conservatives of the old type, vacillating and perched betwixt two stools. Now ensues terrible and responsible a time. And only the more fiery and profound ideas can win out over the darkness, by which we are engulfed. New souls have to come, a new spirit has to descend upon our haplessly beleaguered with suffering and nigh close to perishing native land. There is little, all too little hope that you, people of the old spirit, of inert thought, radically degenerate, should know your culpability, and escape the circle of bewilderment, that ye should open your gaze to the acceptance of a new light and your ears for the sounds of a different world, dissimilar to your musty underground world, a world of monstrous coterie circles. Many of you are hopeless, ye -- are the doomed, and ye die thus blind and deaf. New people have to arrive in Russia, in order to create a new life. The whole texture of your existence is worthless for the creativity of life. Ye -- are the end of the old, ye -- are not the beginning of the new. And likewise never can be termed new people, those various renovators and outward counter-revolutionaries.

The revolution provides enormous a quantity of vital material for socio-philosophic thought, the inner shocks and impulses convey it. Ye were always lethargic and immobile in your thinking. Ye loved to repeat rote-learned thoughts and expound them with your horrid jargon in your light-weight brochures. In pockets ye carried about your small catechisms and at every opportunity perused their hackneyed thoughts. Henceforth it will be impossible still to do this. Henceforth it will be necessary to burn all your catechisms and all your brochures and to bestow a curse to all the triteness of your grey and impersonal thought. Why was your thought never individual? Why were your writers never their own person? This -- was not by chance. In this -- is your condemnation. The time has ensued for the shattering of all your utopias of an earthly paradise, of the dull grey, impersonal, empty utopias, utopias of delimited equality and delimited happiness in non-being. There has ensued the time of an healthy social pessimism, more noble, more complicated and refined, than the optimism of the type of the social fanatics. Now is necessary more severe an attitude towards social life, more responsible an attitude. The social day-dreaming is become a debauchery. The fruits of this debauched day-dreaming are already evident. They always were alike. The striving for an abstract social perfection is a wanton and godless striving. The attempts at the realisation of an earthly paradise have always led to hell on earth, to malice, to hatred, to mutual destruction, to blood, to violence, to orgy. And thus it was during the era of the Reformation, when the Anabaptists created their New Jerusalem. Man has no right to be naive and day-dreamy in social life, cannot be a wastrel in his sentimentality. He has to be a man responsible, he has to see the evil and sin, he has to learn to discern spirits. Too dear has been the cost of your day-dreaming, your sentimentality, your naivte, your non-recognition of evil. Become severe, become responsible, know the evil in the fiery tribulation. Become men. The Russian people has to fulfill a law, a law of culture, a law of governance, a law of existence relative to earth. Such is the lot for sinful mankind. The path to higher creative life lies through law and through redemption. The Russian people -- is a great, but sinful people, filled with weakness and temptations. And the expectation of a social miracle is one of the weaknesses of the Russian people, one of the most grievous of its temptations. This was a temptation spurned by Christ in the wilderness. The Russian people faces having to go through a severe discipline of toil. The revolution teaches us, that there is a tragic lack of correspondence and disharmony between the spiritual summits of Russian life and its darkness beneathe. At the summits long since already there is occurring a crisis of culture, at the same time as at the bottom parts there is not even any sort of culture. Ye revolutionaries -- ye are people mediocre. Ye do not know yet the crisis of culture, since ye do not yet know culture. Ye -- are people half-fastly enlightened. And it is not for you to say, that the Russian people is of an higher culture. Ye yourselves are lower than it. The Russian people needs to proceed by steps, climbing out of the darkness towards the light. There is the complex problem of Russian messianism, and in the understanding of it one can go astray along a path of the most terrible falsehood. Too often Russian people have gone astray along this path of falsehood. And the biggest lie is that of revolutionary messianism. Bolshevism has shown, what such revolutionary messianism is, and in this is its service. Moreover, it has served to expose the lie of humanism, in which the socialist-revolutionaries abide. Within Boshevism, humanism passes over into its opposite, into the destruction of man. There remains always the contrast between the majority and the minority, between the spiritual heights and the material bottoms of life. Yet eternal remains the truth of the aristocratic spirit, of the ancient truth of mankind, which cannot be thrown down by any sort of revolution. The human spirit has to manfully resist the pressure of the empirical. It cannot receive from the empirical with its elemental chaos and darkness its own higher values, it must find these values within its own depths. The revolution teaches this yet once again. The revolution is of the realm of the empirical, destabilising for the freedom of the human spirit. But after the revolution will occur a revision of the dark masses. In this is the positive significance of the revolution. In my letters concerning social philosophy I want to contrast the freedom of the human spirit to the chaotic empirical and chaotic darkness. My social philosophy has religious a source, set at deep a layer of life. The eternal truth of Christianity yet once again is revealed within the tribulations of the revolution, but its revealing within social philosophy is an eternal creative task. I want to write not concerning the abstract, but about a concrete social philosophy.

Second Letter

Concerning the Religio-Ontological Fundamentals of the Societal Aspect

The prevailing consciousness of the XIX Century, which opined itself as at the "forefront" and "progressive", replaced theology by sociology. Society became the gospel of the "forefront" vanguard people of the century. They began to seek God in the social aspect, in the societal aspect. Your sociological worldview and world approach tended to eclipse for us the mysteries of God's world, to tear us off from cosmic life. Ye "forefront" people of the century, ye precipitated out from the Divine world-order and consolidated yourself upon the delimited surface of the earth. Everything by you was rendered social, the product of social categories, everything was subordinated to the social aspect. And therefore everything for you became superficial, everything was deprived of its deep basis, and even the social aspect itself became bereft of any deep foundations. Your social aspect, your societal aspect is an abstraction from out of an abstraction. The sociological world-concept of A. Comte and K. Marx -- is an abstract world-concept. Your sociologism has torn you away not only from cosmic life, but also from historical life. Abstract sociologism is contrary alike both to concrete cosmism, and concrete historicism. Indeed, this abstract sociological worldview has begotten the deep isolation of man, transforming him into an atom. The isolated atoms seek mechanically to unite, in order not to feel so their helplessness and isolation. All ye, so extreme on the societal aspect, and preaching the religion of the social aspect, ye are all splintered atoms. The worldview of one of the first of your apostles and prophets -- K. Marx -- is an atomistic worldview, spurning all organic realities, with everything devolving down into interests. Your socialism is a most extreme nominalism, is a most extreme denial of real ontological communities -- churchly, national, cultural etc. of realities cosmic and Divine. Tell us, placing your hand over your heart, and forgetting for the moment about the social struggle and social denunciations, speak for yourself, of your own inward depths, your utmost truth, what for you is it that is genuine? For you everything long since already has been transformed into an apparition and mirage, in a rapidly changing and deceptive play of human passions and interests. The deceptive social veil of being has replaced being itself for you. And with you there are none, long since already there are no ontological and vital foundations of life. Your social aspect has not brought you to the good, it but desolated your souls. People of former times, of more organic and real eras know more deeply the forms of sociability and community. Ye -- are proponents of the societal out of a bitter need, from out of an emptiness of soul. Your societal aspect is all noise and shouts, but there is not in it a deep realism, within it there is no connection with the mysteries of life, with the mysteries of man, the world and God. Long, long already it is time for you to slacken your movement at merely the surface and to begin movement at depth, long already it is time to ponder, to glance into the depths of the soul, truly in which has to be discerned all the infinitude of the world and the infinitude of God. Needful for you is to surmount the shut-in isolation within your social feelings of self, needful it is to get a sense of the societal aspect of the unsundered portion and level of the Divine world-order. Thousands of threads tie together the human societal aspect, set within a nowise large point of the immensity of all the world, of the life of the vast cosmos, of God's world. Eternally is happening the mysterious endosmos and exosmos between societal life and cosmic life. Ye however wanted to arranged things societally upon earth, having forgotten about the cosmos, having spurned the Divine world-order. Ye built utopia after utopia towards the ultimate societal arrangement and societal welfare, nowise wanting to know the flux of cosmic energies, which can topple all your plans, all your utopias, all your societal earthly paradises. Ye wished to lurk away in your earthly and rationalistic societal aspect, to lurk away from both the world and from God, from the mysterious powers, the dark and the bright, from the terrible infinitude and from the weighty eternity. Within the societal aspect ye wanted to hide from the fear of death and decay, and so ye fashioned short-lived figments of life. Ye deluded yourselves in this, imagining that ye were situated in a genuine life. But ye move about in the realm of death. Each coming instant devours for you the preceeding and will be devoured by the instant after. And not at any single point of your outward and noisy movement is genuine life affirmed. Because all genuine life is a communing with eternity, a victory over death and decay. The ancient Egyptians, having erected their pyramids in the name of eternity, are better still than you, the "forefront" people of our century, for they knew the mystery of life. These ancient builders of the pyramids best of all tend to confute your contrived "economic materialisms", all your suffocating and enslaving sociological abstractions. Indeed, it would be less utopian to have built these foolish pyramids for life eternal, than to build all your perfect societies for life temporal and corruptible. Your social tendency towards day-dreams and your social utopianism -- are begotten from the sundering apart of your sociological consciousness from the cosmic consciousness. Your social utopianism represents an extreme rationalism, it ends with a lunacy in judgement, the vilest and most monstrous of all forms of madness. The folly in your day-dream is to create a perfect and happy societal order in an imperfect and suffering world whole. Both a folly and dishonest is your desire to create a perfect and happy societal order in the world, set within evil, in a world, in which chaos has not yet been transformed into cosmic a condition. Indeed perfect and fine can only be the whole cosmos, only amidst the cosmic condition of the world entirety is there possible a perfect society. And this means also, that perfection and felicity are possible only within the Kingdom of God. The human societal aspect bears upon itself all the sin and imperfection of the world entirety, upon it lies the imprint of worldly servility and worldly necessity. It is necessary to redeem and set free all the world, all of creation, in order that the human societal aspect should be redeemed and set free. Ye however, given so to folly in your judgements, in your rational limitedness, ye are locked up in the isolation of your subjective caprice, in your societal psychologism, so deeply contrary to a societal ontologism, and ye construct your flimsy utopias, your fantasy paradises, as long as the iron tread of worldly necessity does not topple you and compel you more deeply to ponder over the mysteries of life. If freely ye do not turn to the vista of cosmic life, then ye will be compelled to turn towards it by severe necessity. Because indeed, necessity -- is a great good for the unfree in spirit.

Your sociological worldview was always detached from genuine historical activity. And therefore it was merely rationalistic and utopian. Ye isolated your societal aspect not only from the worldly cosmos, but also from the historical cosmos. In your theories ye abstractly subordinated man to the natural and social medium, ye rejected his spiritual freedom and transformed him into a passive reflection of the natural and social cycle. Yet you however have declared, that man of himself arbitrarily and in a break with the past can begin an history, in accord with your adjusted intents. Ye have loved to speak about "leaping from the realm of necessity into the realm of freedom", which is made by this slave of the social medium, a reflection of natural necessity. And namely therefore, in that you have not admitted man as a free spirit, ye therefore have also torn him off from the concrete, the historical activity, behind which stands the living spirit of peoples. By you everything has been rendered abstract -- abstracted, rationalised is your necessity, and abstracted, rationalised is your freedom, whereby the living man and living history have all vanished into abstractions. Truly, the historical actuality -- is a living and concrete reality, an unique reality, distinct from other stages of being, living in accord with its own law, knowing its own good and evil, incommensurate with judgemental criteria of good and evil. Ye have denied this historical actuality, ye have failed to see within it the inner organic life and have replaced it with sociological abstractions. The application of abstract sociological categories to the concrete historical actuality has deadened it, has snatched away its soul and made impossible a living and intuitive contemplation of the historical cosmos. By your sociological abstractions ye have corrupted the historical actuality, as an hierarchical stage of the cosmic whole, and devolved it into the simplest elements, revealable by other sciences, preceeded by your sociology. Ye -- are simplifiers and jumblers. Reality therefore eludes you, is not given you, since in your hands remain only abstract clumps of reality, only the splinters of being. Ye long since already have been committing a pogrom upon being, upon its concrete whole, upon its hierarchic harmony. This rationalised and frenzied pogrom ye commit both in your science, and in your politics. Ye love to moralise over the historical actuality and the historical past. Ye love to transfer your own limited individual moral values onto the supra-personal historical life. And ye relate malignantly to the past history of your own people and all mankind, ye fail to see in the past anything except evil and violence. Ye are incapable of conceptualising, that in the violent deeds themself, committed within history, there was their own justification, that there were gleamings of Divine Providence into the darkness. Tolstoy was a man of your spirit, when he spurned the whole of history, as constant evil, when he committed an unprecedented pogrom upon history in the name of his own individualistic moralism. But he was more radical and more consistent than you. He applied his own consistent individualistic moralism also to all the societal aspect. Ye however repudiate and debase history both in the name of an individualistic moralism, and in the name of the societal aspect, which is constructed by you upon new, unprecedented deeds of violence, upon a new, unprecedented enslavement of man. Ye ought to be acknowledging the autonomous nature of historical activity, to see in it its own law of good, rationally incommensurate with the law of the good of individual activity. Within historical activity it is impossible to see merely the accomplishing of the fates of the individual man -- of an atom and the mass, mechanically having united with these individual atoms, the arbitrary human collectives; in it mustneeds be seen the accomplishing of the fates of nations, of mankind, of the world, as realities, as concrete communities. Societies -- are real organisms. For you however there exist merely the atoms and the masses. Ye wanted as though to convey the whole of history through a general elective rule, and ye know beforehand, that the voting masses will not admit their history. By majority vote history not only cannot be accomplished, and indeed it can never even be begun. The world has remained as though in a primieval darkness and undisclosedness, in an equality of non-being. The atoms and the masses would not take to making those sacrifices, by which history is bought. It is impossible to apply to history the general elective rule and majority vote, it is impossible to moralise over history and demand of it a levelling of the atoms.

Ye rationalistic-utopians, in the grip of a judgemental folly, ye have not learned by the lessons of history, ye have not grasped the meaning of the tribulations sent down upon you. Ye had the possibility to learn and perceive much after the experience of the French revolution. The spiritual reaction against the revolution quite sharpened the cognition of the creative, the vanguard people of spirit. Ye have regarded these people as "reactionaries". But they in many respects brought to fruition that science of the XIX Century, which ye also are compelled to admit as your own. The spiritual reaction against the revolution was likewise a reaction against all the rationalism of the XVIII Century. In this creative reaction was discovered a feel for history and the irrational fundaments of the societal aspect revealed. After the experiment of the revolution, in the grip of rationalist folly, it became clear, that society never was and can never be based upon purely rational principles, fully understood by the small human reason and the capricious positings of this reason. The groundings of human society are lodged within the Divine world-order. There is a mysteried basis to human society, just as mysterious, as is the basis of all organic nature, from which it is impossible to tear away the human societal world. A rather deeper, a revolutionary era consciousness perceived the mysterious working of history, the connection between times, and it limited the human arbitrariness in the construct of society, the arbitrariness of human judgement. J. de Maistre stood upon religious a grounding and religiously he contended against the spirit of the revolution, against the spirit of the rationalistic enlightenment of the XVIII Century. But in this spiritual struggle of consciousness he discerned the legitimacy of societal life, the objective grounding of the societal aspect. There was recognised the organic, rather than the capriciously-artificial nature, of human society and the state. And thus the "reactionary" thinking of J. de Maistre and those akin to him in spirit ultimately begot the sociological naturalism. Even the Darwinism in sociology can be connected with this reaction against the rationalism of the XVIII Century. And A. Comte directly admitted his affinity with J. de Maistre. Espinas accurately demonstrates, that it is for both J. de Maistre namely and the theological school of the early XIX Century that there arises the discerning of the truth, that society is a creation of nature, and not of human caprice, and the representatives of this school he is prepared to acknowledge as the founders of scientific sociology. Then already, although in a partial and limited form, but still all the same, there was discerned the connection of the human societal aspect with the involvement of nature. For the religious consciousness this objective basis of the societal aspect, this natural legitimacy within it, is an expression of the sinfulness of the human world. The world, situated in evil, has to be made subject to some measure of law. Elsewise, through evil, the chaos tends to topple every world-order, to undo every cosmic harmony. In this revealing of a law for the natural and societal order there is its own moral truth, evidencing Original Sin. It is impossible to violate nature. It is necessary to expiate its sins. And thus the objective legitimacy of societal life is revealed in two aspects -- in an aspect religious and an aspect naturalistic.

Ye have not only acknowledged science, ye have made a god of it, ye have transformed it into a rationalistic utopianism. But ye were never humble in facing objective knowledge, ye never held in check the passions and desires of your unvaunted demands on knowledge.

Ye were positivists and materialists to the extreme, but the pathos of knowledge was foreign to you. Ye had never the thirst for knowledge. Your knowledge was a thing subjective, and not objective. It was merely an instrument for destroying. It was not knowledge, not science, that inspired you, but the rather a negative "enlightenment", which is pseudo-enlightenment and nihilism. In place of the objective legitimacy of nature and society ye made the deduction, that everything is permissible and that in accord with your own arbitrary whim you could restructure life. And long since already it is time for you to assume a condition of seriousness about strict science, knowledge with no strings attached. Your science was always self-serving, and therefore not true science per se. Ye imagined, that there exists a science "bourgeois" and a science "proletarian", and by this you killed off for yourself the possibility for an entire knowledge, by this you destroyed the very idea of science. The granule of objective science within Marxism was ultimately swallowed up by its subjective-class pathos, was surrendered over for rending apart by human interests and passions. A sense of serious humility in the face of knowledge, of the apperception of the objective foundations of the societal aspect would have diminished your malice and destructive rage, would have led to a catharsis for your sick spirit. Ye would have ceased to see everywhere the evil will of the governing and ruling classes, ye would have penetrated down deeper into the causes of the evils and woe of human life. But for this ye would have had to show some humility not only afront science, but also afront religion, and turn towards an higher source of light. Society and the state can only be based upon religious and spiritual principles. Society and the state become atomised and disintegrate, when these sources of human community and rule are undermined. You will attain to an understanding of this elementary truth only then, when catastrophe breaks out and when you yourselves are threatened by ruination.

Rarely, all too rarely do people of your type, of your sense of life and your consciousness ponder over the primal wellsprings, over those primal wellsprings of world life, which determine also societal life. Ye do not seek after the meaning of life. Ye seek only the blessings of life. Suchlike a direction of your spirit veils away for you the knowledge of the mysteries of life cosmic and life societal. Within the field of your vision falls merely a limited slice of nature and the societal aspect, subjected to rationalisation within your impoverished thought. I say -- within your thought, since in actuality irrational passions eternally storm about you and there pours forth the darkness of an unfathomable wellspring imperceptible for you. There is indeed a dark, unfathomable wellspring of infinitude within our life and the life of the world. And your judgemental light is powerless to enlighten the dark infinitude surrounding us. Two infinitudes surround us -- the upper and the lower, the light and the dark, a good and a bad infinitude. Yet neither of these infinitudes can be grasped by your small ability of reason. For your limited consciousness there obtains neither the Divine infinitude, nor the infinitude dark and chaotic. Your consciousness snatches only a limited immediate point of the sphere, subjected to rationalisation. Upon these paths is impossible any sort of profound cognition, and impossible also any profound cognition of the societal aspect. The world of the human societal aspect comprises an entire small world, in which is reflected those selfsame principles, in which act those selfsame energies, that are in the larger world. *Within the world societal, just like in the larger world, just like in all the universe, struggle cosmos and chaos.* And the cognition of the societal aspect ought to provide an assist to the cosmic principle to conquer the chaotic principle. In true cognition there is an ontological light, conquering the chaotic darkness, there is a cosmological principle. But your limited rationalism lacks ability not only to overcome the chaotic darkness, it lacks ability even to see it, to recognise it. Therefore ye are situated within its grip.

To the old German mystics was revealed the truth concerning the dark wellspring of being, about the abyss, lying at its foundation. The greatest of them, J. Boehme, taught about the Ungrund, groundless, an abyss, which is deeper than God. And Meister Eckhardt taught about the Godhead, Divineness, which is deeper than God. The Divine light blazes forth within the unfathomable darkness. This dark abyss cannot even be called being, it lies beneathe all being, to it is inapplicable any sort of category, any sort of definition. This is primordial, a blazing forth of light within eternity and it is a theogonic process of the birthing of God. But it would be inaccurate to understand the theogonic process by analogy with evolution, occurring within this world; it does not make eternity subject to time with its law of decay, with its devouring of the moment before by the moment after. It is a revelation of light within the depths of eternity itself. And our small reason meets here with irresolvable antinomies, with insurmountable contradictions. That which occurs within eternity, is reflected also in time, in the temporal world process. Dark waves gush forth from out of the abyss, and the raging chaos has to be conquered in the world and in man, so that the image of man and the image of the cosmos should neither be overcome nor perish, so that there be continued the deed of God's victory over darkness, of God's creation of cosmic being. The birth of light in the darkness, the transition from chaos to cosmos represents the arising of an inequality of being within the equality of being. And in human society there is not only the mysterious, but also dark principle, within the mass of mankind there rages chaos, whereas the societal cosmos is created and preserved only with great effort. Ever and anew the waves of darkness, demanding a new effort of transformative light, within history is termed the influx of barbarians, outwardly and inwardly. Both ancient Egypt and ancient Rome knew these inroads of barbarity. The barbarian Scythic principle bespeaks the abyss, concealed beneathe the most tranquil and conservative of societal aspects. The incursions of barbarism were useful and instructive for era that tended to be too satisfied, tranquil, fettered and stifling. Man always lives over the abyss, and no sort of conservatism can conceal this truth. In the mass, in the crowd there is always the dark abyss. And revolutions always have become the selfsame gushing forth of the chaotic darkness, as with the incursion of barbarians. Both barbarians and revolutions are needful for a world grown decrepit. It is impossible to deny the significance of these historical waves. But their significance is not in this, in what ye suppose, in the ideologies of barbarity and revolution.

Cosmic life -- is hierarchical. Hierarchical also is societal life, insofar as in it is cosmic harmony and an unsundered organic connection with the cosmos. Here is a mystery, imperceptible to people of your spirit. Every fracturing of the cosmic hierarchy atomises being, fractures both the reality in common and the reality individual (of the state, nations etc., of real communities in some measure, as also the person) and instead links and fetters the atoms together into mechanical collectives. From ancient times within human society has occurred the struggle of principles cosmic, i.e. hierarchical, with principles chaotic, i.e. atomistic and mechanical. The hierarchical principle, just like everything else in this world, can degenerate, wherein it cannot fulfill its light-bearing mission and begets the most frightful abuses. The hierarchical principle can become stagnant and inert and present hindrance to all creative movement. Thus, from ancient times the hierarchical power structure of tsar and priest not only guided the people and led them to the light, but it also arrested creative movement. Too often the hierarchical structure of tsardom and priesthood stood in an hostile attitude towards free propheticism. And every time, when too many a sin had accumulated behind the hierarchical principles and unfulfilled went the duty of radiating the light of its bearers, from below arose dark chaotic wills threatening to disorder the societal cosmos, to annihilate every cosmic aspect of harmony within societal life. The hierarchy of tsardom and priesthood has to provide space and freedom to the prophetic spirit, otherwise it degenerates into a moribund legalism and receives merited chastisement. But it is necessary to separate the actual principle, the idea itself from the factual sinful condition. The shining of light in this world has to happen in steps. There is an eternal distinction between the esoteric and the exoteric; it serves to protect the possibility of an higher creative spiritual life for a select portion of mankind, for its genuine aristocracy. There cannot instantaneously be brought to higher light all the vast chaotic darkness of the human masses. The human masses are guided out of the realm of darkness, from the captivity under chaos by degrees, in a process of education. The hierarchical blockage against the overflow of the chaotic darkness, against the momentary triumph of the numerous masses tend to save the wellsprings of light, protects the lamps, defends the light-bearing spirit from a rending apart by a chaos emotional and material. Everywhere in the ancient world it was spirit, roused towards an higher consciousness, that led the struggle against the buffetings of emotional and material chaos within the life of the people. All the great religions knew the distinction between the esoteric and the exoteric, and they created an hierarchical order, oriented not towards an hidden world, but towards the external world. By this path the qualitative was safeguarded against its being rended apart by the quantitative, and the quantitative itself was led towards enlightening. In the religions of the ancient East there was a mysterious and hidden side, providing a definite influence also upon the loftier achievements of Greek culture, in it there were genuine revelations, as it were, anticipating Christianity. But the religion among the people in Egypt did not know these loftier revelations, -- it was still submerged in the pagan darkness. It was the same also in Greece. Buffetings of elemental and chaotic revelations of spirits and demons of unenlightened nature from all sides beset Greece and threatened to drown the awakened spirit. Paganism could not free the people of antiquity from the terrible grip of demonolatry, of demon-worship, from the demons of chaotic nature that were lacerating it. But every hierarchical structure was an attempt to protect spiritual life from the might of this chaotic nature, to create formative principles and set limits to the elemental dissolution. It is impossible to seek the higher achievements of the spiritual life of Greece within the religion of Dionysos, in that mysticism of the people, situated within the grip of the dark chaotic elements. They need instead to be sought out in Orphism, in the Eleusinian Mysteries, in Pythagoras, Herakleitos, Plato. In the dissoluteness of the Dionysian orgies the people was tormented by demons and sought liberation and deliverance from a woeful and restrictive existence by a communing with the elemental cycle of nature. The ultimate and total triumph of Dionysianism would have been the ruin of Greece. And the principle of Apollonian form had to set limit to these Dionysian elements, so that the human visage might rise up out of the darkness. The Dionysian principle -- is democratic. The Apollonian principle -- is aristocratic. Dionysianism lends itself to an elemental, popular basis. Limited by nothing and subject to nothing is the triumph of the popular element, wherein the governance of democracy is transformed into a Dionysian orgy, dissolving away the face of man, plunging the spirit of man into the chaos of nature. Dionysianism is hostile to every hierarchism and every esoterism. Dionysianism tends to triumph during eras of revolution, in the mass movements of peoples. This triumph always subjects to danger the greatest spiritual values, it surrenders to a rending of the greatest spiritual realities. The aristocratic principle, the principle of hierarchic harmony, of form and limit, establishing distinctions and distance, preserves the higher spiritual life, guards the sources of light and protects the human person from being torn apart. The existence of the person presupposes distinctions and distance, forms and limits. Revolutionary Dionysianism abolishes all the distinctions and distance, all the forms and limits, and therefore it is profoundly hostile to the person, it neither admits nor recognises the human visage. When the Christian Church led the struggle against the elemental demonolatreia, the demon-worship, it safeguarded the countenance of man, the image and likeness of God, it helped him stand on his feet. In all the revolutions the elemental demonolatreia in secularised form anew takes hold of man and tears at him. The personal principle is bound up with the hierarchical principle, it is revealed in cosmic order and perishes in chaos. The personal principle -- is by its essence an aristocratic principle, it presupposes distinctions and limit. Person does not tolerate of chaotic confusion, the plebian erasing of all limits and distinctions. The personal principle is a qualitative principle, and it is of an unrepeatable quality, not permitting of quantitative jumbling. Only the mystery of Christ's love leads to unity, not destroying the person, affirming the visage within each. All of you however, situated under the grip of Dionysian elements, harried by the demons of chaotic nature, know not the person and know not freedom. Your revolutions bear with them the enslaving of man, plunging him into primordial darkness. Your spirit is submerged within the collective emotional body and is bereft of higher attainments. The spiritual principle -- is aristocratic, and not democratic. Democratic -- are the emotional-corporeal elements. The arising of the aristocratic principle in the world has represented a struggle of light against darkness, the birth of the person, the liberation of spirit. Your revolutionary Dionysianism always was and will be the momentary triumph of the quantitative, the jumbling of the boundaries of faces and images, the rising up from the darkness of the impersonal and form-lacking plebism. Here is why the principle of organic developement through steps, through light, pouring out from above to below, within historical life has moral and religious significance, -- it safeguards the person, freedom and spiritual life.

Many of you love to speak about freedom and liberation. But who of you is free, about what freedom is it that you speak, does there exist for you a subject to have freedom? The liberation of the chaotic element is not a liberation of man, the chaotic element cannot be the subject of liberation, for it -- is the source of enslavement. Man is situated first of all in captivity by the chaotic element. The dark abyss pulls at the image of man, pulls the visage of man downwards, it hinders man from rising up and standing up in all his total stature. The liberation of man, of the human person is also a liberation from captivity to the chaotic element, and not the liberation of the chaotic element within man and the people. Here is why all the profound people have thought, that true liberation presupposes a moment of ascesis, of self-discipline and self-limitation. Letting loose the elemental passions tends to enslave, make one a slave. When man is situated under the grip of his own chaos, he -- is a slave, his person is pulverised by passions, debilitated by sins. For you, as the "liberators" of man and the people, having snatched away from the elements all the fetters, it is long since time already for you to ponder more deeply over the problem of person. Why in your revolutions is there not the person, why is it surrendered to the rending by elemental furies, why is the image of man dragged down into the elements, to which you sing praise? Ye had never the wherewithal to resolve, let alone to posit the problem of the relationship of the person and society. You have wiped away the realities, for you both the person is not real, and society is not real, for you everything long since already is dissolved away. Your "revolutionary" world-view represents an extreme nominalism within social philosophy, an extreme atomism. Your collectivism is merely the reverse side of this nominalism and atomism. Ye have lost touch with the authentic realities and in their place ye desire to put forth a new, artificial, phantasmic reality. Your world-concept and world-view is in denial of all ontological realism. Your forebears -- are the sophists. Ye have spurned the fundamentals of ontological social philosophy posited by Plato. Plato is too much the aristocrat for you, and ye have seen in him the source of world "reaction". The socialism of Plato was an aristocratic socialism, and it was based upon the acknowledging of an hierarchy of ontological realities. Plato acknowledged the ontological reality of the totality, the reality of a supreme good and truth. Your truth however -- is arbitrary, subjective, a class truth, begotten of special interests and passions. You begin with your matter after all the realities, all the entirety, all in common, have been dissolved away and atomised. Truly indeed, you seek to construct your affair on the basis of no thing and from nothing. And this was directly expressed by the most radical and boldest of you, Max Stirner, although he was not of especially popular use among you. But even Stirner was not ultimately consistent and radical. He admitted of the "singular", having for this no sort of rule, and without any grounds for this. Truly therefore his "singular" is bereft of any reality, the "singular" is stripped bare, hungry and naked it goes desolate in the world. The "singular" is bereft of the reality of the "I", of the reality of the person. This is because person is an ontological reality, it enters into the hierarchy of ontological realities. Person presupposes the reality of other persons and the reality of that, which is both higher than it and deeper than it. Within nominalistic individualism the person dissolves away and disintegrates. In it the human person becomes atomised in the same way, as is the nation, the state, the church, the cosmos and God tend to become atomised. If there be no sort of integrally whole realities, then also there is no integrally real wholeness of person, it divides apart the fate of all the realities in the world and it collapses together with them. If there be no God, then also there is no human person. Person is bound up with universalism, and not with individualism. The perishing of the human person has to finally finish up into your human collective, in which perish all realities, within your impending anthill, that terrible Leviathan. About this yet anon I shall speak. Your collective is a pseudo-reality, which then has to arise to replace the ruination of all the authentic realities, the reality of the person, the reality of the nation, the reality of the state, the reality of the church, the reality of mankind, the reality of the cosmos, the reality of God. Truly, every reality is of person and is of a living soul -- whether man, or nation, or mankind, and cosmos, and church, and God. In the hierarchy of persons no sort of person is abolished and no sort of person perishes, but rather is fulfilled and enriched. All the realities enter into the concrete all-unity. Your impersonal collectives however, bereft of soul, torn off from their ontological grounding, bear with them death for every personal being. And therefore its triumph would comprise a triumph of the spirit of non-being, a victory of nothingness. In revolutionary collectivism there is nothing human, just as there also is nothing of the supra-human, in it there is something inhuman and godless, there is the destruction of both man and God. The fate of man and of God ultimately are inseparable in the final end. And the devil himself is powerless to alter this praeternal commonality of fate, amidst which God Himself was crucified on the Cross, as man.

Ye deny and ye destroy the person, all ye proclaimers of materialistic revolution, socialists and anarchists, radicals and democrats of various stripes, levelling and making an hodge-podge of all, ye proponents of the religion of equality. Ye want as though to transform people into atoms and human society into a mechanism of atoms, into collectives of impersonal atoms. But truly, man is not an atom, he is rather an individuum, an individuality, a diverse being. Each man has his own unrepeatable individual destiny both in this earthly life and in the life beyond, in eternity. It is not by chance, not by external and meaningless reasons that there falls to the lot of each man his destiny with all his tribulations and sufferings. It is not by chance nor meaningless that there fell the tiny tear of the small child, about which Ivan Karamazov speaks. The revolt against the tiny tear of the small child, against the sufferings, as the price by which is bought the world and historical process, is a rejection of an higher meaning to life, the non-acceptance of the Divine world-order. The atheist does not accept the tiny tears of the small child and all the sufferings of life, he revolts against God, in the name of the happy and good lot of man upon earth. But herein however he is ready to cause the shedding of an innumerable quantity of tears and cause an innumerable quantity of sufferings, so that all the more quickly should be attained an happy and healthy human life. Suchlike is the moral contradiction of all the revolutionaries. You, ye Russian revolutionary-intelligentsia, you have spoken much always about the tiny tears of the small child, about the interminable sufferings of the people, and this was your beloved theme. Ye fell into a false sentimentality and you harrangued, you promised a paradise without ill. But when ensued the hour of your dominion, ye manifest an unheard of cruelty, you transformed your land into a sea of tears and caused your people an innumerable quantity of sufferings. Sentimentality often ends up with cruelty. A more severe, harsher a glance at life tends to safeguard against such cruelty. The grasping and acceptance of an higher meaning of all the tears and sufferings of life enlightens man. For everyone, with whom there is religious an awareness and seeing the human countenance, the destiny of man is mysteried and cannot be resolved within the confines of this not-large slice of the enormous eternal life, which we term as the earthly and empirical life of man, from birth to death. The fate of each man is submerged within eternity, and in eternity mustneeds be sought the enigma of its meaning. All seems accidental, meaningless and unjust within the bounds of this short-spanned life. All finds meaning and receives justification within eternity. But you, in your revolting against the Divine world-order and rising up against eternity, you neither sense nor see the actual countenance of man, ye sense and see merely bits and pieces of the person, only its transitory condition, only its temporal sufferings and satisfactions. Your humanistic and sentimental intercession for man, your frenzied desire to free him from sufferings reflects also both your non-belief in God and your non-belief in man, your atheism. And this always leads to a destruction of the person in the name of freeing man from sufferings. The acceptance of the meaning of suffering, of the meaning of destiny, which from the sidelines appears so unjustifiable and unjust, represents also faith both in God and in man. To the apportioned lot of people there falls a varied fate, full of suffering and tears, namely because man -- is a diverse, deeply individual being. It is necessary to perceive man concretely, and not abstractly, with all his unrepeatable history, empirical and metaphysical, in all his organic world connections. Then only can there be something comprehended of his fate. Ye treat man however, as an atom, and all people appear to you as equal and meriting equal a fate. Thus ye want to free man from injustices and suffering, but ye thus tend to kill man in the process. In front of you stands not man, but an abstract atom. And upon these abstracted atoms ye smash the whole of being. Significant for man as a concrete and unrepeatable individual is his connection with his ancestors, with his native land, with his history. But merely fortuitous also is the connection of man with either this or some other social standing or class. Man however, in being abstracted and bereft of qualification, is treated as outside of history, outside the past, apart from his native land, apart from his fathers and grandfathers. But this already is not man, not person, rather only an atom, an abstraction from an abstraction. Meaningless and quite godless is your wish to compare the sufferings of people and rationally calculate, who is to suffer more, and who less, what sufferings can be justified and what not justified. It is not for you to be deciders of human fates and Divine fates. For you is given merely by active love for neighbour to alleviate their sufferings, to bring joy into their life. But this act of love and help for people cannot have anything in common with the rationalistic calculating out of the fates of people, a rationalistic equalising of these fates and their levelling. Your revolutionary religion of equality is likewise atheism, the denial of any higher meaning to world life. It leads not to the creativity of a better and higher life, but to the destruction and annihilation of all the riches within being.

I know, that everything I tell you, ye will term "reactionary" and see in my thoughts a justification of social evil. But I long since already have ceased to ascribe any significance to all your definitions. All your words sound for me, like nasty a noise. And therefore all your wailings and condemnations will not stop me. Inequality is religiously justified by the unrepeatably individual fate of the human person within eternity. This does not mean, certainly, that the earthly lot of man ought not to be alleviated and bettered. On the contrary, this mitigation and bettering is a fulfilling of the command of love. But this means, that it is impossible to revolt against the primal foundations of the Divine world-order, to destroy them, and instead oppose your own limited and arbitrary meaning to that of the Divine meaning of life. Inequality is at the basis of all the cosmic construct and harmony, it is the justification of the very existence of the human person and the source of every creative movement in the world. Every birth of light in the darkness is the arising of inequality, every creative movement is the breaking forth of inequality, an elevation, a separating out of qualities from the qualityless masses. The very appearance of God is an inequality from within eternity. From inequality was born also the world, the cosmos. From inequality was also born man. An absolute equality would have left being in an unrevealed condition, in undistinctness, i.e. non-being. The demand for absolute equality is the demand for a return back to the initial chaotic and dark condition, all level and undifferentiated, which too is a demand for non-being. The revolutionary demand for a return back to equality in non-being is begotten of the lack of desire to bear up under sacrifices and sufferings, through which leads the path to an higher life. This is indeed a very terrible reaction, a denial of the meaning of all the whole creative world process. The pathos of revolution -- is a reactionary pathos. The coercive demand for equality, issuing forth from the bottoms of the chaotic darkness, is an attempt at the destruction of the cosmic hierarchical structure, formed by the creative birth of light in the darkness, an attempt at destruction also of the human person itself, as an hierarchical step, as having been born of inequality. Thus transpires the enroachment upon the royal place of man in the cosmic structure. And it is because this place has been acquired by a terrible inequality and process of separation. The demand for equality can be expanded also downwards, towards the non-human rungs of cosmic life. In the levelling rush there is always thrust upwards not the human, the essentially already aristocratic principles, but rather the lower sub-human principles in man himself, elementary elements, the elementary spirits of nature. In all the communistic mass movements there is always sensed something non-human, some lower elements of nature rearing their head, obstructive to the revealing of the human image in the masses themselves. Differentiating a light needs ultimately to be brought into the darkness of your confusions. The pathos for equality is a jealous envy towards a being alien to one, the incapacity to advance one's own particular being without glancing at one's neighbour. Inequality however permits of affirming the being of everyone, independent of the other. Ye levellers unto non-being, ye love to make use of even Christianity for your aims, ye are not loathe even to resort to the Gospel, in which ye do not believe and which ye do not acknowledge. But within Christianity ye can find nothing for yourself, save for outward sounds and combinations of words incomprehensible for you. The Christian mysteries remain inaccessible for you. Christianity acknowledges the absolute value of every human soul and the equality of value of all human souls before God. But from this it is impossible to make any suitable deductions for the external mechanical processes of levelling and jumbling together. Christianity did not produce revolt and revolution even against slavery at a certain stage of world developement, it acknowledged only but that the soul of man, situated in a social condition of slave, has absolute value and equality before God with that of the soul of the master. Slave and master would be brothers in Christ, and the slave might in the Church of Christ occupy even higher a position, than the master. The Christian equality of souls before God belongs to the graced realm of the Spirit and is untransferrable to the social material plane. For the Christian consciousness, the human soul possesses an absolute value, an absolute value that the earthly empirical life of man does not possess. The value, the sacred, the spiritual reality has greater a significance, than the earthly empirical life of people, than their well-being and satisfaction, than their life itself. Christianity does not reject the sufferings on earth, it accepts them and acknowledges their significance in the supreme fate of man. For the Christian consciousness, suffering and tears cleanse the soul. This consciousness does not teach returning one's ticket to God, as demanded by the atheist Ivan Karamazov in the name of the suffering of people, out of the impossibility to make sense of the evil in life. With Christianity there is nothing for you. Ye -- are apostates from Christianity.

Ye have risen up loudly in defense of perceivable aims in human life against aims mysteried, in defense of man against God. Ye have revolted against the sacrifices, which everything mysteried and great demands. In the name of the conceptual and rational, ye made revolution and revolt, in the name of philistine utopias, of a notional and small earthly felicitude of each and all, ye spurned the greatest sanctities and values. The human well-being of each and all ye set in opposition to the supra-human values. And thus there clashed two irreconcilable world-views, two irreconcilable feelings for life. We, the people of a religious world-view and a religious feel for life, religiously having accepted the Divine order, bowing before the religious meaning of life, we accept the sacrificing in the small, the closely proximate, notional earthly human life and earthly human contentment in the name of the mysteried and great aims of human and world life. We do not revolt against history and culture, won at great price, the sacrificed blood of countless generations of our forefathers. We religiously repudiate, as craven betrayal, the very thought itself about the creation of happiness and felicitude upon an earth, in which be buried all the generations of our suffering and sacrifice-bearing forefathers, in the graveyard of the great reposed and great monuments of the past. Ignoble and godless is this very thought of yours to free from the sacrifices and suffering a generation to come, at the price of generations past. From a deeper, a non-materialistic and non-positivist point of view it is inconceivable even, why the generations to come ought for us to be endowed with a greater reality, and to interest us moreso, than generations past. There is something craven and ugly in this triumph of the temporal over the eternal. Oriented exclusively towards the coming happy life, you have fallen under the grip of the spirit of death, and not the spirit of life. How profound N. Fedorov was, when he posed before the prodigal sons the problem of the resuscitation of all the dead forefathers. This -- is a task more radical, more grand and worthy, than all your rationalistic and moralistic judgements regarding history, than your destroying of the past in the name of the good to come. On that day, when ultimately would triumph the point of view of the good of each and all and would be vanquished the point of view of a supra-personal and supra-human value and sanctity, within the world would become impossible still anything great, anything truly mighty and beautiful. Human life will have fallen to the utmost depths, it would become elementary and simplistic, half-animal a life.

The triumph of the point of view of personal good will have led to the downfall of the person. But the point of view of supra-personal value leads however to an heightening of the person. This -- is an incontrovertible historical fact, which demands investigation. The person rises up and becomes ascendant, when within it are revealed and created the supra-personal values. The human in the true sense of this word is affirmed, when within it is affirmed the Divine. Every value is but a cultural expression of the Divine within historical activity. The Divine demands sacrifices and suffering. The will to the divine within man does not grant his tranquility, it makes impossible any sort of felicitude upon earth, it draws him into the mysteried remoteness, towards the great. The point of view of the personal good of each and all is directed towards the displacement of the Divine, in essence it is anti-religious. The thirst for the Divine in the human soul acts, like a blazing fire, and the strength of this fire can produce a demonic impression. Many of you -- as moralists -- see a demonic power in every historical fate, in the creation of states and cultures, in their glory and grandeur. K. Leont'ev sensed this problem with an alacrity of genius, when he said: "Is it not frightening and an outrage that one should have to think, that Moses went up Sinai, that the Hellenes built their elegant acropolises, the Romans waged the Punic wars, that the handsome genius Alexander in a feathered sort of helmet crossed the Granicus and struggled on neathe Arbela, that the Apostles preached, the martyrs suffered, the poets sang, the painters painted and knights shone forth resplendid at tourneys only *for this*, so that the French, the German or Russian bourgeois in his ugly and comical garb should "individually" and "collectively" be rendered complacent at the ruins of all this past grandeur?"

Ye have stood up for "individual" and "collective" complacency, for a grey social paradise, against Moses and the handsome genius Alexander, against the acropolises and Punic wars, against the Apostles and martyrs, against the knights, the poets and the painters. The past greatness was founded upon sacrifices and sufferings. Ye however want no more sacrifices and sufferings in the name of a mysterious remoteness, imperceptible to each separably nor by all the mass as a whole. Ye want to put the past greatness to a general vote and hand it over for trial by everyone on the matter of a perceived human happiness in this short earthly life. But ye do not even know of love for neighbour, alive in flesh and blood, the concrete being. Man for you is not neighbour, he is only an abstraction. Only Christianity knows love for neighbour and unites it with love for God.

Ye have attempted to base your sociology upon this false presumption, that society has to be all one of a kind, simplistic, undifferentiated, so that the person might become developed, differentiated and varied. The blossoming forth of the person, of the person of each and all ye wanted to connect with the fading away of society, of the state, the nation, with their transition into a condition, which K. Leont'ev termed "simplistic confusion". With you there was always repugnance towards the complex blossoming of culture, towards the glory and grandeur of states, towards the great historical fate of nations. In this complex blossoming, in this glory and grandeur ye have espied a peril for the person, for his happiness. But in truth, ye always were concerned not so much about the person, as rather about the equality of persons. Always ye were glancing about at the neighbour of each person and sought to make sure, that he did not prove higher, did not flourish more than the other. What interested you always was the impersonal person, the person of everyone, the levelling of persons. But equality for you dwells in a sort of median realm of non-being, in emptiness, having within it not one living, concrete person. In the name of the levelling of persons ye are prepared to destroy every person, to chop off the possibility of its every blossoming. Every creative impulse in the person is indeed an impulse towards inequality, the destroying of equality, an upsurge. N. Mikhailovsky with his theory of struggle for individuality was an expresser of that sociological teaching, by which a levelled-down and simplistic society is favourable to the blossoming of each person. L. Tolstoy taught this same thing, though his teaching was not sociological, but rather moral-religious. The moralistic individualism of Tolstoy demanded the cessation of world history, the abolition of all states and all cultures, in order so that the centre of gravity in life should ultimately be transferred to the human person of each and all. Both Tolstoy and Mikhailovsky radically refuse a societal division of labour, as a principle, hostile to person. Socialism also demands a simplification and mixing together in society, the levelling to a societal median and from this awaiting the felicity of persons each and all. At the polar opposite to Mikhailovsky was K. Leont'ev, a thinker more profound and original, than all your teachers and ideologues. He tied in the complex blossoming of the person with the complex blossoming of society, with complex statecraft, with the great historical destiny of the nation. The simplistic confusion of society, which bears with it the triumph of liberal-egalitarian progress, the age of democracy, is bound up with the fading of the person, with depersonalisation, with the extinguishing of creative and vivid persons. The age of the Renaissance was an age of the complex blossoming of society, of enormous inequalities in the structure of society, but it was also however an age of the complex blossoming of persons, the flowering forth of geniuses. The saints were a vivid and extraordinary example of the personal principle, but the greatest growth of sanctity occurred in eras of great inequality. In an age of equality and simplistic confusion, in an age of the triumph of democracy there is already no sanctity and true genius, such as with which are connected the greatest victories of the personal principle. Unity within diversity -- is the criterion of an accomplished beauty of cultures. The romantic teaching of K. Leont'ev can be given also a fully scientific sociological basis. Thus, G. Simmel, in opposition to Mikhailovsky, objectively bases this truth, that the differentiation of the person is not inversely proportional, but the rather directly proportional to the degree of differentiation with a society. Favourable to the growth of the person is not the one-sided condition of levelling into a societal average, but rather its differentiated and complex condition. Without a societal division of labour the person never could arise, nor become distinct from out of the primordial communism of mutual darkness. Individuality, the human person does not initially obtain within the natural and historical world, it slumbers in potential a condition in the chaotic darkness, in a beast-like equality, and it is set free, rises up and developes only by way of a tragic history, by way of sacrifices and struggles, through the greatest inequalities and divisions, through the state and culture with their hierarchical structure and forceful discipline. To people of the XX Century, so tempted by knowledge, under so many a tribulation, it is already unbecoming to yet build idyllic theories about the blissful natural condition, about the natural order, in which would triumph the individual and personal principle, and about the destruction of this blissful condition and this triumph in the natural state of individuality and the person by inequality, by the violence and discipline of state and cultures. Every time, when an hierarchical structure is toppled, when they seek to free the person from every discipline and state and culture, there arises a beastly chaos, it destroys the person, and kills off the image of man. The freedom of the person always has its own correlative thousand-year discipline from a complex culture, transforming chaos into cosmos, cosmic order. Every world of cosmic order -- is differentiated, based upon inequalities and distances. The person is affirmed and blossoms forth in a cosmic world, in the cosmic harmony of societal life. In a world chaotic, in the masses, ultimately there is lost every hierarchical discipline, and the person languishes and perishes.

Person is something ye know not, you have drowned it in the masses. You have become bereft of the sense of distinction and distance. And bound up first of all with this is that you have ceased to feel and be aware of the radical evil of human nature. Evil has gained the victory over you, compelling you to deny it. Some of you are ready still to admit of God in whatever indistinct form, but none of you is capable of seeing the evil. This radical denial of radical evil has received the appellation of humanism. Ye had hoped to liberate man by way of the denial of evil. Upon this sinlessness of human nature albeit corrupted and enslaved by the illusions of religion, and the coercions of the state and social inequalities, ye have constructed your own theory of progress. In mankind's past ye have seen much evil, but this was not a radical evil, lodged within the metaphysical depths, this was always a social evil, lying at the surface of the societal midst. In the future, however, ye see alone only good. Your social philosophy is optimistic. Humanism always is optimistic. But is there a basis for such optimism, is it justified, if one peer into the depths of life? I think, that the social optimism always is superficial. One mustneeds oppose your humanistic optimism with more profound, more severe and healthy a pessimism. Your social optimism and your social day-dreaming bespeak the absence in you of the asceticism needful for every liberation, bespeaks the dissoluteness of your spirit. For spiritual health it is needful to be an ascetic, disdaining the unhealthy social day-dreaming. Rosy theories of progress and the perfect society yet to come too often in practise have led to cruelty and to lowering the level of man. Humanism has had its own significance within the history of human culture and it was necessary to have passed through it. But the final fruits of humanism, as an abstract principle, tend to destroy man, they -- are suicidal. Nietzsche was conscious of this with profound an alacrity, after which the pathos of humanism has become already impossible.

Ignoble and ugly are the indeed spiritual groundings of your revolutionary worldview and world approach, very murky its underground wellspring. At the basis of this worldview and world approach lies the psychology of the outraged, the psychology of the stepsons of God, the psychology of slaves. The sons of God, free in their spirit, cannot have suchlike a feeling of life. The free sons of God, conscious of their lofty origin, cannot undergo the feeling of the slave's being outraged, cannot conceive itself a spiritual proletariat, to foist an uprising, since for them there is nothing to lose and nothing to gain. Indeed, there exists not only a social, but also a spiritual category of proletariat, a particular spiritual type. The spiritual type of proletariat makes all the outward revolutions, torn off from the depths of life, from the world as a whole. Affront, malice, envy --

here is the emotional element, here is the underground psychology of the proletarian spiritual type. Upon such an emotional basis it is impossible to build a fine and free human society. The free sons of God sense not an affront, but rather guilt. The consciousness of guilt correlates to the royal dignity of man, it shows the seal of his Divine filiation. And the proletariat in their social position can have this royal, this Divine filiation consciousness, they can discover within themself the freedom of spirit. The nobility of the human spirit does not depend upon external social position. But when affront, envy and vengeance have poisoned the human heart, the spirit ceases to be free, it is in slavery, it is not conscious of its filiation of sonship to God. And therefore the true liberators of man have to summon him to an awareness of guilt, and not affront, have to awaken within him the awareness of the freedom of the sons of God, and not the slavery of the sons of ashes, the sons of necessity. Here is why those that are free in their spirit cannot confess a proletarian-revolutionary worldview.

Third Letter

Concerning the State

How flimsy and sterile are all your rationalistic theories of the state. In the XVIII Century you wanted rationally to explain the nature of the state by the theory of a societal concordat, and during the XIX Century you attempted to explain it on the basis of the struggle of classes and economic factours. But all, all the explanations, old and new, jam up against the rationally whatever irresolvable remnant, upon the ungraspable mystery of power. In the state there is a mystical basis, and this mystical basis has to be admitted even from the positivist point of view, as a definite fact, not subject to explanation. The principle of power -- is a completely irrational principle. There is an hypnotic effect in every power, be it an holy or a demonic hypnosis. No one yet and no power in the world has devolved in accord with rationally judgemental grounds. Power never was and never can be as an organisation of human interests, an organisation of rule of whatever the interests equally-acting interests. Power always is the pervasion of whatever mysterious principle within human relations, issuing forth from God or from the devil. The state is an especial sort of reality, not devolvable into elements purely human and of purely human interests. The existence of the state is a fact of the mystical order of things. The state is not deducible from whatever the human interests and considerations, and it is impossible to compel an acknowledging of the state, to make the state subject to any sort of rational trends of reasoning. Upon the basis of the nominalistic and atomistic worldview, held by a large part of the positivists and materialists, it is impossible to admit of the state and have meaning in subjecting oneself to it. The state itself by fact of its existence witnesses to an ontological realism, concerning the existence of realities of an other order of things, than those, which you admit of and see -- ye empirico-nominalists of various hues. To you it seems, that the organisation of the state -- is a rational organisation. But truly then a folly is subordination to the power of the state, as all the revolutionary ideologies are designed in the name of a rationalistic revolt against this power. Revolution always seeks to destroy the sacral hypnosis of power. But there exists an indestructible magical aspect to power, which merely passes over from one condition into another. And the new revolutionary ruling powers possess the magical aspect of power, they borrow on it from the magic of the old ruling powers, and employ the old and eternal hypnosis upon the masses. No sort of rational judgemental motives can prevent the masses from subjecting themself to the state and bear sacrifices for it. And this cannot be justified on the basis of any sort of interests. The submission of the masses to every state power is always a matter of folly, is a condition of hypnosis, is a trembling of the people afront realities, such as be beyond the empirical life of people. The objective ontological element of state power is present and acts in all forms, howsoever bad they be or subject to some manner of dissolution. It is active also in the Soviet power. It is impossible to jumble together and identify the nature of power with any whatever form of power. The state cannot be defined by any given human generation. The state maintains a real connection of the times in the life of peoples, and therefore it cannot stand dependent upon the times, as might wish those, who would consign it to the course of time. The state cannot be created and cannot be undone by some particular human generation. It is not in the capacity of people, living in some particular period of history. In this sense, the state possesses a supra-temporal and a supra-empirical nature.

Ye want to dissolve away the state into society, to make it identical with society and by this to rationalise it away without a trace. But indeed the state cannot be entirely narrowed down into society and derived from society, always in it there is an irrational residue, included not from society and not comprised of either the mutually interactive or counteractive societal powers. With the residuum, independent of society, is also bound up the specificum of the state. This specificum is not bound up with any particular form of state, it is present in every form, if the state be neither abolished nor annihilated, it survives revolution and revolutionary teachings about the state. Your societal teachings about the state always arrive at a false construct of power. These teachings see in power not obligation and gravity, but rather a right and pretension. They provide a shove along the path to a savage struggle for power. By this they sap the moral support of power and negate moral meaning for it. Amidst such a construct of power it would have to be a matter of equally-acting interests and the accommodating of interests. And the powers would have to seek paths for the upholding of the interests, for securing the interests. Upon these paths thus occurs an atomisation of the state and it becomes bereft of all its ontological foundation. The state likewise cannot be of a mutual interaction of persons as singular realities. The state is a reality sui generis, a reality of a different order, than the person. The reality of the state and the reality of the person are mutually interactive, they interact each upon the other and are necessary each for the other, but they can also clash, and from their clashing can be born tragic conflicts. The state can transgress the limits, set it by God, and trample the realities of an other order. Then begins an unhealthy process in the life of the state and great upheavals threaten it. But persons also, societal groups can overstep their limits and infringe upon the reality of the state. Then likewise occur unhealthy processes in the life of society and the state. Often the unhealthy processes of these orders get caught up each with the other. In revolutionary movements and the revolutions of persons, societal groups and society, matters go out beyond the limits and violate the hierarchical order and harmony.

The ruling power of the state possesses a religious primal-basis and religious source. Your rationalistic theories have not succeeded in overturning this ancient truth. This truth stands as a positive fact. Power possesses an ontological basis, and it springs up for the primal wellspring of everything, that has ontological a reality. The ontology of power issues forth from God. The Apostle Paul with genius proclaimed this to all the Christian world, when he said, that "every power of authority is from God" and that "the ruling authorities bear the sword not in vain". Not by chance is there the hostility against the Apostle Paul by all of you, who want Christians to provide justification for anarchism. The Apostle Paul -- is the largest obstacle upon your path. By this he did not permit the transforming of Christianity into a Jewish revolutionary-apocalyptic sect, and by this he led Christianity into world history. Ye however, the anarchist Christians, the sectist Christians, want anew to bring Christianity back out from world history. Ye want as though to undo the matter of world history. It is a lie, that Christianity -- is anarchistic, that Christianity denies the state. Christ Himself taught to render unto Caesar that which is Caesar's. But He forbade rendering unto Caesar that which is God's. Christ admitted the autonomous sphere of the kingdom of Caesar, He admitted the significance of this sphere for the Kingdom of God. Ye however, anarchist Christians, want to impoverish the Kingdom of God, to cast out from it an ultimately large autonomous sphere, by your maximalism ye want to bring it into a minimum in expanse. Truly, your maximalism is a minimalism, it neither sees nor wants to know of the manifold and worth of being, in it there is a Judaic miserliness. Christian anarchism thinks of Christianity as a small sect, in opposition to the world historical fates of mankind. And therefore the anarchist Christian outlook -- is an irresponsible outlook. The Apostle Paul rendered the Christian outlook responsible.

Ye, that want to unite Christianity with anarchism, ye, spurning the state in the name of Christ's truth, ye have drowned within you the sense of Original Sin, and have forgotten, that the nature of man doth lie in evil. Your rosy optimism is incompatible with the religion of Golgotha. The state is in opposition to the sinful chaos, it hinders the ultimate falling apart of the sinful world, in subjecting it to law. Vl. Solov'ev finely said, that the state exists, not in order to transform the earthly life into paradise, but in order to hinder it ultimately from being transformed into an hell. Sinful mankind cannot live outside the state, outside the ontological grounds of the power of authority. It has to be subject to law, has to fulfill the law. Abolishing the law of the state for a mankind, wounded by sin, would be a return to beastly a condition. The state is an unifying, stabilising and organising power, directed against the darkness and sin. The compulsive and coercive power of the state itself per se is not evil, though it is bound up with evil, it is a consequence of evil and a reaction to evil. The compulsion and coercion can be for good, acting upon evil and the dark element. But this does not mean, certainly, that every act of compulsion and coercion by the state is fine, it itself also can be evil and dark. In light of the Christian consciousness there have to be admitted ascetic groundings of the state. In the nature of the state is severity. The state awareness sees the power of evil and the weakness of good by nature in man. In it there is not that sugary sweet optimism, in it there is severe pessimism. In the idea of the state there is no dreaminess about an earthly paradise and earthly bliss. Such a dreaminess is always bound up with a denial of the state. The state tends to be less pretentious, and more elementary and simple. In the idea underlying the state is an ascetic severity. A dreamy denial of the state in the name of the utopia of an earthly paradise and bliss represents a perversion in societal life, the absence of an ascetic self-discipline and restraint. Your anarchist social dreaminess is morally just as reprehensible, as is sexual phantasy, eternally imagining oneself in loving embraces. Be more severe and sober. This even aesthetically is more attractive. The unbounded social phantasising is anti-aesthetic. In it is an anti-aesthetic dissoluteness. An iron necessity strikes at this dreaminess and orients it towards activity. And in this necessity there is a learning principle, there is a limiting of subjective caprice. Healthy a religious pessimism has to acknowledge severity in the state, the truth of having law for evil and the beastly human nature, the nature of the old Adam. In the state there is the truth of a restraint and self-delimitation, there is its own beauty of an aristocratic aloofness and form. Stateless utopias and phantasies do not know form, borders, expanse, and in them is always to be sensed an insufficiency of spiritual aristocratism.

All of you, who confess a democratic metaphysics, tend to rise up against the hierarchical nature of the power of authority. Yet in truth power cannot but be hierarchical, and the casting down of every hierarchism is the casting down of every power of authority, i.e. the return to a primieval chaos. Up til now even in all the democracies the hierarchical principle has been preserved. A consistent democracy, in casting down every hierarchism, never was and never can be. Such a consistent democracy would also be an anarchy. It is possible only as short-term transitory condition, after which a power forms anew through differentiation and inequality, through the restoration of an hierarchical principle, though it be in totally new forms. After the French revolution and all the following revolutions, happening after that of the French, Europe remained hierarchical. Europe tries to combine the hierarchical principle with the democratic. This process takes its course into an uninterrupted struggle, and it signifies to an utmost degree a non-organic condition of all the European states and peoples. But civilised peoples cannot permit the casting down of their existence into an anarchistic chaos and therefore they adhere to an hierarchical principle eternally restorative and renewing. Every state is founded upon inequalities, upon differentiations in the structures of society, upon distinctions and different segments within the element of the people, in the masses. The history of the Soviet Socialist Republic vividly demonstrates this. There was no state and no ruling authority, although indistinct they do exist, as chaotic jumblings of the elements and masses. In these elements and masses everything sinks down and vanishes, there is no direction and no sort of goals are realised. The directive and goal-realising power of authority would be born only on that day, when inequality arose, when there occurred segmentation and differentiation, a division into qualitative elements. State power was born upon acts of violence, but these acts of violence were favourable and they set goals of peaceful movement in a darkness, incapable of particular distinctions. The first man of violence, having formed the power of authority in the chaos, having set goals, was a benefactor of mankind, and upon him began God's anointing. Ye however wreak a process against this first man of violence and against his kind, in him you see the source of the evil, from which ye want to liberate the world. In this is your mistake. The origin of the power of authority -- is monarchistic, and not democratic, it arose from the veneration of heroes. Ye tend to think falsely about the nature of man and the nature of the world, you, believing in nothing higher, you positivists, materialists and rationalists, falling nonetheless into a sugary optimism and pretty idealisation, when the talk involves the primordial nature of man and human society. Ye do not see the evil, do not see it in the primal depths of human nature, you forget about that chaotic beastliness, about which teaches the positive science acknowledged by you, and ye therefore ascribe evil to the arising of the state, in the social differentiations and inequalities, in which have formed all cultures. One of your teachers, J. J. Rousseau, thought up the absurd theory of a societal concordat. At the basis of this theory lay a pretty-feelings optimistic reflection about the sinlessness and goodness of man in the natural state -- conjectural, and directly the opposite to everything, that both religion and science teaches. From this theory all the organic unities were fractured, human society was atomised and the reconstruct of society and the state was set as though dependent upon a mechanical sum of the atoms. It was not only society and the state in this theory that lost organic wholeness, but man also ceased to be an organic individuality, always unrepeatable in his uniqueness and his destiny, he was transformed into an atom. Thus at first the state becomes dependent upon human caprice, and then man becomes dependent upon the caprice of the state. In this is a destructive contradiction. That identification of the state with society, which is asserted by theory of the societal concordat and the sovereignty of the people, leads to a total despotism. Indeed, a state is less despotic, than is a society, calling itself a state. Denied are the religious wellsprings of the state, thus rendered independent upon human will and human caprice, but namely then also is affirmed the unbounded power of the state-society over man. The teaching of Rousseau is a self-destruction of man, a most bitter of constraints -- the constraint of man by men, and not by any higher principles, than of man. The state, as an objective principle, does not assert, that man belongs wholly to it, it makes pretense only upon part of man. Human society however, arbitrarily created by people, does not know limits to its pretensions, it is ready to entirely seize hold of man. The state saves man from a collectivism, swallowing up the person. In this is one of the missions of the state. Man is held in check by two objective principles standing over him and by this he is guarded. The theory of the societal concordat is not only religiously and scientifically inconsistent, but it is also frightening in its tyrannical consequences. Another teacher of yours, K. Marx, admitted of an objective necessity, he loved to appeal to an iron force of law. But in this was not his pathos. The pathos of objectiveness, of natural necessity and the measure of law would not enthrall you. You thence have followed along with him, wherein that he proclaimed an unbounded class subjectivism, in that he made a god of the will of the proletariat. The objective side in the teachings of Marx, oriented towards measure of law and necessity, ye never could ultimately accept, and ye quickly forgot about it. But ye have been captivated by the teaching of this, that the state is an organisation of class authority. In this superficial and pitiful theory what tickled you was the subjective human arbitrariness, by which could be toppled one class's rule while replacing it with another. For this mindset, societies and states are composed of not by abstract atoms, but rather by abstract classes. But in both one and the other case your pathos is a pathos of hostility to everything ontological within the life of society, to everything, issuing forth from the greater depths.

In societal philosophy, in the teachings about the state, healthy an antidote against revolutionary arbitrariness, against the subjective dislodging of all objective realities, might involve also a sociological naturalism. Within sociological naturalism is a limitedness, which does not see the ultimate, ontological and spiritual groundings to be in the life of societies and states. But in it too is a certain partial truth against the falsities of sociological subjectivism, which holds sway in all the revolutionary ideologies. It is not by chance that the great "reactionary" J. de Maistre might be admitted as one of the inspirations behind the naturalistic sociology of the XIX Century. He provided religious a foundation to this teaching about society, which was to the highest degree thus favourable to the affirmation of an objective, natural legitimacy of societal processes, and which received scientific a basis. The pathos of an objective legitimacy and necessity can disinfect the consumptive revolutionary atmosphere, it tends to yield afront immutable and intractable realities. And it is necessary in regard to the state. The state is an objective natural and historical reality, which neither can be created, nor destroyed, on human whim. And those, who neither want nor can accept this reality religiously, ought then instead to accept it naturalistically, on the strength of its compelling scientific legitimacy. Objective necessity, the iron weight of law will pound upon those, who deliberately and intentionally ignore the historical realities. Rebellion is chastised by the law of necessity. And if all revolutions finish out as counter-revolutions, sometimes very fierce and ugly, then this will have transpired through necessary reactions of historical realities, reactions in the very depths by their nature, not consenting to be transgressed, and not merely as the effect of the evil will of people and groups of people. Suchlike is the ontologically existing side of "reactions", quite inconceivable for your "enlightened" consciousness, and not merely their superficial side, in which always has occurred much that is humanly ugly.

It is impossible to deny the significance of the struggle of races and aggression in the formative influences of the state. Through these "naturalistic" paths the state power of authority is organised in the initial stages of the developement of societies. In severe struggle and war there is formed the race of rulers, a selective process of the finest, and there is strengthened the aristocracy of power. In the life of human societies, in the historical process of the race, it has enormous significance. Without the formation of the race of the finest and most powerful, of a ruling race, the human world would never have emerged out of the dark indistinct chaos. Within the wellsprings of history, the differentiation and qualitative selections have occurred by way of the military struggle of races and peoples, by way of conquests and victories of the stronger over the weaker. And these "naturalistic" means of the formation and organisation of states nowise contradict the religious and mystical foundations of the state. In the sociological naturalism of L. Gumplowicz there is an indisputable bit of truth, and it can be taken entirely separate from the positivism of L. Gumplowicz. The state is based upon racial inequalities, upon the predominance of the strongest and most adept. And in a predominance of natural strength at the initial stages of human history there is its own truth. If we justly rise up against a predominance of power over law, then a final truth is still not yet expressed by this. This idealistic judgement has to be brought to some realistic grounds and effects. Humanistic declamations concerning the relationship of power and rights nowise resolve the problems. At greater a depth, power has to be admitted as the source of rights, but as a power, possessing an ontological basis. Natural power however at certain stages of the developement of mankind can be an expression of an ontological power, i.e. through it can be realised a certain truth. Without power, arising from the loins of nature, truth can neither begin nor triumph in the world. Through power, the power of nature and a natural selection, light has to be brought into the darkness. And there cannot be an humanitarian attitude towards this darkness, there cannot be constructed an attitude towards it upon the rights of the powerless. The surging waves of the primieval chaos, of darkness and savagery, would engulf human civilisation, were it not for a victorious power through a selectiveness of the higher qualities and moreso light-bearing principles. All states are born of bloody violence. The first ruler was the one most violent. But so pitiful are all your declamations against those acts of violence, all your revolts against those ruling makers of violence. Indeed, in the Old Testament right and beneficial were these acts of violence, and without them never would we have risen from the darkness and chaos into the human cosmic condition. Without these sacred coercions the human race would have drowned in a beast-like chaos at the very beginnings of its history. Ye have to submit to the Divine world-order, or ye will be crushed by natural forces, which for the rebelling assume the form of external law and necessity.

The most reasonable of you are ready to admit the significance of the state. But you admit of the state in too utilitarian a manner and therefore you would limit it to some bare minimum. But the state is not a matter of building water-closets. The state reflects a certain value, and it pursues certain great aims within the historical fate of peoples and of mankind. The state is connected not only with the small, but also with the large-scale matters. By its nature the state strives towards increase and expansion. The power of the state reflects a value. The power of the state possesses not utilitarian a purpose, it exists not for the philistine well-being of the people, but rather for the fulfilling of an higher mission. The state cannot endure, that its wings should be clipped, -- it aspires to the historical distance. An irresistible fate draws every great state to the attaining of might for itself, to the increase of its significance within history. A great state cannot of its own good will consent to a restrictive philistine existence and never in history has it consented to this. Imperialism is the fate of great a state, its dream of grandeur and world expanse. Imperialism is not only the realpolitik of great states, with pretense to a world historical role, but also underlies their romance. Imperialism is the completion and blossoming forth of every great state, its limit. In the imperialistic dream there is something demonic and consuming. The great states of great historical peoples are subject to an irresistible imperialistic dialectic, through which they attain might and then perish, they scale the heights and then fall. Within imperialism at the heights of its attainment the boundaries of the state are shattered, the state exceeds its bounds and passes over into a world unity, which no longer can be termed a single state, distinct from all the other states. Empire always strives to be a worldwide empire. And by its idea there can be only one, a single world empire. An empire only with difficulty tolerates the existence alongside itself of other empires. Such is the pure form of the idea of empire, and this

-- is the idea of a worldwide unification. This idea empirically within history however is not realisable in the pure form, it is liable to get muddled and side-tracked. The imperialistic idea is contrary to every philistine aspect in the state's existence, every limitation, restriction and being fettered down to a small bit of the earth. You, who raise shouts along the streets against imperialism amidst denunciations of it as "bourgeois", you -- are genuinely the philistine and in the name of philistine ideals ye rebel against the great historical tasks unperceived by you. Ye desire, that the state and society should live exclusively by the perceived, the rationally thought out goals, small, near at hand, limited, and ye revolt against anything historically remote, mysterious and irrational, ungraspable for the majority of people. Ungraspable for a majority of people the same, is why Alexander of Macedon with enormous sacrifices needed to form a great monarchy and unite East and West, why the Roman Empire was needed, why the finest people of the Medieval period lived with the thought of a worldwide monarchy, about an holy empire, why Napoleon undertook his absurd campaigns into the distance fraught with perishing, why in our day blazed forth the terrible world war amidst the clash of imperialistic wills for predominance. All this -- is folly, mindless and a transgression as regards the fate of the reasonable philistine mindset, knowing only the welfare of people and generations of people. Out of ignorance, out of fear in the face of everything remote and mysterious, ye conduct your philistine revolts against great historical forces and great historical tasks. Ye snipe at modern imperialism as "bourgeois", but ye have forgotten, that everything in modern life has "bourgeois" a style, that upon it lays the imprint of modern economism. How less so "bourgeois" is your socialism, how less so "bourgeois" your revolutions? Is not perhaps "bourgeois" the style of your soul, are not perhaps "bourgeois" all your goals? In the bustle of our days ye have forgotten about the ancient sources of imperialism, ye have forgotten about the existence of a "sacred" imperialism, so dissimilar in its style from the modern industrial-trade imperialism.

Imperialism is old, as old as the world, it did not arise in our bourgeois-capitalist era. Imperialism -- is one of the age-old worldwide principles. In ancient Egypt, Assyria, Babylon, and Persia there was already an imperialistic will towards the formation of a world empire, to go beyond the bounds of a mere philistine state. In the formation of the great Eastern monarchies, always striving towards worldwide unification, there were active, it would seem, factours very natural and economic. In the ancient East occurred a natural struggle of monarchies, the natural replacement of one monarchy by another, the process of a selection of the strongest and a perishing of the weakest. But in this natural medium, through these natural forces was realised some sort of remote and mysterious aims of history, there was realised the meaning of history. Ancient imperialism had not only a natural, but also a sacred basis, and it was sanctified religiously. The greatest achievement of ancient imperialism was the world monarchy of Alexander of Macedon. Alexander the Great received the religious sanctification of his power of authority from Egypt, from the Egyptian pagan-priests. All the prior great imperialistic formations, and immediately so the Persian imperialism, led to the world monarchy of Alexander. In it had occurred an as yet unprecedented collision, the coming in contact and unification of two worlds -- East and West. Both worlds emerged beyond their isolated condition, and formed an as yet unprecedented breadth and extent of the horizon. The whole Hellenistic period was a spiritual unification and enrichment of mankind upon the basis of imperialistic struggle, imperialistic attainments. Usually within history is not attained and realised that, which was posited as the immediate aim. The world monarchy, towards which Alexander the Great aspired, proved very fragile and short-lived. But the results of the deed of Alexander the Great for the world and for mankind proved innumerable and eternal in their significance, -- there was forged the oneness of mankind. The following imperialistic stage -- the Roman Empire -- was the greatest achievement in the history of empires, in it was attained a true world universality. But those Romans, who created the Roman Empire, also did not suspect, that they would serve more remote and mysterious a goal, than the formation of a great world state, did not suspect that they would create the natural basis within a single mankind for the Universal Church of Christ and that their deed would remain even after the great state created by them had been destroyed. Thus always it happens within history. The most proximate real goals serve but as a temporal means for remote and mysterious historical goals. English imperialism pursued quite egoistic sea-mercantile and industrial goals. But it served the deed of the world unification of mankind, the emergence of European culture beyond its bounds onto the world stage. And the competition of modern "bourgeois" imperialistic wills to world might has a certain higher and mysterious meaning to it. But for you philistines of democracy and socialism, compressed by rational outlook, this meaning does not obtain for you to perceive. It is time already to stop the straight-ahead moralising over history and transferring over to historical activity the criteria of individualistic morals. Morally both right and not right were the Persians and the Greeks, when they struggled for their power and predominance, and morally both right and not right were the Germans and the English, when they struggled for their own power and predominance. The struggle of imperialistic wills within history is not a struggle of good and evil; this is a free competition of peoples and states, amidst which there is no complete rejection by God or exclusive chosenness by Him. And is the English imperialist J. A. Cramb not so already not right, when he says: "If at some point in time there be fated to occur the terrible event of war with Germany, then the earth will see a clash, which more than anything will be reminiscent of the great Greek wars... And we can imagine for ourself the ancient mighty Divinity of the Teutonic tribes, dwelling neathe the clouds, tranquilly gazing down to earth, at the clash of his beloved children, the English and the Germans, rushing into mortal combat; the Divinity, smiling upon the heroism of this combat, of the children of Odin, the God of war". The god of Cramb -- is a pagan god, but the Christian God also presupposes for His peoples freedom in the manifesting of their spiritual and material might. No sort of victorious power can be exclusively material, it always possesses also a spiritual basis, a spiritual wellspring. Within the historical process is necessary a natural selection amidst spiritual-material powers. The triumph of weakness would lead to the lowering of the level of mankind. Ye have cast about the problem of imperialism merely upon the surface. It mustneeds be considered at greater depth. Then only will be revealed for us the twofold nature of every great, powerful and growing state: on the one hand, the state wants to be a distinct national state alongside others, possessing boundaries and individual forms, but on the other hand it strives to go beyond the bounds of a particular state and instead become a world state. The national state -- is a philistine state, it can be the more tranquil and satisfied. The imperialistic state however is situated in the grip of a mysterious historical fate, which offers it either greatness or ruin, it steps into an historical tragedy, from which there is no exit. But a great people are moreso attracted by the remote and captivated by glory, than they are by a philistine tranquility and smugness. It is necessary, moreover, to point out, that upon the paths of its tragic historical destiny imperialism also creates the philistine smugness, which it utilises for its own ends. But imperialism is merely a path, the fate of peoples and of states. It bears within it the seeds of death. As its replacement there comes an imperialistic world communism. But the very idea of a compulsory world unity and rule is a false and phantasmic idea.

The existence of the state within the world has a positive religious meaning and justification. The authoritative power of the state possesses a Divine ontological source. The denial of the ontological source of the power of authority in our times represents a shattering of organic realities, a transgression of the cosmic structure of things. But the state is not endowed with a sinless and pure nature, in it can be discovered evil and even a diabolical principle, it can degenerate and serve ends, contrary to its proper destiny. Every principle can turn into its reverse, a downfall. The state has not only a natural, but also a Divine grounding. It is an acting of the Divine principle within the murky natural medium, the refracting of an absolute principle within the relative. But making a god out of the state is impermissible, and impermissible too is transforming it into an absolute, impermissible is bestowing upon it Divine honours. Absolute imperialism is an anti-Christian lie. The state ought not to be autocratic, unbounded, nowise subject to any sort of higher, supra-state principles. This higher truth was still hidden for the pagan consciousness. The ancient pre-Christian world did not know limits for the state. It was not capable of distinctions in this. The divine for it was submerged in the natural, and natural necessity was not delimited by Divine truth. The state was a matter of natural necessity, setting bounds to the beastly chaos. The problem indeed of the limitation of the state itself could not as yet be put before the consciousness of the ancient world. All the peoples of the ancient world strove to create a mighty power, which should hold mastery over the chaotic elements, lead a way out from the savage condition. This power of authority was sanctified by the religious consciousness of the peoples of the ancient world. In the great monarchies of the East the regal power of authority was bestown a divine significance and to it was accorded divine honours. Ancient Egypt was a cradle of this religious sanctification of regal power. Kings there were directly descended from the gods. And in this separating off of the regal line from the rest of the race of mankind there was its own wisdom. Human nature was not yet sufficiently freed from the elemental forces of lower nature, not lifted upwards, for its rights to be opposed to those of the state with limitations to its power. Through the despotisms of the East man gradually and with difficulty emerged from the naturo-chaotic, elemental-savage condition. The state was not of a delimited and sketched-out sphere for the people of the ancient world, for them it was everything. And the people of the ancient world so appreciated the power of the state defending them from the natural elements, that even in Greece, the most human and humanistic Greece was not able to set limits to the state. Even the divine Plato did not know those limits.

The religious sanctification and apotheosis of regal power in the East contained within it a seed, from which afterwards at Rome, in a different spiritual atmosphere, in a different stage of mankind's spiritual developement, there arose the cult of the Caesars, the acknowledging of Caesar as a man-god. And then occurred the clash of the cult of the Roman Caesars bestown divine honours, clashing with the light of Christ, enlightening the world. When the first Christian accepted a martyr's death, not wanting to bestow divine honours to Caesar, he forever religiously limited the pretensions of state power, he opposed to it the infinite nature of the human spirit as a spiritual boundary-line. Upon the blood of the martyrs was raised the Church of Christ and was formed the new spiritual kingdom, in opposition to the pagan kingdom of Caesar and its boundless pretensions. The spiritual autocracy of the state was at an end. there opened forth a new spiritual source of truth, independent of the state. Only to the Christian consciousness opened up first the limits to the power of the state, only for it first became possible a distinction and division of the two realms. From the words of Christ -- "bestow unto Caesar that which is Caesar's and unto God that which is God's" -- there began a new era in the history of the states in the world. The "kingdom of Caesar" and the "Kingdom of God" are distinct and they enter into very complex, entirely dramatic correlations. The dramatic interaction and clashing of the "kingdom of Caesar" and the "Kingdom of God" have not ceased even at present, it will exist until the end of time and but enter into new phases. The Christian consciousness repudiates every autocracy of state power, be it the autocracy of Caesar or the autocracy of the people. It has set limits to every human power of authority, be it the power of one, or many or of all. This Christian truth is ascendent over all forms of state power and does not signify preference of this or some other form. In the Christian world the kingdom of Caesar is limited by the Church of Christ and the infinite nature of the human spirit, revealed but through Christ. The source of the limitation of the authoritative power of the state -- is purely religious, spiritual. At its primal basis this is not a limitation of the state by society and societal groups, demanding these or some other constitutional guarantees, this is first of all a limitation of the state by the church and the human soul. In the Christian revelation there is included an altogether special "declaration of rights" of the human soul, in its filiation through Christ to God. In the Christian world the state can no longer make pretense to man in toto, its power does not extend to the depths of man, to his spiritual life. The depths of man belongs to the church, and not to the state. The state has to do only with the outward man, it regulates only the external relationships of people. And in the Christian world the state too often oversteps its bounds, intrudes upon an area not its own, and violates the human soul. But this is already a sin of states, a deviation from the correct path. Spiritually there are forever set limits to the state, and the rights of the human soul acknowledged. This is true also in regard to autocratic monarchies, which are not limited by society nor societal groups, but are still limited by church and the rights of the human soul. Insofar however as autocracy has overstepped the bounds of the national-historical form of monarchy, religiously sanctioned, but not made a god of, and tended yet towards an apotheosis of Caesar, it has betrayed the truth of Christ and entered upon the path of the cult of the man-god. This tendency always was stronger in the East, in Byzantium and Russia, than in the West. In the West, in Catholicism, with particular a power there was set and established limits to the power of the state, to the kingdom of Caesar. The cult of Caesar from Rome returned to its birthplace, to the East. The rights of man were sensed more strongly in the West. And all ye, being apostates from Christianity, and having forgotten your spiritual birthplace, ye demand the liberation of man and the limitation of the power of the state over him, not knowing, from whence derives this liberation and limitation. Ye have lost the religious kenning of your fathers and haplessly, distortedly, in secularised form ye express the old Christian truth. Every limitation to the pretensions of the state and every affirmation of the rights of man has as its source the Christian Church and the Christian revelation concerning man's filiation of sonship to God. The people of our time tend to have forgotten this.

And therefore, when they wanted to liberate man with revolutions and affirm his rights, they created instead a new and more terrible tyranny -- an autocracy of society and of the people. They but unfettered the old chaos, and then the old truth of the state intruded upon their rights.

The affirmation of the mystical aspect of the state, of the religious character of the power of authority does not mean invariably a theocratic conception of the state and its power. Theocracy is first of all an ancient Jewish principle. The Christian theocracy, the Western form -- is Papist, and the Eastern -- Caesarist, and it signified a predominance of Old Testament principles within Christianity. The larger truth was not in the papal theocratic idea and not in the imperial theocratic idea, but rather in the dualistic conception by Dante, who not only expressed the Medieval spirit, but was also an herald of modern times. The sacred sense of imperialism does not signify invariably its theocratic conception. In imperialism there is an exertion of the human will, of the will of peoples, and in this historical exertion considerable freedom is predisposed to man and to the people. The task of creating a great empire cannot be merely a simple fulfilling of religious law, of a religious command, as the theocratic grounding of the imperialistic idea might want. The imperialistic will always transcends the limits of the law. As heroes of the imperialistic idea there was Alexander the Great, Julius Caesar, Peter the Great, Napoleon, Bismarck -- people of demonic will. Theocratic imperialism -- is too slick a conception, rubbing open the deepest and the tragic contradictions of the human soul. The antinomy of the "kingdom of Caesar" and the "Kingdom of God" can never be reconciled and overcome within the bounds of earthly empirical life. State and church can neither be ultimately united, nor ultimately divided, -- they are situated in an antinomic interplay, they both assist each the other, and oppose each the other. Christianity justifies and sanctifies the state, but in a strict sense of the word a "Christian state" is impossible. In the nature of the state always there will be, even if not anti-Christian, then at least in any case external to the Christian, the pagan elements. The state cannot consistently be Christianly pious. The state is not a revelation of Christian love and grace, of the brotherhood of people in the Spirit. The state -- is a phenomenon of the natural order, and not the graced. And in all the arrangements of the Christian state there is sensed falsehood and the lie. The Kingdom of God is a matter of grace, a supernatural kingdom, and in it there is no compulsory state. But it would be mistaken to see in the state a necessary minimum, a necessary evil, a least of all evils for sinful mankind, which will be abolished, when mankind rises to higher a stage. Many of you however think thus, with sympathies towards a Christian anarchism. No, you will not succeed in shunting off the state into a dark corner. The state has positive tasks, it aspires for the maximum. The imperialistic idea eternally stirs the state. The "kingdom of Caesar" is an autonomous sphere, necessary for the richness and might of God's world, in it are realised certain creative tasks, not to be realised along other paths. The kingdom of Caesar -- is an enormous aspect of the hierarchy of being. It becomes of the kingdom of evil only then, when it demands for itself divine honours, when they would make a god of it, when they substitute it for the Kingdom of God, when it enroaches upon the depths of the human spirit, upon his infinite nature. Here is why the distinction and delimitation of the two kingdoms is so important, as forever foretold by Christ. The state possesses a religious grounding, and the disintegration of this religious grounding subjects it to the danger of disintegration. The immanent grounding of the state -- is spiritual, and not material. But in the secularisation of the state there is its own relative truth. The state then emerges out from the old, the transcendent religious sanctions. It proceeds through a splintering apart of its original composition. But insofar as it loses its inner spiritual religious basis, it becomes subject to processes of disintegration and experiences great upheavals. We have to directly and fearlessly admit, that the state's existence in the world amidst the judgement of the religious Christian consciousness is antinomic and that this antinomic aspect cannot be surmounted by any sort of slick

Christian theocratic or Christian anarchistic formulations. God wanted the state for the fulfilling of His foreordained plans. And it is not for you to redo and correct the will of God. There remains but for us to live out to the end the religious contradictions of the state. For every Christian, his attitude towards the state begets tragic conflicts. It is impossible to flee them, it is needful up to the end to accept them. The Christian truth, that the human soul stands more precious, than all the kingdoms of the world, is not a denial and abolishing of the state. All of you, ye enemies of the state, are incorrect in wanting to use the Christian truth for your own ends. Ye love sometimes to use Christianity for your own utilitarian ends. And in these instances, on what you stand, there does not enter in even a grain of Christian truth, it entirely eludes you. Ye have only the empty husk remaining, only the outward formulas and words, bereft of their meaning. How misused the Gospel becomes, by those who do not believe in it. There is something inwardly ugly in this. This ugliness reaches monstrous proportions in Tolstoy. Ye would quite like to rework Christianity into an humanistic facsimile. But in this you will not succeed. All your "Christian" objections against the state -- are essentially humanistic objections. All your anarchism, for the basis of which ye also draw upon Christian arguments, is based upon positivist humanism, whereas Christianity for you is but an empty husk.

The relationship between the state and humanism is very complex. Active in the state is not only the Divine principle, from which it has come about and by which it is sanctified, but also the humanistic principle, purely human a principle. This humanistic principle has always been active in the ruling power of authority. It was there in Alexander the Great, and it attained to an extreme expression in Napoleon. The purely human activity was there also in the Russian ruling power of authority and the bureaucracy, perhaps the sole historical activity in Russia. At the basis of states and empires lies an aristocratic humanism. But there is another, a debilitating democratic humanism, which leads to the disintegration and breaking up of states and empires, which is hostile to every historical power and to every historical aspect of greatness. It does not want to permit the sacrifices by human persons and by human lives, since it cannot justify these sacrifices within the bounds of the empirical earthly life, and another life it does not admit of. Your democratic and anti-religious humanism is filled with mollifyingly soft and sentimental repudiations of the severity, the fierceness and coldness of the state, since you do not believe in a meaning to life, such as transcends the empirical shell of human life. Democratic humanism arises as a chastisement for the false paths of aristocratic humanism. In your spiritual outlook you cannot admit, that with the state is connected a value, passing over into eternity. Your humanism permits of the state only as an utilitarian means for the well-being and satisfaction of the earthly life of people. You would render the state into an organisation of interests and want to transform it over into a commercial economic institution, to transform it into a mercantile-industrial counting office. And ye rip apart the state as an autonomous reality and value. The state cannot be justified on the basis of interests. It limits the interests of every living generation and subsumes them to the great past and to a great future. Within it act not only those now living, but likewise deceased ancestors and the not yet born descendants. All your liberal, your democratic and socialistic teachings concerning the state merely bypass the nature of the state. Your teachings fail to get down to the essence of the state, they merely let off steam, trying to dissect this essence. The fate of the state and its dialectics are suchlike, that, when in an absolute monarchy is discovered an humanistic self-affirmation, betraying the religious mission of the power of authority, when Ludvig/Louis XIV says "L'etat c'est moi", -- the revolutionary people answers with another humanistic self-affirmation and democracy says: "L'etat c'est moi".

All the utopias of a perfect and godly state upon earth are based upon a confusion of various planes, the confusion of this world -- with the other world; they all manifest futile attempts to transpose a fourth dimension upon the three-dimensional expanse. Upon this are based also all the utopias, denying the state, the utopias of a stateless perfect condition upon earth. The state is an arduous and sacrificial human path in the three-dimensional, and not a fourth-dimensional expanse, within the natural world, set within evil. The state cannot be grounded only upon love. The realm of love is the realm of grace, the Kingdom of God, and not the kingdom of Caesar. Upon love is grounded the church, and not the state. The Kingdom [of God] is of a different dimension of being, than is the state. These two realms co-exist, co-contact, interact, but never do they merge, never become identical nor exclude each other, nor supplant each the other. All attempts to hitch Christian love to the state, as its sole grounding, lead to tyranny. Christian love can only be as the free flowering of human life and human community, and not with a compulsory basis for them. The rule of law thus also possesses such an enormous significance in human community, in that it serves as a guardian and guarantee of a minimum of human freedom, in that it preserves man from this, that his life be entirely dependent upon moral traits, whether from the love or hatred of some other man. Freedom and the independence of man demand, that at the basis of the state be set not only love, but likewise force and the rule of law. In this is an higher truth. Monism in societal life, the exclusive predominance of but one principle always leads to tyranny, to a quenching of the multiplicity and richness of life. The combining of multiple principles provides for the greatest freedom and multiplicity, the interacting one with another, whilst inwardly subordinated to the spiritual centre.[1] All utopias strive towards an extreme social monism and therefore lead to tyranny. And, perhaps, the most terrible tyranny is that, which is captivated by a total denial of the state in the name of this or some other principle, whether of class or the individual, international or of the people. The greatest freedom obtains then, when man senses and

[1] The French occultist Fabre d'Olivet constructed a sharp-witted social system, based upon the combining of three principles -- Divine Providence, necessity and human freedom. In this there is much that is accurate.

perceives for himself an immanent, and not transcendent state, as also all the supra-personal realities and unity.

Fourth Letter

Concerning Nation

People of your ilk, hostile to me, have given little thought concerning nation and the national problem. Ye are wont even to acknowledge the state on utilitarian grounds. But ye have proven incapable of penetrating into the intimate mystery of the national manner of life. True, you admit of the rights of oppressed nationalities and for these nationalities ye are ready to become quite extreme nationalists. Many of you tend to posture under your sign for the right of self-determination of nationalities. But this proves also, that to the mystery of national lifestyle you only can approach at it externally, that inwardly it is beyond you. You are ready to admit of the national lifestyle and national rights of the Jews or the Polish, of the Bohemians or the Irelanders, but amidst this, the national lifestyle and national rights of Russians ye never could admit. And this is because, that it is the problem of oppression which has been of interest to you, while completely uninterested by the problem of nationality. Ye proclaimed the right of the free self-determination of nationalities, not so much out of any interest for the nationalities themself and even not believing in the existence of such sort of realities. You merely need this "free self-determination" as a means of struggle for your political and social ideals, for an abstract equality and freedom, and nowise for the concrete national manner of life, not for a national flourishing. Indeed, in the national lifestyle there is for you an ungraspable irrational mystery, hidden deep in the earth. Ye have never penetrated thence, ye always remained at the surface. You are very sensitive to the Jewish question, ye struggle for the rights of the Jews. But do you have a sense of the "Hebrew", do you have a feel of the soul of the Jewish people, have you ever once penetrated into these mysteries, into these mysterious fates of Judaism, deriving back from the ancient wellsprings of mankind? No, your struggle for the Jews is not out of any desire to know the Jews, not to acknowledge the existence of the "Jewish", it is merely the international struggle for levelling an equality, a struggle for man in the abstract, for an abstraction of man. Ye do not know the concrete man in flesh and blood, in race and tribe, the man national. your struggle for the liberation of oppressed nationalities and for their equality is an international struggle, a geometric struggle, a struggle abstracting and tearing the national man off from the living countenance, from his maternity and fatherland. The "oppressors" of nationalities sometimes acknowledge them more, than do the "liberators". "They oppress" is of the living national man in terms of race and tribe, flesh and blood, whereas "they liberate" is of an abstracted geometric man. I do not want to "oppress" the Jews and the Jewish, but I also do not want to "liberate" man abstractly, as an abstraction, bereft of all his Jewishness. I deeply feel for the Jews and Judaism, all the uniqueness and unrepeatable aspect of the Hebrew fate, all its exclusiveness and unvanquishability. And as my feeling this passes over into sympathy. But I do not believe in the watering-down and making a mish-mash of resolving the Jewish question. The secrets of every national manner of life merits sympathy. It is needful to get down into it even then, when the discourse goes hostile to us as a nation. The German people was our enemy and we had to fight against them. But the unrepeatable uniqueness of the German, the most intimate thing in the German spirit, the genuinely individual in the expression of the German visage always, even at the moment of struggle, seemed to me to merit of sympathetic consideration. In our international struggle for the liberation and equality of nationalities there is no feel of perception of national visages, there is not in it the love for the national image. K. Leont'ev was correct, when he declared your national politics merely a weapon of worldwide destruction and espied in it merely the triumph of democracy and cosmopolitanism. your principles of the "right of the self-determination of nationalities", so bally-hooed about in the Russian revolution, is anti-historical an abstraction, of contrived themes, which deny the unrepeatably unique reality, which is called nationality. Nationality cannot be severed off away from the concrete history, and its right cannot be merely a matter of abstract investigation. Each nationality within the various periods of its existence possesses various rights. These rights cannot be merely watered down. there exists a complex hierarchy of nationalities. It would be thoughtless and absurd to compare the rights to self-determination of the Russian nationality and the nationality of the Armenian, the Gruzinian or the Tatar. It would be thoughtless and absurd to approach with the same abstract measurement the rights of the German nationality and the Spanish nationality at a given moment of world history. In the life of nations there occur periods of flourishing and periods of waning, periods of the high exertions of their powers and periods of weakness. And their rights to self-determination in these instances are varied. The question about the rights of the self-determination of nationalities is not some abstract-juridical question, this is first of all a question biological, in the final end a mystically-biological question. It rests upon the irrational grounding of life, which is not subject to any sort of juridical and moral rationalisations. All the historical nationalities possess quite varied, unequal rights, and they cannot be put forth under the same pretensions. In the historical inequality of nationalities, the unequalness of their real weight, in the historical predominance now of some, now of other nationalities there is its own great truth, there is the fulfilling of a moral law of historical activity, so dissimilar to the law of individual activity.

Nation is a category predominantly historical, concretely-historical, and not abstractly-sociological. It is the product of a totally unique historical activity, and its secret eludes those, who are totally bereft of the sense of historical activity, who dwell entirely within the sphere of abstract sociological categories. You people of an abstract sociological world outlook, ye cannot grasp the secrets of a national way of life, since you dissect the nation in general into abstract sociological elements. After your analysis nothing remains of the nation. And indeed, the nation is not liable to any sort of rational definitions. No sort of rationally persuasive signs explain its manner of life. All ever farther and afar, into the mysteried irrational depths recedes the lifestyle of a nation in the measure of the application to it of rational psychological or sociological definitions. The manner of life of a nation is not to be defined nor explained, be it by race, nor by language, nor by religion, nor by territory, nor by state sovereignty, although all these signs more or less are extant for the national manner of life. And most correct are those, who define the nation as an oneness of historical fate. The awareness of this unity is also what comprises the national consciousness. But the unity of an historical fate is also an irrational mystery. In this viewpoint the national consciousness is immersed within the depths of life, within the bosom of historical reality, such as is singular and unrepeatable. The Jewish people has deeply a sense of this mysterious oneness of historical destiny, although it has lost almost all the signs of a national lifestyle, and language, and territory, and state, and has fallen away from its old faith. One can conceive of this mysterious unity of historical fate in terms of the element of mixed blood, occurring from the complex confluences of races. On biological grounds, the historical nationality is not a matter of pure blood, of pure races. The formation of an historical nationality is already the result of the complex interaction and mixing of races. Race itself per se is a factour naturo-biological, zoological, and not historical. But this factour not only acts within the historical forms, it plays also a defining and mysterious role in these forms. Truly, in race there is a mysterious depth, there is its own metaphysics and ontology. From their biological sources of life the human races enter into the historical activity, within it they are active as more complex historical races. Within it a different place belongs to the white race and the yellow race, the Aryan race and the Semitic race, to the Slavic and to the Germanic race. Between the zoological race and the historical nationality there exists a whole series of intervening hierarchical stages, which mutually interact. Nationality is that complex hierarchical stage, at which most concentrated is the keenness of historical fate. In it the natural activity passes over into historical activity. The formation of the historical Jewish nationality was already the result of the interbreeding of races and the mixing of blood, in it the purely Semitic element met up with the non-Semitic elements. H. S. Chamberlain sees an effect of negative sides to the Jewish nationality in this, that the mixing was a transgressive blood-mix, the uniting of the pure Arab-Semitic with the Syriac. But however one might explain the racial origin of Judaism, the singular and mysterious historical fate of the Jewish people began after the Jewish nationality was formed. In this fate, blood plays an enormous role. But the Jewish nationality represents already a different hierarchical stage, than for example, the Semitic race, in which have transpired various historical fates. It is the historical fate of the Jewish people, namely, quite inexplicable on rational grounds, that provides us an exceptional sense of history, of historical reality. The formation of historical nationalities is not the interweaving of aspects of the biological character with aspects of the sociological character, this is rather the formation of the historically concrete, of an historical individuality from the natural racial chaos. The formation of an historical nationality is the struggle against the primitive chaotic darkness, it is the visage becoming distinct, of a countenance from out of impersonal and formless nature. This is a beneficial process of the arising of differentiations and inequalities within historical activity, where all is concrete. Even with a lop-sided and incredible exclusively anthropological, racial philosophy of history (Gobineau, H. S. Chamberlain etc.), there is in it all the same some amount of truth, which is altogether not there in the abstract, sociological philosophy of history, in ignoring the mystery of blood and according everything to rational social factours. Historical differentiations and inequalities, by way of which the historical cosmos tended to form, cannot be razed and abolished by any sort of social factours. And the voice of the blood, the instinct of the race cannot be eradicated in the historical fate of a nationality. In the blood is lodged already the idea of race and nation, the energy of the realisation of their summons. Nations -- are historical formulations, but they are lodged already in the depths of nature, in the depths of being. In the very loins of cosmic life there is a potency for national destinies, and there is an energy, pulling towards the realisation of these destinies. History is inculcated within nature. Historical activity is an enormous hierarchical step of cosmic life. In it the cosmic energy is concentrated and decides the fate of the world. Race, as a cosmic principle, acts in a concentrated manner within nationality, just as in the historical principle. Within historical activity occurs the formation of the cosmos, a verymost great struggle and vanquishing of chaotic principles by cosmic principles. Historical nationality is an attainment of cosmic being. And its destruction is a destruction of the cosmos, a return to chaos.

The nation is not an empirical phenomenon of this or some other fragment of historical time. The nation is a mystical organism, a noumenon, and not a phenomenon of the historical process. The nation is not merely the generation alive today, nor is it the sum of all the generations. The nation is not a mere composite accumulation, it is something primordial, an eternally alive subject within the historical process, in it there live and dwell all the past generations, no less so, than the contemporary generations. Nation possesses an ontological core. The national manner of life conquers time. The spirit of the nation forestalls the devouring of the past by the present and the future. The nation is always striving towards imperishability, towards a victory over death, it cannot allow the exclusive triumph of the future over the past. Here is why in the national manner of life and the national consciousness there is a religious grounding, a religious depth. Religion is the establishing of bonds and kinship, the surmounting of differingly alien a lifestyle, and in the native land first of all it is that man finds this bonding. And every attempt to sever nationality off and away from this religious depth tends to throw it off onto the surface and subject it to the danger of disintegration. The true national consciousness is a consciousness at depth, it affirms not the eradicating and death-bearing power of the historical process, but rather preserving it all by its living and resusciative power. The national consciousness is conservative not because, that it is hostile to creativity, but because that it preserves authentic life, the wholeness of life from the death-bearing destructions that await; it acknowledges our grandfathers and fathers, our forefathers, just as alive, as we ourselves, as also our descendants to be. The life of the nation, national life is an inseparable bond with forefathers and an honouring of their legacy. In the national there is always the traditional. And insofar as our revolutionism sunders the bond of time, it annihilates the memory about the past, about ancestry, and it is deeply anti-national. Internationalism is a religion of the future, not knowing boundaries in its pretensions, and not a religion of the eternal, it heralds to everything alive about death and destruction, and not about life and resurrection. Revolutionary internationalism is also a resultant religion of death, the denial of imperishability. This religion has no respect for gravesite memorials. It is directly the contrary to that great resusciative spirit, which impelled the ancients to build their cemeteries and gravesite memorials. This religion of the all-devouring what is to come has no wish still to concern itself over any connection with ancestors, over the graveyards of their forefathers, over their imperishability and with what they have in common with them in life. The national consciousness is profoundly the opposite to this spirit. And superficial and contradictory is that national consciousness of modern European peoples, who are torn away from their religious roots. The modern nationalism of the peoples of Europe has gone false at its roots. But also through an impaired and insufficiently deep national sense, the modern peoples tend to get involved in religious life, in order for themself to strive for imperishable life. In nationality, life is affirmed against the death, which internationalism threatens all peoples with. Every nation in terms of its healthy instincts strives for a maximum of power and flourishing, towards revealing itself within history. This -- is the creative side of nationalism, and internationalism is hostile to it the same, as it is to its preserving and resusciative side. Internationalism wants as though to halt the growth of the power of peoples, wants as though to pluck the bloom from them. It wants as though to divert the vital movement of peoples off to the side, into the wastelands, the distant expanse, into the dreadsome abstractions of what is to come.

It wants as though to quench the will to being for nations, the will to historical ascendency. It morally traps the national egoism into an ascetic renunciation. But behind the renunciation, with its push onto the path of non-being, lies hidden human self-assertion, class and personal egoism, the thirst for well-being, the refusal of sacrifices, such as are demanded by historical destiny, the historical movement of peoples upwards. Revolutionary internationalism destroys the past of nations and does not want to allow them to have their own future. It would subject them to a different future, dreadful in its emptiness, its abstractness. And in the most elementary, instinctive national egoism there is a greater vital truth, than in your internationalism.

Ye internationalists of all shades have made a very horrible substitution: you have replaced the being of all-mankind, of the one concrete mankind, with non-being, to which ye have given the name Internationale. You have made an hopeless hodge-podge of universality and internationalism. And ye have seduced many, have drawn the heart of many by the guileful appearance of good. The confusion, the substitution and fraud began earlier, prior to the birth of the socialist Internationale, -- in the humanist pacifism, in liberal cosmopolitanism, in Masonism. Therein already the concrete all-mankind was replaced by an abstract mankind in general. Within the positive, the concrete all-unity of mankind there enter in all the degrees of the being of man, all the fullness, in it nothing is ignored nor abolished, everything attains to its greatest power and expression. But of a concrete all-unity ye know not. It is provided for first of all within the Universal Church, and in it the oneness of mankind is conceived religiously. But completely foreign to you is the idea, that mankind is a concrete reality, as it were some person within the cosmic hierarchy. In your negative and abstract unity of mankind all the hierarchical degrees of the being of mankind are abolished, and from them occurs merely abstraction. In the concrete all-unity there cannot be an opposition between the nation and mankind: in the all-unity of mankind all nations are affirmed, and in it they attain to strength and flourishing. In the abstract unity of mankind the being of nations gets displaced -- mankind is not in the nations nor through the nations, and the nations are not in mankind nor through mankind. Mankind becomes an abstraction constructed from out of all the degrees of concrete individual being. In universality the nation and mankind -- are inseparable and presuppose each the other as members of one cosmic hierarchy. In internationalism the nation and mankind mutually excludes each the other and in the final end there is neither nation, nor mankind, since there is no sort of concrete reality, no sort of concrete individuality, there is only abstraction. There is no concrete man, but instead merely the abstracted man of class, there is no concrete mankind, merely instead an abstract mankind, an abstraction from everything organic, living, individual. Internationalism is contrary not only to nationalism, but also to universality, and to the positive sense of all-unity; within it acts the spirit of non-being, destroying realities in the name of illusions.

I know of nothing more repulsive and false, than the attempts of certain of you to give internationalism a Christian grounding and justification. Some naive and weak Christians are seduced by this. But Christianity can only be hostile to internationalism, it is hostile to the spirit of non-being, to a spirit, destroying concrete realities in the name of abstractions. Christianity affirms the concrete positive all-unity, into which enters all the richness of being. But it cannot and does not have anything in common with that abstract monism, wherein vanishes both God and the world, and there flounders man, the nation and mankind. For Christianity there exists foremost of all the soul of each man, the soul of the people, the soul of mankind. But it does not know that which has no soul. And has your Internationale a soul, your internationalised mankind? Abstractions cannot possess a soul. And indeed your internationalism asserts not a single mankind, merely a single proletariat. Ye create a greatest division within mankind, such as ever known in the history of the world. Ye deny the image and likeness of God in man and instead assert to him the image and likeness of economic position. For you man and mankind do not exist, for you there exist only economic categories, only that, what materially a man has or materially has not. And downright sacrilegious is every comparison of your internationalism with Christianity. This you deny, ye internationalists, you deny that mankind is of a single sort before God, and ye yourself are the worst enemies of the oneness of mankind. Ye would ultimately destroy within humankind the spiritual bond of the future with the past and the spiritual bond of a class chosen by you -- the proletariat -- from the remaining rejected portion of mankind. And ye therefore -- are murderers of mankind and of man. Christianity calls for the brotherhood of peoples, just as it does for the brotherhood of people. But the brotherhood of peoples presupposes the existence of people, of human persons. True love is always the affirming of the visage of the beloved, in the unrepeatable individuality. And my Russian love for the Frenchman, the Englishman or the German cannot be a love for the abstract man, the man in general, it can only be a love for the French, the English or German man, -- for the French, the English or German is what comprises his individual image. Ye however do not know love, do not know brotherhood. For you nothing exists, except abstract economic and sociological categories, comprising a great wedge within mankind. The love for some whatever nationality, the brotherly attitude towards it presupposes the affirmation of the eternal being of this nationality, does not permit of its vanishing away into an abstract mankind. And is it for you to be the heralds of the brotherhood of peoples? Internationalism is an ugly caricature, a distortion from the universal Christian spirit, its false likeness. Thus also the Anti-Christ will be in a false likeness of Christ, simply a caricature.

In the French language there are two words for denoting two completely different concepts -- *nation* and *peuple*. In Russian there are no correspondingly good words. The opposition between *natsiya (nation)* and *narod (the people)* sounds bad, since it is a oppositional contrast of a foreign word and a Russian word. But with this terminology having been established for us, it is an opposition we are compelled to deal with. Upon the word "narod" for us lies the fateful imprint of the narodnik-populist mindset, from which it is so difficult for Russians to get free of. For all of you, ye Russian narodnik-populists, consciously or unconsciously lovers of the people and worshippers of the people, it is very difficult to accept a national consciousness, and ye tend to confuse it with a narodnik-populist consciousness. Your narod-people is not a nation. You apply to the people the category of quantity and the category of social class. But to a nation these categories are inapplicable. Your narod-people is first of all an empirical quantity, a tremendous sum total of the Peters and the Ivans. Your narod-people is not a great organic whole, encompassing all classes and all generations, it is merely the masses of the common folk, the peasants and workers, only the physically toiling classes. There are quite many excluded from your narod-people, be they the intelligentsia, the gentry, the bureaucracy, the merchants, or the industrialists. And you demand service to the people, as to something outside the bodily flesh of everyone not belonging to the physically toiling classes, as to a supreme principle of life and idol. I am thus deprived of the right to sense myself of the people, within the people, and the people in myself. Hence the people's aspect was not in the depths in me. The people's aspect was outside me and above me. I have to serve the people, have to see in it the criteria of truth and right, have to bow before the people and in the name of the people have to renounce the greatest values. Upon this social class and quantitative construction of perception of the people was based traditionally the opposition between the intelligentsia and the people. The populist consciousness sundered the organic wholeness of national life and created insurmountable oppositions. The populist intelligentsia wanted to overcome the abyss between the people and the intelligentsia, they went to the people, renounced everything in the name of the people, but their populist consciousness merely made seemingly eternal the chasm between the people and the intelligentsia, since it provided it the push onto the path of social-class struggle and opposition. This chasm vanishes only upon the grounding of a national consciousness, oriented towards greater a depth. Ye have remained but on the social surface of life, ye have never gotten down to that spiritual oneness, in which disappears the opposition between noble and peasant, between the intelligentsia and the people. It is impossible to set the intelligentsia or the gentry in opposition to the nation. The national aspect is in my own particular depths and in the depths of everyone, at more deep a level, than our social trappings, in which also is found the Russian, the French, the English, the German, connecting the present with the remote past, uniting the nobility and the peasantry, the industrialist and the worker.

Nation is not this or some other class, nor is it the numerically empirical quantity of the now living people. Nation is a mystical organism, the mysterious life of which we grasp in our own particular depth, when we cease living merely at the surface of life, the life of external interests, when we get ourself free of the exclusive grip of the mere trappings, that divide people. The peasant can be less of the narod-people, than the nobleman or intelligentsia person, if his life is sundered off from the depths and thrown out on the surface, while at the same time as the life of the nobleman or intelligentsia person can be found situated at this depth and drawing upon creative power from the deep wellsprings. Thus, all your revolutionary democrats, all your workers councils and peasantry deputies have nothing in common with the people, as a nation, as a mystical organism. A thousand times moreso of the people was the nobleman Pushkin or the intelligentsia person Dostoevsky. A nation attains its most perfect and highest expression in genius. Genius is always of the people, national, in it always is heard the voice from the bosom, from the depths of national life. The spirit of the nation always is expressed through a qualitative selective process of persons, through select persons. No sort of a rational democracy with its quantitative mechanism can be the expresser of the spirit of a nation. And the will of a nation is inexpressible arithmetically, in quantities, there is not the will of the majority. In the nation speak not only the living, but also the dead, bespeaking a great past and the still enigmatic future. In the nation enter in not only the human generations, but also the stones of churches, palaces and manor-houses, gravestones, old manuscripts and books. And in order to grasp the will of the nation, it is necessary to listen to these stones, to peruse the unperished pages. But with your revolutionary-democratic din ye want to drown out the voice of the dead generations, you want to kill the sense of the past. For you is hidden off the approach to the great organic entirety, conquering the destructive power of time. And therefore ye cannot know the will of the nation, nor can ye express it. Ye set opposite the nation from the people, which ye want to transform into a revolutionary democracy. But the nation is not democracy and is inexpressible in democracy. There are more mysterious paths of its expression. And that generation, which breaks every connection with a national past, never will express the spirit of the nation and the will of the nation. This is because that in the spirit of the nation and the will of the nation there is a power resusciative, and not death-bearing. It is time, it is time already to orient ourselves not towards the "people", but towards the nation, i.e. to pass from the surface down to the depths, from quantity to quality. The national principle in societal life is a principle qualitative, and not quantitative. The *national aspect* is lodged within the ancient loins of nature, and these potential energies of the national way of life reveal themself within history. Immeasurably deeper is lodged the national, than your democracy, than your "people", than all your quantities and masses of the present day. The nation is spirit, God's plan, which the empirical people cannot realise nor undo. The empirical people has to subordinate itself to the nation, to its tasks in the world. In the nation is a noumenal, ontological core, which is not in that empirical phenomenon, which ye call the "people". It is not narodnik-populists, but rather Russians you should be. *Russia* ought to be infinitely more valuable, more sacred for you, than the people, than the human population of this or other times, in this or some other part thereof.

The state is not the definitive sign of the way of life of a nation. But every nation strives to form its own state, to fortify and strengthen it. This is healthy an instinct of the nation. The way of life with a state is a normal manner of life for a nation. A nation's loss of its state, of its independence and sovereignty is a great misfortune, a grievous ill, crippling the soul of the nation. The fact, that the Jewish people in antiquity constantly already fell under the foreigner's yoke and lost its state independence, and then altogether was deprived of a state and lived as wanderers in the world, shattered and crippled the soul of the Jewish people. There accumulated for it a nowise good feeling against all the other peoples, living in their own states, and they tended towards a revolutionary splitting away towards internationalism, which is but the reverse side of its impaired nationalism. But for the Jewish people also there has not ultimately died the will towards the forming of their own state, and the passionate dream about it is resurrected in the utopia of Zionism. The relationship between the lifestyle of the nation and the lifestyle of the state is very false. Every nation strives to form a state and reinforce itself in it. Through the state, the nation reveals all its potentials. On the other hand, the state has to have a national grounding, a national core, although the tribal composite of the state can be very complex and manifold. The Russian state was the *Russian* state, it possessed at its basis a Russian core and realised the Russian idea in the world. A state, possessing no national core nor national idea, cannot have creative life. Such a state, as Austria-Hungary, was an exception, and its existence was determined not by inner energies, but by the course of external historical circumstances. A state that is exclusively dynastic -- presents a sickly phenomenon of historical activity. The dynastic principle cannot be self-sufficing. It has to be subordinated to the national principle. But the state by its nature strives to go beyond the framework of the self-contained national state. It is only the states of small nations that remain purely national. Larger nations, conscious of their mission in the world, strive to form an imperialistic state, which goes out beyond the bounds of the national manner of life. The will of great nations is directed towards an imperialistic unification, in which also is realised the national vocation. There is a dialectic of national lifestyle, which destroys the boundary lines of nationalities and strives to transform the national state into an imperialistic state. The empire of Great Britain represents the end of England, as a national state, it is the emergence of the English nationality out onto the world stage. And the national question is there equally alike for nations small and weak and for nations large and powerful. For nations small and weak the national question is a question of liberation and independence, a question of the formation or preservation of the national state. For nations large and powerful the national question is a question of world might and a world mission, the question of the formation and extension of an imperialistic state. The national movements of the XIX Century, with which the democrats and revolutionaries sympathise, were struggles for the independence of nations small and weak, and for the reunification of partitioned nations. In this was realised the historical tendency towards individualisation, which is an indubitable part of historical truth. But alongside with this there occurred the struggle for the large historical unities, for the great historical bodies, in which was realised the historical tendency towards universalisation, which is another part of historical truth. Ye never could grasp the truth and meaning of this demonic will of the great nations, this devouring thirst for the realisation of their world missions. For you the national question was always exclusively a philistine question. You always denied the existence of the national question for Russians, for Russia itself, the Russian national question. And you drowned out the Russian national question with the question of the Armenians, the Gruzinians, the Polish, the Finns, the Jews and many others. The false state of politics under the old ruling authority, failing to understand, that the imperialistic politics of a great people can only be in the assisting and benefiting small nationalities, instead was morally conducive for you and helped in your deed of destruction. The national consciousness at certain stages of the historical might of a nation passes over into an imperialistic consciousness. But the national consciousness exceeds all limits and reaches its height in the messsianic consciousness. Messianism is a foolish state of consciousness for a people, and by its nature it is contrary both to nationalism, and to imperialism. Nationalism and imperialism stand in the natural order of things. Messianism goes beyond the natural bounds, it is a thing mystical. In messianism there is a degree of sacrifice, nowise found in nationalism and imperialism. The messianic consciousness moreover demands from a people a world service, the service of the saving of the world.

Every messianic consciousness possesses as its source the messianic consciousness of the Jewish people. The spirit of messianism is foreign to the Aryan peoples. It reveals itself only in Judaism, in the Jewish intense expectation of the Messiah, in the Hebrew consciousness of itself as the chosen people of God. The Hebrew consciousness was not a nationalistic consciousness and still less was it an imperialistic consciousness; it was a messianic consciousness. Christ the Messiah appeared within the Hebrew people, but He appeared for all the peoples of the world, for all the world. And after the appearance of Christ the Jewish messianism was impossible still within the Christian world. There could no longer be a chosen people of God, in which would appear the Messiah. But there could be the exclusively intense consciousness of a people regarding its religious and spiritual vocation in the world. This sense of chosenness and calling in a people, is similar to that, which an individual man might feel, quite irrationally, and his pretensions can be deluded. The fulfilling of a messianic calling is a free exploit of spirit, leading out beyond the bounds not only of nature, but also of history. Within the bounds of history the messianic calling is unfulfillable. The Christian messianic calling within the world always was oriented towards the end, it was always apocalyptic, its remote aspects always supra-historical. A positive historical groundwork can be undertaken only within nationalism and imperialism. Messianism however is a flash of lightning, is the folly in Christ. Messianism is not subject to any sort of rationalisations. The messianic consciousness within Christianity readily deviates towards the ancient Jewish messianism. This deviation is to be found there both in Polish messianism, and in Russian messianism. Those, who have regarded the Russian people as a God-bearing people, have adopted much from the ancient Jewish spirit. In the messianic fire can be scorched away both the national manner of life, and the imperialistic manner of life. The Polish messianism came about in consequence of the perishing of the Polish state, whereas Russian messianism preceeded the perishing of the Russian state. The way of life of every nation has religious a basis. The messianic consciousness however comprises its religious summit. Moments national and religious get interwoven and at certain points they mysteriously tighten. Thus, at the basis of Russian nationality was Orthodoxy, and our people was spiritually strengthened by it. However, at the summits of our consciousness blazed a messianic religious light. It was impossible to separate the Russian idea from the religious idea. But this splicing together of religious and national moments also created a very complex relationship between nationality and church in Russia. The Church was subjected to too great a nationalisation, and the Christian consciousness as universal was weakened. Russian messianism transitioned itself from Christian into ancient Jewish a mode. And it became necessary for us first of all to restore to health the religious foundations of our national consciousness. Russian messianism severed itself away from its religious foundations and appeared in the new guise of revolutionary messianism. And this revolutionary messianism has inflicted terrible wounds upon Russia. In the most national Russian element was discovered a principle of self-destruction.

If ye want to get in touch with the mysteries of the national lifestyle, then ponder more deeply and more seriously the Jewish question. If the indestructible, unrepeatably original and mysterious power of Judaism within history does not give you the feel of nationality, then ye are hopeless. You have contrived various methods of deciding the Jewish question, in order to quash all the acuteness of this question. Never, never will you get it right on the "Jewish", it is stronger than all your teachings, all your jumblings and simplifications. Judaism exists in the world for this, in order to demonstrate to all peoples the existence of a mystery national and a mystery religious. Indeed, too easy and too superficial do the philo-

Semite and the anti-Semite relate to Judaism. It is necessary to tackle this question at greater depth. In this question is to be sensed the judgements of God within history. Judaism has its own mission in world history, and this mission passes beyond the borders of national missions. It bespeaks the existence of wider an extent, than the national existence. Within history there is the formation and unification of larger an expanse, than with national formations and unifications, there are the spirits of races and the mission of races. There is the Latin world, which brought to mankind a particular spirit and a particular culture, there is the Germanic world, there is the Slavic world. There is a shifting within history of the spiritual mastery of these races and these missions. But there are spiritual totalities of still larger an extent -- the Aryan world, the Semitic world, the Mongol world. The Aryan race, which it is so difficult to define by investigations anthropological and ethnological, possesses its own idea within the world, its own spiritual mission. The Aryan world through Christianity has accepted into it a Semitic graft and by this has been salted. But it cannot allow the triumphing of the Semitic spirit, and it liberates Christianity also from the exclusive domination of Semitism. The unconscionable self-opinion of the Germans in this also consists, in that they regard themself the sole pure Aryans, bearers and expressers of the purely Aryan spirit. With the Germans there is their own messianic consciousness, but this messianism is not so much religious, as rather racial and spiritual-cultural. In the German messianism there is nothing apocalyptic. If the temptation for Russians is that the sole true Church is the Russian Church, that the true Christ is the Russian Christ, then the temptation for Germans is that true culture is German culture. But such a cultural messianism is an inward contradiction, since messianism has a religious, and not cultural nature. Culture can only be national, and not messianic. Messianism always thirsts to emerge out beyond the bounds of culture. German cultural messianism is just as false in its pretensions, as is the Russian revolutionary messianism.

There are perhaps two types of nationalism, two types of the understanding of nationalism. Nationalism can be the idealisation of the elemental traits of a people, of self-sufficing a people. It can be enraptured with these traits and not permit of any criticism nor of self-criticism. This -- is an elemental nationalism, and in its lower manifestations it can be a zoological nationalism. This type of nationalism can likewise pass over into a negation of the national idea and sees in the weakness of the national and the national awareness -- a national peculiarity. Russian internationalists not seldom become nationalists of such a type. The self-denial and self-destruction of Russia can readily be admitted as a Russian national peculiarity. The Russian revolutionary intelligentsia was bereft of all national feeling and national awareness. But within it were characteristically Russian traits. They destroyed Russia, but they destroyed it in a Russian way. Russian nihilism was a Russian national phenomenon. But it destroyed our national way of life. To this type of elemental nationalism, however, belonged also the moreso rightwards Slavophil currents, affirming the national idea. These currents became intoxicated with the national peculiarities, irrespective of whether they should enable or whether they hinder the resolution of national tasks, or whether they increase our power and our value in the world. But there exists another type of nationalism, a creative nationalism. For this type of national consciousness, the national manner of life is a creative edifice. This type of national self-consciousness not only permits of, but also demands a self-critique, it calls for self-criticism and rethinking in the name of the national lifestyle. The second type of national consciousness is the more lofty. But it too can become sundered off from its national groundings and roots, the national ontology. It bears light into the dark aspects of the loins of national life. An integrally whole and organic understanding of the national problem rests upon a mystical and irrational basis. A mechanical understanding of the national problem leads to various theories of federalism, of personal autonomy etc. To what your inorganic approach to the national problem leads to, your mechanical deductions, your rationalistic utopias in this area, is demonstrated by the hapless fate of Russia. The denial of the organic national manner of life in the name of abstract thoughts, in the name of an abstract justice, equality, unity etc. is always an incitement to the murder of the living being. And all of you, internationalists, levellers, simplifiers, confusers, ye are all murderers, with blood on your hands. You have killed our rodina, our native-land, a living being, bearing the name Russia. And ye were murderers always, and everywhere.

Fifth Letter

Concerning Conservatism

I want to speak at present about conservatism not as a political view and political party, but as one of the eternal religious and ontological principles of human society. Unknowable for you is the problem of conservatism in its spiritual depths. Conservatism for you is exclusively a slogan in the political struggle. And this sense of conservatism does exist, and it created both its adherents and its antagonists. Conservative political parties can be very vile and can distort the conservative principle. But this ought not to obscure the truth, that the normal and healthy existence and growth of society is impossible without conservative forces. Conservatism supports the connection across time, does not permit of an ultimate breaking of this connection, it unites the future with the past. Revolutionism is a surface phenomenon, severed off from the ontological groundings, from the core of life. This imprint of the superficial lays upon all the revolutionary ideologies. Conservatism however has spiritual a depth, it is oriented towards the ancient wellsprings of life, it has connection with its roots. It believes in the existence of an imperishable and indestructible depth. In the great geniuses and creators there was this conservatism at depth. And never would they cleave to the revolutionary superficiality. Without the conservative means there would be impossible the appearance of great creative individualities. Can you count off many a creative genius amidst the ideologues of extreme revolutionism? The best of people were not with you. They all drew upon creative energy within the depths of life. And if foreign to them was the conservatism external and political, then still the principle of conservatism both deep and spiritual could always be found in them. This conservative depth is there in the greatest people of the XIX Century, it is there with Goethe, with Schelling and Hegel, with Schopenhauer and R. Wagner, Carlyle and J. Ruskin, with J. de Maistre, with Villiers de l'Isle-Adam and Huysmans, with

Pushkin and Dostoevsky, with K. Leont'ev and Vl. Solov'ev. It is with these, who thirst for a new and higher life and who do not believe in the revolutionary paths for its attainment.

The exclusive dominance of revolutionary principles destroys the past, it annihilates not only the perishable in it, but also the eternally precious. The revolutionary spirit wants to create its life to come over the graveyards, having forgotten about the gravestones, it wants to build over the bones of its dead fathers and grandfathers, it nowise wants and it denies the resurrection of the dead and deceased of life. The revolutionary spirit wants to surrender human life to the destructive power of time. It casts all that is past into the yawning chasm of the future. This spirit makes a god of the future, i.e. the flow of time, and it has no anchorage within eternity. But truly, the past has no less a right, than does the future. The past is no less so ontological, than the future, the reposed generations are no less so ontological, than the generations to come. In that which was, is no less so of eternity, than that which will be. And as regards the sense of eternity we have a sharper sense of it in our turning towards the past. In what is it that attracts us the mystery of the beauty of the ruins? It is in the victory of eternity over time. Nothing provides such a sense of the imperishable, as with ruins. Having gone to ruin the walls, overgrown by moss on old castles, palaces and temples, present us the appearance of another world, glittering forth from eternity. In this other world the genuinely ontological is contrast against the destructive flow of time. The destructive flow of time bears away with it everything too temporal, everything, arranged for earthly well-being, and what is preserved is the imperishable beauty of eternity. In this is the secret of the beauty and the charm of memorials of the past and memories of the past, the magic of the past. And it is not only ruins that provide us a sense of the victory of eternity over time, but also the preserved old temples, old houses, old clothing, old portraits, old books, old memoirs. Upon all this lies the seal of a great and beautiful struggle of eternity with time. No sort of modern, recently constructed church, even though it represent a perfect copy in the style of ancient temples, can give that tremulous and numbing sensation, which the ancient church gives, since this sensation is begotten in us, whereby that time has attempted to put there its fatal seal but then withdrawn. And it is instructive for us, how imperishable beauty, not the destruction and decay of time, but rather the struggle of eternity against this destruction and decay, is the contrasting of another world within the process of this world. Everything new, contemporary, recently designed and built does not yet know of this great struggle of the imperishable with the perishable, of the eternity of the other world with the stream of time of this world, upon it there is not already the imprint of a communing with an higher manner of life, and therefore already there is not in it such an image of beauty. It is necessary to ponder more deeply upon this magic of the past, upon this its mysterious enchantment. This attracting and strange magic is there also in the old manor-houses, and in the old parks, and in the familial remembrances, and in all the material objects, bespeaking the old human attitudes, and in the old books, and in the very mediocre portraits of ancestors, and in all the remnants of things of old cultures. Nothing new, modern and of tomorrow, can provide such an acute feeling, since there has not occurred in it yet the great struggle of the world of eternity with the world of time. The attracting beauty of the past is not the beauty of that, what was, what was once present-day and new, this -- is the beauty of that, what is, what eternally abides after the heroic struggle against the ravaging power of time. I well know, that in the past not everything was so beautiful, that much in it was hideous and ugly. But the secret of the beauty of the past nowise is to be explained by this, that we may tend to idealise the past and imagine it quite otherwise, than it was in actual fact. The beauty of the past is nowise the beauty of that present, which happened in actuality three hundred or five hundred years back then. This beauty is the beauty of that present, which is at present, after the transformation of this past by the struggle of eternity against time. The beauty of an old church, just as the beauty of familial traditions, is the beauty of a transfigured church and transfigured familial life. The image of beauty is no longer still the image of that church, which was built a thousand years back, and is not the image of that familial life, which two hundred years back transpired on earth with all its sins, vices and human abnormality. We know a greater beauty, than our forefathers. Here at a certain depth it becomes necessary to search out the groundings of conservatism. True conservatism is the struggle of eternity against time, the resistance of incorruptibility against decay. In it there is an energy not only preservative, but also transfigurative. About this ye tend not to think, when ye judge conservatism according to your criteria.

Your revolutionary attitude towards the past is the polar opposite to the religion of resurrection. The revolutionary spirit is incompatible with the religion of Christ, since it desires not resurrection, but rather the death of all the past and departed, since it is exclusively oriented towards future generations and nowise thinks about dead ancestors, does not want to preserve the connection with their legacies. The religion of revolution is namely the religion of death because that it is exclusively immersed in the present and future earthly life. The religion of Christ is the religion of life namely because that it is oriented not only towards the living, but also to the dead, not only to life, but also to death. Whoso averts themself from the face of death and flees from it towards the anew arising life, that one is situated under the destroying grip of death, and knows merely a snatch of life. The fact, that revolution buries its own deceased in fine graves, and replaces the religious funeral singing by instead revolutionary songs, and does not put up crosses at the graves, also signifies, that it does not desire a restoration of life, the resurrection of the dead, and that everyone reposed is for it merely a tool and a means, only an opportunity for asserting the present-day and tomorrow life. The religion of revolution submissively accepts this vile law of the natural order, under the force of which the future devours the past, the moment after squeezes out the moment before; it bends the knee before this woesome and stagnant aspect of a natural life, with a fatal and death-bearing viciousness. This religion of death not only willingly reconciles itself with the death of former generations, of the fathers and grandfathers, but even would like to destroy the very memory of them, not allowing of any continuation of their life within our remembrances and paying respects, in preserving any bond with them by traditions and legacies. You, the people of a revolutionary mindset, having spurned every truth of conservatism, you do not want to hearken to the depths within you, in which ye would have heard not only your voice and the voice of your own generation, but the voice also of the departed generations, the voice of all the people throughout all its history. Ye do not want to know the will of all the people in its history, ye want to know only your own will. Ye ignobly and vilely take advantage of the fact, that your fathers, grandfathers and forefathers lay in the ground, in the graves, and cannot have their own voice. Ye do nothing wherein they might rise from the graves, ye take advantage of their absence, in order to set about your own doings, in order to use their legacy, with no regard for their will. At the basis of your revolutionary feeling of life lies a profound non-belief in immortality and non-wish for immortality. Upon the triumph of death is built your kingdom. Conservatism, as an eternal principle, demands, that in deciding the fate of societies, states and cultures, that there be heard not only the voice of the living, but also the voice of the dead, so that there be acknowledged the real manner of life not only of the present, but also of the past, in order that there not be sundered the bond with our reposed. The teaching of N. F. Fedorov concerning the resuscitation of dead forefathers is in direct contrast to revolutionism, and is a religious grounding of the truth of conservatism. The truth of conservatism is not a principle, restraining the creativity of the future, it is a principle, resusciative of the past in its imperishability. In the teaching of Fedorov there is much utopian phantasy. But his basic motif is extraordinarily profound. And in comparison with the radicalism of Fedorov all else seems quite stale and superficial.

The revolutionary denial of the connection of the future with the past, the connection between generations, as regards its religious sense -- is a denial of the mystery of the praeternal connection of the

Son and the Father, of the mystery of Christ as the Son of God. In revolution there is asserted sonship without fatherhood, as though the Son of Man has no father. The sons of revolution -- are parvenus. Revolution in terms of its spiritual nature is a sundering of the hypostaseis of fathers and sons. It as though destroys the mystery of the unity of the Holy Trinity in the world, in history, in society. And in truth, the Divine Trinity acts not only in heaven, but also upon the earth. And mankind can be of the unity of the Trinity or depart it and rise up against it. In Christianity there is affirmed the praeternal bond of the Father and the Son, and the Son is begotten of the Father. But the breaking of this bond can come from two sides, can have two opposite sources. When conservatism denies the creativity of new life, when it holds back the movement of life and represents merely a force of inertia and stagnation, it likewise is destructive of hypostasis regarding father and son, it asserts a father without son, a father which is non-begetting. Fathers, having risen up against the creative and non-destructive life of the sons, in undertaking persecution against everything dynamic in the life of the sons, likewise as though destroy the unity of the Divine Trinity, just as the sons, in a revolutionary breaking every connection with the fathers, -- is destructive of the past. They become quenchers of the Spirit. And therefore the conservative principle cannot be the sole and abstract principle, it has to be united with the creative principle, but in the preservation and resuscitation of the eternal and imperishable in the past. But in the past also there was much of the corruptible, sinful, evil, and it is consigned to the fire. The guarding of all the empty husks of the past, of all its chaff, of everything non-ontological in it is a bad, wicked and negative conservatism. It causes revolutions and becomes the reason for them. Rotting and decaying processes of the past have no right to preservation.

The nature of the conservative principle is poorly understood not only by its enemies, but also by some of its proponents. There exists a type of conservator, who is most of all constituted for the compromising of every conservatism. In the true preservation and guarding there has to be a transfigurative energy. If in it is only inertia and stagnation, then this is evil, and not good. Great is the significance of historical traditions and accounts. But in the traditions and accounts there is not only a conservative, but also a creative principle, there is a positive energy. The traditions and accounts tend eternally to be created, preserving a successive aspect. Thus, in churchly life everything is based upon sacred tradition. But tradition does not signify a stagnant tradition. There is a tradition regarding religious creativity, there is a creative tradition, a creative conservatism. And the fidelity of the tradition signifies the continuation of the creative work of the fathers and grandfathers, and not merely the remnants. In the past, in the life of the Church there was creative movement, there was a start, a commencing of human activity. The commencers and the creators were the apostles, the martyrs, the teachers of the Church, the saints. And we are unfaithful to the tradition concerning them, if we in ourself do not sense the commencing of creative religious energy. The same thing can be expanded also to all the entirety of cultural and civil life. The false and stagnant conservatism fails to understand the creative secret of the past and its connection with the creative mystery of that which is to come. Therefore in its reverse side it appears as a revolutionism destructive of the past. Revolutionism is a chastisement, lying in wait for the false conservatism, for betraying the creative tradition. In revolutionism there triumphs Hamism, the parvenue spirit. In true conservatism, however, there is a nobility of ancient origin. The historical antiquity possesses a religious, a moral and aesthetic value. The nobility of sacred antiquity is something everyone is compelled to admit in the finer moments of life, when free of the fumes of the present-day. But this value and this nobility of the remote, ancient, old, the thousand years ageless, is the value and nobility of a transformation by the spirit of eternity, and not inertia, not aridness and ossification. We religiously, morally and aesthetically revere the life in everything old and remote, not the death, a life greater, than the quickly gone moments of the present day, in which being has become indistinguishable from non-being, and wherein the bits of the imperishable get jumbled together with the vast quantity of the perishable.

The truth of conservatism is a truth of historicism, a truth of the sense of historical realness, which is completely atrophied within revolutionism and radicalism. The denial of an historical successiveness is a denial and destruction of historical reality, a lack of desire to know the living historical organism. The denial and destruction of historical succession is likewise a transgression against real being, just as is the denial and destruction of the succession of the person, of the individual human I. Historical reality is an individuum of a special sort. In the life of this reality there is an organic long length of time. Within historical activity there are hierarchical degrees. And in the destruction of the hierarchical structure of the historical cosmos there is the destroying, and not accomplishing of history. Within the historical cosmos there are utilised and established qualities, dislodgeable and undestroyable in their ontological grounding. This hierarchy of qualities, crystallised within history, ought not to hinder the formation of new qualities, ought not to restrain the creative movement. But also no sort of creative motion, no sort of formation of new qualities can destroy and topple the already crystallised historical values and qualities. The maturation of life and the increase of values is accomplished through the conservative principle, transfiguring the old life for eternity, and through the creative principle, creating new life for the selfsame eternity. The rift between fatherhood and sonship, which is wrought by a false conservatism and a false revolutionism, represents a debilitation of life, represents the spirit of death for the past or for that to come.

Incorrect, false and ugly is your exclusive faith in the future. This futurism -- is your root sin. It destroys and dissolves the whole historical and cosmic manner of being. That futuristic world-feeling, which is manifest in connection with new trends in art, has a quality of radicalism, it leads ultimately to a revolutionary denial of the past while making a god of the future, and makes thence final bold deductions. All you social revolutionaries of various hues, you are so half-fast and hopelessly shallow, that ye cannot plumb the depths of the futuristic sense of life. Your futurism proves extreme and radical only on the social plane. But all your thinking, all your sense apperception of life is so outmoded, so inert, your consciousness is so hemmed in by the categories of the past. Your idolatry of the future belongs to the bad aspect of the past and is derived from it. Indeed, a new sort of soul would not sin with this idolatry, it would be free as regards the times. Every pitiful illusion -- imagines the future tinged in a radiant happy light, whereas the past -- is in a light gloomy and black! Every pitiful delusion sees in the future a greater reality, than in the past! How can it be that upon quickly-fleeting time should depend the reality of being and the quality of being! What a slavery there is sensed in such an attitude towards life! Truly, one mustneeds at a greater depth to seek out the authentic realities and qualities of being. A true and a total attitude towards life ought to affirm the eternal, the eternal in the past and the eternal in the future, as a single life prolonged, has to seek out the genuinely ontological. And indeed, it is the ontological, and not the illusionistic attitude towards life that has to reveal the creative stirring within the depths of being, the ontological stirring of the most absolute actuality, and not your superficial stirrings, fragmenting being into phantasmic moments of motion. The conservative principle possesses a religious significance, as affirming the fatherly hypostasis, eternally of value and existent in the past, as a will to a resuscitation of the past into life eternal. And it nowise contradicts the creative principle, likewise oriented towards eternity in the future, in its affirming the hypostasis of sonship. The emergence of a radical futurism was inevitable, and it is necessary moreover to welcome it. Within it is ultimately exposed the lie of the revolutionary attitude towards both the past and the future, wherein is revealed the abyss of non-being, which the half-fast and shallow revolutionaries fail to see.

There exists not only the sacred tradition of the Church, but also the sacred tradition of culture. Without tradition, without a continuity and successiveness, culture is impossible. Culture is derived from the cult. In the cult however there is always a sacred connection of the living and the dead, of the present and the past, always there is the veneration of ancestors and an energy, directed towards their resuscitation. And inherited from the cult, culture has received this revering of gravestones and memorials, this sustaining of the sacred bonds of time. Culture per se strives to assert eternity. In culture there is always the conservative principle, preserving and prolonging the past, and without it culture is unthinkable. The revolutionary consciousness is hostile to culture. This came about from its hostility to the cult, at its very start it had fallen away from the cult, from the established cultic connection. Initially it was there in the Iconoclastic heresy, rebelling against the cultic aesthetics. All of you, ye people of the revolutionary spirit, ye are all iconoclasts. It is impossible to believe you, when you say, that you will be for culture, when ye establish your own "prolekults" and other deformities. There is much you have need of from the tools of culture for your own utilitarian ends. But hateful for you is the soul of culture, its cultic soul, sustaining the fire in the unquenchable lampada, preserving the connection of the times within eternity, oriented towards those at rest, as also towards the living. Ye want as though to force out the soul from culture and leave from it only the outward trappings, only the skin. Ye desire civilisation, but not culture. In true conservatism they tend to respect the creative doings of the predecessors, who started and created the culture. Ye however have spurned this matter of respect, since the great predecessors are stifling for you. Ye want as though to set things up and stroll at freedom, without the past, without predecessors, without any connecting bonds. Your revolutionary rebelliousness is indicative of your creative impotence, your weakness and insignificance. Since why would the strong, sensing in themself a creative might, rise up against reposed creators, and commit outrages over the graves? Culture presupposes a conservative principle, a principle, preserving the past and resusciative of the dead, and this conservative principle cannot be timid and forced into the boldest creativity. The creative principle and the conservative principle cannot be set in opposition. New temples ought not without fail to destroy the old temples. The future is compatible with the past, when the spirit of eternity is victorious. The revolutionary, however, or reactionary opposition of principles conservative and creative reflects a victory of the spirit of corruptibility. Culture presupposes both the same a conservative principle, just as it does a creative principle, preservation and initialisation. And culture tends to perish, when one of these principles triumphs exclusively and squeezes out the other. The flourishing of culture demands also a reverent regard towards the graves of the fathers, and creative boldness, initiative of the unprecedented.

The image of Rome represents an eternal image of culture. The complex composite of Rome, and the accumulation within it of many cultural epochs, preserved in it as the traces of world history, tends to teach us to acknowledge this eternal, this conservative-creative nature of culture, this great connecting bond of the times, this preservation and transfiguration of the past within the present and the future. At Rome are the memorial testaments of human creativity, and the memorials of history have been transformed into phenomena of nature. The ruins of Rome provide a mighty and stirring sense of eternity. With an especial intensity this enticing feeling pervades one, when one looks upon Campania, upon the Appian Way, upon the ancient graves. Thereof is the domain of those at repose, thereof a land not still of birth, but rather wherein the past has inherited eternity, has entered into the undying life of the cosmos. Thereof it is recognised, that human history is an inseparable part of cosmic life. One sees at Rome many a temple of complex construct, combined of several cultures and cultural epochs. On the ruins of an ancient pagan temple is set a temple of the early Christians, and upon this a yet later Christian temple. Thus, for example, the charming temple of St. Marie in Cosmedin and the more reknown St. Clemento. This provides an exceptional sense of the indestructible, the eternally abiding reality of history. The construct of Roman culture is similar to the geological construct of the earth, it is a manifestation of the cosmic order. Rome deepens immensely the sense of historical life. In it the graves -- are a domain of life, and not death, the catacombs speak to the eternal foundations of our culture and history, speak about the possibility of their passing over into eternity. All this is difficult and vexing in a first experiencing of Rome, the comprising and the co-dwelling of the Rome of antiquity, the early Christian Rome, the Rome of the Renaissance and the Baroque Rome convincingly speaks about the eternal connecting bonds of time within culture and history, about the combining and confluence of principles conservative and creative. The revolutionary denial of all conservatism is barbarity. And the revolutionary elements -- are barbarian elements. The revolutionary spirit is the reaction of the barbarian element against culture, against the cultural tradition. But within culture there can occur stagnation, the dessication of creativity, which makes this reaction inevitable. The whole of European culture, which foremost of all is the Latin culture, is grounded upon the tradition of antiquity, upon the organic with its connections and therefore already it includes within it a conservative principle. Ye fail to have a sense of this because ye are indifferent towards culture, and since your ideal of sociability is not a cultural ideal. The conservative principle tends to be completely denied by those, who deny the uniqueness of historical activity. The admitting of the very fact of the existence of this activity already presupposes the admitting of the conservative principle, i.e. the preservation of its unity and successive flow. Ye however seek to replace the concrete historical activity with an abstract sociological activity, and therefore the conservative principle presents you an obstacle upon the path of your abstraction.

The conservative principle in societal life does not allow for the casting down of the societal cosmos, formed by the creative and organising work of history. This principle holds in check the pressure of the chaotic darkness from below. And the meaning of conservatism therefore is not in this, that it hinder movement forward and upwards, but the rather in this, that it hinders movement backward and downwards, towards the chaotic darkness, with a return to the condition, prior to the formation of states and cultures. The significance of conservatism -- is in the hindrances, which it sets for the manifestations of the savage-chaotic element within human societies. This element is always there latent within man, and it is connected with sin. And you, ye ideologues of revolutionism, denying all and any rights for conservatism, are yourself under the grip of delusions and lead others astray, when ye repeat your trite commonplaces to the effect, that revolutionism always is movement forward, and conservatism -- is movement backwards. Quite often within history the revolutionary movement forwards was an illusionary movement. And instead it was really a movement backwards, i.e. the intrusion into the societal cosmos such as was being formed by the creative process of history, the intrusion by a chaotic darkness, which drags downwards. And therefore the struggle between conservative and revolutionary principles can seem a struggle between principles cosmic and chaotic. But conservatism can render itself a principle, restraining movement forward and upwards and hence negative, in the instance where it conceives itself as the sole cosmic principle of human life and stands in hostile regard towards the creative principle. The checks in place guarding against the chaotic darkness below, formed by many generations in the societal cosmos itself per se, are insufficient. The chaotic darkness, possessing a wellspring unfathomable, ought not only to be held in check and not permitted within the societal cosmos, it ought likewise to be subjected to light and creatively transformed. The conservative and the creative principles have to serve one and the same cosmic deed, the great deed of the struggle against the worldwide chaos and against the sin, which has given over human societies into the grip of this chaos. And if the chaotic and formless darkness itself per se be not as yet evil, as merely rather deriving of the unfathomable wellspring of life, then it becomes evil, when they attempt to sanction and sanctify it, and attempt to make it into a guiding principle of human life. Within the revolutionary ideologies, chaos receives rationalistic sanctions.

The life of individual people, of human societies and of all historical mankind receives eternally new sources of renewal from vastly still dark, chaotic, barbarian powers. These powers renew the decrepit and congealed blood of mankind. New human races and new human classes come into communion with the historical cosmos. This -- is an inevitable process for the good. The darkness has to enter into the kingdom of light, in order to become enlightened and to support the sources of light by new powers, rather than resulting with this, the casting down of all the lanterns and spreading the realm of darkness. The entrance of new powers into the historical cosmos and the historical light is a process organic, and not mechanical. As with every organic process, this process presupposes hierarchic principles, and hierarchic vital structure. The total casting down of the hierarchical principle topples in turn all the lanterns and extinguishes the light gotten with such toil and pain. The lanterns ought to be guarded ,so that the darkness should come to commune with the realm of light, and not cast down the realm of light. Within the cosmos there is an unfathomable chaotic grounding, and from it spouts forth the source of new powers. But the cosmos has to preserve its hierarchical structure, its central source of light, in order not to be ultimately overturned by the chaotic powers, in order to fulfill its own Divine pre-ordained plan, in order that the darkness be in-lightened, in order that the chaos should be communed into cosmos. The revolutionary mindset does not understand these profound relationships between chaos and cosmos, hidden beneathe all the societal turnabouts and changes. The pure, the abstract revolutionary consciousness, quite contrary to nature and monstrously so, seeks to unite the chaotic and the rationalistic, it bows simultaneously to chaos, and to rationalism. It is opposed to the cosmic and the mystico-organic. The revolutionary consciousness does not want to account with the organic nature of man and human society, with their physiologies and psychologies, possessing great stability. It does not want to know, that these physiologies and psychologies have deeply "mystical" a basis. And this is a feature of extreme rationalism, which leads to a rationalistic violation of nature, which avenges itself. Societal developement and societal changes have to reckon with organic nature and its inexorable laws. But this rationalistic violation of the organic nature of man and of society transpires through powers chaotic, digressing from the cosmic rhythm or not yet having entered into it. This uniting of chaos with rationalism is one of the paradoxes of societal philosophy, which bespeaks the contradictions of human existence. In the growth and blossoming of the tree there is neither chaos, nor rationalism. It is the same also for the nature of human society, immersed in the bosom of cosmic life. But the chaotic element and rationalism within the life of human societies appears as the result of the evil issuing from human freedom, of that capricious freedom, which is a sign of human slavery. The laws of nature, holding chaos in check within the cosmos, crumble down upon human society, bringing it onto the path of chaotic and rationalistic violence, and they return man to the prison of his old physiology and psychology, nowise conquered nor overcome by revolution. Chaos cannot free man, since it is the source of the slavery of man. Revolution is powerless to change human nature; it leaves it remaining organically old, subject to the old and unsurmounted physiology and psychology, whilst making pretentious claims to mechanically create a new society and life. This also renders revolutions to a remarkable degree illusionary, not having roots. This powerlessness of revolutionary chaos to alter human nature, to overcome the laws of its physiology and psychology, this being sundered off from the mystical depths of organic life, -- also provides the basis for the truth and rights of conservatism. If revolutionism had the power really and substantially to alter and transform human nature and make a new and better life, then it would be justified. But since revolutionism is lying, when it says that it can do this, since it is but the attainment of illusions, then the reaction of conservatism against it is a necessitated reaction from a violated, non-transformed nature.

The conservative principle is not a violence-prone principle nor ought it to be. This -- is a free-organic principle. There is in it an healthy reaction against the violation of organic nature, against the attempts of the murdering of life, which seeks to prolong itself. The conservative principle itself per se is not opposed to developement, it only demands, that developemental growth be organic, that the future not destroy the past, but rather should continue to develope it. Woesome is the fate of that land, in which there is no healthy conservatism, lodged within the people itself, and having no fidelity, no connection with its forefathers. Hapless is the lot of a people, which loves not its own history and wants to start it all over again. Such is the unhappy fate of our land and our people. If conservatism exists only with the ruling authority, severed off from the people and opposed to the people, and not being within its people, then all the developemental growth of the people is rendered impaired. In conservatism, as a connection with eternity, there has to be not only power, but also truth, stirring the people's heart, and grounded in its spiritual life. A despised and repugnant conservatism is powerless, it can coerce, but it cannot attract to itself nor maintain itself. And unhappy is the land, in which all conservatism renders itself loathed and coercive. When conservatism is associated in the mind of the people with the hindering of developement and hostility towards creativity, then in the land revolution awaits. Culpable in this become both those conservative powers, which have permitted within them the deadening and ossification, and those revolutionary powers also, which rise up against the eternal principles, against the non-transitory values and sanctities. The conservative energy likewise has to be immanent to the people, just like the creative energy, it cannot be exclusively external for it. Revolution signifies an extreme transcendent aspect for everything Divine and spiritually of value. In the final end every healthy conservative tendency, without which there cannot be the preservation of the societal cosmos, has its support in the thousand year feeling of the people, which it is impossible to destroy in a single day, minute or year. The spiritual turnabouts in the life of a people however occur not by those paths, by which occur revolutions. The greatest spiritual turnabout within the history of mankind -- the appearance of Christianity in the world -- was not a revolution in our sense of the word. The greatest freedom for man obtains by a combination of the conservative principle with the creative principle, i.e. the harmonic developement of the societal cosmos. New revelations of the spiritual world however arose on different a plane, eluding our gaze. Ye both want to preserve memory of yourself in generations to come, and ye want a longevity in historical life. And by this ye assert some whatever truth of the conservative principle. And if indeed ye do want, that there be preserved memory concerning you and that you should continue to live on, then ye ought to preserve the memory concerning your dead forefathers and ye ought to resuscitate them unto life eternal. "Honour thy father and thy mother, and well will it be with thee, and long-lived wilt thou be upon the earth". Within the religious depths is lodged the conservative principle. Therein also is lodged the creative principle.

Sixth Letter

Concerning Aristocracy

Love for the aristocratic idea has become allotted to few in your democratic age. They consider aristocratic sympathies either as the manifestation of class instincts, or as aestheticism, having no vital significance. But in truth, there is more a depth, more vital groundings, within aristocracy. These groundings have now grown dim, and about them they begin to doubt. But for one interested in the essence of life, and not its superficial aspect, one would have to admit, that it is not aristocracy, but rather democracy which is bereft of ontological foundations, that namely it is democracy which does not have in itself anything noumenal, and that its nature is purely as phenomenon. The aristocratic idea demands a real predominance of the finest, democracy -- the formal predominance of all. Aristocracy, as the governing and rule by the finest, as the demand of a qualitative selection, remains forever the highest principle of societal life, the sole worthwhile utopia of man. And all your democratic outcries, with which ye fill the squares and bazaars, do not drown out from the noble human heart the dreams about the dominance and rule by the finest, the select, nor do they drown out this call from the depths, that the finest and select should appear, in order that the aristocracy should enter into its eternal rights. For our craven times it is seemly to remember the words of Carlyle from his wondrous book, "Heroes and the Heroic in History": "All the social processes, such only as you can observe in mankind, lead to one end -- they either attain it or they do not, but this other question, -- namely: to ascertain their able man (the capable man) and invest him with *the symbols of capacity* by grandeur, veneration or whatever else you please, yet only that he should possess the actual possibility to guide people in accord with his own capability. Constituent assemblies, parliamentary proposals, bills on reform, French revolutions, all strive, essentially, towards my indicated goal or in the opposite instance exhibit complete thoughtlessness. You seek out the most capable man in a given land, you set him up as loftily, as you can, invariably you honour him, and you receive in full complete governance, and no sort of ballot box, parliamentary eloquence, or speech-making, constitutional institute, no sort of anything mechanical can further improve the position of such a land even one iota". And it is not improper in our times to bring to mind Plato. In his aristocratic utopia there is something eternal, though its trappings be temporal. The aristocratic principle itself cannot be surpassed. It was there in the Middle Ages and will be there in the times to come. As long as the human spirit be alive and the qualitative image of man not be ultimately smothered by the quantitative, man will strive towards a domain of the finest, towards a true aristocracy. And what can ye oppose to this utmost human dream, this sole worthy utopia? Democracy, socialism, anarchy. I shall examine still further all these, your dreams and utopias. The aristocratic principle -- is ontological, organic and qualitative. All your principles, be they democratic, socialistic or anarchistic, -- are formal, mechanical and quantitative, they are all indistinct and indifferent to the actual realities and qualitative aspects of being, for the sustaining of man.

In essence, it is impossible even to contrast aristocracy with democracy. This is a matter of concepts incommensurable, quite totally different qualitatively. Although it is conceivable, that democracy can posit as its goal the selection of the finest, and thus the establishing the domain of a true aristocracy. Amidst this goal can be posited the searching out of a real, not merely formal aristocracy, i.e. the setting aside of that aristocracy, which is not of that domain of the finest, and the opening up of free paths for a true aristocracy. All the democratic forms portrayed by you but poorly serve these ends and are forgotten about in the name of the shallow interests of the present-day. Democracy is all too easily transformed into the formal tool of an organisation representing special interests. The search for the finest is replaced by the search for the moreso answerable to interests, better at accommodating them. Democracy itself per se possesses no inner, ontological content, and therefore it can accommodate itself to ends quite very contradictory. This in essence renders it distinct from aristocracy, which is an ideal of nobility, of nature, of quality. One is thus not outwardly a fraud, is not subject to too pitiful the illusions. From the very creation of the world there always have ruled, do rule and will rule a minority, and not the majority. This is true for all forms and types of governance, for monarchies and for democracies, for eras reactionary and for eras revolutionary. From the governance of a minority there is no escape. And your democratic attempts to create a domain of the majority, in essence, appear but a miserable delusion. The only question is in this, whether the minority that rule be of the finest or of the worst sort. One minority gets replaced by another minority. Here it is in all its entirety. The worst sort topple the finest or the finest topple the worst. Direct goverance and rule of authority by the human masses cannot be, this is possible only as a moment of elemental mass outpouring in revolutions and revolts. But very quickly occurs the differentiation, wherein is formed a new minority, which snatches the power into its hands. In revolutionary eras there rule a throng of demagogues, who craftily manipulate the instincts of the masses. Revolutionary governments, accounting themself to be of the people and democratic, always become tyrannies by the minority. And seldom, seldom does this minority become a selection of the finest. The revolutionary bureaucracy usually becomes even more vile, than the old bureaucracy, which the revolution topples. The revolutionary masses always become merely the atmosphere for the realisation of this tyranny by the minority.

The triumph of democracy is always indeed illusory and short-lived, it lasts but a mere moment. And illusory the same would be the triumph of socialism, if it were even possible. You would have to free yourselves of wordplay and the external trappings, and penetrate with clearer a look into the very essence of life. In the most real and authentic actuality the question always comes down to this, whether what triumphs be aristocracy or ochlocracy, mob-rule. In essence, only two types of power exist -- aristocracy and ochlocracy, the rule by the finest and the rule by the worst. But always, always but few do the governing; such is the invariable law of nature. The governance by all signifies nothing real, besides a dark, indistinct and jumbled chaos. Every arrangement by this chaos presupposes the distinction and separating out of these or other elements, of an aristocracy or an oligarchy. There exists an invariable tendency towards the formation of a nobility. The nobility remains forever as a model more qualitatively lofty a condition, begotten of differentiation and completion. The bourgeois have imitated the nobility, and the proletariat also copy and imitate it. All the parvenue desire to be nobility. And in socialism the proletariat desires to be the new nobility, the new aristocracy. In the world, evidently, there has to be a minority, set within a privileged position. The destruction of the historical hierarchy and the historical aristocracy does not mean the abolition of every hierarchy and every aristocracy. There forms instead a new hierarchy and a new aristocracy. Every vital level -- is hierarchical and has its own aristocracy, non-hierarchical only is the pile of dust and only in it is there not separated out any sort of aristocratic qualifications. If a true hierarchy is broken and the true aristocracy destroyed, then there appear false hierarchies and a false aristocracy is formed. A bunch of swindlers and murderers from the dregs of society can form a new pseudo-aristocracy and represent the hierarchical principle within the structure of society. Suchlike is the law of everything living, of everything, endowed with vital functions. Only a pile of sand can exist without hierarchy and without aristocracy. And your judgemental denial of the hierarchical-aristocratic principle always leads to an immanent chastisement. In place of an aristocratic hierarchy there forms instead an ochlocratic hierarchy. And the dominion of the black elements creates its own select minority, its own selection of the best and the strongest among the rogues, the foremost of the rogues, the princes and magnates of the rogue realm. On the religious plane, the toppling of the hierarchy of Christ creates the hierarchy of the Anti-Christ. Without the pseudo-aristocracy, without a reverse sort aristocracy you would not survive a single day. Everything plebian wants as though to fall into an aristocracy. And the plebian spirit is a spirit of envy towards the aristocracy and hatred toward it. The simplest man of the people cannot be a plebe in this sense. And thus in the peasantry there can be features of a genuine aristocratism, never given to envy, there can be the hierarchical features of its own bearing, foreordained of God.

Aristocracy is inborn, having ontological a basis, possessing one's own unique and unaffected features. Aristocracy was created by God and from God it receives its qualities. The toppling of an historical aristocracy leads to the establishing of another aristocracy. Both the bourgoise, the representatives of capital, and the proletariat, representative of labour, can make pretense to be aristocrats. The aristocratic pretensions of the proletariat exceed moreover the pretensions of all the other classes, since the proletariat, inn the teaching of its ideologues, has to conceive of itself as a chosen class, a class -- messianic, the sole genuine humanity and higher race. But every desire to emerge out into the aristocracy, to rise up into the aristocracy from some lower condition, essentially is not aristocratic. There is possible only the natural, the inborn aristocraticism, the aristocraticism from God. The mission of a true aristocracy -- is not so much to ascend to still unattained and higher conditions, as rather to descend to lower conditions. Aristocraticism, both the inward, and outward, -- is something innate, and not obtained. Proper to aristocraticism -- is generosity, and not greed. True aristocracy can serve others, can serve man and the world, since it is not concerned with self-advancement, for to begin with it stands sufficiently high. It -- is sacrificial. In this eternal value is the aristocratic principle. In human society there has to be those, who have no need to exalt themself, who are free of the ignoble features, connected with self-advancement. The rules of aristocracy -- are innate rules, and not of acquired goods. There have to be in the world people, in whom there are innate rules, there mustneeds be the emotional type, free of the atmosphere of the struggle for the acquisition of rights. Those, who in toil and in struggle acquire their rights and advance their living condition, are not free of many bitter feelings, of being wronged, often from spite, they are smothered by the aspect of their lower past. I speak, certainly, not about those exceptional people, for whom such laws be not writ, but concerning rather the average level among people.

There is possible and can be justified only the aristocracy by the mercy of God, an aristocracy by spiritual descent and calling and an aristocracy by nobility of origin, in connection with the past. That which presents itself to you as unjust and disturbing in the position of the aristocrat, is that which is the justification of his existence in the world, the privilege by origin, by birth, and not by personal merits. One can be the aristocrat irregardless of personal merits, personal toil and personal attainments. And this has to be so in the world. Genius and talent belong to the spiritual aristocracy, because that genius and talent -- are gifts, not merited, not earned repayments. Genius and talent are received innately through birth, through spiritual origin and spiritual legacy. The spiritual aristocracy possesses that selfsame nature, as does the social and historical aristocracy, and this is always a privileged race, endowed with the gift of its preeminence. and such a spiritually and physically privileged race has to exist in the world, in order that there should be expressed the features of the nobility of soul. Nobleness is likewise the emotional grounding of every aristocratism. The nobleness is not something acquired, not earned, it is a gift of destiny, it is a trait of nature. The nobleness is a special sort of emotional grace. The nobleness is directly contrary to every pettiness and jealousness. The nobleness is an awareness of its belonging to a true hierarchy, of its initial and by birth abiding within it. The noble aristocrat knows, that there are hierarchical ranks standing higher. But this does not arouse in him any sort of bitter feelings, does not devastate him, does not shake his sense of dignity. His consciousness of dignity is likewise an emotional grounding in aristocratism. This dignity is not something acquired, but rather is innate by birth. This -- is the dignity of the sons of noble fathers. Aristocratism is sonship, it presupposes the connection with fathers. Those lacking in origin, not knowing their paternity cannot be aristocrats. And the aristocratism of man, as an higher hierarchical degree of being, is the aristocratism of sonship to God, the aristocratism of the nobleborn sons of God. Here is why Christianity -- is an aristocratic religion, a religion of the free sons of God, a religion of the gifted grace of God. The teaching concerning grace -- is an aristocratic teaching. Non-aristocratic however is every psychology of being wronged, every psychology of pretension. Such indeed -- is a plebian psychology. But aristocratic is the psychology of guilt, the guilt of the free children of God. It is more characteristic for the aristocrat to sense himself at fault, than to feel wronged. Christianity is pervaded by this aristocratic psychology. The Christian awareness is that of the sons of God, and not slaves of the world, the children of freedom, and not children of necessity, -- this is an aristocratic awareness. Those, who sense themself stepsons to God, and wronged by fate, tend to lose the noble and aristocratic features. The aristocrat as noble, has to feel that everything, that elevates him, is received of God, and everything, that diminishes him, is the result of his guilt. This is directly opposed to that plebian and ignoble psychology, which senses everything uplifting as earned, and everything diminishing, as through the fault of and wronging by others. The aristocrat type is directly the opposite to this type of the slave and parvenue. These are different variants of soul. The aristocratic stock of soul can also be that of the grimy worker, while at the same time the nobleman can be a rogue.

Ye want as though to drag down the quality of the human race, want as though to abort the aristocratic features from the human image. Aristocratic nobility is all rot to you. Ye build your realm upon the plebian psychology, upon the psychology of affront, envy and malice. Ye take everything, that is of the worst from the worker, from the peasant, from the intelligentsia bohemian, and from this worst of everything ye want to create the life to come. Ye appeal to the vengeful instincts of human nature. From this is begotten your sense of good, blazes forth your light of this darkness. Your Marx taught, that in evil and from evil has to be born the new society, and the arousing of the darkest and most monstrous human feelings he reckoned upon as the path for it. He set the emotional type of the proletariat in contrast to the emotional type of the aristocrat. The proletarian is also one, who knows not his own descent and reveres not his ancestors, and for whom there does not exist kin and native land. The proletarian consciousness infers vexation, envy and vengefulness as among the virtues of the new man to come. He sees liberation in that selfsame revolt and uprising, which is a very terrible slavery of soul, its captivity by outward things, by the material world. The proletarian is cast out upon the superficial surface. The aristocrat however has to live at greater a depth, having deeper feeling of connections and roots. The proletarian consciousness rends the bonds of time, destroys the cosmos. The proletarian psychology and the proletarian consciousness does not have to be, is not obliged to be that of the worker, of a man, standing at the lower rungs of the social ladder. And the slave can sense himself a son in regard to God, and to native land, to father and mother, can deeply experience his connection with the great national and cosmic totality, his place within the hierarchy. I have known grimy workers, who were moreso the aristocrat, than many a nobleman. But ye want not, that the worker should be in so noble a condition, ye want to transform him into a genuine proletarian and into a plebian by conviction. In the foundation of your realm, hostile to every aristocraticism, ye stoke up the revolt of the slave and the rebelliousness of the plebian. In the revolt and rebelliousness there is something of the slave and the lackey. One that is noble, and conscious of his own higher dignity, guarding within him the higher image of man, be he an aristocrat of spirit or an aristocrat by blood, if he not degenerate and fall, -- will find other paths to stand up for truth and right, to expose falsehood and the lie. From the inner aristocraticism, from the ennobling of soul there can be born a new and better life. But never will it be born from the slave's rebelliousness, from the lackey's denial of every sanctity and value. Your type of the proletariat is the embodied negation of eternity, the assertion of perishability and temporality. The true type of the aristocrat is however oriented towards eternity.

In aristocraticism there is a Divine injustice, a Divine whimsy and caprice, without which would be impossible cosmic life, the beauty of the universe. The ungifted, the plebian-proletarian demand of a levelling justice and requital to each according to his quantitative toil is an infringement upon the blossoming of life, upon the Divine profuseness. At still greater a depth this is an enroachment upon the mystery of Divine grace, the demand for a rationalisation of this mystery. But in the injustice of the Divine superabundance can lie hidden the higher meaning of the world's life, its blossoming. The aristocracy within history can fall and decay. It usually tends to fall and decay. It can readily become too brittle, too ossified, and locked off from the creative impulses in life. It has the tendency towards the formation of castes. It begins to stand in opposition to the people. It betrays its destiny and in place of service and demands for itself privileges. But aristocraticism is not a right, aristocraticism is a duty, an obligation. The aristocratic virtue -- is in giving, and not in taking. The aristocrat is one, to whom moreso is given, who can share out from his abundance. The struggle for power and for special interests is by its nature non-aristocratic. Aristocratic power, the power of the best and most noble, the strongest in their giftedness, is not a right, but an obligation, not a pretension, but rather service. The rights of the finest -- are rights innate by birth. The struggle of the finest and their efforts are directed at the fulfilling of obligations, directed at service. Aristocracy as regards its very idea -- is sacrificial. But it can betray its idea. Then it becomes too entangled in its external prerogatives and it falls. But always it must be kept in mind, that the masses of the people emerge from darkness and commune with culture through the effort of the aristocracy and the fulfilling of its mission. The aristocracy was the first to emerge from the darkness and received God's blessing therein. And at certain stages of historical developement the aristocracy has to renounce certain of its rights, in order to continue to play a creative role within history. If there is in Russia still a genuine aristocracy, then it ought by way of sacrifice to renounce the struggle for its violated privileged interests. The aristocracy is not a social estate or class, the aristocracy is a certain spiritual principle, by its nature indestructible, and it acts in the world in various forms and formations.

Certain of you are ready to admit of a spiritual aristocracy, although not very enthusiastically. But too simplistically do ye tend to make a connection between a spiritual aristocracy and the historical aristocracy. You think, that the historical aristocracy is representative only of the evil of the past, that it has no right to existence and that it possesses no sort of correspondence to a spiritual aristocracy. In actual fact, everything is more complex, that you imagine it. Everything indeed becomes more complex, than it seems to you, ye simpletons. No one, certainly, should tend to confuse and regard as identical a spiritual aristocracy with the historical aristocracy. The representatives of the historical aristocracy can stand quite low in the spiritual regard, and the very utmost representatives of a spiritual aristocracy cannot emerge and even usually do not emerge from the aristocratic strata. This -- is indisputable and elementary. But it is impossible to deny the significance of blood, of inheritance, of a racial social selection for the working out of an average type of soul. You are too inclined to take man in the abstract, as an arithmetical unit, ye abstract man off from his ancestors, from his inherited traditions and customs, from his upbringing, from the centuries and millennia, alive in his blood, within the cells of his organic being, from all the organic connections within man. But your abstract, arithmetical man is a fiction, not a reality, it is bereft of any content. You consider man that he is alike with all others, -- two hands, two legs, two eyes, one nose etc. But what eludes your glance namely is that man, even to greater a degree, is dissimilar with every other. In the human individuality there cross many a current in forming the nature of man. Man is organic, by blood he belongs to his race, to his nationality, to his social condition, to his family. And in the unrepeatable, belonging only to him alone individuality there are uniquely refracted all the racial, national, societal, familial inheritances, traditions, wonts and customs. The human person takes its crystalline form upon this or some other organic soil, it has to have the supra-personal compactive medium, in which will occur the qualitative selective process. One of the greatest errors of every abstract sociology and abstract ethics -- is this failure to admit the significance of the racial selection, in forming the nature, in the working out of the emotional as well as physical type. The racial aspect does have an enormous significance in the type of man. But man can surmount the racial delimitation and pass on into infinitude. And he ought to possess such an individualising nature. The nobleman, in surmounting the limitations of the nobility, having gotten free of the class biases and special interests, might remain of the nobility by race, by emotional type, and yet the very victory over being of the nobility can be a manifestation of the nobleman's nobility.

Culture is not the work of a single man and not a single generation. Culture exists in our blood. A culture -- represents the work of a particular race and racial selection. The "enlightened" and "revolutionary" consciousness, always shallow and limited, has set a distorted imprint upon science itself, although from science it has derived its knowing. For scientific cognition it has tended to obscure the racial aspect. But an objective and disinterested science has to admit, that in the world exists a nobility not only as a social class with defined interests, but also as a qualitative emotional and physical type, as a thousand year culture of soul and body. The existence of a "white bone" is not merely a class prejudice, this is likewise an insuperable and ineradicable anthropological fact. The nobility in this sense cannot be eradicated. No sort of social revolutions can abolish the qualitative racial advantages. The nobility can die as a social class, can be deprived of all its privileges, can be deprived of all property. I do not believe in a future nobility as a social class, and I myself as a member of the nobility do not desire privileges for the nobility. But it remains as a racial matter, as a spiritual type, as a plastic form, and the dislodging of the nobility, as a class, can increase its emotional and aesthetic value. This occurred also to a remarkable degree in France after the revolution. Nobility is a psychical aspect of race, which can be preserved and act under every social order. For the world and the world's culture there is necessary the preservation of this psychical aspect of race with its crystalline aristocratic features. Its total disappearance would represent a diminishing for the whole human race, a total triumph of the parvenue, the death of the age-old nobility in mankind. The selection of the features of nobility of character was accomplished over millennia. The psychical results of this long process cannot be destroyed by any sort of revolutions. The abolition of the feudal structure in the West was not a total abolition of these psychical traits, which were worked out under feudal chivalry. These traits began to be imitated also in other classes. In the knighthood chivalry there was forged the person, there was wrought the tempering of character. The sense of honour in modern man, in the modern bourgeois world, derives from the tradition of chivalry. Chivalry wrought an higher type for man. In chivalry there were the temporal and corruptible trappings, of which nothing still has remained. With these trappings was connected much that was bad. But in chivalry there is also an eternal and undying principle. Chivalry is likewise a spiritual principle, and not merely a socio-historical category. And the ultimate death of the chivalrous spirit would represent a degradation of the human type. The higher dignity of man was forged and formed within chivalry and the nobility and from it passed on into wider circles in the world, it -- is of aristocratic origin. The selection of noble traits of character occurs slowly, it presupposes an inherited transmission and familial traditions; this -- is an organic process. There is suchlike an organic process also in the formation of an high cultural medium and high cultural traditions. In the genuine, in the deep and refined culture, there is always sensed the racial aspect, the blood connection with cultural traditions. The culture of people of the present-day, without a past, without organic connections, always is shallow and coarse. And one, for whom the culture is already a matter of many generations, tends to possess an altogether different cultural style and different cultural fortitude, than for one, newly come to culture.

The pity for us is that in Russian history there was no chivalrant knighthood. What explains it is this, that with us the sense of person was not sufficiently worked out, that the tempering of character was not sufficiently strong. The force of primitive collectivism remained too great in Russia. Many a Russian thinker, and learned writer also, has taken pride in this, that in Russia there was no genuine aristocracy, that our land was essentially democratic, and not aristocratic. Morally pretty was thus our wonted democracy, our simplicity, characteristic also to the genuine Russian nobility. But in the absence of an aristocracy there was also our weakness, and not only our strength. And in this was to be sensed a too great dependence upon the dark element of the people, the inability to separate out from the enormous quantitative a guiding qualitative principle. From the times of Peter the role of an aristocracy for us was played by the bureaucracy, and in the bureaucracy there were certain features of an aristocratic selection. But all the same, the bureaucracy cannot be acknowledged a genuine aristocracy in its type of soul. With us there triumphed a bureaucratic absolutism at the top and populism at the bottom. Creative developement, in which would have played a guiding role of qualitatively selective elements, with us was rendered impossible, and at present we are fiercely getting the payback for this. Yet all the same it would be unjust to deny the tremendous significance of the nobility in Russia. The nobility was our vanguard cultural stratum. The nobility created the Russian great literature. The estates of the nobility, the nobility families were our first cultural medium. The beauty of the old Russian lifestyle -- was a gentryfied beauty. The noble style of Russian life -- was first of all a gentry style. The sense of honour first of all and most of all was developed amongst the Russian nobility. The Russian guardsman in its time was as a school of honour. The intrusion into Russian life of the commoner and his too great a predominance for us quickly lowered, rather than raised, the type of soul to be found in a man. Our life has lost all its style. The finest, our most stylistic and beautiful epoch, the most worthy to be termed our Renaissance, remains the beginning of the XIX Century, the time of Pushkin, Lermontov and an entire pleiade of poets, of the mystical movement, of the Decembrists, Chaadayev and the conceiving of the original

Slavophilism, the time of the empire style, i.e. the age of the guiding role of the nobility, of the gentry intelligentsia, of the gentry cultural stratum. Back then still we were not nihilists. In place of the gentry culture, insufficiently durable, with us there then came nihilism and the nihilistic style. But everything most remarkable in Russian culture was connected with the nobility. Not only the heroes of L. Tolstoy, but also the heroes of Dostoevsky, are unthinkable outside the connection with the nobility. Remember, what Dostoevsky said in "The Adolescent" ["Podrostok"], concerning the nobility and its significance. All the Russian great writers were nourished on the cultural medium of the nobility. In the flames of the bonfires, stoked up by the revolutionaries, they burn up not only the empire style manor houses, but likewise also Pushkin and Tolstoy, Chaadayev and Khomyakov, and there gets burnt away all the Russian creativity and Russian tradition. The destruction of the Russian nobility is a destruction of cultural traditions, the rending apart of the bonds of time in our spiritual life. Your parvenue hatred for the nobility -- is a craven feeling, diminishing the level of man, it is directed at not only the privileges of the noble, of which long since already there are none, and which it would be folly to restore, but also against the psychical features, which are indestructible and which inherit eternity. But then too it must be admitted, that the nobility for us both morally and spiritually fell earlier, rather than having been toppled by the revolution.

Chivalry and the nobility ought not psychologically to disappear from the earth, they ought to provide the basis for a realm of nobleness and honour, for an higher type amidst the broad circles of the people. It is not the democratisation, but rather instead the aristocratisation of society that has the inner spiritual justification. The seeds of aristocratism, of nobleness of nature are there present in each class, and not the rejected classes only. The liberating process in human life has only one meaning -- the opening up of wider paths for the discovering of aristocratic souls and for their prevailing. Within history there occurs a tortuous process of all ever anew searchings out of a true aristocracy. An harsh and contemptuous attitude towards the common people -- is not aristocratic, this is the trait of the boorish fellow, the trait of an upstart. An aristocracy ought to provide for the common people from its surfeit, to serve with its light, by its riches of material and of soul. With this is bound up the historical vocation of the aristocracy. Ruskin dreamt about such a socialism, which would be produced by consequence of the aristocracy. He was an ardent advocate of the hierarchical structure of society with the aristocracy at the head and together with this, just as ardent an advocate of decisive social reforms to the benefit of the deprived classes. In this he followed upon an eternal truth of Plato. Ye too ought to follow Plato and Ruskin. The average mass of the historical aristocracy and nobility tend easily to betray their destiny, to fall into an egoistic self-assertion and degenerate spiritually. Those, who especially hold dear their aristocratic privileges and oppose them for others, become least of all aristocratic in their emotional type. Boorishness in the aristocratic and nobility circles is very widespread. When the betrayal of their destiny by the hierarchically upper classes goes far enough with a spiritual corruption in them, then revolution boils up, as a just punishment for the sins of the high and mighty. And what for the future can save more lofty a culture, always based upon the hierarchical principle, can only be a sacrifice by the historical aristocracy, the readiness to renounce class reparations, the readiness to renounce privileges and bear out their own service, to fulfill their mission.

But there exists in the world not only the historical aristocracy, in which is wrought an average level by way of racial selection and inherited transmission, -- in the world likewise exists a spiritual aristocracy, as an eternal principle, independent of the mixings of social groups and historical eras. The historical aristocracy can possess features in body and soul of aristocratism, but within it there is still not the feature of a spiritual aristocraticism. Spiritual aristocraticism comes to be realised in the world by way of individual grace, it cannot have obligatory and predominating a connection with any sort of social group. The appearance of a spiritual aristocraticism, of genius, presupposes a propitious spiritual atmosphere in the life of the peoples, but it is not bound up with any selective process within nature nor the working out of the average cultural level. Genius as such is not inherited, just as saintliness is not inherited. Great people are born at providently preordained moments. But they emerge out of the average level, from the upper aristocracy, just like from the midst of the peasantry or philistine element. The relationship between the spiritual aristocracy and the socio-historical aristocracy has its own degrees. But at the same time the higher and more auspicious appearances of a spiritual aristocracy do not possess any sort of connections with the socio-historical aristocracy, with organic selection and inheritance, yet in its average degrees they do have a certain connection, since they are in a greater dependence upon the trans-individual tradition, upon the selective process, through which crystallises the cultural medium. For the genius there is no law written, but for talent it does yet remain written.

In the world there eternally live and act two aristocracies -- the exoteric and the esoteric. The exoteric aristocracy is formed and acts within the external historical plane. In the manifestations of the exoteric aristocracy there is a persuasive legitimacy and a naturo-biological basis. The esoteric aristocracy forms and acts within the inner hidden plane. In the manifestations of the esoteric aristocracy it is impossible to persuade by suchlike a legitimacy and result upon such a naturo-biological basis, it belongs to a graced order, to the realm of spirit, and in the realm of nature, into which also enters the historical plane. The esoteric aristocracy forms as though a mysterious religious order within history, and in it are conceived all that is creatively great. In the exoteric plane of history all this creative life tends to fall into an already altered aspect, perceptible for the average human level, for culture with its demands and tasks. This variance is clearly visible in the life of the Church. The domain of the saints or holy elders represents the esoteric religious aristocracy. In it are realised the lofty and real attainments of churchly life. But in the Church alongside with this exists also an exoteric aristocracy, the outwardly legitimate historical churchly hierarchy. It is necessary for the historical life of the Church, for the religious educating and guidance of peoples. In it there is a selectivity and preeminence, necessary for the crystallising aspect of the churchly average aspect. The historical churchly aristocracy possesses its own great and positive mission, but it is not the final and most deep thing within the religious life. The spiritual attainments of the inwardly hidden life of the saints passes over in an altered exoteric form into the historical churchly life with its external hierarchical stages. The same correlation between the esoteric and the exoteric exists also in all the spiritual life of mankind, in every culture. There exists an aristocracy and hierarchy of the average, the exoteric culture. In it there is a selectivity and preeminence. It demands a consensus, a consensus first of all in education and upbringing, a consensus of mind and ability. It lives and developes in the cultural tradition and account. But when you set upon the path of a denial of mental and formative consensus, you cast down the qualitative in the name of the quantitative and prepare a kingdom of darkness, you shove the people backwards. You appear as agents of regression. Qualitative consensus of upbringing, education, of mind, capabilities is necessary for cultural work, for every civil and societal activity. This consensus creates its own hierarchy, its own aristocracy. But this is an exoteric aristocracy, acting in the average domain of state and cultural existence. Deeper and beyond it stands the esoteric aristocracy, the higher spiritual aristocracy, in which is conceived everything creative, every discovery and revelation, in which man passes beyond the bounds of this world. The higher spiritual aristocracy is a kingdom of sanctity, of genius and chivalry, a kingdom of the great and noble, of an higher human race.

The personal principle is revealed, becomes crystallised and developes first of all in the aristocracy. This -- is the first emergence of the person within history from out of the dark collective element. Afterwards by complex and tortuous paths there occurs the search of conditions, propitious for the revealing of an aristocracy of select persons, of a qualitative selective process of persons. Beyond the aristocracy at the first stage there is established the aristocracy of successive stages. Not only does the aristocracy exist as a class, as a social group, but also each class, each group works out its own aristocracy. There is separated out and gathered up an aristocracy whether peasant, merchant, professorial, literary, artistic etc. And if there did not occur everywhere this differentiating process of the separating out and formation of an aristocracy, then a formless and chaotic philistine element would pull matters downward and not allow for the creativity of values. Facing each historical epoch there stands the complex task of working out and fortifying its aristocracy of varied stages. And it is not so simple to decide, what sort of political and social order is favourable for the working out and strengthening of such an aristocracy. All of you, devoted to levelling, have your own various monistic theories, in any case. But all your theories stand for little. The complexity of life always capsizes them. It is not the exclusive triumph of some whatever principle, but only a more complex combination of several principles that favours a true aristocracy. A subsidiary role in this great work can be played also by the democratic principle, when it is delimited and subordinate to more lofty principles. Aristocracy and democracy -- are two inwardly opposed principles, metaphysically inimicable and mutually-exclusive. But in social actuality the clash of these principles gives complex results, and the triumph of the aristocratic principle can be enabled by the democratic, when it is not given to smug pretensions. Facing both monarchist society and democratic society alike stands the task of working out and selection of a guiding aristocracy. A pure monarchy is an abstraction, monarchy concretely realises itself through an aristocracy. And the value of a monarchy is first of all in the capacity to gather up a guiding aristocracy and strengthen it. A monarchy tends to fall, when it gathers the worst around itself.

The spirit of democratism in its metaphysics, in its morals, in its aesthetics bears with it the greatest peril for the aristocratic principle of human and world life, for the noble qualitative principle. The metaphysics, the morals and aesthetics of the quantitative would be to divide and destroy everything qualitative, everything personally and in common uplifting. The realm of democratic metaphysics, of democratic morals, democratic aesthetics -- is a realm of the worst, and not a realm of the finest. The realm of democracy ultimately casts down the ancient ideal of valour and the nobility of descent, it shatters the biological and spiritual grounds of aristocraticism. The triumph of the democratic metaphysics represents a greatest peril to human progress, for the qualitative uplifting of human nature. Ye want as though to create such conditions, as would render impossible the further existence of aristocraticism in the world, the working out and selection of the finest. There is the greatest of delusions from your side, when ye say, that you want to set free human nature. You actually want to enslave human nature, you want to set up limits and obstacles for it. Ye deny alike the biological grounds for aristocraticism, its racial grounds, and its graced grounds, its spiritual grounds. Ye doom man to a grey, qualityless existence. True, you want as though to lift the enormous masses of mankind to higher a level, ye want as though to force it to this higher level. But the reason ye want as though to do this, is not because you value and love the "higher level", but because you want a levelling of everything, and you tolerate no distinctions nor anything uplifting. The human uplifting impulse itself has never interested you. And you tend to forget, that the uplift is attained by a free struggling and free selectivity. It is not the uplifting, but rather the forcing of events that interests you most of all. And it is beyond you, for your consciousness the mystery of history lies forever concealed. The mystery of history -- is an aristocratic mystery. It is realised within a minority. The minority aspect bears within it the spirit of universality. The spirit of universality -- is an aristocratic spirit. The spirit of the majority aspect, the democratic spirit -- is a provincial and particularistic spirit. Within history exists the leadership of the minority, the leadership of an aristocracy. The revolt against this guiding leadership is an infringement upon the mystery of history. Ye will not succeed in destroying the ontological distinction between souls, nor succeed in erasing the distinction between the intelligent and the stupid, the gifted and the ungifted, the noble and the craven, the beautiful and the ugly, the graced and the graceless.

Seventh Letter

Concerning Liberalism

The word liberalism has long since already become bereft of all its charm, though it derives from the beautiful word freedom. It is impossible to charm the masses with freedom. The masses do not trust freedom and lack the wherewithal to connect it with their daily interests. Indeed, in freedom there is something moreso aristocratic, than democratic. This is a value -- moreso dear to human a minority, than to the human majority; it is oriented first of all to the person, to individuality. Within revolutions liberalism has never triumphed. Not only in social, but also in political revolutions it has not triumphed, since in all revolutions it is a matter undertaken by the masses. The masses have always a pathos for equality, and not for freedom. The liberal spirit per se is not a revolutionary spirit. Liberalism is an outlook and worldview of cultured segments of society. Within it there is no stormy element, no fire, enflaming the heart, in it there is moderation and too great a formality. The truth of liberalism -- is a formal truth. It never says anything either positive or negative about the content of life, it wants as though to guarantee to the person his beloved content of life. The liberal idea does not possess the ability to transform itself into a semblance of religion nor arouse towards it feelings of a religious manner. In this is the weakness of the liberal idea, but in this also is its fine side. Ideas democratic, socialistic, anarchistic, make pretense to bestow a content to human life; they readily become transformed into pseudo-religions and arouse for them the attitude of a religious character. But in this also is rooted the falsehood of these ideas, since in them is no sort of any spiritual content and nothing at all, worthy of a religious pathos of attitude. The attachment of religious feelings to unworthy objects is a great falsehood and temptation. And it mustneeds be admitted, that liberalism does not urge this. The democratic idea is still more formal, than the liberal idea, but it has the capacity to pass itself off as a content of human life, for a special type of human life. And therefore within it lies concealed a poisonous temptation. The socialistic idea is distinguished by its unlimited pretentiousness. It makes pretense at setting the goals for human life, at the same time as it relates to the means of life, relates to its material implements. Ye have long since already made a god of and absolutised the relative means, and have attached to them the sense of almost a religious order, and the goals of life have become moribund for you. Your religion of sociability, of the social aspect, is a religion of means, and not of ends. True, in the outward societal aspect everything relates to means; the ends however present themself at greater a depth, the ends -- are spiritual, not societal. And the verymost spiritual community of people, their most inward societal aspect is indefinable by the external criteria of the societal aspect. It is because the ends and the content of life obtain from the spiritual depths and are rooted in Divine activity. The social medium represents however a complex combination of means for the realisation of these ends and this content. All the social ideas therefore prove hopelessly and insurmountably formal and within them it is impossible to arrive at genuine content and ends, it is impossible ever to get at the ontological core in them.

Is there such an ontological core within liberalism? In people, too caught up in the liberal idea and confessing the doctrine of liberalism, and in liberal movements and parties there is too little of the ontological. And in a majority of cases this reflects merely shallow people and a superficial movement. But in the sources of the liberal idea there is moreso a connection with the ontological core of life, than in the sources of ideas democratic and socialistic. It is indeed because freedom and the rights of man, of the human person, of the human spirit possesses a greater connection with the spiritual foundations of life, than the right of universal suffrage or the socialisation of the means of production. Freedom and the rights of man, inalienable in the name of utilitarian ends, are rooted in the depths of the human spirit. And insofar as liberalism tends to assert them, it is connected with the nature of the person, which possesses an ontological basis. It is impossible to ground liberalism on positivist a basis, possible only for it is a metaphysical basis. On positivist grounds, man can be deprived of his most sacred right, if need be. Chicherin well understood the metaphysical nature of liberalism and he grounded it upon a sufficiently extreme and one-sided form. There is no basis to acknowledge an inalienable freedom and inalienable rights for the human person, if such does not have an eternal spiritual basis, if it is all just a reflection of the social medium. Rousseau consequently thus admitted the sovereignty of society and was compelled to deny all the inalienable freedom and rights of man. Marx likewise denied this freedom and rights. The liberals -- positivists only by the inconsistency and superficiality of their consciousness -- are prepared to admit of the inalienable freedom and rights of man. The spiritual sources of the freedom and rights of man are manifest as freedom and rights by the religious consciousness. And in this point the formal truth of liberalism coincides with the ontological core of human life. The rights of man and the citizen have their own spiritual basis in the freedom of conscience, proclaimed in the English religious revolution. This truth has become all more and more generally admitted. But more deeply still, the inalienable and sacred freedom and rights of man are grounded in the Church of Christ, acknowledging the boundless nature of the human spirit and defending it against the unrestricted infringements of the external state and society. This -- is the eternal truth of the Universal Church, in the Reformation it received only one-sided an expression, called forth by complex historical conditions. The abuses of Catholicism in its human, all too human manifestations (very exaggerated) ought not to overshadow this truth, that within it was already lodged the acknowledging of the infinite rights of the human spirit. The Reformation spiritually received everything from the Church, though in impaired form.

That the true freedom of the human person is of Christian origin, is evident already from this, that the ancient world did not know personal freedom, it knew only a public freedom. Benjamin Constant has already stressed the deep distinction between the ancient and the modern understanding of political freedom. And this -- is a distinction between the pagan and the Christian consciousness. Upon the basis of the pagan religious consciousness freedom could be understood, only as it was understood in Greek democracy, but it would be impossible to understand it, as it was revealed to the Christian religious consciousness, perceiving the infinite spiritual nature of the human person. The teaching of Rousseau was something residual from the pagan consciousness. It does not know of personal freedom, does not know of the spiritual nature of man, apart from society, does not know of his inalienable rights. It denies freedom of conscience, it enslaves the human conscience to society, to the sovereignty of the people. And its consciousness of political freedom -- is a pre-Christian consciousness. And all of you, deriving from Rousseau, deriving from Marx, in place of the real freedom of the person substituting instead an illusory societal freedom, all of you are mere pagans, renegades from Christianity. For you man does not exist in his inner, his spiritual actuality, man exists merely in context of his social trappings. In the name of your new god -- the sovereignty of the people -- ye deprive man of all his rights. Man possesses a profound ontological bond with such authentic realities, as church, as nationality, as the state. But what is there ontological in the right of universal suffrage, in the socialisation of production, in all your production, in all your collectivism? Why does man have to renounce his rights, to hedge off his nature in the name of such fictions and phantasms?

In the idealistic liberalism there were the blessings of a finer consciousness, and there was a greater attention to human nature. But these blessings were closed shut by a shallow "enlightenmentism". "Enlightenmentism" never did mature a deep consciousness. Its light -- is not a solar light. This -- is an artificial light of lamps, diminishing the actual need for the true light. And better it is to proceed through complete darkness, through the night of the consciousness, in order to sense the thirst of being in communion with the realm of the authentic light. The widespread liberal ideology is too overgrown with this shallow enlightenmentism, and within it drown the gleamings of an higher truth. Liberalism draws upon an existence, bereft of all ontological groundings, it lives the bits and pieces of a sort of befuddled truth. And they have ceased to regard it as an autonomous manifestation of spirit. Liberalism has become so basically weather-beaten, has become so lacking in soul, that it is possible still to admit some element of liberalism, but impossible already it is to be a liberal by faith, by one's ultimate worldview. Liberalism has ceased to be an autonomous principle, it has been rendered into something of a compromise, something of a semi-democratism or semi-conservatism. It opposes to the democratic or socialistic faith a different tactic, different interests, but it is powerless still to oppose with a different faith, a different idea. Too often are made into liberals those, who are weak of faith, who do not love to belabour themself with ideas. In the liberal camp proselytism is impossible. Too often the liberals themself fall for more radical and extreme ideas, they give way before the revolutionary type and consider themself unworthy to join in with the revolutionary faith and revolutionary activity. Liberal has become a synonym for the moderate, the man of compromise, an opportunist. But can one be called a moderate and opportunist, one who has his own idea, differing from that of the social-revolutionary, his own faith, and who is faithful to the end in his principle? Liberals usually tend to fall morally before the revolutionaries and are powerless to oppose them with some other, more lofty a moral truth. How to explain the weathered aspect and emptiness of liberalism? Why have they quenched in them the gleams of truth higher than those, which are impelled by democratism and socialism?

"Know the truth, and the truth will set you free". "Where the spirit of the Lord is, there also is freedom". Herein at whatever the depth has to be grounded the liberating principle. In truth, Christianity seeks to set man free from slavery, from slavery to sin, slavery to the lower nature, slavery to the elements of this world, and within this has to be sought the basis of a true "liberalism". The true liberation of man presupposes his liberation not only from external slavery, but also from inner slavery, from the slavery to himself, from his passions and his cravenness. About this ye have failed to understand, ye enlighteners and liberators. Ye let man remain in his inner slavery and ye proclaim his rights, i.e. the rights of a slave, of the lower nature. At the basis of your liberalism was an inner defect. And why could it not but fall. Your liberalism in fatal a manner betrayed its solely possible spiritual basis. Ye made a declaration of the rights of man and ye tore off from it the declaration of the rights of God. In this was your original sin, for which ye have been chastised. Higher than autonomy, self-law, stands theonomy, God's law. This was profoundly understood by the French Catholic school of the early XIX Century, with J. de Maistre at the head. And this school demanded the promulgation of the forgotten rights of God, demanded this sacred declaration and to oblivion with the indisputable rights of man. Since ye have forgotten about the rights of God, you have forgotten also about this, that the declaration of the rights of man has to be connected with a declaration of the duties of man. The path, upon which the rights of man was torn off from the duties of man, will not lead you to good. Upon this path, your liberalism has tended to degenerate. The demands for rights without a consciousness of duties has tended to shove matters upon the path of a struggle of human interests and passions, with contention among mutually-exclusive pretensions. The rights of man presuppose a duty to appreciate these rights. In the realisation of the rights of man the most important thing is not the proper legal rights pretensions, but an appreciation of the rights of the other, respect for each human image, i.e. the obligations of man to man and of man to God. The obligations of man lie deeper than the rights of man, and they provide the basis for the rights of man. The right flows out from the obligation. If everyone were to be very strongly conscious of rights and yet very weakly conscious of obligation, then the rights of no one would be respected and would not be realised. Both the rights of man, and the duties of man are rooted in his God-semblance nature. For if man -- has likeness only to the natural and social medium, if he be merely the reflection of external conditions, merely the child of necessity, then he has no sacred rights, nor sacred duties, then he is merely a matter of interests and pretensions. The rights of man presupposes the rights of God, and this is first of all a matter of the rights of God in man, the rights of the Divine within man, his God-likeness and sonship to God. Man has infinite rights, only because that he is infinite spirit, because that his depths enter into the Divine activity. The human person does not suffice unto itself, it presupposes the existence of God and Divine values. Is it possible to proclaim the sacred rights of man, as those of a perfected and disciplined beast, as the pinch of ashes, in which in a moment life burns itself away? The rights of man have to possess an ontological basis, they presuppose both the existence of the human soul in eternity, and the existence, far infinitely exceeding that of this soul, the existence of God. About this your enlightened liberalism and your radicalism tends to forget, and this is why it has to appear weather-beaten in aspect, for it cannot realise any sort of the rights of man. An abstract and doctrinaire liberalism, pretending for support upon its own emptiness, is an intolerable lie, and against it ought to be undertaken movements, seeking for real content in social life.

The liberal ideology tended to degenerate in the intellectual atmosphere of the XVIII Century, which was inclined to assert a natural harmony. This ideology was pervaded by faith in the natural harmony of freedom and equality, in the inner affinity of these principles. The French revolution completely confused equality with freedom. The whole XIX Century shattered the illusion of a natural harmony, it vitally revealed the irreconcilable contradictions and antagonisms. It was discovered, that equality bears with it the danger of a very terrible tyranny. It was discovered, that freedom is no guarantee from economic slavery. The abstract principles of freedom and equality do not create any sort of a perfect society, do not guarantee the rights of man. Between freedom and equality there exists not an harmony, but rather an irreconcilable antagonism. The entire political and social history of the XIX Century is the drama of this clash of freedom and equality. And the dreaminess about an harmonic combining of freedom and equality is merely an unrealisable rationalistic utopia. There never could be concord between the pretensions of the person and the pretensions of society, between the will for freedom and the will for equality. An abstract liberalism is just as powerless to decide this task, as is an abstract socialism. This -- is a squaring of the circle. On the plane of a positivist and rational task this is unresolvable. Always there will be the clash of the unrestrained striving for freedom with the unrestrained striving for equality. The thirst for equality always will be the greatest danger for human freedom. The will for equality will revolt against both the rights of man and against the rights of God. All of you, ye positivist-liberals and positivist-socialists, but poorly understand the tragic aspect of this problem. Freedom and equality are incommensurable. *Freedom is first of all the right to inequality.* And equality is first of all an infringement upon freedom, a limitation of freedom. The freedom of a living being, not a mathematical dot, is realised in a qualitative distinction, in an ascent, in the right to increase the capacity and value of its life. Freedom is connected with the qualitative content of life. Equality however is directed against every qualitative distinction and qualitative content of life, against every right of uplift. One of the most remarkable and refined political thinkers of the XIX Century, de Tocqueville, first clearly conceived of the tragic conflict between freedom and equality and he perceived the great dangers, which the spirit of equality tends to bear. "I think, -- says this noble thinker, -- that it is quite very easy to establish an absolute and despotic governance of the people, who be in a societal condition of equals, and I submit, that if suchlike a governance were once established of suchlike a people, then it should not only but oppress people, but over the course of time would bear off from each of them many of the verymost chief aspects, present in man. It therefore seems to me, that despotism most of all has to be guarded against in democratic times". This noble alarm in the face of the levelling, in the face of an European mongolisation, was there also in

J. S. Mill. And he was distressed by the fate of the human person in a democratic society, obsessed with the spirit of equality. The illusions of the XVIII Century, the illusions of the French revolution were shattered. Freedom unleashed an unrestrained will for equality and had concealed within it the seeds of self-negation and self-destruction. Liberalism gave birth to democracy and unrestrainedly passes over into democratism. Such was its consequent developement. But then democracy destroys the very foundations of liberalism, equality devours freedom. This was seen already over the course of the French revolution. The year 93 destroyed the declaration of the rights of man and the citizen, from the year 89. This was a fatal process. The contradiction between freedom and equality, between the rights of the person and the rights of society was insurmountable and unresolvable in the natural and rational order, it was surmountable and resolvable only in the graced order, in the life of the Church. In the religious community, in the churchly society is removed the opposition between the person and society, and in it freedom is brotherhood, the freedom in Christ is brotherhood in Christ. Spiritual sobornost', communality, resolves this squaring of the circle. In it there is not the distinction between right and obligation, not the opposition. But also in churchly society there is no mechanical equality, in it there is only brotherhood. And freedom within it is not the setting of oneself in opposition to the other, to one's neighbour. Religious community is based upon love and grace, which neither liberalism nor democratism tend to know. And therefore are resolved in it the fundamental antinomies of human life, its brutalmost conflicts.

The inner developement of liberalism leads to democratic equality, which comes to be in an inevitable opposition to freedom. But on the other hand also, liberalism is subject to the danger of degeneration and decay. In the liberal idea, per se, there is nothing as yet "bourgeois". There is nothing "bourgeois" in freedom. With disgust I employ your illusionary words, shallow and superficial, bereft of any ontological meaning. Neither do I think that you have known, what such a "bourgeoisness" is, nor that you have had any right to speak about it. You indeed yourselves are quite immersed in it. But it is impossible not to admit, that the dominance of abstract liberalism in economic life has borne its own negative and evil fruits. If the Manchester school also had a relative justification at a certain historical moment, then at the utmost its unlimited dominance has but compromised and watered down the liberal idea. It is an economic individualism nowise limited by anything, surrendering all economic life wholly into the grip of an egoistic struggle and competition, not admitting of any regulatory principle, and it has as it were no sort of an obligatory connection with the spiritual core of liberalism, i.e. with the affirmation of the rights of man. The insolvency of the so-called economic liberalism has long since already been apparent. And around the idea of liberalism has coalesced an atmosphere, imbued with unpleasant associations. Indeed the ideas generally, and even not so much the ideas, as rather the words, their expression, sounds suspiciously corrupt. Human interests are capable of distortion and defilement even with the most lofty words, connected with the religious life. The word "liberalism" belongs to a series of very corrupted words. But has many a word remained uncorrupted, in many of your words has there remained still the luminous and active energy? The corruption of liberalism began with the mixing up of ends and means, with the replacement of the spiritual ends of life by material means. The freedom of man, the rights of man are a lofty spiritual end. Every political and economic order can but be the relative and temporal means for the realisation of this end. When liberalism sees in the freedom of man and his inalienable rights its lofty end, it affirms an incomplete, but indubitable truth. But when it begins to ascribe an almost absolute significance to temporal and relative political and economic means, when it begins to see an impermissible transgression against its abstract doctrines in the searching out of new forms of social organisation, it degenerates and decays. And upon this basis has been created very complex and entangled relationships between liberalism and socialism, which it is impossible to express in abstract form.

Ye love to contrast in opposition liberalism and socialism as two eternally hostile and incompatible principles. This is accurate relatively so, as are also all abstract formulas. The liberal ideology and the socialist ideology took form around differing vital tasks, and their pathos has different sources. The will to freedom gave birth to the liberal ideology. And what gave birth to the socialist ideology was the will for the securedness of daily bread, the satisfying of elementary vital needs. And if liberals are those, for whom the elementary vital needs are satisfactory and secure and thereupon want freely to have their life, then the socialists are those, for whom it is still necessary to see to the satisfying of the more elementary vital needs. In the individual perspective, socialism is more elementary than liberalism. In the societal perspective however, this correlation is reversed. In principle as it were we should consider it a liberal socialism and a socialistic liberalism. Liberalism does not possess any sort of obligatory connection of idea with the Manchester school, with economic individualism, and this connection -- is by chance factual. Liberalism is fully compatible with social reform, it can permit of all ever and anew means and methods for the securing of the freedom and the rights of man. The liberal declaration of rights bears formal a character and permits of whatever the satisfactory social context, so long as it does not infringe upon the rights of man, such as are termed inalienable. A certain sort of reform-based socialism is even more compatible with the ideal groundings of liberalism, than it is with extreme forms of a democracy, bereft of social based a character. And on the other hand, there is possible a liberal socialism. The socialism of a reform type can ground itself upon liberal principles, can consider the social reforming of society within the settings of the declaration of the rights of man and citizen. Liberalism imbues within it elements of socialism. Socialism however can be rendered more liberal, can consider moreso not only the economic man, but also man, endowed with inalienable rights in the fullness of the individual life, with the rights of spirit, outside the scope of utilitarian considerations. But such a liberal and reform socialism is certainly not there in the modern socialism. It is most important of all to recognise, that liberalism and socialism -- are relative and temporal principles. The liberal faith and the socialist faith -- are a false faith.

The liberal principle is one of the principles of human life, but it cannot be assertable as the principle singularly and solely dominant. Taken by itself per se, it proves split off from ontological a grounding. Liberalism ought to be combined with deeper and non-external a conservatism, equally as also with a social reformism. Religiously, liberalism is Protestantism. In liberal freedom there is a portion of truth, just as there is in the Protestant religious freedom. But Protestantism is sundered off from the ontological groundings of the Church, it affirms the principle of religious freedom abstractly, and not within the fullness of human life. The same occurs with liberalism. Liberalism is sundered off from the ontological groundings of the societal, it affirms the principle of political freedom abstractly, and not within the fullness of human life. And just like with religious freedom, where the freedom of the religious conscience has to be oriented towards its ontological groundings, to the fullness of churchly life, so too with freedom and the rights of man, which have to be oriented towards their ontological groundings, to the fullness of the spiritual life of man. Philosophic liberalism, as an abstract type of thought, is inclined to deny real communities and totalities, the ontological reality of the state, of the nation, of church, and to admit of society only as mutually-interacting persons.

The pure liberal ideology transforms everything into the person as the sole reality. But by this nominalism is ultimately shattered also the reality of the person itself. And this is because the reality of the person presupposes other realities. About this I have spoken more than once already. Rationalistic liberalism denies the existence of an ontological hierarchy. But by this it denies also the person as a member of the hierarchy of realities. Liberalism tends to degenerate into a formal principle, if it does not unite itself with principles moreso profound, moreso ontological. Individualistic liberalism severs off the individuum away from all the organic historical forms. And suchlike a sort of individualism desolates the individuum, steals off from it all its supra-individual content, such as is derived from history, from the organic belonging of the individuum to its race and native land, to state and church, to mankind and the cosmos. The liberal sociology fails to understand the nature of society. And the liberal philosophy of history fails to understand the nature of history.

Liberalism, as an entire mindset and worldview, -- is anti-historical, just as anti-historical, as is socialism. And from this side lurks its severe fate. All the rather more profound attempts at providing a foundation for liberalism rest upon the idea of a natural right. And they attempted to provide the basis for natural right idealistically. But the teaching about a natural right is bound up with faith in the "natural condition". Natural right gets set in opposition to historical truth, just as the natural condition gets set in opposition to the historical condition, to historical actuality. All the teachings concerning a natural right have long since already been subjected to merciless criticism, and there is left remaining not a stone upon a stone. The idealistic revival of a natural right and the attempts to give it a normative ground with the help of the philosophy of Kant do not get down to the final depths, to the ontological groundings. The inalienable and sacred rights of man cannot be termed as his "natural" rights, as rights derived from a "natural condition". And in vain do ye idealise the nature of man, in vain do ye seek to rely upon it in the aspirations for a better life. "Historical" man is all the same better than "natural" man, and the setting loose of "natural" man begets only evil. The "historical" condition is higher than the "natural" condition, and "historical" right is higher than "natural" right. Man possesses inalienable and sacred rights not as a "natural" being, but as a spiritual being, from his grace-born nature of sonship to God. And this means, that it is proper to seek out the grounds of the rights of man not in "nature", but in the Church of Christ. The boundless right of the human soul is not "natural", but an "historical" right of the

Christian world. The human soul, as revealed by Christianity, is not the "natural condition" of man, since in the "natural condition" it was profoundly stifled and shut inwards. The human soul had its revelation from out of the depths within the Christian historical era, and this revealing was anticipated only in the ancient mysteries and in Platonic philosophy. The grain of truth in liberalism was derived from this higher source. Your philosophy however of a "natural condition" and of "natural right" is superficial. Deeper is the philosophy of an "historical condition" and an "historical right". The faith in a perfect "natural condition" long since already has crumbled away, it does not hold up to the criticism by either the scientific consciousness, or the religious consciousness. Man by his "nature" is neither good nor sinless. All "nature" lies in evil. In the "natural" order, in the "natural" existence rules hostility and harsh struggle. The "historical" order is an higher condition of being, than is the "natural" order. Humanism has falsely gotten the "natural" man confused with the spiritual man, with the graced rebirth and sonship to God, and at its limit has arrived at a denial of man. You, ye people of the XX Century, should have gotten free from the remnants of the XVIII Century, from the backward ideas of the century before last. There is no sort of a "natural" condition, there is no sort of a "natural" right, and there cannot be any sort of a "natural" harmony. Already in the XIX Century ye should have turned to the "historical", to the depths of historical actuality. And insofar as liberalism sets itself in opposition to the "historical" and bases itself upon the "natural", it degenerates into an abstract emptiness. The "historical" -- is concrete, whereas the "natural" is an abstraction. Within the "historical", in the historical organic totalities there is a conquering of sin and evil of the "natural" condition". And yet higher than the "historical" condition and "historical" right stands the "spiritual" condition and "spiritual" right.

Faith in the ideal of liberalism has become already impossible. Everything has quite changed and become complicated from the times, when this faith was still fresh. It has become quite apparent, that this faith was based upon a false teaching concerning human nature, nowise wanting to know about its irrational sides. We do not much already believe in a constitution, cannot much already believe in parliamentarism as a panacea for all ills. One might admit the inevitability and the sometimes relative usefulness of constitutionalism and parliamentarism, but to believe, that by these paths can be created a perfect society, that there can be cured the evil and suffering, is already impossible. Nor does anyone have such a faith. And the most recent doctrinisers of a liberal constitutionalism and parliamentarism present pitiful an impression. Parliamentarism in the West is undergoing a serious crisis. There is a sense of the exhaustion of all the political forms. And insofar as liberalism believes too much in the political form, it does not stand at the heights of the modern consciousness. Socialism likewise does not stand at the heights of the modern consciousness, insofar as it believes too much in economic organisation. All these faiths -- are remnants of the old rationalism. Rationalism was based upon a narrowing down of human experience, upon the ignoring of that irrational human nature, which makes impossible the complete rationalisation of society. People of the modern age can no longer still believe in the saving aspect from any political and social forms, they know all the relativeness of them. All the political principles are relative, not one of them can pretend to an exclusive significance, not one of them can be a solely-saving means. The faith in a constitution -- is a pitiful faith. Constitutions can be set up in accord with the demands of the historical today, but to believe in them is meaningless. Faith ought to be directed towards objects more worthy. To fashion oneself an idol out of a legal state is unworthy. In this there is a certain limitedness. A legal state -- is a thing very relative. And if in liberalism there be some eternal principle, then it is not becoming to seek it in these or some other political forms, nor in this or some other organisation of representation and rule, but rather in the rights of man, in the freedoms of man. The rights and freedoms of man are immeasurably deeper a matter, than for example, the right of universal suffrage, a parliamentary order etc., and in them is a sacred basis. But it is namely because the rights and freedoms of man demand more profound a basis, than that given them by liberalism, a basis metaphysical and religious. There is a partial truth to liberalism -- the freedom of religious conscience, and its basis -- is in Christ and His Church, in the freedom of the Church from the pretensions of the "world", since only in the Church of Christ is revealed the boundless nature of the human spirit. Outside of Christianity, the pretensions of the secular state and secular society as regards to the human person would be unlimited. By the blood of the Christian martyrs was won the freedom of the human spirit. Concerning this it would be proper for you to remember -- in imagining yourselves as liberators. But ye want as though to free man also from the Church of Christ, which is the realm of freedom, and by this ye do surrender man totally into the grip of natural necessity.

In our time it is rarely possible to encounter a pure liberal, expressing the abstract liberal principle. Usually the liberalism becomes very convoluted and combined with various other principles. In the liberal purity and emptiness is impossible to get a grip. Either liberalism gets mixed in with conservative principles, and then it becomes deeper and more viable. Or else it gets mixed in with democratic obfuscations, with socialistic and anarchistic principles, and then it generates a shallow and insipid radical. You, the radicals, -- are the most unnecessary sort of people in the world, the most superficial, the most indirect, living off others, and not yourself. Ye live by foreign, moreso the leftist, revolutionary ideas, which ye are powerless to oppose and powerless to give up, and powerless to see through. And for mankind ye cannot be anything even of a tragic lesson, an instructive essay, as compared to the authentic revolutionaries, socialists and anarchists. You radical-liberals have not those firm principles, which might be defended to the very end, which might be set up in support of the left in opposing the destructive elements. In this sterility is sensed the fruits of liberalism, having no ontological groundings. Ye never were sure, whether there are ontological groundings in the state, the nation, in all the historical totalities. And you get carried away by tendencies more extreme and resolute, more credulous and fanatical. Ye liberal-radicals, -- are sceptics in your spiritual type and therefore cannot affect history. A false faith has to be opposed by a true faith, and not by disbelief and scepticism. Disbelief and scepticism, duplicity, glancing about at the sidelines, living on a borrowed account, on the account of foreign ideas for lack of one's own -- are the wonted traits of the radical. here is why the liberal-conservative stands higher, than the liberal-radical, he is more a man of principle, he knows, what to oppose to foreign ideas. Liberalism, as a self-sufficing abstract principle, in standing forth for the freedom of the person, readily passes over into anarchism. This anarchism becomes very guileless, very ideal, altogether non-destructive, but also very powerless. Suchlike a liberal-anarchist appears, for example, with Spenser. Suchlike was W. Humbolt. This finds its expression in the wish to bring the state to an extreme minimum and gradually abolish it altogether, amidst a lack of understanding of the basic nature of the state. In such a liberal anarchism there is no genuine pathos and no activity, it conveys a theoretical and stuffy-study character. But this anarchistic inclination inwardly debilitates liberalism. All the defects and weaknesses of liberalism are bound up with this, that it all still abides in the formal freedom of the old Adam and does not know the material content of the freedom of the new, the spiritually reborn Adam.

Eighth Letter

Concerning Democracy

De Tocqueville presents thus his impression of the progressive growth of democracy at the beginning of his brilliant book, "Democracy in America": "All the following book was written under the impression of a certain kind of religious foreboding, produced in the soul of the author in view of this irrepressible revolution, having traversed over the course of several centuries through all the hindrances and now apparently it moves forward amidst its progressive destruction". This sense of foreboding is well known to me. I experienced it long ago, very long ago, at first almost still in childhood, then as a youth, it was acutely enough sensed in the first Russian revolution of 1905 and reached a tormentive intensity in the springtime of 1917, when there began the outpourings of the second, the "great" Russian revolution. Democracy -- is not a new principle and is not newly come into the world. This -- is an old, an age-old principle, well known already to the ancient world. But newly in our era, the question of democracy has become a religiously-alarming question. It becomes such already not on the political, but on the spiritual plane. It is not about political forms that they happen to speak, when it is a religious foreboding they are experiencing over the progressive march of democracy, but rather something deeper. The realm of democracy is not a new form of governance, this rather -- is a peculiar spirit. Never yet has the idea of democracy triumphed in the world in a pure form, and scarcely indeed is this triumph possible. But the spirit of democracy has celebrated already a few victories. Democracy, as a self-sufficing abstract idea, subordinate to nothing higher, is the apotheosising of man into a god and a denial of the Divine source of power. The people is sufficient unto itself. The supreme principle of its life is that of its own will, independent in whatever the direction, what it wants, whatever its content. The people's will assumes the role of a god, because it is affirmed formally, without connection with its content. The content behind the people's will presupposes already some sort of supra-human values. Yet actually in turning one's attention to the content of the people's will, one would no longer tend to make a god of it. And this is because the people's will can be directed towards evil, whereupon it is subject to censure, or it is directed towards an higher good, to the Divine content of life, and then it is not merely the people's will, but rather then this good itself and this Divine content have to be acknowledged as a supreme principle. Ye have herein insufficiently pondered this. The admitting of the people's will as a supreme principle of societal life can only be as the worship of a formal and content-lacking principle, in making a god out of human caprice. The important thing is not, what a man wants, but the rather that there should be this, -- that he should want. I desire, that there should be this, this whatever I desire. Here is the final formula of democracy, of the people's power of authority. Deeper it cannot go. The very content and condition of the people's will lie outside the interest of the democratic principle. The people's will can desire a most terrible evil, and the democratic principle cannot protect against this. Within the democratic principle are no sort of guarantees, that its realisation will not lower the qualitative level of human life nor destroy the greatest values. In the abstract idea of democracy there is quite great a contempt for the qualitative aspects of man and the people, for their spiritual level. This idea desires as though to abstract human attention away from human life and the totality of life, and direct it instead wholly to forms and manifestations of will. The people's sovereignty bears purely a formal character. It remains uncertain, what the sovereign people does desire, when everything will be put to its will, as to what sort of structure of life it will desire to create.

You have come to believe in democracy, because you have lost faith in truth and what is right. Yet if ye had believed in the objective existence of truth and right, then ye would have had to posit truth and right as higher than the will of the people, and subordinate the will of the people to such. But for you truth and right are whatever the people wants and whatever it says. Ye seek to surrender truth and right to be decided by a majority of voices as proclaimed by a right of universal suffrage. This is a faithlessness, this also is godlessness, set into the foundation of all the democratic ideology. You want truth and right concerning the societal arrangement to obtain from the majority, from the quantitative. But can truth and right have any sort of relationship to the criteria of the majority, the quantitative? Truth and right have an other, a Divine source, independent of human caprice. Truth and right can be there in the minority, and not in the majority, and even always it abides in a minority. And it is almost monstrous, how people can arrive at such a condition of consciousness, that in the opinion and will of the majority they should see the source and criteria of truth and right! The justification of the principles of democracy, the principles of the majority and the quantitative, can only be a matter of scepticism. Those who, having succumbed to doubt, desolate, sundered off from the ontological groundings of life have to have recourse to the decisions of the majority, to the criteria of the quantitative. If there is no truth and right, then we shall reckon as truth and right, as whatever the majority admits it to be. If however there is truth and right, but I do not know it and do not know the real paths to it and am eternally in doubt about it, then it but remains to be put to the majority and to the humanly quantitative to seek out substitutes to the unworthy qualities in me myself! A democratic revolution in the world therefore also evokes a religious shock, since it witnesses to a spiritual collapse of mankind, to a growth of godlessness, to a terrible scepticism, to the loss of all the qualitative criteria of truth and right. Democracy is a sceptical societal gnosseology. This gnosseology acknowledges themes, which have become bereft of the sources of spiritual life. Here is why the growth of democracy in the world bears fatal a meaning. It runs parallel to a weathering-down of the soul, to the loss of God in the soul. *Democratic equality is the loss of the capacity to distinguish the qualities of spiritual life.* This is a matter of jumbled themes taken for granted, which have ceased to appreciate qualities. The democratic ideology based on quantities cannot but lead to a kingdom of the worst, and not the finest.

At the basis of democracy is not posited a will to the uplift of life, to quality and values. Democracy of itself creates no sort of new values as such, nor can it create such. It is set up outside of any thought about the value and content of life. And the all-levelling democratic era of human history represents a lowering of the qualitative value content of life, a lowering of the human type. Democracy does not possess the interest for the raising up of a lofty human type, and therefore it is powerless to create a better life. The apostle of democracy, J. J. Rousseau, believed in the natural goodness and felicity of human nature and he thought, that it would be discovered in all its beauty, when there was established the form of the people's power. This engrained lie was overthrown by life itself, by the experience of history, and by thought more complex and deep. For Rousseau's mindset it was not a task of victory over sin and evil, not a task of re-educating man and the people and creating an higher human type. Instead, it was needful merely to snatch off the chains from the people, to give the people the possibility to express its will and by its will to set up society -- and there would thus ensue the perfect natural condition. During the XIX Century they lost faith in the natural condition of man and the natural condition of society, they could not ground democracy upon this philosophical basis and moreover they were unable to replace it with anything. It remained incomprehensible, why anything of a nowise limiting nor restraining discovery of human nature in its non-transformed condition should lead, through democracy and the people's power, should lead to well-being, and beget societal truth. The positivism of the XIX Century was already unable to believe in any sort of felicitous natural condition. But still it readily sanctions and makes a god of democracy, demands a formal bowing before the given, the natural man and his sinful will. True, the democratic metaphysics asserts, that each individual man tends to err, he is situated in non-truth and falsehood, but unerring and correct is the will of all, the will of the people, the will of the collective. And here arises a very complex philosophical problem, over which ye democrat-positivists have failed to ponder. Of what sort of nature is this collective, which is termed the people, and which ye acknowledge as sovereign? Does the people, for which ye admit the supreme power, does it represent a certain real unity, does it possess an ontological core? Ye indeed are nominalists, and not realists, and the people, as an human collective, cannot be for you an ontological reality, it is merely a mechanical sum-total. In your will of the people occurs only an arithmetical combination. You believe in a majority of voices. From the summarised will of all is not received the general will of all. Marxism, which was an extreme expression of the worldwide spirit of levelling, displaced the democratic illusions, and killed the democratic metaphysics. And to its merit this has to be admitted. Social-democracy denies the existence of the people as a real unity, it dissects it into classes and groups with opposing outlooks and interests, and for it there does not exist the will of the people, there is no sovereign principle. Higher than the will of the people stands the will of the proletariat, to which are transferred all those divine attributes, which the democratic metaphysics ascribed to the people. The proletariat becomes higher than the people, it is a real unity. This -- is a new fiction, a new fetish, but it dislodges an old fiction, an old fetish -- "the people". The people in that sense, in which democratic metaphysics asserts it, does not exist. This "people" cannot have any sort of will. It is merely a complex of interactive social groups with varied inner outlooks and interests or a mechanical complex of separate human unities.

The people is likewise however a mystical organism, as it were a person in communality. In this sense the people is a nation, it encompasses all the classes and groups, all the living and the dead. But of the people in such a sense, democracy does not want to know and does not know, it lies completely outside the field of vision for democracy. Not only is it improper to confuse and regard the people and democracy as identical, it is also necessarily in vain to separate and set them in opposition. The words "democracy" and "democratic" are employed in too dim and indistinct a sense. Under democracy they tend to posit the working classes of society, the peasantry, the workers and labour intelligentsia, and the broad democratic outlook and the people's power, i.e. the political form, and the people as the sovereign economic owner of the land. There transpires an uncritical confusion between democracy, as human a condition among the people, and democracy, as a certain political direction and political mindset. They tend to say -- "he is a democrat", i.e. a man of the common people or close to the common-people average, he comes from the lower levels of society, but they are also wont to say -- "he is a democrat", i.e. a man of democratic outlook and democratic convictions, though he be of aristocratic descent. And in both the one and the other case the word "democratic" and the word "people" have little connection between them in common. The *people* does not signify the "democratic" classes, and the "people" can have convictions that are not "democratic". The people can hold to an altogether non-democratic form of thought, can be altogether non-democratic in outlook. Thus also it has transpired within history amidst the organic condition of the people. Democracy is already an egress from the organic condition, the breaking up of the unity of the people, a division within it. Democracy by essence is mechanical, it says that the people as whole an organism no longer is. Democracy is an unhealthy condition of the people. In the "organic" epochs of history no sorts of democracy occur or arise. Democracy -- is the offspring of "critical" epochs. Democracy cannot be the expression of the spirit of the people, since the spirit of the people is expressible only within the organism, whereas democracy is mechanism. Democracy regards man as an arithmetical unit, mathematically equal to every other. For it the people, as an organic whole, is dissolvable into atoms and then is gathered as mechanical collectives. The people however does not comprise arithmetical units and atoms. The people is an hierarchal organism, and in it each man is a diverse being, unrepeatable in his qualitative aspect. And therefore also the will of the people is inexpressible within the human sum-total, within the opinion of the majority. Universal suffrage -- is an inappropriate means of the expression of qualities in the life of the people. The minority can better and more perfectly express the will of the people as an organic whole, endowed with a spirit of sobornost', of communality. And one alone can better express the will and this spirit, than all, than all the human numbers. Upon this is based the significance of great peoples within the historical life of peoples, of leaders, of rulers. The people is not the human numbers, not the human masses. This is what ye have forgotten in the democratic ages. In your democracies governs the human numbers, and ye are wont to think, that behind you stands the people. But this is your great lie, which has to be exposed. The human numbers are a flickering, borne on the whims of the wind. And the will of this human number cannot be the will of the people. This will cannot be a matter of a chance sum-total, wavering with every breeze. One fact already, that your realm of democracy is torn by the struggle of parties and that to the parties in it gets surrendered the fate of states, tells against you and does not permit of the belief, that the people finds in it its expression. Democratic governance is in the final end a fiction. I have said already, that in actuality there is possible only an aristocracy or an ochlocracy. The tyranny with parties rarely comes by aristocracy. For therein occurs a process of selection of the finest and most capable. In the people's sovereignty perishes the people, it drowns in the mechanical numeric and does not find expression for its organic spirit, whole and indivisible. It finds its expression only irrationally. In the people's sovereignty man also perishes. For the autocracy of the people does not delimit itself regarding the inalienable rights of man and provides no guarantee of the untouchable aspect of these rights. To the autocratic democracy ought to be opposed both the spirit of the people, and the rights of man, since it is readying a most terrible of tyrannies.

The most advanced peoples of the West have long since already sensed a dissatisfaction with democracy and have attempted to find an egress into new forms. The crisis of the democratic ideology has long since already occurred. And you, ye pure democrats, believing in the supremacy of the democratic idea, -- are people of a stale mode of thinking and an outmoded form of feelings. In the European world there was a democratic deluge, in which all more and more Europe became immersed. The deluge is continuing and has not yet reached its climax. But there has begun already a reverse motion. In the sphere of thought long since already has begun an ebb-tide. The limits of democracy are perceived, and the more perspicacious minds have espied the democratic danger and dead-end. Quantity cannot create quality. Society, having splintered apart into atoms, into mathematical specks, cannot be gathered up, reunited nor assume an harmonic form by way of mechanics, by way of counting up voices and entrusting power to the majority. The will of the people is something qualitative, which cannot be attained by any sort of quantitative combinations. And it is particularly then, when democracy has been proclaimed as the supreme will of the people, that the will of the people is not shown, is rendered dead. *Democracy also is an hopeless search for the dead will of the people.* All the systems of a democratic goverance by the people's will represent hopeless attempts to gather together a fallen-apart will. In democratic governance the will of the people is rendered fallen-apart and part rises up against part. The democratic parliament is an arena of struggle for special interests and for power. It is difficult to hear within it the voice of an unified people. It is heard only at exceptional moments and through exceptional people. The counting of votes, dependent upon a million chance incidents, says nothing concerning the qualitative aspect of the people's will. The right of universal suffrage, which up to now for many of you appears to be an irrefutable dogma, evokes the greatest of doubts. The right of universal suffrage is a totally mechanical, numeric and abstract principle. The right of universal suffrage does not know of concrete people, with their different qualitative aspects, with their varying import, it deals exclusively with abstract people, with atoms and mathematical specks. It also does not know organic social groups. The right of universal suffrage is an abstraction of the qualitative aspect of life, and it does not want to know of any sort of qualitative selective process. From whence however do ye derive the assurance, that by such a path it is possible to receive for society higher a quality? This -- is hypnosis under the idea of equality. You have come to believe, that equality, not a proportional but a mechanical equality, is so great a truth and great a good, that it is all so fine, that all will flock to it, and it will handle everything. But this making a god of equality is also an original sin; it leads to the replacement of the concrete, qualitative, individual nature of man by a nature that is abstract, quantitative and impersonal. Basic to the false equality underlying the right of universal suffrage is a denial of man. In the results of this universal right truly is something inhuman and anti-human.

Every man, if he be taken not as an abstract mathematical speck, has his own point of consensus, his own qualitative attainments. The principle of consensus -- is a true principle, more human a principle, than its complete denial. The principle of consensus -- is qualitative, and not quantitative, and in this is its truth. The principle of consensus can be distorted and degenerate, can become understood totally materialistically, as a material consensus. But this nowise says anything against its basic truth, since everything degenerate can come to light and everything in the light can be misused. But one thing beyond doubt both for the religious consciousness, and for philosophic thought: it is necessary to deal with man in his qualitative aspect, i.e. to make selection of the finest and most capable. There are no sort of external societal means to deal with man in all his unrepeatable individual uniqueness. But there are also group qualities of people, signs of which can be perceived and established. Suchlike are the qualities of education, the qualities of societal experience, the qualities of historical preeminence, the qualities of more lofty a cultural experience. Consensus essentially ought to be spiritual. But a spiritual consensus has also material signs of its expression. A more lofty cultural level is connected also with the material structure of society, with the accretions by historical formations. In order that the representation be not exclusively mechanical and numeric, it is necessary to consider in it the historical accretions and the qualitatively selective forces. Societal experience and societal preeminence possess a quality, which it is impossible to disregard and which it is impossible to destroy in the name of abstract doctrines and ideas. Thus, for example, in Russian the Zemstvo represented suchlike a qualitative historical formation, in it societal experience had accumulated, the knowledge of matters, traditions. The destruction of the Zemstvo, the rural self-government, and the lack of desire to give it preference in representation is a destruction of societal qualities and a submersion into the darkness of the quantitative. I think, that in the bureaucracy, amidst the danger of its nowise limited rule, there are the qualities of experience, knowledge and succession, needful to be considered. It seems strange to have to argue the preference of more lofty a cultural segment, which should have to bear a different weight in societal life, than a segment, standing qualitatively lower. Man -- is not an abstract being, he needs to be taken within the historical medium and preeminence. Tremendous a significance bears upon man's descent, and his upbringing, his instincts and traditions, his recollections and bonds. Here is why also the historical classes have had quite greater a significance, than is apparent in your abstract sociology and abstract democratic ideology. Under these external forms lies concealed something essential for life. The problem of democracy cannot be put abstractly and in isolation, it has to be bound up with the problem of culture. And then collapses the ideal of an abstract democracy. Democracy cannot topple the hierarchical order of society, which is rooted in the hierarchical order of the cosmos. The rebirth in France of the Medieval idea of a corporate representation bespeaks a deep dissatisfaction with an abstract, mechanical, quantity-based democracy. They have begun to realise, that it is impossible to take man as an isolated atom and from these atoms create a society and a state. There exists an hierarchy of organic formations, to which man belongs. These organic formations have to have their own representation. It is misfortunate, that all the organic formations have been almost destroyed by the democratic age, wherein isolated and alone man and the new corporations are bound up exclusively with economic interests. French syndicalism has inflicted strong blows upon the democratic idea and in it consequently there is active the spirit of an enormous corporation -- the workers syndicate. But this corporation has exclusively an economic basis and its spirit moves along the interests of class struggle. It arose during an era of the falling-apart of the people's will. Under the rule of such a sort of corporation there cannot arise an organic structure of society. It leads only to permanent revolution. But syndicalism, just as with the rebirth of the idea of corporate representation, signifies the serious crisis of democracy. They will begin to suspect, that the people is not a mob, a numeric mass, when it possesses a complex structure and qualitative differentiations. And needful is a more complex system of representation, not so mechanical and levelling, as the system of the right of universal suffrage. In the very principle of the soviet representation there is a bit of truth, remaining still. But never will you find a perfect system of representation, since representation itself is one of the subordinate, relative and transitory principles of societal life. To spiritual culture belongs the primacy over every political form, and corporations ought first of all to have spiritual a basis.

The democratic ideology is an extreme rationalism. It rests upon faith in the possibility of rationalising human life and ultimately to construct it upon human powers alone. Democracy consequently has to deny the existence of irrational principles within societal life and cannot tolerate them. Society, as based upon mechanical numbers, upon the right of universal suffrage, understanding man as a mathematical speck, is also a totally rationalised society, intolerant of the incursion of any irrational powers. A democratic republic with parliamentary governance is also a rationalised society. This is an attempt to identify the state, always possessing an irrational and mystical basis, with a fully rationalised society. Democracy wants wholly and without any remnants, to dissolve the state into society. The ideology of democracy cannot admit of the state as a specific and autonomous reality, it wholly folds the state into society, i.e. sees in the state only a function of society. Society however gathers people into relationships. And thus vanish all the ontological groundings of the state and society. There remain only interests, only the will and reason of man as the sole justification of the state and society. No sort of other, loftier and more mysterious powers then act with the state and society. Such a levelling process in the state and society, such a rationalisation of society and constructing it by human powers alone represents a grave danger for the human person also. The human person in all its uniqueness and originality stands guarded by the societal irrational principles. An irrationally grounded state moreso esteems the human person and has less a pretension upon it, than a fully rational society. But the irrational element of human society is indestructible, and it thwarts all the pretensions of your rational democracy. Ye cannot succeed in controlling the irrational element. The complete rationalisation of human society would be a victory of the quantitative over the qualitative. And it is needful to give thanks for that "dark" principle in the life of human societies, which makes impossible their ultimate rationalisation, so fatal for the human person. The conditions of varying qualities of the people is inexpressible in any sort of democracy. Individual powers are too active in the life of the people. And this thwarts all your democratic constructs.

A pure, abstract, autonomous democracy is most terrible a tyranny, it murders man. The unbounded power of all is more terrible than the tyrannical power of merely one. In the mere short-term moments only is possible the triumph of such a democracy, but these moments have always become a most terrible infringement upon the freedom of man. With these moments has arisen the darkness from below and it engulfed society. But short is the life of such a democratic autocracy, it stands at the edge and slides down. It is thwarted by powers, unforeseen by the democratic ideology. And this is fortunate for mankind. If an ultimate democracy were possible, then mankind would perish, drowned in the darkness. In the very idea of the people's power, limited by nothing and subject to nothing higher, there is no sort of truth, also not the truth concerning man, concerning the human image, about his infinite spiritual nature, upon which is impermissible any sort of infringement. The sacred rights of man are not enclosed within democracy and do not derive from it. A sovereign people can take away from a man everything, that it wants, that it finds necessary for its well-being. An autonomous people -- is a most terrible autonomy, since in it man is dependent upon an unenlightened quantity, upon the dark instincts of the masses. The will of one and the will of a few cannot so distantly spread its pretensions, as the will of all. From the will of a single autocrat it is possible still to protect a part of one's existence, but it is incomparably more difficult to protect it from the will of an autocratic people. Democracy in its extreme expression does not want to allow even the rights of a partial life, it has the tendency to transform all the entirety of human life into something public. It is difficult, very difficult to stay concealed from the all-prying and unbounded extent of democracy in its pretensions. It intrudes into our dwellings, penetrates into our thoughts and feelings. It seeks to render man into a being exclusively societal. The style of life of democratic societies all more and more leads to uniformity. This style does not tolerate solitude and solitaries, it does not leave a place and time for contemplation, and it is hostile to the uniquely original creativity of the few. Ye have declaimed much about the despots and tyrants of the old societies and have promised to create a society of the free. This is all illusions, deceptions and deceits. Amidst the most terrible despotisms of the past there occurred a vivid blossoming of persons, there occurred geniuses and saints, there was possible a life intimate and contemplative, there were great creative upsurges. K. Leont'ev was right, when he said: "Under the Turks there were martyrs for faith; under the Belgian constitution there is scarcely anyone godly!" Democracy is unfavourable for the appearance of strong, vivid, creative persons, it creates a levelling to the societal average, which strives to completely swallow up the person and subordinate it to itself. Your democratic societal outlook is a most terrible of tyrannies, it oppresses the human spirit, clips its wings. The old tyranny with the bon-fires of the Inquisition left more room for human individuality, reckoned more with it. A most terrible intolerance can all the same be an expression of respect for the human individuality, for the spiritual life of man. When the church cuts off and anathematises heretics, it admits of the infinite value of the human soul and is attentive to its unrepeatably individual fate. The inattention and contempt of democracy for the human soul, for its individual life and fate is truly terrible and deadly to man. Your realm of a soul-less, materialistic democracy is a realm of a most terrible of Leviathans, a monster of millions of voices. It is terrible for man to be tossed into this abyss of numbers, into this all-engulfing impersonal societal aspect. It is not as terrible, when they oppress, hem in, even torture, while admitting on principle the person, than when in actual principle they deny it and replace it with impersonal principles. The old Russian autocratic realm no little tended to oppress and even torture the human person, but insofar as it was a Christian, an Orthodox realm, it acknowledged the human person, the value of the human soul. And spiritually it was not so terrible a despotism. The old despotisms had a religious basis and therefore they acknowledged the spiritual life of man, they did not view man as a societal atom. Your new and democratic despotism has no desire to have any religious basis, it completely ignores the spiritual life of man and values man only from the perspective of societal usefulness. For this despotism nowise sacred already is the mystery of birth of man, nor the mystery of his life, nor the mystery of his death. Man becomes the slave of societal utility, of the majority of voices, of societal opinion, the slave of special interests.

Your democracy is profoundly hostile to the spirit of freedom, and it would become you to leave off with declamations about a liberation from tyrannies and despotisms, which your democratic movements would bring about. Freedom is aristocratic, and not democratic, it is oriented towards the person, and not towards the masses. Your societal freedom can however prove a most terrible tyranny, it can turn out to be an enslavement of all. Your democracy is profoundly hostile to the spirit of creativity. It not only does not open up paths for creativity, as rather narrows off all the paths, it crushes all the creative impulses. The most creative eras in the life of mankind -- are aristocratic, and not democratic. Your democracy is profoundly hostile to higher culture. It wants as though to lower the level of culture, to diminish in culture the qualitative element for the increase of the quantitative. Democratic movements are moved with envy towards higher culture, with the evil remembrance of dislike for alien qualities. And this sets a seal of ignobility upon the style of democratic culture. Your democratic age began with the denial of great people, of geniuses and saints. It fights against the prerogatives of creative persons. The egalitarian passion torments your consciousness, distorts the quality of your will, your thoughts and your feelings, it hinders the understanding of anything higher. The egalitarian passion always leads to a lowering of the level of the person and of culture in a democratic age. Those pervaded by the pathos of democracy can posit themself only vulgar and vulgarising tasks within spiritual culture. The ideals of democracy -- are philistine ideals. The will of democracy is directed at a lowering of the human race. This will seeks as though not only the abolition of social classes, but also to destroy all the qualitative differences within society, all the qualitative results of the racial selective process. This is unattainable. The qualities of a people cannot be ultimately stripped away and destroyed. But democracy is motivated in its will towards this. Democratic society desires as though to be totally simple and mixed. This also would be a most arrogant of tyrannies.

There is no more bitter and humiliating dependence, than a dependence upon the human will, on the caprice of those like oneself. One can subject oneself to an higher will, to an higher truth, to higher principles, one can limit oneself and deny oneself in the name of these principles. But the dignity of the God-like nature of man, the noble pride of man tends to revolt against a situation, wherein one's life becomes wholly subject to men, those one's equal and lower. Submission to church, to state, to nationality, to higher realities and values -- is sweet and noble. But why should I have to be subject to the interests, the instincts and impulses of the human masses? Spiritually it is impossible to compel me to this. Possible herein is only physical coercion. Democracy thus seeks to force me to be subject exclusively to men and the human. Subordination to an hierarchical order can be the respecting in it of an higher and supra-human principle. In it is a sacred symbolism. In the priest and the king what is venerated is not the man, not the equal and not the lower, but rather the hierarchical structure of the societal cosmos. Democracy however abolishes all the sacred symbolism. For the dignity of man and the freedom of man what is necessary is to limit democracy, to combine it with other principles and subordinate it to other principles. The people's power is merely human power. The people's power however does not know its limits and it intrudes upon the freedom and rights of man. The freedom and rights of man are guaranteed only by principles, possessing a supra-human nature, rising above human arbitrariness. The maximum of freedom obtains by a combination of several principles. And this is because every autocracy, except the autocracy of God, is dangerous for man. For the true freedom of man, for the guarding of his dignity and the guarantee of his rights, it is important, that the will of the people be directed towards the good, so that truth and right should rule it. The liberation of man and the people is a liberation of the will of man and the people from evil, its subordination to God's truth. If the will of a people be subjected to evil elements, then it -- is an enslaved and enslaving will. Yet how can ye attain to this, in acknowledging the will of the people itself per se as the supreme good and in it to seek out the source of liberation? Ye have fallen into the sin of worshipping man and have gone the path of worshipping man. In order to liberate himself and others, man has to admit of an higher will, than his own, and to seek it, its realisation in the life of society. The formal principle of the people's power itself per se is already godless. It is possible to admit of democracy as one of the underlying principles of societal life, but religiously it is impermissible to admit it to be the supreme principle. Christianity has nothing in common with democracy and cannot provide a foundation for democracy. The attempt to align Christianity and democracy is the great lie of our times, an hideous substitution. Christianity -- is hierarchical. The Christian revelation about the infinite value of the human soul, about the equal-value before God of all human souls is not a democratic revelation, is not a democratic equality. Christian brotherhood is not democratic equality. Everything qualitative in Christianity, everything unrepeatably individual, everything unique, is all connected with the person and therefore hierarchical. Here is what ye never could understand: the connections of the person with hierarchism. Ye think, that favourable for the person is a levelled, a simple and mixed condition of society, and that the hierarchical principle is hostile to the person. But this is also based upon your lie, your spiritual churlishness. The very existence of the person presupposes an hierarchical structure to the cosmos, qualitatively distinct and set apart, from the societal and worldly average, and which thus would not represent a formless abyss, all levelled and jumbled in together.

Peoples have to proceed forth through the experience of democracy, have to have the experience of democratic self-activity. Not in order to forever build at a democracy, but for this, in order to perceive the corruptness and emptiness of the pretensions of democracy. Democracy -- is a transitory condition. In the very conception of democracy was allowed a lie. Democracy was conceived through demagoguery, through a craven flattery to the interests and instincts of the masses. From this impure wellspring cannot be born any sort of societal truth. The self-activity and self-affirmation of the human masses have been implanted in the basis of democracy and cannot come to good with those societal formations, which were created in such a psychical atmosphere. Democracy becomes rendered a tool to human special interests and human passions, an arena of struggle for power and for mastery. Democracy has intensified the sinful lust for life. Democracy understands power as a right, and not as an obligation. And every higher idea in democratic societies withers away. The prevailing of democracy signifies the prevailing of the interests of various societal groups and their struggle for power. And this also is a source of the decay of democracy. A sort of worm gnaws away at democratic societies. At their basis sits spiritual a lie. The experience of democracy demonstrates, that man cannot build by his own powers, cannot ultimately rationalise societal life through his own limited reason. The betrayal of destiny on the part of the hierarchically leading segments of the societal organism has tended to thrust peoples onto the path of the democratic experience. And the restoration of the old organic order has proved impossible and sterile. The old organic manner of life was destroyed in the democratic revolutions, and a thirst for a return to it was merely a romantic whimsy. It is impossible to externally force peoples back to the old monarchic-aristocratic order. Peoples pass through division and dissolution, through the death of the old organic condition. But they do not create new truths and new beauties, they fall into untruth and ugliness. They would have to experience much, to survive much, to suffer much, before they come to a new organic condition, before they come together in the name of an higher idea. And therein remains the tormenting question, can the peoples indeed upon this earth arrive at a justly true and beautiful society? It is difficult to believe in this and Christianity does not teach us this. The cosmic principles continue to exist in human society, they possess an indestructible ontological grounding, lodged within the Divine activity itself. But very complicated is the relationship of these ontological foundations for the phenomenology of the societal aspect. Behind the visible and external societal aspect acts a societal aspect not seen, inward. It likewise saves the world from going to pieces, prevents its return to chaos. Within human societies are mysterious forces, which are not taught about in all the rationalistic theories of society.

From the profound crisis of democracy is possible no egress exclusively political and social. In the European world is sensed the hopeless and fatal vanishing of all political forms. They anew repeat and re-combine the already well-known old principles. Political creativity has dried up. It is difficult to conceive of something new. And long since already it is time for all of you, believing so much in politics and in the external societal aspect, to turn towards greater a depth, it is time to really think, to stop with dissipating energy outwards and direct it inwards. The crisis of democracy is not a political crisis, this is first of all a spiritual crisis. In this crisis is exposed the lie concerning the religious grounds of democracy. Attempts to provide a theocratic grounding and justification to democracy represent still a greater lie and temptation, moreso than with the theocratic grounding and justification of Caesarism. I am not an advocate of the idea of a byzantine-theocratic autocracy and I do not believe in the possibility of a return to it. But in this ancient idea there is a greater depth, a greater beauty and nobility, than in the idea of a theocratic democracy. The anointing by God cannot rest upon the human throngs, the human masses. The anointing is a chosenness. A theocratic democracy is a negation of this chosenness. Mankind has lost faith in any singularly-saving principles of societal life, pretending to some exclusive mastery. The idol of the people's power is toppling the same, as is the idol of a singular power of rule. The tasks of the societal aspect are infinitely complicated. In democratism there remains only the one moral truth of simplicity, in opposing the gentry in regards to the people. The brotherly relationship of man to man ought to be at the spiritual basis of every worthwhile society. Christianity inwardly long since already has set limits to the pretensions of all the principles of the societal aspect as being chief and supreme. The theocratic dream of the Christian world finds itself no adequate expression in whatever the singular principle of the societal aspect. And the Christian consciousness in the final end has to arrive at the realisation, that in the visible world of the societal aspect there is no singularly sovereign principle, by which can be built God's kingdom of truth. An higher principle mustneeds be sought in the depths of spirit. Democracy has to be, first of all, limited by spiritual life and subject to spiritual life. This is the task of inner educating of democracy. It is acutely conceived by the finest political thinkers and activists. But how helpless they are in its resolutions! A triumphant democracy cannot be taught anything, it remains at the surface level of life and does not want to plumb the depths. Only the terror of life, only the ruination of all hopes can compel a self-satisfied democracy, just the same as with a self-satisfied monarchy and aristocracy, can only compel to a deepening, to a search for an emergence into spiritual life. Thus hinge all the political crises within a religious crisis. Democracy is too captivated by the goods of earthly life. It has ceased to believe, that human society possesses also a trans-earthly purpose. The worldwide democratic movement, having evoked in refined and profound people a religious distress, leads to a bitter pessimism. But in this pessimism is an healthy principle. It turns man towards a supra-earthly life. The experience of man in democracy has to orient him to God. In this -- is the significance of democracy.

Ninth Letter

Concerning Socialism

Socialism is not an invention of our own days. Socialism -- is one of the age-old principles, active already in the ancient world. From Robert von Pohlmann (Pel'man), in his remarkable book, "History of Ancient Communism and Socialism", one can peruse much that is instructive in this regard. One would recognise that already back then there occurred a savage struggle of classes, there were uprisings of the masses, there was the greed of the avaricious classes of the haves, the envy and vengefulness of the classes of the have-nots, and that back even then already were constructed social utopias. Von Pohlmann, Eduard Meyer and others have demonstrated, that the economy in Greece was more varied and complex, than it seemed at first, that back then already there was capitalism and it bore with it all the contradictions. During every time in which there has existed the struggle of classes, there was hatred between the haves and the have-nots, there was poverty and want and the question about daily bread tormented man. The sources on the social question are to be found already in the ancient Biblical curse: "In the sweat of thy brow thou shalt obtain thine bread". The Bible knows of this economic materialism. But during the XIX Century there begins to appear the socialistic principle in an extreme and limited form. It becomes all more and more the prevalent and defining style of the era. The economism of our age has been rendered all-pervading and all-defining. Nowhere is there anything safe from it. The economic materialism of Marx was not a theoretical fabrication, it was reflective of a sort of activity. In actual fact something happened, that evoked the teaching of Marx as a reaction within thought. Modern socialism has a reflective nature. In it there is no creative principle. Socialism -- is flesh from flesh and blood from blood of the bourgeois-capitalist society, a phenomenon within this society. It is wholly determined by the structure of this society and its inward movement. It spiritually remains on the same plane. Socialism is bourgeois in its very depths and never rises above the level of the bourgeois sense of life and the bourgeois ideals of life. It desires merely the equal for all, an all-encompassing bourgeoisness, a bourgeoisness, fortified for the forevermore, a bourgeoisness ultimately rationalised and regulated, healed from the inner but yet gnawing at it ailment, having overcome the remnants of the irrational in its principles. Socialism has connected its fate with class, begotten of the "bourgeois" structure, with the child of capitalism -- the proletariat. The ideologues of socialism -- are slaves to necessity, not knowing spiritual freedom, -- they have come to imagine, that the proletariat, comprised of the step-sons of capitalism, can be class-messiahs. Ye have imputed to this class, like to the chosen people of God, all the virtues and valiant traits and have projected it as an higher race, as creators of a new life. The position of the working class in capitalistic society is woeful and meriting of sympathy and help. But in the emotional type of this class there are no especially lofty features. It is compelled by want, it is poisoned with envy, malice and vengefulness, it is bereft of creative originality. From these inner emotional elements can there be born an higher human type and an higher type of societal life? The "proletarian" type is sooner a lower human type, lacking noble features, the features of the free in spirit. These noble features, these noble features of the free in spirit can be there in the simplest workers and peasants. But for this type there does not have to be in it the "proletarian" consciousness and the "proletarian" psychology. Upon the ignoble, the slave in spirit and upon evil, it is that ye want to create your new kingdom. The image of your class-messiah betrays your spiritual nature.

Both the "bourgeoise" and the "proletariat" are of that historical era, which possesses a style capitalistic and socialistic, and they reflect a betrayal and falling-away from the spiritual foundations of life. The first that made the betrayal and falling-away from the sanctities was the "bourgeoise", and then after came the "proletariat". It is from the "bourgeoise" that the "proletariat" learned atheism and materialism, from it appropriated for itself a spirit of superficial enlightenmentism, through it the spirit of economism was imbibed, and pushed it upon the path of the struggle of class interests. I well know, that the "bourgeoise" and the "proletariat" represent abstractions, inconsistent with living reality and never covering it. Ye have invented the "bourgeoise" and the "proletariat", ye have called to life these abstract spirits and, having given them names, you have imputed to them an almost magical power. In the life of human societies the fictions possess no less a significance, than the realities. And the fictions of the "bourgeoise" and the "proletariat" have poisoned our life. These fictions have to be reckoned with, for they are endowed with a reality in the psychology of man and society. And here, without bestowing an all-encompassing ontological meaning to the abstractions of "bourgeoisness" and the "proletariat", it has to be admitted, that many of the sins and vices of the "proletariat" have been transmitted by way of an inheritance from the "bourgeoise". In our "proletariat" there is nothing original, all it has, is borrowed. The possessing "bourgeois" classes represent a very complex activity, in them there is the good and the bad, the lofty and the lowly, a mixture of light with darkness, just as in everything human. The both godless and transgressive climate of this class is shameful, cutting them off, despicable, spurning in them the image of man and the image of God. This too is your godless transgression, an impediment to the accepting of baptism and of accepting the revelation concerning the brotherhood of all people in Christ. But in the realm of the abstract categories of the "bourgeoise" and the "proletariat", the "proletariat" has received from the "bourgeoise" what it seems to me to represent its vices, though for you representative rather its virtues. Marx also essentially taught this, that the "proletariat" is a child of the "bourgeoise", that socialism is a reflection of "bourgeois" economic activity, a defensive reaction to it. The nature of socialism -- is reactionary and class-based, in it there is no creative discovering, no soaring. Revolutionary socialism itself is shackled like a slave to economic activity, condemned to serve an earthly idol, compelled thus by necessity. Socialism is begotten of a bitter necessity, and not from freedom.

But here is something ye ought always to remember, whilst being puffed up with pride in the new spirit of proletarian socialism. Socialism was created by the bourgeoise, an higher cultural stratum. It emerged in the world as an idea, germinated within the bourgeois classes, the thought of which was unmercenarily directed at the resolving of social contradictions and at the surmounting of social evils and injustices. Thus arose the socialism of Saint-Simon, Charles Fourier, Robert Owens, thus also in antiquity arose the socialism of Plato. And indeed even your Marx and F. Lassalle were "bourgeoise" and not proletarians. Only in the "bourgeois" classes can socialism be a noble and non-avaricious movement of the human spirit, ideas as such. In the "proletarian" classes socialism involves interests, and not ideas; in a fatal way it assumes a materialistic character, in it can no longer be anything of sacrifice. Only the "bourgeoise" can ennoble socialism. And any nobility in socialism is merely of the Platonic type, in an aristocratic socialism. There is nobility in the hierarchical socialism of J. Ruskin. Proletarian socialism is not noble, it is craven and avaricious as regards its primal-bases of soul. It lowers human nature, the human type. Proletarian socialism is impelled by malice, envy and vengefulness, which also set the tone of your mass socialistic movements from ancient times up to the present day. At all times the psychology of the revolting masses, in its downward flow, has been alike. Always this psychology has been unpleasant and ugly. The greater share of guilt in this monstrous and sick psychology rests upon the upper classes, which failed to fulfill their calling, and were the first to have betrayed the common sanctities and the higher truth, but this does not change an evaluation of the "proletarian" psychology. In this psychology, the Christian sense of the guilt of each man was overshadowed by the non-Christian consciousness of a proletarian victimised. To sense oneself a proletarian is a great misfortune of man, a gnawing apostacy, a rupture from fatherland and fathers, instead of higher a condition, from which can be born an higher type of life. A worker might also not sense himself a proletarian, and great is the culpability of those, who would thrust him upon the path of such proletarian feelings and mindset regarding himself. The monstrous aspect of the proletarian psychology and the proletarian socialism born of it loudly witnesses to the truth of hierarchism, the nobility and beauty of the type of soul, living in an organic hierarchism. The "bourgeois" psychology is the reverse side of the proletarian psychology, it is likewise non-hierarchical, it likewise is a falling-away from the organic order and is likewise ignoble. The "bourgeois" inner feeling and self-consciousness of the haves is the same improper and vile a condition, as is the "proletarian" inner feeling and self-consciousness of the have-nots. The "bourgeois" and the "proletarian" -- are nigh close. These two types copy each other and sustain each other. The orgy of acquisition within capitalistic society had to spawn socialism. Yet within socialism is its own negative truth, a greater truth, than in democracy.

The social question was born not by outward, but by inward causes. And it cannot be resolved by external material means. The social question is posited and decided in the psychological medium, and at the basis of its resolution rests either these or yet other elements of soul. Only cooperation among classes can create an healthy atmosphere of soul in the resolution of the social question. When it is decided exclusively by movements from below, in this resolution are elements unhealthy and malicious of soul. The social movement is constructed exclusively upon the principle of class struggle, and it cultivates not the higher, but rather the lower instincts of human nature. It manifests itself not as a schooling of self-affirmation, but rather a schooling in avarice, not a schooling in love, but rather a schooling in hate. Coming from below, the exclusively by class resolutions of the social question rend the oneness of the human race and instead divide it into two hostile races. This movement lowers the psychical type for man. It denies the cosmic, i.e. the hierarchical structure of society. This revolutionary resolution to the social question presupposes a breaking away from the spiritual foundations of life, the denial of them and contempt for them. The revolutionary, the class socialism thinks and acts thus, as though there exists not the human spirit and spiritual life, as though there was nothing inward, only along the outside. It represents a terrible abstraction of spiritual life, of the true content of life. In it man ceases to exist, and it is only economic categories that act. The movement however from above downwards in resolving the social question, hierarchical as regards its principle, acknowledges the existence of man and his spiritual life, and it is oriented towards the non-avaricious and noble instincts of human nature. Such a movement acknowledges, that needful is a spiritual rebirth of man and human society, that by material means alone the social question is irresolvable, that the human race is a single race for God and possesses an organic hierarchical structure. And thus, the English socialist movement represents higher a type, than the German or French socialist movement. Within it the class struggle aspect is toned down, in it is realised a cooperation of classes, in it practical realism is combined with idealistic impulses. Carlyle, Ruskin, the Christian socialists were inspirers of this movement. After the orgy of capitalist acquisition, after Manchesterism, the ruling classes of the haves began to become aware of their vocation and the finest amongst them accepted part in the social reformation of society. And the sting of a revolutionary socialism was removed. A semi-socialism can be combined also with conservatism.

The comparison and alignment of Christianity with socialism has always seemed to me to be a mockery. The affinity between Christianity and socialism is asserted only by those, who remain at the surface and fail to penetrate down to the depths. In the depths however is revealed the total opposition and incompatibility between Christianity and socialism, between the religion of heavenly bread and the religion of earthly bread. There exists a "Christian socialism", and it represents a very guileless phenomenon, in much even meriting of sympathy. I myself am ready to consider myself a "Christian socialist". But "Christian socialism" essentially has too little in common with socialism, indeed almost nothing. It tends to term itself such merely out of tactical considerations, it arose for a struggle against socialism, it was a reaction of Catholicism in regard to socialism and it preached social reforms on a Christian basis. In the past, within the history of Christianity there was many a "socialistic" movement upon religious a basis, but these movements were usually anti-church, heretical and sectarian. All these religio-social currents were pervaded by apocalyptic and chiliastic ideas, they expected the immediate realisation of a sensory thousand-year reign of the Kingdom of Christ upon earth and they attempted by force to realise it. All these Christian socialist currents tended to forget, that the Kingdom of God cometh not with notice and that the Kingdom of Christ is not of this world. The era of the Reformation especially was rich with such movements, jumbling together Christianity with socialism. But bitter were the fruits of this mix. Chiliasm for example, based upon a confusion of Christianity with socialism, can serve as a warning threat. The religious lie of such a sort of chiliasm has long since already been exposed. John of Leiden once founded an heavenly Jerusalem upon earth, he brought to realisation his form of a sensory thousand-year reign of the Kingdom of Christ. And this hell, which this heavenly Jerusalem presented, these acts of violence, blood and nastiness which accompanied it, ought to cause all religiously sensitive people to pause a moment and think. The attempts at a creation of the Kingdom of Christ upon earth, amidst the old nature, without a transfiguration of man and a transfiguration of the world, always have been and always will be the creation of an earthly hell, and not an earthly paradise, a terrible tyranny, destructive of human nature leaving not a trace. It is impossible by violence to seize hold the Kingdom of Christ and it is impossible to situate it within the old nature, whereas the coming of this kingdom signifies a transfiguration of the old nature and a graced transference from the realm of violent coercion into the realm of freedom. The confusion and identification of Christianity with socialism, with an earthly kingdom and an earthly felicity, is an experiencing of Jewish apocalyptics, the manifestation of Judaism upon Christian a grounding. And it is not by chance that Marx was Jewish. This is a manifestation of Hebraic apocalyptics, of an Hebraic chiliasm at late an hour of history, in an atmosphere of an atheistic and materialistic age. This is an illustration of the anti-Christian nature of the Hebrew apocalyptic, of the Jewish apocalyptic expectations. The old Jewish apocalyptics was revolutionary and anti-historical. Upon its soil occurred the uprising of the Zealots. The apocalyptic spirit differed from the prophetic spirit, which was not revolutionary and which was pervaded by a sense of history. And the new, the socialistic Jewish apocalyptics is likewise revolutionary and anti-historical. It is needful to penetrate down deep into the anti-Christian nature of socialism. Socialism, as a worldwide phenomenon, has a religiously Judaic origin. Within it act those selfsame principles, in the name of which Christ was repudiated by the Jews. Jewish chiliasm, full of hopes for a sensory Kingdom of God upon earth and the expectations of a Messiah, who would realise the earthly kingdom and the earthly bliss of the Jewish people, does not accept the mystery of Golgotha, in conjunction with the appearance of the Crucified Messiah. The Jewish people, in the flaring apocalyptic atmosphere, awaited not the Christian Messiah, but rather a socialistic messiah, not a Christian thousand-year kingdom, but rather a socialistic thousand-year kingdom. The temptation of socialism, the temptation of an earthly kingdom and bliss without the sacrifice of Christ and the Crucifixion, without the passage through Golgotha also led to a refusing of Christ and to the torment of His Passion. Herein was determined the tragic fate of the Jewish people upon the axis of world history. The question concerning socialism is more intimately and more deeply bound up with the Jewish religious question, than it would appear, to all of you societal-rationalists. If the democratic movement in the world evokes religious an alarm, then still moreso does the socialistic movement also evoke religious an alarm. Within the problem of socialism is a religious depth, and this is one of the ultimate problems of history, leading us to apocalypsis. Socialism has very old, ancient roots, not only social, but also religious. Yet only at the summits of history, when all the contradictions of human life are laid bare, is laid bare also the nature of socialism, and there is revealed, of what sort of spirit it is. Socialism makes pretense to be not only social reform, not only an organising of economic life, but also a new religion, seeking to replace the religion of Christ. Socialism now comes into the world with a religious pretentiousness, it seeks as though to be all things to everyone, it demands towards itself an attitude on the order of the religious. The religion of revolutionary socialism accepts all the three temptations, spurned by Christ in the wilderness, and upon them it wants to create its kingdom. It wants to transform stones into bread, it wants salvation through social miracles, it wants a kingdom of this world. Socialism is an edifice of mankind upon earth without God and against God. Dostoevsky prophetically perceived this. Socialism is a constructing of the Tower of Babylon. Socialism completes the deed, initiated by democracy, the matter of the ultimate rationalisation of human life, squeezing out from it all the mysterious, supra-human and Divine powers. Socialism desires still more broadly and deeply to seize hold of human life, than does democracy. It makes pretense to create a new life fully and completely. Christ brought into the world not peace, but the sword. He divided people by spirit. Socialism likewise bears into the world not peace, but a sword. It divides people by economic position. It does not acknowledge the existence of spirit. It does not acknowledge the existence of man. It replaces man with an economic category. The religion of socialism is a murdering of man. It begins with a denial of man's sonship to God. At its basis lies the experience of a revolting slave, and not a son, the feeling of underground insultedness. Having arisen from the dust he wants to be a god. Socialism is a kingdom of the people from the ashes, with the conceit of themselves as gods. Man's Christian consciousness of himself as a son of God cannot lead to socialism. This noble state of mind is incompatible with class hatred. Socialism transgresses upon the freedom of the human spirit, upon his birthright. It promises man bliss for denying his birthright. It promises a complete rationalisation of the societal aspect for denying the mystical foundations of the societal aspect. And correct was the gentleman with the retrograde and mocking physiognomy in Dostoevsky, who wanted to dispatch to the devil all the social felicity and to live according to his own will. The Kingdom of God upon earth, in our physical nature, amidst our slavery, sins and vices, -- is impossible, and the very wish to affirm it is under these conditions -- a godless wish. For you it is difficult to understand, how the very wish to force the Kingdom of God upon earth can be a godless wish. But this is what is necessary to understand. In this forcing of the Kingdom of God upon earth there would be acting not the spirit of Christ, but rather the spirit of the Anti-Christ. Revolutionary socialism is one of the Anti-Christ temptations.

Your socialism represents a compulsory virtue and a compulsory brotherhood. Here is what is repellant in your socialism, here is why aesthetically and morally it is repulsive. Your revolutionary socialism does not admit of that basic Christian truth, that the brotherhood between people can only be as the fruition of free a love, only as an higher spiritual blossoming of human community. Ye however want as though to forcibly compel people into brotherhood. The idea of brotherhood is borrowed by you from Christianity, you pilfered it and unconscionably used it, whilst having no sort of right to it. The brotherhood of people is possible only in Christ and through Christ. The brotherhood of people cannot be something of the natural order, a natural condition among people and their societies. In the natural order man is not a brother to his fellow man, but rather a wolf, and people conduct a fierce struggle one against another. In the natural order Darwinism is triumphant. Your socialism also derives from this natural struggle and through a most vicious struggle wants to assert brotherhood upon earth. And all your socialism is inwardly eaten away by inner vice and sickness. In evil and through evil it intends to assert its good. Not through Christ, not through graced love do ye desire to assert the brotherhood of people, but through hatred and the rising up of class against class. Ye hopelessly confuse brotherhood with a grouping and unifying of economic interests. Never, never in your kingdom can man become brother to his fellow man, he can only become a "tovarisch", a comrade. But what does "tovarisch" (an aesthetically low-down word) have in common with brother? All the difference between socialism and Christianity -- is in this difference between "tovarisch" and brother. The brother respects in a brother the man, as the image and likeness of God, the brother becomes one with his brother, as sons of the same father. Brotherhood presupposes a common paternity. And those, who do not know father and who renounce father, cannot be brothers. The tovarisch-comrade honours in the tovarisch-comrade not the man, but rather the class, an economic category, the tovarisch-comrade unites with the tovarisch-comrade in a commonness of material interests. Tovarisch-comrades do not recollect their paternity, do not want to know of the same one father, they -- are prodigal sons. Your socialistic category of "tovarisch" signifies the greatest of contempt for man. Your "tovarisch-comrade" ultimately divides the human race into two hostile camps and everything is considered permissible against the hostile camp. Your religion unites and divides as regards material interests. Can there be anything more hostile to the spirit of Christianity? Indeed, monstrous is every would-be alignment of tovarisch-comradeship and Christian brotherhood. Socialistic "tovarisch-comradeship" wants as though to transform the world into a commercial-industrial enterprise, in which everything is united by material interests alone and wherein are no reasons to wage between them a material struggle. Christian brotherhood posits itself different ends, not having anything in common with commerce nor the uniting of material interests. Your socialism with its craven, spiritually plebian "tovarisch-comrade" ideal shows yet again, that brotherhood is impossible in the natural order, that it is possible only in the graced order. Brotherhood is impossible outside of Christ, outside the grace love of Christ. Criminal and ugly are all your pilferings from Christ, of treasures belonging to Him, without the acceptance of Christ Himself. Brotherhood without Christ is slavery, coercion, tyranny. Only with Christ is brotherhood a realm of freedom. Brotherhood without Christ, without Divine Love is also a forced comradeship, summoned to life by material violence. Graceless brotherhood -- is terrible a thing, it is the death of man, the death of the human person. Through love for Christ is affirmed each human person in his singular uniqueness. Brotherhood in Christ is an unity of persons.

Brotherhood without Christ, a tovarisch-comradeship, is an unity of the impersonal, in it is impossible to distinguish the countenance of persons. A socialism ultimate and to the limit is also an ultimate and to the limit denial of the freedom of man. It is possible to force me to act with respect for the dignity and rights of every man, from me can be demanded the admitting of the citizen in each man. But nothing and no one in the world, not even God Himself, can force me into brotherhood, can demand from me a brotherly regard towards those, whom I have not chosen to nor loved. This -- is an act of my freedom, which I will not cede to you for any sort of good in the world. I reserve for myself the right of a modicum of distance, and I acknowledge distance as necessary in the natural order. It is impossible to compel me to a greater closeness, a greater love in regard to the fellow man, than that which I freely want and choose to have. Your socialism wants to force me to this, and I scorn its forceful intrusions. In the political order I acknowledge citizenship, in the religious order I acknowledge brotherhood. But at its root level I deny tovarisch-comradeship as a monstrous bit of confusion of various planes, as the monstrous pretension of a social category to play a religious role and substitute as a religious category.

Many are the transitory forms of socialism. Certain of them can seem religiously innocent. But in order to discern the age-old nature of socialism and catch sight of the lie and the evil, which it conveys into the world, one mustneeds take socialism to the limit, collectivism taken to the limit. And your collectivism taken to the limit is the most terrible, that can await man and mankind. This collectivism taken to the limit no one ever has ever imagined for oneself sufficiently and concretely. It would however be proper to remember, that in the utopia of T. More it is difficult the same for people to move about, as it is in the soviet republic, and in the teachings of Etienne Cabet permits of only one government newspaper. The Russian revolution hints at this, that there will come of it a paradise of collectivism. But the majority of you, socialists indeed, are incapable of conceiving your aspirations and dreams, taken to the limit. The majority of you, socialists indeed, are constituted eclectically and confuse various principles. You yourself know not, of what sort is your spirit. Ye -- are but foils of inhuman, of human-destroying powers. Collectivism taken to the limit is the collectivising away of all the whole man leaving not a trace, of all his body and all his soul. Collectivism wants to leave nothing in the individual aspect of the man himself. It wants to subsume everything in man to its all-devouring control. Collectivism, in its unlimited and pseudo-religious form, makes pretense to all the whole of man. No sort of state, even the most tyrannical and despotic, has had this sort of pretensions. Much in man remained free and individual, not regulated and not rationalised away even amidst the most terrible of tyrannies. Every state, however despotic its form, has nonetheless acknowledged the individual human being, it was aware of its limits. The state could oppress man and even torment him, but it did not have pretension to forcibly organise the total man and total mankind, to inculcate compulsory virtue. And therefore one could at least breathe freely. Nothing more terrible in the world can there be than compulsory virtue. In the name of the dignity of man and the freedom of man, in the name of his higher nature, it is needful to reserve to man a certain freedom to sin, the freedom of choice between good and evil. If it were fated at some point in time to realise collectivism in its ultimate form, then the freedom of man would ultimately be destroyed. Not only the material tools of production, but also the spirit of man, and the body of man, would be collectivised and socialised. The collectivisation and socialisation would tend to go all further and further deep down. And from this fatal process it would be impossible anywhere to escape, with no salvation from it. This process cannot limit itself to the material side of life. In vain do ye want to quiet the matter with the consideration, that the forced collectivisation would be of the material side of life, whereby the spirit would become more free. This is a very deep-rooted lie, the greatest of self-deceits and delusions. Ye indeed begin with this, that ye collectivise the human spirit, that ye kill the person. By this collectivisation of spirit ye seek to create a spiritual pseudo-communality, a pseudo-sobornost'. Your sobornost' communality is a false one, since true sobornost' communality obtains within the Church of Christ, it obtains already open to the human soul. True spiritual sobornost' communality has room in it for the person of man and for the freedom of man. Your sobornost' however does not tolerate the human person and human freedom. Your forced collectivism abolishes every material basis of free spiritual culture. All the material means, without which is impossible any sort of appearance and embodiment of spiritual culture in our sinful world, ye want to exclude from individual useage and free evaluation, ye want to betray them to your Leviathan. A free individual initiative upon anything with be impossible. Only the state, the central commune, the collective, will possess the means and implements of expression and embodiment of spiritual life. Not having them will be the person and the free association of persons, positing itself ends, not in accord with the central and ruling collective. There would even become impossible the free publishing of books, journals and newspapers, since all the printing aspect will be in the hands of the central collective and would be subservient to its interests and ends. There would be possible only a "prole-cult", and not a free culture. There would be preserved only the freedom of the unembodied spirit, and the human spirit would become disembodied.

Ye have jumbled together the sphere of law and the sphere of morals, and in regarding these two spheres as identical you want to erect your compulsory collective. And this tempting jumble bears with it a greatest of dangers for human freedom. Law is a compulsory principle, defending and guarding human freedom. It makes possible the living together and community of people also in the case, when people are sinful and evil, when they are given to violence and greed. Human society cannot be constructed upon love as an all-binding and compulsory principle. Love between people can only be as the free flourishing of human community, only with the graced order within it. Obligatory and forced love is a monstrous contradiction and an insult to the very nature of love. In the natural order human society has to have obligatory and compulsory groundings, preventing a chaotic dissolution. Human society in this sinful world, in this old nature has to be governed not only by love, but also by law. And in the law, in law there is active a Divine energy. Those, who allow for human society only the principle of love and spurn every other principle, tend to deny Christian love and they replace it with some other sort of compulsory and non-Christian love, a love, terrible in its gracelessness. Upon such a graceless love L. Tolstoy wanted to base human community. All ye collectivists want to bind people one to another, even though inwardly they have nothing in common between them and may even hate each other. Ye want to bind people to one another on the basis of necessity and common interests. Your socialistic love is an iron necessity, an evil forcing together. And hateful to you is the right of the defense of human nature, its free choosing. You want to leave nothing for the freedom of man and for the free love of man. Ye have not only jumbled up law with morals, ye have likewise jumbled the sphere of private law with the sphere of public law. Ye totally deny private law and replace it with the public. And this means, that you confuse freedom with necessity and replace freedom with necessity. Ye desire a compulsory and necessary freedom. Ye do not allow for freedom of choice and a falling-away, not because that man for you is rendered perfect and ye want to perfect man, but the rather, because man for you in his inner nature does not exist, and is merely a reflection of economic necessity.

There is a lie set within the very basis of the moral pathos of socialism. This lie tends to tempt sentimental people. The socialistic declamations concerning rich and poor in a majority of cases is false at its very foundations. The moral pathos of socialism is an hodgepodge of a false sentimentality and affectation of sympathy, together with a vicious and evil vengefulness. Sentimentality often leads to viciousness. This -- is a law of emotional life. Socialism, as regards its moral composition, is a sentimental ferocity and a fierce sentimentality. The subjectively-moral, emotionally-passionate side of socialism is something verymost ugly and deceptive, and it also threatens to turn human life into an hell. The objective, scientific, intellectual side of socialism is more neutral and innocent. The morals of socialism, taken to the point of fanaticism, for many so imposing, is also its most godless and terrible side. Salvation from this ugly, man-killing morality has properly to be sought out in the pathos of objectivity, and with a perceptive humility in facing the necessity and legitimacy of the social process. The pathos of objectivity would cool down your blazing souls, would weaken your malevolent feelings. You live in an unhealthy and overwrought emotional atmosphere, in which class hatred reaches the boiling point. Entire whole classes seem to you bent upon evil and evoke from you malevolent feelings. This maliciousness of entire whole classes of society is asserted also by the so-called "scientific socialism", and despite the objective side of its teachings, it sets great hopes upon enflaming the malevolent feelings of other classes. The lie is set within the primal basis of your understanding of the origin of social evil and inequality. The moral pathos of socialism is born in you of that false awareness, wherein social injustice, poverty, sufferings occur chiefly from the evil will of the ruling classes of the haves. You love to declaim regarding this even then, when you are adherents of an "objective", "scientific" socialism. But such a misuse of moral categories within the understanding of social activity leads to a moral distortion and immorality. It is not good, it is bad to see an evil will in people and whole classes even there, wherein are active causes of an objective character, where natural necessity impels its own iron grip. You at a stroke both misapply moral categories in social life, while totally denying moral responsibility and its imputation to the human person. This combination of extreme moralism with a total amoralism creates an unhealthy spiritual atmosphere.

Objective bases of the societal aspect do exist, deeply lodged within nature, within the structure of cosmic life. The structure of society does not depend upon the evil caprice of these or some other classes of society. Society is a phenomenon of nature, and its legitimacy is bound up with the legitimacy of nature. A graced society, having conquered the natural legitimacy, belongs already to a different plane, a different dimension; it is a fourth dimension of society in comparison with its other three dimensions, in which transpire legitimate social life. From more profound a point of view, the objective necessity itself within societal life can be said to have a spiritual and moral meaning. In it is active Divine truth, refracted the dark and sinful nature. The root causes of human woes and human want are lodged within the sinful nature of man and the world. The sinful nature becomes subject to a severe rule of law. Into the realm of freedom can only enter a transfigured and reborn nature, not only the nature of man and mankind alone, but also of all the world and the whole cosmos. Facing man is set the difficult task of a victory over nature and mastering of its elemental powers, with their regulation for higher cosmic ends. The poverty and want in human societies is bound up first of all with the low degree of a victory and mastery over the elemental natural forces, with a dependence upon these natural elemental forces. Marxism from its objective scientific side tended to understand, that the whole social structure of society, with its class differences and inequalities, is determined by arbitrary forces, by the degree of victory over nature, by its already attained material values and riches. But Marxism is inwardly a contradictory teaching; the objective-scientific side in it clashes with the subjective-class side, with which is bound up the revolutionary and moral pathos of socialism.

In the philosophy of socialism are two elements: in one of them the class aspect is ascendant over the objective aspect and across all the expanse of history alike there is seen a truth in the uprisings of the have-nots and of evil in the very existence of the haves; in the other -- the objective spirit is stronger than that of the class and in various historical epochs are admitted various classes progressing and having various tasks set before them. In fact, revolutionary socialism always moves by and is inspired by the first element, it sympathises with all the uprisings of the masses, all the revolts of the black elements in history and at all times alike condemns and curses all the upper classes, all the haves and cultured segments. Throughout all of history it follows along a single line, dividing the human race into two races, into two realms -- the "bourgeoise" and the "proletariat". In Marxism both elements of socialism get jumbled together. But with the revolutionary social-democrats is a predominance of this association with the "proletariat" over all the course of history, acknowledging it as the revolutionary-progressive class, along with hatred for the "bourgeoise" as a class of oppressors and the culprit behind social evils. Kautsky's history of socialism was written in this spirit. The progressive and revolutionary role of the "bourgeoise", about which Marx taught, does not evoke for it any sort of positive moral attitude. Decidedly at another point of view stood Lassalle, who rose many heads higher over the socialistic mental average and who has to be admitted among the finest of socialists. Lassalle acknowledged, that in various historical eras various classes appear as bearers of a world progressive "idea", that the bearer of such an "idea" was the third estate, and now the fourth estate appears as its bearer. Lassalle therefore very highly values the historical role of the bourgeois classes and condemns the uprisings of the working classes, when out of step with the "idea" of the historical era, as for example, the peasant armies of the era of the Reformation. Russian socialists ultimately are incapable of assuming an historical perspective, and the spirit of Lassalle is foreign to them. They -- are avid moralists, and their moralism all too often passes over into moral idiotism.

Herein is the problem, over which ye have too little pondered and by which ye become repellent by your distorted moralism. Does social inequality appear not only a matter of necessity and measure of law, but also as favourable, and good and correct? Why then have you acknowledged as a moral axiom, that social inequality is evil? At a certain step of the developement of material productive powers, inequality provides the maximum benefit, the maximum of satisfying the demands of the people. Levelling then would instead lead to impoverishment, to a weakening of the productivity of labour, to a destroying of the sources of the people's wealth and the people's sustenance. At a nowise high level of developement, when man has as yet insufficiently mastered the elements of nature, social inequality, with its stratifying out of a privileged class of the haves, -- this is a sole saving factour and is good even for the have-nots, for the masses of the people. The fact of the existence of a nowise numerous segment of the haves and of the rich itself per se cannot be the source of social evils and woes. To assert this -- means falsely to play around with numeric categories. The taking away of the material means from this nowise numerous segment cannot essentially alter the position of the masses of the people, in their enormous numbers. For the increase of wealth and of raising the favourable condition of the masses, of the great numbers, what is needful is not the impoverishing of a small number, but rather the growth of productivity, the developing of the material productive powers. The social question is really first of all decidable upon the paths of productivity, and not redistribution. Levelling down to the bottom element, who tend to demand much from you, is a pillaging of human culture, a lowering of the level of life. A socialism of impoverishment -- is a most terrible socialism. The course of events after the world war has shown, that socialism is begotten of poverty, and not wealth. Far more bearable still would be a socialism based upon wealth, a socialism of abundance. When the fanatics of revolutionary socialism demand, that it would be best for all to be worse off, rather than that there should exist a privileged bit of the haves, providing the possibility of sustaining higher a level of culture, -- their moralism is stirred with envy and malice rendered into a god. Healthy moral judgement would have to admit, that it were better that some few should be at an higher level of culture, than that all should be at the bottom level. *Inequality is a condition for the developement of culture.* This -- is axiomatic. It remains unshown, -- why that equality is morally higher than inequality? And is perhaps inequality itself per se a truth and good and something proper to strive for? *Even in the Kingdom of God will be inequality. With inequality is connected all being.* In the world ought not to be the poor and the hungry, all ought to be vouchsafed an humanly dignified existence. But this does not require equality. In the very uprising against the foundations of the social order in the name of justice there is a religious lie, begotten of evil feelings. For us it is not given to know, why one is rich, and another poor, why to each falls the lot to these or some other tribulations. People ought not to think, that they are holier than God and can set straight the injustice deigned by Providence. The revolutionary struggle for justice begets hatred. It is not the struggle for justice, but rather love that ought to guide us in help for the poor and suffering. And to the abundance of love is set no limits. It is not the struggle for an abstract justice, but rather a creative instinct that ought to guide us in social improvement.

Christ taught, that it is easier for a camel to go through the eye of a needle, than for a rich man to enter into the Kingdom of Heaven. Here is what for many, outwardly in regard to Christianity and not delving into the mysteries of the Christian religion, -- tends to sound almost socialistic. Ye socialists love to misuse the Gospel and mention it, when it suites your irreligious and anti-religious ends. In these references to Gospel texts, in these non-religious interpretation of texts there is something ugly and sacrilegious. The words of Christ about the rich have a meaning, directly the opposite to that, which ye seek to impart to them. For everyone, who inwardly and not merely outwardly approaches the mystery of life, it has to be clear, that Christ was concerned about the fate of the rich, about their soul, when He said, that it is very difficult for them to get into the Kingdom of Heaven. He tended to say, that that the rich more readily become slaves to the material world, to material things, that they become bereft of freedom of spirit and therefore it becomes difficult for them to gain entry into the Kingdom of Heaven, into the kingdom of free souls, loving God far more than all the world and everything that is of the world. Christ wanted to spiritually liberate the rich, He thus was interested in their salvation for eternity the same, as also for the salvation of all human souls. He came into the world for all, alike for the poor and for the rich. And when He spoke words about the difficulty for the rich to enter into the Kingdom of Heaven, He was thinking not about the material interests of the poor, but about the spiritual interests of the rich. He therefore revealed the absolute significance of every human soul, independent of its social position. For Him there could not be the chosen and the repudiated as regards social position. The socialistic declamation about the rich however occupies a pole, directly the opposite to Christianity, it is pervaded by hatred of the rich and jealousy of them. Socialists want also to make it difficult for the poor to gain entry into the Kingdom of Heaven. The words of Christ are oriented towards the inner man, towards the human soul. The socialistic words are oriented towards the outer man, to the material trappings of the man, and in them always is to be sensed an ignorance of the inner man. Christ taught about a graced, blessed, Divine poverty as an higher freedom and beauty of the soul. It is only but for the few. The poor one of God, St. Francis of Assisi, in perfection realised this image of the beauty of poverty. But what in common does this have with socialism? Christ taught, that the poor have spiritual advantages over the rich, that for them is made easier the entry into the Kingdom of God. Socialists however forever speak about the great advantages of the rich, they are jealous of these advantages and they want to take from them these advantages and transfer them to the poor. Christ taught about one giving away one's wealth. The socialists teach about taking away the riches of others. Christ called for feeding the hungry and giving away one's last shirt. And this has to be by an act of abundant love. Christ with this turned towards the inner man, to the depth of the human soul. This was not a recipe for an external social order, about which the Gospel said nothing. The socialists do not call for feeding the hungry and giving away one's last shirt to one's neighbour. They are oriented towards the outer man. They call upon the hungry to take away by force. They instill into a poor man the thought, that wealth is wonderful, that the lot of the rich -- is an enviable lot, and by this they poison his poor heart. Christ wanted, that there should not be the hungry, that all should be fed, that all should be clothed. And the Christian attitude towards life demands caring about the hungry, the unfortunate and deprived. And difficult it will be for the rich to have to be answerable for this. But how contrary and opposite is the spirit of Christ to the socialistic spirit! Christ revealed the eternal truth about the spiritual composition of man, and not a temporal truth about the social construct of society. The entire Gospel preaching of Christ even presupposes the existence of private property and social inequality, and leaves untouched the social structure, which is always determined by complex natural and historical conditions, it teaches the eternal truth of love and self-sacrifice. The socialists want to render impossible and unnecessary the Christian virtues of love, sacrifice and charity. Great is the wisdom of Christianity, for which the absolute value of the human soul does not depend upon social position and is affirmed in every historical setting. Both master and servant can be brothers in Christ, whilst remaining in their social position. Christianity demands, that the soul of the master and the soul of the servant should be acknowledged absolutely of value and equally of value before the Lord, so that the master should respect in the servant the image and likeness of God. But it does not appeal for social revolution, does not teach, that some particular structure of society at all times is alike obligatory. The Apostle Paul taught, that the slave, remaining in the social position such as has befallen his lot, can attain perfection and can go the path of Christ. Social-revolutionary elements were quite foreign to the Christian Church; these elements were there only in heretical and sectarian movements. Christianity has had an enormous significance for the abolition of slavery in the world, but the activity of Christianity in this regard was spiritual, and not social, inward, and not outward. Christianity admits, that all social changes are determined by a special legitimacy, that historical advantage on the external plane cannot be abolished and destroyed. The social question has its own technical side, its own scientific methods, its own material conditions. The wisdom of universal a Christianity admits all this, as distinct from sectarianism. The ultimate healing of social evils and sufferings is possible only in the cosmic harmony, only in the Kingdom of God. Until this, however, there is possible only relative steps. The social question is irresolvable, resolvable only are social questions. The Christian sense of good involves freedom and therefore presupposes a certain freedom of evil.

The ideology of socialism is the ideology of a material and unqualitative toil. It is hostile to toil that is spiritual and qualitative. And it would be erroneous to assert, that socialism takes under its wing toil in all its entirety, work as a worldwide principle, and is thus representative of the idea of labour. Socialism represents a mechanical and quality-lacking material sort of labour and denies the creative nature of labour. The problem of work as creativity is nowise at all of interest to the socialistic mindset, it is situated off its horizon. In this regard, socialism is situated in a servile subordination to the bourgeois capitalistic society despised by it, and is powerless to rise above it. Socialism tends to make a god of the proletariat, but has no respect for work. The materialistic nature of socialism hinders it from perceiving the religious nature of work. The liberation at its limit for the socialist consciousness is a liberation from work. The ideology of work passes over into an ideology of hostility to work, based upon envy of those, who are freed from working. In the pathos of socialism there is no obligation of work. And the socialists want as though to summon to work only the bourgeois classes out of a sense of malice and revenge. The attitude of socialism towards work exposes its negative and merely reflex nature, its dependence upon that, against which it manifests a reaction. Socialism has not conveyed into the world the idea of the ennobling aspect of work and its uplifting creative and qualitative character. It bases itself upon an abstraction of the quantity of work. The quality of work is something that socialism does not want to know, it despises it. But work has its own sacred rights, inseparable from its sacred duties. When capital denies the sacred rights of labour and oppresses them, it becomes an evil principle and against it there is the necessity to struggle. Capital is a necessary principle in economic life, without which there cannot be turned out work, but it can transform itself into a self-serving abstract principle, and then it falls out of place in the organic hierarchy. Socialism however wants to represent work, also fallen out of place from the organic hierarchy and transformed into an abstract principle. There exists a qualitative hierarchy of work. And sacred only is that work, which dwells in this qualitative hierarchy. Plato knew this well. Ruskin knew this in modern times. But the socialists do not know this. Material work, as an abstract numeric principle, does not exist. This -- is a fiction, upon which Marx constructed so much. Work has spiritual a basis. And the productivity of the so-called material work is dependent upon the spiritual condition of man. The discipline of work is a spiritual discipline. In the final end it has religious groundings. Without the religious groundings, without the spiritual discipline work falls apart, disintegrates and economic life is transformed into an ant-hill. Your materialistic socialism is powerless to straighten out the problem of discipline and the organisation of work. Discipline and the organisation of work can only be hierarchical. And herein ye clash with a contradiction that is to your undoing. Socialistic society considers itself a working society. But materialistic socialism lacks the powers to organise work, it rather disorganises it, since it denies the hierarchical order of work. It destroys the spiritual foundations of labour. At its very conception, socialism rose up against a division of labour. And the division of labour is at the basis of human society and human culture, the basis of the discipline of work and its qualitative hierarchical aspect. The casting down of the division of labour is a casting down of the societal cosmos, an ending of a qualitative culture. The qualitative levelling of work is an insult to the finest and a selection of the unfit, a denial and destruction of abilities and talents, of experience and education, of vocation and genius. And in vain do certain of you, the freedom loving, tend to think, that the complete uniformity of the material, the cramping of every quality into the quantitative, can free up space for a manifold of the spiritual, for qualitative distinctions in spiritual life. The abstraction of material life and the abstraction of spiritual life does not exist. Everything is connected and interwoven within the societal cosmos. Howsoever ye might want to avoid it, ye are compelled to admit the supremacy of material work and deny every aspect of autonomy for spiritual work. You despise spiritual work and its representatives. You want to enslave their work to the material. For you this is merely -- two abstractions, and you want as though ultimately to subordinate one of them to the other. And therefore socialism is terrible not only for capital, it is even more terrible for spiritual work, for creativity, i.e. in the final end for the spirit of man. *Your socialism is an uprising of matter against spirit, the conflict of matter with spirit.* The "bourgeois" kingdom of capitalism was likewise a kingdom of matter, destructive of spirit, and you -- are its continuation, the heirs of this kingdom, quenchers of spirit.

Your idea of worldwide social revolution, of the Zusammenbruch shattering of capitalistic society, represents a monstrous jumbling of ideas of a scientific and social-political order together with ideas of a religious order. The grand leap from the realm of necessity into the realm of freedom, about which Marx and Engels taught, is already a transition from the historical process to a process supra-historical, an apocalypsis of world history. Social revolutions, in the sense of a world catastrophe, initiating a new historical era, -- there never were nor ever can be. The social process, by its nature, is a process molecular. In the natural order it can only be evolution, and not revolution. Social processes tend to have nothing in common with a political coup d'etat, with an overthrow of power, such as might transpire over the course of a single day, with the burnings, the uprisings and clash of weapons. It is impossible by bayonettes and guns to change economic relationships, to create a new structure of society. This is true also in the relationships of social counter-revolutions, and not only revolutions. Social growth presupposes the growth of the power of man over nature, the growth of economic productivity and a moral change in the attitude of man towards man. These economic and moral processes do not bring to mind revolutions and cataclysms. The objective scientific side of Marxism leads to a denial of the idea of worldwide social revolution. And if

Marxism nonetheless called for social revolution and believed in it, then it is because that it is not only a science, but also a faith, it possessed not only a social, but also a religious, a pseudo-religious pretension. The awaiting expectation of a social revolution is also a false religious expectation, a substitute and self-deception. The revolutionary social maximalism has always been based upon a confusing of the relative and the absolute, of the social and the religious, of means and ends. In the natural order, within historical activity there ought to be asserted a plurality of means. The resolution of the social question within the limits of the three dimensions of this world can only be by the complex and the relative. "Social revolution" is possible only as a process of disintegration. Social reformism, directed at the defense of the interests of labour and workers, ought to be aligned also with historical advantages and traditions, and with the inalienable rights and freedom of man. What is needful is the combination of free individual initiative, of a free societal cooperation together with a state regulation. This means, that the socialist principle, taken within its relative and partialised truth, has to be in accord with other principles, principles conservative and liberal. The social reformation of society, the regulation of production, the organisation of labour ought to be in accord with the principles of private property. And this is because the principle of property possesses an inseparable bond with the principle of the person. The principle of property has deep religious and spiritual groundings, it is rooted in the spiritual freedom of man, in his organic, spiritual connection with ancestors and descendants. But with the principle of private property can be bound up very ugly abuses, it easily can become a tool of greed and avarice, it can become transformed into a tool of oppression. The principle of private property is not an utmost and absolute principle, it ought to be subordinated to higher principles, it ought to be within limitations. An autonomous, abstractly sufficient unto itself private property produces a terrible desolateness within human life, it becomes a principle vampire-like. And then a social uprising falls to the lot of truth. Private property ought to be something inwardly spirit-bearing, and then it is justified, it has its own mission. And it then represents one of the eternal principles of human life. To the spirit of greed, avarice, egoism, to a spirit, in the grip of a thirst for pleasure and tempted by insipid and ugly luxury, -- there has to be opposed another spirit. There is needful a spiritual struggle against the "bourgeois" spirit. Socialism has not the powers to conquer this "bourgeois" spirit, since it itself was propagated by this "bourgeois" spirit, it -- is its offspring. And never ever will ye socialists, children of this "bourgeois" age, be able to tear yourself away from the three-dimensional "bourgeois" world. The passing over into the fourth dimension of human existence is an inner spiritual turnabout, a religious revolution. The victory over poverty and hunger, the guarantee for each member of society of the necessary minimum of human existence is a task more modest and elementary, its solving does not mean a transition over to another dimension, into a supra-historical existence. A final and total socialism is impossible and would be ruinous for man, for his spiritual nature, for his higher dignity. A triumph of the religion of socialism would halt the growth of productivity and would paralyse creativity. It destroys the motivation for work. The triumph would render impossible a creative abundance, *since abundance presupposes inequality, competition and selection.* For the enormous majority of the proletariat, within which mankind would tend to become identical, the higher qualitative culture would become needless, and unnecessary would be the higher creative upsurges of spiritual life. To the proletariat would belong the supreme power, nowise limited. *But in the name of the freedom of creativity, in the name of the blossoming forth of life, in the name of the higher qualities, inequality has to find its justification.* It is not by chance that the positivists and materialists most of all rise up against inequality. They cannot grasp its meaning. Because only for a religious outlook on life and man's fate that there obtains meaning within the mysterious world-order and every man has his own apportioned lot beyond the pale of earthly life. It is monstrously unjust and cruel to demand for all people equal conditions. The conditions of life, for one man customary and comparatively easy, for another would be unbearably tormentive and weighty. The coercive levelling of a man uncultured and coarse with that of a man refined and of high culture can only be dictated by vengeful malice and hate. The capacity for passion is dependent upon the constitution of a man, upon the stirring within him of the blood of ancestors, upon education, upon level of culture, upon his calling. The bourgeois-capitalistic age is ugly in this, that it topples and levels everything, kills everything individual.

At the basis of the socialistic religion lies a denial of immortality and a revolt against the Divine world-order. Dostoevsky profoundly understood, that socialism is a consequence of the denial of immortality. And therefore in socialism is an avidness for death, an avidness for earthly life. How trite and vile all your utopias are, they are all -- philistinism taken to the limit! A spiritual lie lays at the basis of your social day-dreams. By means of this unhealthy social dreaminess ye seek to swallow in yourself the fear of death, ye gain a sort of surrogate for immortality. The social day-dreaming, the social utopianism has swallowed up the religious feeling within you, has weakened the consciousness of the meaning of life and has hidden away eternity for you. An healthy social pessimism would be something salvific for you, from it would issue a spiritual restoration of health. Your socialism makes pretense to be a new religion, a new spirit, and not merely a social arrangement, not only the gaining of daily bread for the hungry. And in this pretension perishes also the not-large portion of truth of socialism. Ye not so much provide earthly bread for the hungry (quite often ye instead deprive of that bread, which was had earlier), as rather that ye proclaim a religion of earthly bread against the religion of heavenly bread. Your pretensive socialism is profoundly anti-historical, does not understand the mysteries of history, and therefore it is essentially reactionary. It aspires to the Anti-Christ's end of history. And only universal Christian brotherhood, oriented towards Christ's end of history, can conquer the temptation of socialism.

The idea of democracy and the idea of socialism -- are contradictory ideas. A democratic socialism on the type of Jean Jaures is not an authentic socialism. All of you, ye socialist-revolutionaries, mensheviks, rightest socialists of every hue, -- are not genuine socialists, ye are all moreso democrats, than socialists. The genuine socialists -- are the communists. And the communists are correct, in opposing their socialism to democracy. Democracy -- is formally without content, it is unable to distinguish the direction of the people's will. In the formal aspect of the people's power, the people's will does not have any sort of object. Democracy is sceptical and moreover it is optimistic to the extreme. Socialism is pessimistic in regard to the formal will of the people, and what it is interested in is this, that the will of the people should have a definite direction and a definite object. Socialism affirms however not the sovereign will of the people, but the sovereign will of a class, the will of a messiah-class, the proletariat. Only the proletariat is free of the original sin of exploitation. And a consistent socialism allows only for the manifestation of will of the proletariat, and deriving not from every proletariat, but only the socialistic proletariat, a proletariat, true to the "idea" of the proletariat. It is not the factually actual, empirical proletariat that ought to rule, but only the "idea" of the proletariat. In the name of the "idea" of the proletariat can be committed whatever sort of violence it pleases over the factually actual proletariat. Supremacy belongs to that minority, which is the true bearer of the "idea" of the proletariat, which preserves the true faith. The socialistic state is not a secular state, as is the democratic state, this -- is a sacral state. On principle it cannot be faith-tolerant and cannot acknowledge any sort of freedoms. It admits of rights only for those, who confess the true faith, the socialistic faith. It comes nigh to an authoritarian theocratic state. The socialistic state is a satanocracy. Socialism confesses a messianic faith. The proletariat is the messiah-class. The preservers of the messianic "idea" of the proletariat is an especial hierarchy -- the communist party, centralised to the extreme and imbued with dictatorial power. No sort of manifestation of will of the people is permitted. It becomes necessary to forcibly subordinate the people to the "sacred" will of the proletariat, and to subordinate the proletariat to the "idea" of the proletariat. They know the truth and the subordinating to truth is through but few -- by whomever should comprise the central committee of the communist party. What a lack of resemblance to democracy in this there is! True socialists have to be sceptical of democracy, so empty and without content. Socialism has a desire to pass over to a content of life, to reveal the true and just will. And in this socialism is more correct, than is democracy. But here it comes nigh close to the utmost limits of non-being. The "idea" of the proletariat -- is completely vacuous, an idea fraught with non-being. The content and ends of life cannot be social and defined via external material signs. The content and the ends of life can only be spiritual. It is impossible to seek a righteous will outside of righteousness itself and the sanctity of the will. All the social and political forms prove to be merely formal. Both ought to be subordinated to the spiritual ends of life. And theocracy is only a symbolisation of the Kingdom of God, not its attained reality. In this was the reason for its historical crash. Socialism ultimately unveils the emptiness of all the external aspirations for a perfect society and a perfect life. Only in the real realisation of perfective spiritual life is there the resolution of the problem of a perfect society.

Tenth Letter

Concerning Anarchism

Anarchism, just like socialism, is one of the vintage strivings, appearing from times of old in human society, and is one of the societal forms of thought of man taken to the limit. The revolutionary pathos of anarchism is different from the revolutionary pathos of socialism. There exists an inwardly conflicting struggle between these two revolutionary elements, but also a subtle passing back and forth from one to the other of these elements. If socialism comes nigh close to non-being in its thirst for equality, then anarchism comes nigh close to non-being in its thirst for freedom. Socialism taken to the limit -- is an empty equality. Anarchism taken to the limit -- is an empty freedom. If socialism believes in the beneficial aspect of compulsory organisation, then anarchism believes in the beneficial aspect of a natural autonomism and anonymity of man. Anarchism believes, that from chaos by means of a natural path can be born harmony. In anarchism there is a greater faith in man, than there is in socialism, although there be no sorts of a basis for such faith within it. Anarchism denies the significance of law for human life, for society, for the paths of history, it denies every sort of historical hierarchism, every right and every state. For a consistent anarchistic consciousness the historical process is completely meaningless and man ought to excise all the ossified warts of the state and culture. A consistent anarchism does not acknowledge any sort of worthiness of duty in the historical path of mankind. It desires to restore the natural man, free of all connections, from all historical remembrances. Everything is rendered merely a constricting box for the man free by his nature, the whole of history -- is merely the chains, holding man down. Anarchism admits of no sort of inner legitimacy of the social process. Man both can and ought completely to free himself at whatever the moment of history, amidst whatever social structure he might please. But revolutionary anarchism includes within it an element of class socialism. Only in rare cases, when anarchism appears in its idealistic forms, does it present man, the human person independent of social position. In the majority of cases, however, anarchism is representative of the same "proletarian" classes of society, as is socialism, and even admits itself an ideology of the lumpen-proletariat, the fifth estate. The anarchists love to declaim over the freedom of man, about the person, but ye breathe the same class hatred, as do the socialists, and ye likewise cannot rise up above the class point of view. And this -- is an inner contradiction of anarchism, in this is sensed its lack of freedom, its dependence upon socialism of a most vile sort. In the emotional composite of anarchism lies a revolutionary rebellious feeling of being wronged, a lack of success in life, of evil memories of those values and good things, which did not prove to be so and are sensed as alien. The ideology of anarchism is nigh close to that of the grimy vagabond, having dispatched to the devil any matter of social hierarchy. The anarchistic passion for destruction is borne out of a sense of hatred and vindictiveness. The anarchist within human society, within human culture senses nothing as his own, nothing near and dear for himself, and everything seems to him alien, imposing and hateful. For the anarchist the state -- is not his state, but alien, imposing and hateful. And what does the anarchist acknowledge as his very own? Nothing. It is not only material property that he may be lacking (sometimes he may also possess it), but first of all he is lacking in spiritual property, he senses himself deprived of any share and from this he heaps up a destructive malice in his heart. Max Stirner, one of the most extreme and interesting philosophers of anarchism, wrote a book entitled, "The Individual and His Property". Max Stirner considers all the whole world as the property of the "individual". But this is a terrible self-deception. In actuality, he has plundered the "individual", he has deprived it of any property at all. The "individual" -- is a spiritual proletariat, who has nothing of his own, all the spiritual realities and al the spiritual values -- are not his, are alien and therefore are hateful for him. The "individual" lives in a void, in a terrible spiritual desolation. He not only arranges his affairs upon "nothing", but also the content of his life, the ends for his life, are based upon "nothing". And all you revolutionary anarchists are likewise spiritually proletarian the same, as is the "individual" of Stirner, likewise hollow the same, likewise empty the same, likewise the same torn away and cut off from all the wellsprings of spiritual life and spiritual riches.

Anarchism is an atomism, the disintegration of all the societal totalities into self-asserting atoms, into individuums, beginning with them all history, denying all higher realities. The triumph of anarchism would be the falling apart of all the hierarchies of reality, of the organic connections between them, the destruction of all cosmic order, the revolt of chaos against cosmos. In this uprising of chaos, first of all, would be subjected to doubt all the cosmic realities, the realities of God's world, begotten in the light. Into the chaotic darkness they would become submerged, and the chaotic darkness would be admitted the sole reality. The chaos would break loose, and the self-asserting atoms of themself would think to recreate a new world. Here is what stirs underneathe the anarchistic teachings, sometimes so very idyllic and charming. From a philosophic point of view, your anarchism is an extreme nominalism, a denial of the reality of all the totalities and entireties, nations, states, mankind, cosmos, God. Anarchism transforms all the realities into apparitions and oppression. It wants as though to lay man bare, to posit man in emptiness and through emptiness. But upon this path is not man transformed into the ultimate of phantasms? Are ye not also destroying man, that individual, which was your ultimate cause, and in the name of which ye revolted against all the world and against God? For you who are consistent anarchists, the human person is but the most vacuous of all phantasms. Ye had to go even further and deeper into the revolutionary process of fragmentation and disintegration. Ye transformed man into an atom. But even your sort of man is falling apart further into atoms. The upheaval goes deep. Man however is a totality, is a real wholeness. The parts rise up against the whole and displace the core of the human person, its spiritual centre. Your destructive nominalism has to proceed ever farther and farther, it is set to preserve no sort of reality. Why is the separate man more real, than all the supra-human realities that you would destroy? Here is the vile bias, from which only with difficulty ye can gainsay. Not many of you hold to the ultimately radical view of the destruction of every reality in the world. Indeed, this destruction would be endless. The infinitude of destruction would reveal the darkly gaping abyss, which would frighten even the most extreme of you. But ye summon forth spirits, bolder, more consistent and radical than you. Ye are all however still too timid. Even Max Stirner, the boldest of you, has preserved the superstitious realities of the "individual". But a consistent anarchism would have to admit only the reality of the dark chaotic abyss of non-being, only an everlasting infinitude of fragmentation and disintegration. The anarchy would seize also the individuum, as also every human "I".

Your anarchism is a self-contradiction and a self-destruction. Upon it there is nothing for you to grab hold of and get anywhere. The dark deluge bears you forth into the abyss. It is not of any sort of person that you can speak. No sort of countenance remains real for you. Ye cannot rightly pronounce any sort of name. The anarchistic path is the path of the self-destruction of the person, the perishing of the human "I". Whoso would blow up with dynamite all the realities set over him, all the values and sanctities, that selfsame one blows up also himself, his own "I", that selfsame one sets ruination to his own person and casts himself into the chasm of the chaotic non-being. The human "I", the human person, the human individuality really does exist, if there exist realities higher than man, than his trapped-in "I". Man down to the depths really is, if God is, and he perishes, disintegrates, if there is no God, if within him perishes God. Man always is sustained by that, which is higher than him, by what renders his own proper reality infinitely deep and infinitely sustainable. The man, in whom is only the surface dimension without dimensions of depth, would scatter about with the wind and lose even the right to his name, bestown him forever by God. But do ye indeed know any other dimension of the human being, than the surface dimension? Man would revolt and rise up, yet having become ultimately trivially flat in plane. The realities, dwelling in man and connecting him with the deep Divine workings, tend to guard man, his image, his countenance, his dignity, they prevent his decay and perishing within the dark abyss, within the chaotic elemental. On a day of anarchism one would always find a person lacking restraint, having lost his image, his spiritual centre. Anarchism is murderous to man the same, as is socialism. You anarchists set no one free. It is not man that you set free, but rather you set free chaotic non-being, in which man perishes.

And those realities, those powers, which anarchism wants to overthrow, they defend man from the elements perilous to his image. Church with its hierarchical structure safeguards the image of man, defends the human person from the demons of nature, from the elements besetting him on every side and threatening him. The state with its hierarchical structure guards the image of man from the beastly elements, from the darkness welling up from below, it acknowledges man as an individual being, it defends against an evil will such as transgresses al bounds. The law guards the freedom of man from the evil will of other people and all society. The law exposes sin, sets limits to it and makes possible a minimum of freedom within sinful human life. Anarchism however denies evil and sin, regards human nature as naturally fine and sinless. But namely by this, anarchism does not liberate man, rather it enslaves him all the more. By this, anarchism hurls man into a chasm, into a beastly and slave-like chaos, it betrays the human person for the rending by demons. Anarchism asserts the freedom of slavery under evil. The anarchist-liberators do not know the freedom of the New Adam, begotten in Christ. Your anarchistic freedom is the final spasm of the old Adam, of the old natural man. A truly free spirit cannot be an anarchist, in having no one and nothing to overthrow. The anarchistic mindset -- is the mindset of the slave. And one truly aspiring to liberation cannot be an anarchist, -- for he wants first of all to liberate himself from his own lower nature, from the grip of the dark elements over him. Anarchism seeks absolutely to set man free, without having changed and transformed his nature, leaving him a slave of sin and passions. It desires a realm of freedom without redemption. But, truly, Christ -- is the liberator, and freedom is there, where the spirit of the Lord is. Ye however have no wish to know Christ and the spirit of the Lord and think of yourself as free, whilst remaining slaves. The freedom of man is not gotten by revolts and uprisings. The anarchistic freedom -- is a negative freedom "from", and not a freedom "for", it is a formal freedom, and without content. This -- is the freedom of children, who want to have the possibility to do anything they might think of, but they still do not know, what to think of. Have you ever pondered over this, for what purpose is your freedom, how you may make use of your freedom, and what sort of a positive content you attribute to it? I tend to doubt, that ye have deeply pondered over this. You want to have the possibility to do everything, that you might want. But is there anything essentially that you want? Have ye already chosen your path? Do you already love something so much, that the object of love should fill your life with an higher content? About this, none of you say anything. You have no sort of goals. Your free anarchist communes -- are idyllic philistine utopias, bereft of any deep content. The means, to which ye resort in the struggle, cast upon you an ill-boding blackish red light and bestow you an almost demonic character. But your ends are vile and insignificant. By terrible and transgressive means ye strive for a philistine sweet idyll of mundane prosperity, for a natural paradise of its little cottages with gardens. Your dreadful bloody revolts and uprisings have to end up with nothing. All your pathos -- is in the means, and not the ends of your struggle. The anarchistic freedom -- is an empty freedom, a freedom from all the bonds of being, from God, from the cosmos, from every human community. But what is it that ye will do on the next day afterwards, when all the positive bonds, filling the life of man, are shattered? You yourselves do not know, what there is for you to do. Ye sense a morbid anguish and lassitude of emptiness, a terror of non-being. You yourself prefer the slavery of the vacuous freedom. And the slavery has not long to wait. The empty, the freedom bereft of content will in a trice be reborn into slavery. Ye will become slaves to yourself and to those like you and to all the untransformed and unenlightened nature. Anarchism does not know true freedom, just as socialism does not know brotherhood. Anarchism lays bare the secret of all the negative currents, that worship the old, the natural man. It bares into the daylight every revolutionism, socialism, democratism. And none of these currents can seriously set anything in opposition to anarchism, cannot contend against it. The radical exposure of the lies of the negative currents is to the merit of anarchism.

The ideology of anarchism in a majority of instances has anti-religious a basis and stirs with a pathos atheistic. Suchlike is the anarchism of Bakunin, the anarchism of M. Stirner, the anarchism of the dynamitists, the anarchists of actions. The anarchism is first of all directed against the Heavenly King, and thereupon against earthly kings. But the ideology of anarchism can base itself also religiously, can pass itself off as a religious teaching and in the name of God deny every power upon earth. Suchlike is the anarchism of L. Tolstoy, the anarchism of Edward Carpenter, the anarchism of the Dukhobors and sectarians, denying every embodiment of Divine principles within the historical process. Religious anarchism -- is a phenomenon of a completely special sort. Towards anarchism can tend only a religion of abstract spirituality and abstract monism. Abstract spirituality and abstract monism assumes hostile a position towards the historical embodiments and towards historical multiplicity. This -- is not the Christian religion, this -- is a monstrous abstraction and castration of Christianity. This is a sectarian dukhoborism, a sectarian "fighting the spirit", passing itself off as Christianity, it combines an extreme individualism, the denial of everything churchly and of all the worldly historical connections of man, with an extreme of monism, with the assertion of an absolute identicalness and impersonality. In this abstract religious individualism and monism is a denial of the organic unity of cosmic life and mutual assurance and responsibility of each human person for everyone and for all. The sectarian dukhobor-like religious anarchism desires to cast off from itself the burden of the world process, the burden of the historical fate of mankind and, having isolated itself, begin of itself to live in absolute freedom. This religious anarchism wants to admit of only the dominion of Divine law within itself. It is repulsed by the concrete multiplicity and by the tragic fate connected with it. It considers itself abiding in an absolute unity, in an unembodied and unembodiable spirituality. It does not want to smear its sacred white robes of anarchism by any attachment to historical bodies and embodiments. Religious anarchism shuts itself off from history, does not want to share in such a dirty affair. Religious anarchism is also an extreme rationalism, it does not believe in the mysterious basis and mysterious meaning of the historical embodiments and it believes, that through the individual consciousness and an orientation to Divine law all the world can suddenly be changed and brought to a new life. Suchlike is the faith of the Tolstoyans, of the Dukhobors, of the spiritual Christians, of the evangelical Christians. Evangelical Christianity rejects not only the whole of world history, but also the whole of religious Christian history. And this evangelical Christianity, in the final end, degenerates into moralism and legalism. The most extreme and typical Christian anarchist was L. Tolstoy. In him can be studied the inner stirrings of the wellsprings of religious anarchism. The extreme spiritualism of the Tolstoyan anarchism is combined with an animal-like materialistic understanding of the content of life; an extreme individualism is combined with a no less extreme monism, completely denying as regards person; a stupid denial of the worldly and historical process is combined with an extreme rationalism, with a coarse denial of everything miraculous and mysteried. The folly of anarchism is always a rationalistic folly, an enraptured reasoning. This is true both in regards to the religious anarchism, and in regards as well to the anti-religious anarchism.

The pathos of anarchism is the pathos of a denial of history. And every denying of history bears within it the seed of anarchism, though it not conceive of itself as anarchist. And thus within the Russian Eastern Orthodox religiosity there is an anarchist wont, a dislike for rule and organisation. The anarchistic tendency was there also in the Slavophils. It is compatible also with autocracy. This is because the organisation of mankind for historical life is contrary to the anarchistic spirit. In Catholicism there are no sort of anarchistic elements, although Catholicism also has struggled against the state power. Orthodoxy has been submissive to the state power, but in it have been possible peculiar anarchistic tendencies. The vastness and unboundedness of the Orthodox soul in the East, the insufficiency of form and limit, the weakness of self-organisation contribute to a pious anarchist aspect. It is erroneous to think, that anarchism is a manifestation of the activity of the human spirit. With outward din and outward gestures ye lead others into error and yourselves ye delude. Anarchism not only can be a manifestation of passivity, but in the final end it is always a manifestation of passivity of spirit. Anarchism is not manly, it is something feminine. The masculine spirit gives form, is disciplined, is organised. The feminine-passive spirit is immersed in the formless, undisciplined and unorganised chaos. And all you, ye most terrible anarchists, you bombers and exploders of the old world, all you people are not manly-active, but of feminine-passive a spirit. Ye are not master of yourself nor do you master the elements, ye are in the grip of elemental spirits unknown to you. Anarchists -- are the most irresponsible of people, they do not want to take responsibility upon themself for anything. And irresponsibility also is a manifestation not manly, of passive a spirit. The masculine spirit takes upon itself responsibility.

At the basis of religious anarchism can be discerned the atrophy of the sense of person. With the Tolstoyans, the Dukhobors and other religious anarchists the person is stunted. In a total impersonality they see the fulfilling of the Divine law of life, and all want to arrive at a complete identicalness and impersonality. The religious anarchist is ready to admit the individual image as a sin. The religious anarchism of Tolstoy was derived from the obtuse facelessness of Platon Karataev. But if religious anarchism knows not the person, then your irreligious anarchism ultimately can no longer pronounce the word "person", since it is completely cut off from this reality. You tend to deny every power and would overthrow every power with such ease and irresponsibility, because that you know not the person nor value the guarding of its image. Therefore you do not dread and even prefer plunging into the impersonal chaos. The pretension to unlimited freedom of the person, not admitting of any power over it, destroys the person and plunges it into the impersonal chaos. This is a fundamental paradox of anarchism. Ye are wont to think, that you are rising up and revolting in the name of the person, in the name of its infinite freedom and it apotheosis. But this -- is a terrible self-deception. The existence of the person presupposes limits and distinctions, presupposes its being guarded against the raging of the impersonal chaos. Person discovers its own ultimate freedom not in the capricious snatching away of all limits and distinctions; not in permitting in itself the dark and all-destroying chaos, but in the cosmic and historical structure and harmony. The human person and human freedom are inseparably connected with hierarchism. here is a truth, hidden from all of you, not only the anarchists, but also the socialists, and the democrats, and the liberals, and all those captivated by the external positivist political and social forms and ideas. *The being of the person is connected with an ontological inequality.*

Person is possible only in a cosmos, and only in a cosmos is there distinguishable the facial countenance, the visage, the image. Differences are also the basis for discerning differences. Cosmos however possesses an hierarchical structure, within it each person has its own unique place and unique destiny, in it all are united, all is unrepeatably so. And every enslavement of the person, every confusion of it with the impersonal and every violence against it by the impersonal is a result of the non-cosmic condition of the world, its enslavement by chaos, with its dividing apart and fettering. Person is impossible in chaos, in chaos the facial countenance, the visage, the image, is indistinguishable. In chaos everything is all mixed up and entangled. In chaos it is impossible to preserve anything especial.

Chaos admits of nothing unrepeatable, unique, differing from everything else in quality and purpose. Chaos does not know limits for its outpourings, for its destructive pressure. The chaotic condition of the world is a totally impersonal condition, in it the individual becomes indistinguishable. In the cosmic structure there is an appreciation for the unrepeatably individual, for the hidden aspects, there is a preservation from all-engulfing confusion. In the chaotic element there is no such respecting of it. This element considers everything its own, everywhere it intrudes, everywhere it appropriates for itself, everything it vulgarises. It does not know of sacred places, does not know of anything not to be touched. Anarchy too is chaos, a denial of the cosmic order of the world, an all-general confusion, the transgressing of all those hierarchical boundaries, which have safeguarded the being of the person. And therefore anarchy bears with it the enslavement and destruction of the person. At its limit, in extending itself over its abyss, anarchy destroys all the realities, and it turns into a condition of non-being. And the charm of anarchy for the tempted is the charm of non-being. Because it is tortuously difficult to then uphold being and increase its riches. The path to the summits of being lies through suffering. Ye however want to instantly overleap the suffering and have landed instead in the realm of non-being. In eras of revolution there occur momentary triumphs of anarchy. Chaotic elements erupt within the societal cosmos and displace every cosmic structure and harmony. All the limits are transgressed, all is in confusion. A faceless god or demon triumphs in revolutions. Certain of you are happily ready to invoke the name of this god. This -- is the god Dionysos. He makes his festive orgies within the elements of revolution. Does he bear with him freedom, does he liberate the person, does he lead man upwards? No, the unlimited autonomy of this god destroys the person, and plunges the human image into the dark and impersonal chasm. And in ancient Greece, in its native land, the god Dionysos was not a god of the person, not a god of the human image. Nor in the religion of Dionysos was there born the person, was there uplifted the human spirit. In the Dionysian orgies of Greece befell and poured forth the chaotic elements of the East, having set out from its own shores, having risen up against its own rulers. The human visage was uplifted and manifest in the religion of Apollo, the god of form and limit. The whole of European mankind and European culture was created by an Apollonian giving of form to the Dionysian element. Thus was forged the image of man. Anarchy attempts to destroy the prolonged work on the liberation of man from the orgiastic elements, on the forging of the human countenance. Christianity freed man from the ancient demonolatry, the demon-worship, and uplifted the person of man. Anarchy seeks as though again and anew to summon the elemental demons of nature and surrender man to them for rending apart. Anarchism has neither the wherewithal nor seeks to enlighten the elements. It wants to believe in their natural goodness, it remains in ignorance of evil. Anarchism is contrary to the human nature and is a contradictory combination of the Dionysian elemental with a boundless rationalism. It believes in the rationality of the elemental itself. And thus chaos assumes the guise of a new reasonable structure of life and manifests itself already as evil, and not as a primieval element, preceeding the differentiation into good and evil.

Historical hierarchism nourishes mankind and man, it makes possible the selection of qualitative elements and the spiritual flourishing of life and creativity in a select portion of mankind, in a spiritual aristocracy. Oh, certainly, never was the position of the select minority, of the spiritual aristocracy in this world, easy and satisfying. In every structure of life the path of this minority lay through suffering, through hindrance and tortuous struggle for its idea. But in principle the existence of this minority allowed for the guarding against being engulfed by the chaotic human masses. Always there was possible an intimate and concealed life, though also suffering, always there was possible an esoterism in history. Anarchism on principle denies all esoteric and concealed life, rises up against it, as against a principle aristocratic and hierarchical. It wants as though to crush this hierarchically higher life with an elemental chaos. In your anarchistic movements it is the lower that displaces the higher. And this has a significance not only material, but also spiritual. The hierarchical structure of the cosmos is a path of the guarding and revealing by degrees of the higher hidden truths, the sources of light. Anarchism wants to spill out everything hidden of the sacred vessels to the chaotic and mass element. And especially threatening with this spilling out is the anarchism religious and mystical. Anarchism is metaphysically and mystically contrary to hierarchism. Therefore it aspires to vulgarisation, it betrays quality for quantities, it does not admit of any sort of untouchable sanctities, no sort of enclosures for temples, no sort of veilings for mysteries. And yet, on the other hand, the anarchistic outlook is striking in its insufficiency of love and condescension towards people, towards the human masses. The anarchistic idealisation of non-structure and chaoticness, the anarchistic hostility towards every vitally living order and structure bears behind it an inestimable woe and suffering for the human masses, for the average man. But who possesses the right to precipitate other people, their own neighbours, into chaos, into disorder and lack of structure across the whole of life, into hunger and cold, into a precarious situation dealing with an elemental level in living concerns and elementary rights? In any case, such an attitude towards people is impermissible for the Christian. And those, who consider themself Christian, should seriously think about this. The organisation of human life, not permitting it to descend into a living hell, is the duty of each Christian. In this is manifest the love for people and the condescension to human weakness. And there is nothing more ugly and irresponsible than that mystical anarchism, which would prop itself up via the abyss and chaos, the vast primitiveness and primieval natural darkness, and which calls for this, to mystically embellish suchlike conditions of the people's life whilst terming as "bourgeois" every attempt at organisation, every structure, every vital order. And least of all, certainly, can there be found in this mystical-anarchist phraseology the spirit of love. The spirit of love is there moreso in the most austhere aspect of the state. In the aspect of the state there is the condescension towards human sinfulness, towards human incapacity, there is a responsible awareness of the evil in life, there is a knowing of that darkness, which envelopes the life of mankind. The apocalyptic interpretations and groundings of anarchism are also a lie. In this is bound up all that selfsame unmanly, irresponsible passive spirit. The denial of the principle of authority and of the state on the basis, that the end of the world is nigh, that everything is over and has become history, is a religious temptation, a religious collapse. It is not for us to know the times and the seasons. Christ indeed speaks about this. And at times we ought to fulfill our duty and show a spirit manful and active. From somewhat deeper a perspective, history itself transpires within eternity and merely is projected within time. And in eternity is posited the task of history. And therefore an apocalyptic anarchism has no justification. It ruptures history within time, as a temporal process. It seeks to emerge from time, but as a slave to time.

The hierarchical principle of authority, the hierarchical law of church, state and legal rights ought to lead mankind to the end of time. These principles are surmountable only within the dimension of eternity, and not in the dimension of historical time. But even in eternity, even in heavenly life the principle of authority will exist in a transfigured form. And there will be no anarchy there. The power of authority can cease to act as a principle of coercion and force, since it acts thus only in the materialised and dark medium, but it cannot pass away. It acts both in the heavenly hierarchy, and in the heavenly cosmos. The principle of the rule of authority -- is an eternal principle, and not merely a temporal reaction against evil. The pretension of anarchism is directed at the destruction of the cosmos, and therefore would want to abolish the rule of authority, such as is governing of the cosmos, upholding it and regulating it. Anarchistic freedom leaves no place for the world and God. This is a narrowing down of freedom, and in its desolation there is no place for any sort of riches. Anarchism nowise wants to render man genuinely free, -- it wants only, that the unfree should be declared free, nowise having altered their nature, i.e. it seeks a substitute and deception. Anarchistic freedom -- is not real freedom. The anarchistic consciousness does not know the truth, known by the seers of humanity, -- this truth, that man -- is a microcosm. If ye had known this hidden truth, then ye would have ceased with your external revolts and uprisings. One who is conscious of oneself as a microcosm cannot revolt against the cosmos. He liberates himself by revealing in himself the cosmos. Here is in what comprises the higher attainment of human freedom. Ye have nowise lofty a concept of the nature of man, of the dignity of man. And ye want to render each man boundlessly free and autonomous an authority. What a shallow, empty pretension! What self-adulation! The inner dialectics of anarchism murders it, leads to a self-devouring and self-destruction. In this dialectic -- is the fate of anarchism. The dialectics of anarchism destroys freedom, destroys the person, destroys every reality. Anarchism bears with itself death, and not life, and not resurrection. The empty thrashings of anarchistic passions is but a great trial for the human spirit. Upon this path man tends to learn much, negatively. Thus is exposed the meonic lie of all the negative "leftist" currents. Anarchism lies inwardly concealed also within liberalism, and in radicalism, and in democratism, and in socialism. What can all these currents oppose anarchism with, what sort of self-sustaining ontological principles are there in them? Unconvincing are all of those, who say they are against anarchism. Anarchism ought to come to an end, as an inward chastisement, as the finish of every such path, having fallen away from the spiritual centre. And indeed, within anarchism there is a sort of ultimate temptation. In surmounting it, mankind would finally emerge towards true life. The final endpoint of anarchism can only be a most terrible despotism, only the autocracy of some false god, which should rise up from out of the ensuing chaos.

The appearance of this despotism would be preceeded by a kingdom of the boorish, a kingdom of the ignoble, lowering the spiritual type of man and mankind. And ignoble is the anarchistic type of outlook. This type denies the good of birth, the good of descent, of belonging to a good lineage. It does not know of any sort of birth and any sort of descent, it does not connect itself with any sort of lineage. Thus as anarchists are so readily rendered all, who sense themself cast off and amidst this thirst to live with the masses and in the masses. People solitary and alone, unperceived, but given to concentration, depth and contemplation, do not esteem life with the masses and in the masses they are not rendered anarchists. Anarchism -- is one of the ways to make a career among the masses. This is a path not possible for those of any innate nobility. It is easy for the literary-artistic bohemian to get caught up with a vague anarchism. But this does not enhance the type of soul for anarchism. And this is because the literary-artistic bohemian is usually one who has lost his spiritual centre and the deep connection with the wellsprings of life. In the anarchistic approach of the bohemian type there is no selection of qualities, there is no aristocratism of soul, there is no consciousness of the higher dignity of man as a son of God, there is no manful spirit. The anarchistic bohemian is of a passive medium sort, obedient to the prevailing currents; he is ready to fulfill the commands of the master of life, and he is ready to worship different gods. And the spiritual medium sort, favourable for anarchism, always is disoriented, and in it are lost the strong features of the image of man. Through the temptation of anarchism the dark powers, the dark spirits seek to disarm man in the most responsible hour of world history, when it is necessary to have a knightly steeling of spirit. And this is not by chance, in this there is an inward plan and an inward significance. Chaos seeks to overthrow the cosmos, appearing in the guise of good, in the guise of the spirit of freedom. And in order to stand up against deceptions and illusions of anarchism, there is needful a manliness and boldness of spirit, there is needful a depth of knowledge and a clarity of contemplation. In anarchism it is not the creative spirit that finds uplift. And the genuine creativity of man cannot but oppose anarchism.

Eleventh Letter

Concerning War

Life in this world is a struggle. Struggle -- is the child of sinful dissension, it issues forth from incompleteness. But through struggle is surmounted this dissension and there issues forth a fulfilling of life. War -- is one of the noble, although also terrifying forms of struggle. War -- is antinomic by its nature, it is a realised contradiction. In the name of life war is waged and it serves for the fulfilling of life. And war sows death. The ends of war -- are peace and unification. Wars have been a mighty means for the unification of mankind. Peoples have engaged in bloody disputes and in clashes. From ancient times, through wars human societies were united into great historical bodies, into enormous empires; through wars peoples were dispersed across the surface of the earth, and by this path prepared for a single mankind and a single world history! And yet war has been, however, an expression of a most bloody discord within mankind, dependent upon the hatred of peoples and the thirst for destruction. War involves both darkness and light, hate and love, brute egoism and lofty self-sacrifice. War cannot be only good or only evil, in it there is both a great good, and great evil. War -- is begotten of sin and is a redemption from sin. War bespeaks the tragic aspect of life in this world, about the impossibility in it of an final arrangement, one of tranquility and endless prosperity and felicity. War inflicts quite terrible blows to philistinism, to the philistine sense of peace and satisfaction. The demon of war has always attracted mankind from afar, has sundered it away from philistine attainments and limitation. War speaks most of all about the irrational, the demonic powers within man, about the fire, which always can burst forth and burn up all human interests. War is an experiential overthrowing of the rationalistic outlook on history. And this is because, truly, people have to periodically lose their mind, to make war. Between the interests of individual people and the aims of peoples and of war there exists an irrational incommensurability. The terrible sacrifices in war are not justified by any sort of interests. These terrible sacrifices demand a supra-rational sanction, they demand faith in an end and its significance, lying beyond the limits of this empirical slice of earthly life. If, in the opinion of the sharp-minded sociology of Benjamin Kidd, reason cannot approve the aims of progress, cannot give sanction for sacrifice by individual interests in the name of the distant interests of the social organism and therefore demands sanctions supra-rational, religious, and then especially true is this in regard to war. In war falls victim not only the individual man, but also whole generations. Can such a self-sacrificing of the interests of individual people and of a whole generation be justified? It is necessary to disavow one's own small sense of reason, in order to justify such a self-sacrifice. A rational justification by any such whatever interests -- would be absurd and impossible. Here is why the rationalists and positivists on principle come out against war, and they typically tend towards pacifism. Religious people however more readily accept war with its terrors and do not rise up on principle against war, though also they are conscious of its evil.

You pacifist-humanists, rising up against war and appealing for eternal peace, ye do not believe in an higher meaning to human life, ye do not believe in eternal life. And the killing in war frightens you more, than it does believing Christians, having accepted in their heart the commandment of Divine love. This is perceptible, and this can surprise only those, who fail to penetrate deeply into the meaning of life. Ye tend to look very superficially at the life of man and see only this surface slice of life. And ye desire, that this surface slice of life should be arranged as possible more tranquilly, more satisfactorily and more acceptably. Farther, higher and deeper for you there already exists nothing more. The physical killing frightens you so, while not so frightening Christians, knowing of unending life, since with physical death for you everything is ended. And ye are nowise bothered, that spiritual killing is a thousand times more terrible than the physical killing. Amidst this, whilst our earthly life is filled by spiritual murder. Without any war we yet tend still to murder our neighbours by our feelings and thoughts, we shoot out on all sides man-killing bursts, we poison with terrible poisons the souls of people. Our peaceful life is filled with hatred and malice, and this hatred and malice kills people. In the Gospel it is said, that those killing the soul need to be feared more, than those killing the body. And herewith in the most peaceful and non-military of times there is a war going on, killing souls, poisoning and lacerating the souls of people. Why does this not scare you? Why does this frighten you less, than the physical killings of war? Every killing in its inner essence is a killing spiritual, and not physical. Killing is not the reshuffling of atoms of matter. Killing is an act of the will, directed at the negation and destruction of an human countenance. And in war, from deeper a perspective, there does not occur such a killing. And this is because the physical killing during a time of war is not directed at the negation and destruction of the human countenance. War does not presuppose hatred towards the human countenance. In war there does not occur the spiritual act of the killing of man. Soldiers -- are not murderers. And upon the brow of soldiers there does not lie the mark of murderers. Upon our peaceful brows even moreso can be seen this mark. War can be accompanied by murders as acts of spiritual hatred, and factually it is accompanied by such murders, but this is non-inherent to war and its ontological nature. The evil mustneeds be sought not in war, but prior to the war, in the times that on the face of it are seemingly most peaceful. During these peaceful times happen the spiritual murders, and malice and hate accumulate. In war however the sown evil is sacrificially redeemed. In war man takes upon himself the consequences of his path, he bears an answerable responsibility, accepts everything, often to the point of death. And true, it is not the endlessly prosperous life upon earth that is manifest as the consequence of all these earthly arrangements in his own name without God, but rather death. War -- is a great revealer. Within it are projected on the surface that, what occurs in the depths. And the earlier committed spiritual murders in it are then manifest on the physical plane. War is not so much evil itself per se, as rather bound up with evil and appears as the consequence of an evil rather more deep. And in the spiritual nature of war there is its own good. Not by chance are the great virtues of the human character forged in wars. With wars is connected the working out of manliness, of bravery, of self-sacrifice, of heroism, of chivalry. Chivalry and the knightly steeling of character would not exist in the world, if there were no wars. With wars is connected the heroic in history. I saw the faces of young people, of their own good will gone off to war. They marched in their striking battalions, almost to certain death. I never forgot their faces. And I know, that war is oriented not only to the lower, but also to the higher instincts of human nature, to instincts of self-sacrifice, love for native land, it demands a fearless attitude towards death. One must not forget, that in war people also die, and not only kill. And therefore war, amidst the spiritually obligatory attitude towards it, ennobles and elevates the human soul. Your pessimism possesses philistine a nature. Your ideal of seemingly apparent peace -- is a bourgeois ideal of earthly prosperity, beneathe which simmers human hate and malice. For sinful mankind, pacifism is a lie and a falsehood, an outright deception. Your fear of physical violence proceeds from an unspiritual attitude towards life, from too exclusive a faith in the material world. But physical violence does not exist as an independent activity, it is merely an expression of the spiritual condition of man and the world. Everything material possesses merely a symbolic, sign-like nature. Ye however want to deal with the consequences, whilst ignoring the causes, and abolish the outward expression, without transforming the inner being. And even in your pacifism there is a side, inpropitious for the characteristics of your attitude towards life. War bespeaks the uniqueness of historical activity, it provides a manly sense to history. Pacifism is a denial of the self-sufficing aspect of historical activity and historical tasks. Pacifism subjects history to an abstract moralism or abstract sociologism. It derails history prior to its spiritually real ends.

The psychology of war is very interesting. In it has to be sought out the riddles of the psychology of the masses of the people, and it represents a most powerful refutation of the rationalistic groundings of the societal aspect. If generally it is impossible to arrange society upon a rational societal accord, then least of all can war be arranged upon it. War always possesses irrational groundings and presupposes the complying of man to ends, standing higher than his perceived interests. It is impossible to wage war in the name of reasonable, utilitarian, well-conceived and thought-out ends. It is folly to make war in the name of reasonable ends, and in the higher sense "sensibly" to make war is merely something in the name of foolish ends. There is a basic paradox in the psychology of war. Every rationalisation of war is to murder it, every attempt to render too perceivable the ends of war impugns its pathos. It is impossible to make war for "land and freedom", just as it is impossible to make war in the name of some abstract benefit of the state, in the name of "facing tight straits" etc. To war well can only be in the name of irrational aims, the mysterious, remote and imperceptible aims of life, on irrational instincts, without reflection and prior judgement, for "Faith, Tsar and Fatherland", for the sanctities of the people, out of love for native land, outweighing all other interests. War mustneeds be considered in its mysterious organicity and let be left in it the revered sanctities, nowise transferrable to any other sort of interests. Democratic demands, that the goals of the war and the significance of the war should be perceived by all those participating in the war, that this war should be conducted through a general elective vote, that each soldier freely and reasonably should decide, whether he wants to make war and whether he possesses understanding of the meaning of the war, is a revolutionary-rationalistic absurdity, a monstrous lack of understanding the nature of war and the nature of an army. The Bolsheviks likewise urge people to make war in the name of the imperceptible and absurd, in the name of worldwide social revolution, in the name of the third internationale etc., and therefore only they also wage war. The masses always have to participate in war in the name of the imperceptible, the mysterious and irrational.

And what is more imperceptible, more mysterious, more irrational an end of war, what is greater than the holy trembling and holy obedience war evokes, what is finer, than an organised and disciplined army, what finer than its trampling forth to war. The human masses can be organised and disciplined only by irrational and for it imperceptible principles, assumed as sacred. Principles too close and perceptible tend to disorganise. You attempted to organise and discipline the Russian army during a time of revolution upon rational-democratic principles. Ye, fools or criminals, imagined, that the army could exist without an hierarchical structure. And you drained the soul out of the army, you destroyed it and directed its military energy towards those ends, to which other elemental instincts had drawn it, another irrationality of the masses. Civil war, the social war of classes seemed possible, since that in it stormed an irrational element, guided by beastly instincts. But a rationally-democratic national war was impossible. During the era of the French revolution the army well and victoriously waged war, since it was pliant to the mysterious instinct of love for the fatherland, and it was directed towards creating a nation. What decides for and wants war is not an empirical people, but a supra-empirical nation.

The army is a mystical organism. And it can well wage war only wherein the person and its separateness are submerged into this mystical organism. There cannot be waged war, wherein there is personal reflection and personal judgement on the matter. Only the mysterious surmounting of its own separateness, its own uniqueness makes possible a facing of the terrors of war. And in facing this terror it is impossible to sense oneself a separate person judging upon the matter. Without an hierarchical submission there is impossible any sort of an act of war. The hierarchical principle in the army is also a principle, irrational for the person. War is an expression of the irrationality of life, it speaks loudly about the impossibility of rationalising life totally beyond any trace. The democratisation of the army is also its rationalisation, i.e. the killing of the singular soul of the army, its dissolution into atoms. The rational and moral criticism of war presupposes the disintegration of all the mysterious spiritual realities. The soul of the masses splits apart, becomes atomised, when the masses fall away from obedience to the mysterious sacred ends of life. And one infinitely higher wages war in the name of a mysterious and sacred goal of life, than one who wages war in the name of an end too perceptible and close. War, just as with all the sacrifices of history, is made also in the name of the Ivans and Peters, obeying while not understanding the aims of the war. The masses of Ivans and Peters can experience for themself the significance of the war only subconsciously, in its mysterious depths, in its humility before the sanctities. All the whole world and the historical process with its sacrifices and sufferings transpires for each Peter and Ivan, for his eternal fate. But this cannot be grasped rationalistically and positivo-empirically, this presupposes the realisation of ends of life beyond the bounds of earthly life. Here is why Christianity accepts war with its terrors and sufferings. And it is difficult to accept for those, who deny immortality, and for whom everything vanishes with this life. When faith has perished in the higher realities, when everything has fallen apart, then it is impossible further to wage war, then it is better to end off the war.

In opposition to the war of peoples ye set off a war of classes, and all the sacrifices of this war seem to you justified. the killings made in war frighten you, but ye are not afraid to do killings in your class and revolutionary wars. Your humanistic declarations cease, when the talk gets around to your revolutionary wars. When nation wars against nation, ye are rendered into meek vegetarians, you abhor bloodshed, you appeal for brotherhood. But when ye succeed in transforming the struggle of nations into a struggle of classes, ye become blood-thirsty, ye deny not only brotherhood, but even an elementary respect of man for man. In the historical warrings of peoples never has there occurred such a denial of man, as in the revolutionary wars of classes and parties. War has its own obligatory ethic in regard to the antagonist. The valiant enemy is safeguarded with military honours. In revolutionary class wars everything is regarded as permissible, and there is denied every ethics common to mankind. One might then deal with an enemy, as with an animal. War does not transgress the cosmic hierarchical order, it is subordinate to it. What transgresses it only is "civil war". War is like a duel. Two peoples live tightly close in the world, they sense themself each insulted by the other, and they meet piling each upon the other, admitting each other worthy of a fight. And war is morally higher, more spiritually so than a social struggle, a "civil war", which is not a war. War is based upon the acknowledging of the realities of totalities, of communities, of spiritual organisms. The social struggle, the civil war denies all the totalities, the communities, the spiritual organisms, it disintegrates them, atomises them. The social struggle knows only the commonness or opposition of interests, it does not know commonness or opposition of spirit. Civil war cannot but lead to brutality. No mysterious ends, no historical fate of peoples is begotten of civil wars, but rather the ends of conceptual judgements, and ends connected with the falling away of man or social groups from the organism, amidst the awareness of special interests. Imperialistic wars by their nature nonetheless stand higher than social wars. In them there is an organic idea, rising above the divergent human interests, to which people are compliant; in them is the historical fate of peoples, victorious over the limitedness of the human horizon. Imperialistic wars from ancient times have had as their aim an universal unity. Through the great wars were mixed together and united races, tribes, nationalities, and mankind was united across the face of the earthly sphere. War does not negate the real unity, begotten not of interests, but of the very loins of being. It bespeaks regarding however the irrational and antinomic life of the hierarchically real unities.

False is that philosophy and that morality of war, for which the war of hostile peoples is a struggle of Ormudz and Ahriman, of light and darkness, of good and evil. In war never can the light and right be exclusively on one side, and evil and darkness on the other. Such an elementary moralisation, concerning war, simplistically transfers over to historical activity the categories of personal morals, and in the final end, leads to amoral consequences. When my people cries out against an hostile people, then morally it would be with biased self-praise to regard one's own people as a people of perfection, and to point to the hostile people as blackguards. In the struggle of peoples there has to be its own "idea" and to want as much as possible to imprint more strongly this idea upon world life. The "idea" of my people is not the sole one only, having a right to existence. Other peoples have other "ideas", and they have their own justification. There occurs a rivalry of such "ideas", as though a natural selection of the mightiest ideas. And God predisposes to the peoples the freedom of such a rivalry. In the struggle for its "idea" a people employs the totality of its spiritual powers. In the clash of peoples the moral rightness of one side can be relative a matter. War is not a struggle for moral truth and justice. It is difficult even to conceive, where there is justice in the great historical clashing of peoples. Why would it be just, that the Greeks should have conquered the Persians or the Persians the Greeks, the Romans the Gauls or the Gauls the Romans, Napoleon the whole world or the whole world Napoleon instead? Why should it be just that there is the increase of some empires or the destruction of others? Would it be just to destroy the Turkish empire or to preserve it? All these questions are irresolvable, since they are incorrectly posited. War is a struggle not for justice, but for the ontological power of nations and states. More appropriate here are biological criteria, rather than ethical. It might be possible to see truth in the victory spiritually and materially of strong and vital nations, situated in a flourishing period, over nations weak, disintegrating and decaying. In war there occurs a contest of the various spirits of peoples, a trial of their powers. War is a struggle for the realisation of their own destiny in the world. A people, sensing itself chosen, moved by a demon of its own calling, cannot halt upon its path. But there awaits it an immanent chastisement, if upon its path it is compelled to commit acts of violence too great, if it bears into the world too much grief and suffering.

Wars become very qualitatively different in their character. There occur wars more or less equal among peoples in their strength and their culture. In this case there occurs an intense rivalry and contesting, which has to decide, to which ought to belong the predominance in the world, and the spirit of which will be more closely inscribed upon remotest history. There occur wars also of peoples mighty and highly-cultured against peoples weak and little-cultured. In this case the aim of the war can be posited as colonisation, the implanting and expansion of the higher culture. The first type of war represents a realisation of imperialistic aims. And there occur wars of oppressed peoples for their liberation, outwardly the more weak, but inwardly still having preserved their spiritual strength. These wars have as their purpose not the realisation of an universal sameness, but rather the retention of individualisation. They cannot of themself bring about the realisation their own weak and small nations, and with them become involved mightier nations, which take under their defense the more weak in the name of their own world tasks. And certainly, there occur wars, in which the stronger, the barbaric and uncultured peoples engulf and enslave peoples of an higher culture, such as has become decrepit and soft, having succumbed to inward moral illness. Suchlike in their time were the invasions of the Germans upon Rome and the Mahometan world upon Byzantium. These incursions could assume a very wild and destructive character. Yet all the same they have a certain inner significance, hidden from our superficial glance. Military incursions of the Mongol world can still threaten cultural Europe. But whatever sort a character such a war might bear, it would be an indicator of the intense *dynamism* of history. Pacifism however tends towards a static outlook on history. Your trite revolutionary-democratic formulae, denying "annexations", also signify a denial of the dynamism of history, they are an unthinkable and unrealisable demand for the halting of history, a victory of the static over the dynamic. The dynamic aspect of history is a complex series of annexations. To these annexations across the span of the whole historical process it would be very difficult to apply the category of justice. Justice -- is a static, and not dynamic a category. It demands a world equilibrium, and not a dynamic process, always resulting in tragic clashes and torments. The dynamic process of history is a clashing and interaction of races, tribes and nationalities, their strengthening and weakening, their movement across the surface of the world stage, their appropriation or loss of territory, the redivision of their role and place upon the earth. There is nothing static in the earthly existence of peoples, which forever would determine to them borders based on justice. The most quiet and secure places on earth are opened up by way of the dynamic. And the annexations of the past, which we tend to perceive in their crystalised results, were no moreso just, than future annexations against them.

History is still not at a finish. The dynamism of history is not waning, but rather intensifying. The world is not approaching towards a worldly felicity, towards a worldly paradise, towards an idyllic eternal peace. Everything compels us to think, that the world is headed towards a terrible struggle, towards ever new clashes of historical powers, towards new tribulations of the manliness of spirit, of a knight-like tempering of spirit. The surface of the earthly stage is still not arranged. There is still many an historical task remaining unresolved. The Eastern question is unresolvable peacefully. Ye however seek to debilitate and inwardly weaken the people for the impending times of the terrible struggle, when their powers of spirit will be subjected to terrible trials. The democratic and socialistic denial of war on principle is a very cunning disarming of Christian peoples, the scattering of the old armies for the formation of a new international army of an earthly kingdom. The socialistic spirit of internationalism substitutes and takes the place of the Christian spirit of universality. Christianity however desires peace for all the world and the brotherhood of peoples. But it desires, that this should be a genuine inner peace and a genuine inner brotherhood. In the Christian peace and Christian brotherhood there would be conquered evil. In your peace however, and in your brotherhood the evil would forever remain unconquered. Your pacifism is a denial of evil, a non-wish to recognise evil, a desire to work with evil as though there were no evil. And therefore, ye will never attain to worldwide brotherhood, nor eternal peace. Your pacifism ultimately destroys the knightly principles, the chivalrant-militant struggle with evil.

Your idea of the eternal peace of peoples -- is a bourgeois idea. You want an outward tranquility and well-being, not having been redeemed of sin, not having conquered the inner evil. You want to continue on with the spiritual killings, whilst averting from you their external consequences, in not experiencing the terrors of the physical killing. You want as though to be contradictory, that the peoples are pacified, and that the evil hostility is conquered. Ye desire as though to weave an outward guise of the brotherhood of peoples, yet without that inward love, which also alone can create it. Ye want as though to proceed from the outward to the inward and along the way ye altogether forget about the inward. The true path however is the path from the inward to the outward. Seek ye first the Kingdom of God and all else wilt be accorded you. Ye however tend to think, that the Kingdom of God is first in accord with the all else. Here is why you will never arrive at the brotherhood of love and of peoples. It is impossible to create brotherhood upon economic and juridical principles, it does not issue forth out of any sort of special interests and cannot be guaranteed by any sort of law. It is the domain of the Spirit. True, ontologically real peace has to be a cosmic peace, and true, ontologically real brotherhood has to be a cosmic brotherhood. War is waged not only upon the limited expanses of the earth, not only upon the physical plane. It is waged on all the planes of being, in all the hierarchies, it is waged also in the heavens. In the higher hierarchies the angels of God battle with the angels of Satan. But their weapons of war are more refined and aethereal. A clear-sighted glance everywhere in the world-edifice, in its most deep and remote layers has to make apparent the aspect of war. The visible material war is but a manifestation of the invisible spiritual war. And how shallow, how pitiful in comparison with this genuine life of peace are all your contrived internationales, eternal peaces etc.

The Christian apocalyptic prophecies do not tell us, that before the end-time there will not be wars, that there will be peace and well-being. On the contrary, these prophecies say, that before the end-time there will be terrible wars. The apocalyptic sense of history contradicts an eternal peace. All the utopias of an earthly paradise, of peace and happiness on earth, smash apart upon the apocalyptic. The apocalyptic sense of history -- is fraught with the tragic. It teaches us this simple truth, that in the world grows not only the good, but also the evil, that the most terrible struggle is still ahead. Ahead, in the spiritual plane, there stands still a most terrible war, the war of the kingdom of the Anti-Christ with the Kingdom of Christ. The war of Christ and the Anti-Christ, of those true to Christ and those allured by the Anti-Christ will also be a final war. This terrible spiritual war will have also its own material manifestations. There was war at the very wellspring of human culture. War was a mighty mover of culture. War also will come at the very end of human culture, at its very summits. The bourgeois and socialistic "eternal" peace will not forestall this final war and the wars, preceeding this final war. There stands still ahead a clash of the Aryan-Christian world with the Mongol East. Apocalyptic war carries over the material clash into the spiritual plane. And it casts a light upon all the past of mankind, upon the spiritual substrate of all the material struggle. The outward, the economically and juridically conditional world veils over the spiritual depths of life, the fire hidden in it. But this veiling cannot be eternal. In pacifism, humanitarian-democratic and international-socialistic, there is hypocrisy, the desire to evade the consequences of evil, but not the evil itself. War -- is antinomic by its nature, and it tends to resist all the slick rationalistic teachings. War is deeply antinomic also for the Christian consciousness. War evokes a tragic conflict in the soul of the Christian. It is not good and evil, not truth and falsehood that clash in this conflict, but rather two goods, two truths. To you is unknowable this tragedy. Ye desire to know only the clash of an abstract good with an abstract evil. But the life of man is infinitely more complex and complicated. The tragedy of human life is rooted in the clash of values of a different order, in the inevitability of a free choice between two like dear values and truths. The fatherland is of unquestionable value, and patriotism is a lofty state of spirit. But love for the fatherland can clash with love for other values just as indubitable, for example with love for man and mankind, for high culture, for spiritual creativity etc. And war can only be perceived tragically. It is only sinful to wish for wars and be elated by war. This -- is indeed godless. It is needful to want peace, it is necessary to sense the grief and terror of war. Love ought to win out over evil and discord. But love is active also in war, refracted within the dark element. According to the teaching of J. Boehme, Divine love, refracted within the darkness, is transformed into wrath. The same transpires in the elements of war. In this is the truth of war. But war is a jumbled actuality, within it act other principles, both the principles of an evil hatred and of evil greed. And therefore it cannot but evoke grief. War sets man face to face with death, and this closeness to the mystery of the death of man tends to deepen man.

But war can inwardly disintegrate and degenerate, it can become bereft of its own idea and its purpose. This has occurred also with the world war of our times after the catastrophe with Russia. The world war did not resolve any sort of tasks and ended with a bad peace. Inwardly the war has continued. Our soiuzniki-confederationists were lacking in a positive idea of the war, a consciousness of mission, connected with this war. The soiuznik ideology was humanitarian-pacifist, and the guiding idea here was a masonic idea. Masonism however, in the final end, seeks to undermine all nations, to deprive them of their individual character, to replace the Church of Christ with a false humanistic pseudo-church, and to replace the concrete all-unity of mankind -- with an abstract unity. The old Christian Europe is perishing from hostility, from the prolonged continuing inner wars of France and Germany. Germany has become noble in its defeat and merits towards it a different attitude, than obtained during the time of war. Powers, hostile to Christianity, have made a muck of the war and deprived it of its inner meaning. Then the truth of the peace will ensue within its own right. There will happen periods of history, when war will become an unconditional evil, when the healthy spiritual-religious instinct will have to demand peace for all the world. And if then the peace be not in Europe, then Europe will find itself threatened by ruin, threatened by the might of the Mongol

East. But it is impossible to delude oneself with optimistic hopes. The spiritual discord of Europe provides but grounds for pessimistic forebodings.

Twelfth Letter

Concerning Economism

Our historical era in tinged in the light of economism. Upon everything lies the imprint of economism, and economism obtains throughout the whole of life. Never before has economics assumed such significance within human life, never before has man sensed such a dependence upon economics, never before has there been posited so high an economic productivity nor has it been transformed into such a self-sufficing end. It is not by chance that in our era was created the theory of economic materialism. This theory but reflected the state of European society. The spiritual life of man fell into slavery to material life. And this manifestation of actuality was passively reflected within thought as the theory of economic materialism, for which the whole of spiritual life is but a supra-structure atop the economic. The "ideological supra-structures", which now the economic materialists and socialists would as though expose, have also been a sign of the nobility of the human spirit, have been demands in the sacred sanctioning of life. They started on exposing these noble "supra-structures" and materialistically explaining them away, when there occurred a lowered level of material life relative to the spiritual. It is not by chance, from the opposite polarity of spirit, that in our time the Christian thinker S. N. Bulgakov created an unique economic religious philosophy in his "Philosophy of Economics", and in it proclaimed the Sophianic aspect of economics. Many of the ideological currents of our time are determined by the ponderous influence of economism. And some of the more profound of these currents are prepared to see in economics an almost metaphysically deep principle of being. L. Tolstoy always too was a slave of economism and to all his Christianity he bestowed an economic character. There is economism also in the "Philosophy of the Common Task" of N. F. Fedorov. Never before has terror in the face of need, in the face of insecurity in life reached such striking proportions. Never before has man felt such a pressure and squeezing from all sides, such abandonment to the whims of fate. The oppressive aspect of economism appeared as the result of the loss of every sacred sanctioning of economic life. Something became terribly aggravated in human life over the course of the XIX and XX Centuries. Human life becomes all more and more difficult. From the extensive toiling of man it passes over into an intensive toiling, from an extensive emotional soul type into an intensive emotional soul type. In nothing still does there remain space for man, everything is under pressure. Tight it becomes for man upon the earth. The growth of the people's population and the growth of needs chains man down to economics. The coming of the machine into human life was one of the most radical revolutions of human history, shaking up all the age-old foundations of human existence. The rhythm of human life changed. All more and more there was lost the rhythm, common to the rhythm of nature. Human life was rendered all less and less natural, in accord with nature. Man goes forth through disintegration and disharmony. What is so necessary, determining the grip of economics on human life? *Need is an expression of the non-cosmic condition of the world.* A final surmounting of the need presupposes the onset of cosmic harmony, the surmounting of the material condition of the world, which signifies its non-cosmic, tattered and fettered condition. The existence of the laws of material nature, life in our physical body, connecting us with the physical corporeality of the world, presupposes an imperfect, impaired necessitating condition of man and of mankind. Those of you are mad, who think to attain a social paradise and bliss, of perfect freedom and without knowing evil and suffering, whilst remaining in the physical body, remaining subject to the realm of material nature and its laws. The natural material realm demands of man the economic aspect, economic work, economic concern. The Gospel words about the lack of concern with the birds of the heavens and the lilies of the fields are oriented towards the inner spiritual man, but are completely inapplicable to the external plane of life, are not directly transferrable to it.

You socialists tend to have imagined that need is begotten of inequality and that the need will cease, when there is established a realm of equality. From an economic point of view, this is one of the most ridiculous judgements, as one can come up with. Upon this theme declaim the socialists in the foaming up of revolutionary passions, in the plane of agitation. But on the plane of cognition, in more tranquil a state of thought even the more pensive socialists do not assert this. Foremost of all, with Marx himself can be found a toppling of this pseudo-moralistic position, that all evil proceeds from inequality. From an economic point of view, inequality was not only necessary, but also was beneficial. Thanks to inequality there was possible a maximum of attainment in economic life, a maximum of the surmounting of need. It is not inequality that creates need, but rather that need creates inequality, as a saving propensity, as an egress, forestalling economic and cultural lowering and ruin. The course of the Russian revolution points this out. Inequality is a most mighty impediment in the developement of productive forces. A levelling amidst poverty, amidst need would render impossible the developement of productive forces. Inequality is a condition of creative process, of every creative initiative, of every selection of elements, more conducive for production. Inequality creates a social setting, in which the people can live and satisfy its own needs even amidst a nowise high developement of productive powers. Your socialistic attitude towards inequality and the division of labour is a completely uncritical confusion of categories economic with categories moral. And only by virtue of this confusion do you identify social inequality with the exploitation of alienated labour, the forms of labour with moral crimes. Indeed, there does exist the exploitation of alienated labour and a morally criminal attitude of the classes of the haves towards the classes of the have-nots. But this is a judgement principally of a different order, than a judgement concerning the arrangement of economic life. Ye are proud of Marx as one having a most objective and scientific mind, for whom cognition was nowise muddled by anything subjective. But all the whole theory of surplus value in Marx was based upon a confusion of economic and moral categories, a muddling of the objective with the subjective. The theory of surplus value also became the source of the subjective moral pathos of revolutionary socialism. If more than doubtful be the scientific qualities of the theory of value obtaining to labour and if it be already a confusion of various categories, then that deduction, which Marx made of it in his teachings about surplus value, is therefore transformed into a declaration of revolutionary morals against the malevolent exploiters. This subjective-moralistic, revolutionary-class teaching is in a striking contradiction to the other side of the teaching of Marx, in which is admitted objective predominance within economics of the productive thrust over the thrust for redistribution and demand. If the form of distribution, if the social structure of society is determined by forms of production, necessitating at a given stage of developement the organisation of production, then collapse all the trite declamations about inequality and exploitation as the sources of all the evils and misery. Even slavery itself can be admitted for its time a relative plus in the organisation of the economy.

The economic task, facing man, is first of all the task of mastering nature and regulating its elemental destructive forces. From this perspective even socialism can be justified merely as a certain form of the organisation of production, of the regulation of elemental forces. Marxism even indeed justifies socialism, first of all, as an organisation of productivity, a raising of the productivity of labour at a certain degree of developement. A socialism, which would lower the productivity of labour and would lessen the developement of productive forces, would be reactionary. Suchlike is Russian socialism, even though it has connected itself with Marxism. It leads to poverty and want, it destroys material values. The growth of productivity, the mastery of the elemental forces of nature is a necessary condition for the victory over want, poverty and hunger on the material plane. The non-fulfillment of this basic condition, of this summoning of the productivity of labour and expectation of a social felicitude is the demand for a social miracle, is the forcing of a would-be miracle by those, who do not admit of miracles and spiritually are unworthy of them. In your social outlook always there predominate the ideals of demand over the ideals of productivity. You have a demand-oriented, and not productivity attitude towards life, and you want ultimately to foist such an attitude upon the working class, denying the obligation of labour and the spiritual discipline of labour. You propose for yourself a social paradise with a maximum of demand and a minimum of productivity. And you would like to completely abolish that class of people, who are interested in building up productivity, interested in productive initiative and productive planning. Your demand-based ideal of life -- is a limitedly philistine ideal. In it are no sort of creative tasks. The "consciously aware" socialistic worker -- wants first of all to be in on demands and to lead the struggle for the interests of demand, and not the interests of productivity, his "consciousness" frees him from all the obligations and inspires him to endless pretentiousness. The "bourgeois" a thousand times moreso than any worker can be engrossed with the most beastly interests of demand, but in this there is no sort of an "ideal" -- this is simply the craven, sinful and transgressive state of man, given over to a bovine-like existence, generally prevailing over human-like an existence. The "consciously aware" worker however has his ideal of an earthly paradise based upon demand and by this he is distinct from the typical worker, from all typical people, with their needs, woes and legitimate dreams about a better life. The socialistic ideals based upon demand destroy the economy, and hinder man from mastering the forces of nature. The maximum wealth of the people and the overcoming of want is attained then, when the whole stands higher than the parts, when the whole stands not upon well-being based on demands and the satisfying of people, but rather upon the well-being and value of the state, the nation, culture. This nowise excludes the fact, that the interests of the state, the nation and culture can hypocritically serve as a veiling for the interests of classes and individual people. But the social ideal based upon demand leads to poverty.

Economic material life cannot be set in opposition to spiritual life, cannot be completely abstracted and sundered. A dualistic sociology, severing apart spirit and matter in social life, -- is erroneous and illusory. The whole of material life is but an inwardly a manifestation of spiritual life and is rooted within it. The partial truth of economic materialism can be turned round also from deeper a perspective, where material life can be perceived as issuing from spiritual life. The significance of the spiritual discipline of the person and of the people for economic life is enormous. The discipline of labour, the organisation of labour and the productivity of labour is dependent upon spiritual factours. In the final end, it is spirit that wins out over nature and masters the elemental forces of nature. Economics, as a transforming of the forces of nature, as their organisation and regulation, is an act of the human spirit. And upon the qualities of spirit is dependent the character of economics. Economics is not the manifestation of a moribund material nature, but is rather permeated through and through by spiritual energies and presupposes an interaction between man and nature, their interpenetration. Work is a manifestation of spirit, not of matter, it possesses spiritual foundations. The growth of material productive powers presupposes whole-imaged an energy, the creative initiative of man as regards nature. And the meeting of material demands cannot be the sole aim of economics. It is motivated also by the creative instinct of man. The social organism cannot be dualistically divided, and it is impossible for the material side in it to be thought of abstractly. Such an abstraction of material life and rendering it soulless gives rise to a whole series of sickly phenomena. Upon this basis issues also the immeasurable exaggeration of the significance of the people's economy, the grip of economics over all the whole of life, amidst an immeasurable disdain for economics, treating it as something but vile and unworthy. And in both the one and the other instance economics is rendered into a stifling and uninspiring force. They tend to forget, that economics is an uncovering of the power of the human spirit and through it is realised the mission of the regal vocation of man within nature. Economic life cannot be the dominant aspect, nor self-sufficing. It has to be subordinated to the higher principles of life. Then only will economics realise its mission of the regulation of elemental nature. Economics obstructs the death-bearing triumph of elemental forces, it limits the grip of death within the natural order. In the economic act is a mysterious side, which our secularised age is little conscious of. The gaining of economic benefits from nature is a spiritual activity, in which the loins of nature open to the coming guidance by its spouse.

But the human spirit variously can be in slavery to material life, such as tends to create its economics. The human spirit can be in a servile dependency not only to the natural medium, but also to the social medium. Capitalism and socialism represent abstract principles, which do not correspond to any sort of simple actuality. In reality, there do not exist and cannot exist in pure form any sort of capitalism and socialism. But these two principles can be thought of as two forms of the slavery of the human spirit by economics, of the economics created by them. In a monstrous capitalistic economics the human spirit evokes and developes forces, which overwhelm and enslave it. Man cannot then deal with not only the elemental forces of nature, but neither with the elemental forces of economics, which live and act by their own law. The spiritual centre becomes displaced, and there occurs a mixing-up of the hierarchical stages of life. Then in place of capitalism comes socialism with its pretensions about regulating the elemental forces of the economy, for a rationalising of the economic chaos. And the human spirit falls into a new form of slavery. We have already seen, what socialism bears with it into the world. Taken to its limit, it ultimately has to destroy man. Socialism wants to use the regulation of the elemental forces of the economy as a ticket to the collective socialisation of man leaving not a trace, transforming him into an economic category. But this process began already in capitalism. Both the slavery capitalistic and the slavery socialistic can only be opposed by an inner freedom of spirit from the oppression of material life. Economics inwardly is posited as a manifestation and means of spiritual life. And it is possible to establish two spiritual attitudes towards economics: it can be based upon work as under a law and illumined by an Old Testament-like truth, or it can be based upon work creative and illumined by a new religious light.

Indeed, a revolutionary turnabout, not in a superficial, but in a more profound sense of the word, has come about with the machine economy. And the problem of the machine involves deep metaphysical problems. Many a noble thinker of the XIX Century feared the victorious advent of the machine, and they sensed the deep opposition between the machine and spirit, they saw in its conquests the materialisation and mechanisation of spiritual life, a quenching of the spirit. So also sensed many a Russian writer and thinker, the finest of them. I do not fully subscribe to this view and I think, that it does not get at the full depth of the question. Though I too sense the dangers, connected with the impact of machines, and experience a morbid vexation at their fumes and noise. Indeed, the machine is as it were a crucifixion of organic nature. It destroys the organic rhythm of our natural life, it breaks apart all the organic wholeness. The machinisation of our life is also a passage through fragmentation, an emergence from the primordial wholeness of natal life, in which spirit and matter are bound up inseparably, in which spirit abides also in the very loins of organic matter. The economic victories of man over nature have to lead to a sundering of man from nature, to a fragmentation of wholeness and division. Man emerges from the loins of nature, from its elements, and he desires to become the master of nature, wants to rule the natural elements. And nature withdraws from man, it shrivels and dries up around him. The victorious appearance of the machine is also a most important aspect of the struggle of man with nature. The machine mows down everything alive in nature. It brings death to animals and plants. Everywhere that there extends the might of the machine, the blossoms fade. The machine as it were destroys one of the most perfect manifestations of organic nature -- the human body, it as though replaces the body. In its victorious advent the machine bears ruin for ancient beauty. This phenomenon is evident in futurism, which is a slave-like reflection of the machinisation of life. The proud dream of man about mastery over nature leads to a monstrosity, to the death of beauty, to a destruction of the blossomings of life. Ye have allowed a sort of non-truth in the very setting of the task of the domination of nature and having mastery over it. Ye have lost contact with the soul of nature. Ye seek not to have a nuptual hold on nature, not united, but rather disunited from it. And therefore arise the bitter and ugly fruits of your domination of nature.

But it would be erroneous to think, that the machine murders the spirit. It is not spirit, but rather organic matter, the flesh of the world, that the machine kills. It bears with it death not for spiritual life, which essentially is indestructible, but for the organic vital tenor of life, for natal lifestyle. The coming of the machine into our life evokes in many a noble soul romantic an anguish over the loss of wholeness and organicity, as regards the old lifestyle arrangement. But for this rending romantic anguish over the past, there is no turning back. The spiritual life of man has to seek out wholeness and beauty upon other paths. The victory of the machine and the ravages provided by it have evoked an hostility towards civilisation, the exposure of its lies and falsehoods, the idealisation of barbarism, and tormentive travails to return to a primordial wholeness. But in this exertion of spirit there is sensed a sterility and fruitlessness. For this however, wherein the spirit should feel itself more at ease and more free, it is needful to perceive the twofold and antinomic character of the appearance of the machine in the world. The machine not only oppresses the human spirit, but also liberates it, it as it were with iron claws frees it out from organic matter, in which it initially slumbered, and then became awakened. The machine produces fragmentation and division, which quite complicate our spiritual life and makes possible its most refined manifestations. The primordial organic wholeness is coarse, and the only thing refined is the romantic attitude towards this organic wholeness in an era, when it is already destroyed. The primordial organic wholeness -- is woeful in the knowing. Knowledge is sharpened and deepened, when man has already passed through fragmentation and division. And a more profound attitude towards the machine is not so straight-forward and simple, as it seems to the romantics of the past. The world has to undergo the triumph of the machine, and the human spirit has to bear up under this process, ultimately has to become free and arrive at an higher wholeness. Economics cannot develope without the machine. It is impossible to deny the machine in the name of more backward forms of an economy. And the denial of the machine is a denial of the economic process, is a returning of man back to a primordial, slave-like dependency of the human spirit upon material nature and the social medium, since it denies, that the spirit can preserve freedom even amidst the transition to more complex forms of an economy. Thus the human spirit is posited as in an exclusive dependency upon a lifestyle setting, upon backward forms of an economy. In this regard Marxism is more correct, than is populism. In the machine is also a principle of dark magic. Behind modern technology lies concealed the same psychology, which was there in black magic, the same greedy thirst for power over the forces of nature with the help of external means. But through technology is revealed the possibility also of a more luminous magic, based upon a creative love for the inner essence of nature. The historical role of the machine has to be looked at dialectically, concerning it is impossible a simple "yes" or "no".

The ends and significance of economic life lie deeper and farther, than presents itself to the typical economic mindset. These ends and this significance can be conceived of only in a frame of mind, going out beyond the bounds of economics. The economic act ought to win out over the heaviness and chained down aspect of the material world, ought to gain mastery over the chaotic elements. But the victory over the chaotic elements of nature and its control by man beset by its materiality cannot be limited to the not-large portion of nature, surrounding man on the earth. Our planetary economics is surrounded on all sides by perils, it is subject to the influence of cosmic forces. Our agriculture is situated under the grip of cosmic forces, and little as yet has been done for the regulation of these elemental forces, by which it is surrounded. Facing man stands the task of the creation of a cosmic economy. A cosmic economy is not some utopia of a paradisiacal bliss, the resettlement from our earthly planet to the heavenly expanses. The very structure of a cosmic economy is determined by a truly realistic, and not abstract, attitude towards nature. Man is all still inadequately conscious of the depths of his connection with cosmic life. In former times he directly sensed the depth of this connection and sensed himself dwelling in the very loins of cosmic life. Man then became free from the demons of nature, he withdrew from Great Pan and began to sense nature as remote from himself and as a stifling mechanism. The consciousness however of a new connection and the association of man with the cosmos was vouchsafed but to few. Man has not yet gotten into the depths of nature, in order to dominate and govern the elements, and not be under their grip and be governed by them. Man has remained at the surface of nature and at the surface he conducts his economy. At the surface many a fiction has presented itself to him and many a fiction has been created by him. Many a fiction, not genuinely real, is also there in the technical powers of modern man over nature, of which he is so proud. All your technical might, all your social regulations do not get to the depths of natural life. How pitiful is all your technical might and how shallow all your utopias in comparison with the "project" of N. F. Fedorov, revealed in his "Philosophy of the Common Task". N. Fedorov posits the daring task of the creation of a cosmic economics, the regulation of all nature, the victory over its death-bearing powers. N. Fedorov pushes to the limit the economic task of man. Indeed, economics ought to be the victory of life over death. But who of you has given any thought to this, that economics ought to win out over the death-bearing powers, that in it ought to be uncovered a resusciative power? Your technology and your socialism but legitimatise death, and are but submissions to the law of death bereft of the desire for resuscitation. For this, that the matter of life should win out over the matter of death, there is necessary a key to the revealing of cosmic life, in which everything is all inseparably interconnected and nothing can be ignored and isolated without deadly consequences.

Magicians in every period of time have sought the keys to the mysteries of cosmic life and by force have wanted to rip out from nature its secrets, whilst remaining remote and alien to the very soul of nature. Black magicians were men of coercion and greedy for power. But they succeeded nonetheless to learn certain secrets of the inner life of nature. All our positive science and technology possesses larger a connection with the magicians, than suggests itself in your mindset. Ye have tended to forget its origin and sources. Technology has become the modern magic. It wants by force to learn the secret of nature and dominate nature for greedy human ends, whilst remaining foreign to the inner life of nature. And technology would tend, in the final end, to be reborn into a sort of magic, as discerning its true nature. In technology there is an element of black magic, and it unleashes powers, the actions of which are still uncertain and not so harmless, as might seem. There is an element of black magic also in modern capitalistic economics. Thus, the power of money over life, truly a terrible power, is a form of black magic. Money is detached from every ontological basis, in it is no genuine being, it leads to a fictitious and phantasmic existence. Yet in it is a magical power and might. And the task of a creation of a cosmic economics, of victory over the death-bearing forces of nature and the regulation of these elements -- is magical a task, it cannot be merely as a task of a positivist technology. But magic can be likewise also luminous. Dark magic ultimately enslaves man. Luminous magic, subordinate to religious principles, frees man. The expanded and deepened approach to the economic problem is there also in the book of Bulgakov, "The Philosophy of Economics". In it, economics is considered religiously. But religion itself receives too economic a character. Bulgakov admits of a Sophianic economics. By this he wants to connect it with the soul of the world. But there is a danger in such an economic approach with Sophia, -- the Wise Virgin, neither begetting nor establishing. It becomes all more and more apparent, that the victory over social evil and want is a cosmic task, -- unfulfillable within the bounds of the limited earthly societal aspect. N. F. Fedorov is correct, and to him belongs the final word on this, on what you call "the social question": the root of evil is not in poverty and want, but in death; poverty and want -- derive from death, and "the social question" in the worldly sense is resolvable only by way of a victory over the death-bearing powers. Economic means alone here do not help. At your surface level of life, in your stifling perspectives are resolvable only social questions, and not the worldwide social question. Socialism, proving hollow by way of its pretension to resolve the worldwide social question, wants only to uniformly distribute the power of matter over man. Socialism's ideal of an economic demand-based redistribution is in essence non-spiritual and anti-religious, this is a slave-like ideal. A complete nourishing from a religious point of view -- is an eucharistic nourishing. In an eucharistic nourishing man is united with the cosmos in Christ and through Christ. And then demand and creativity coincide, man imbibes within him cosmic life and from himself generates creative energy into cosmic life.

Economics is an hierarchical system. It is impossible to consider it atomistically. It cannot but be an arena of struggle of all against all. All economics is an organised work, is a regulation of elemental forces. Economics is the interaction of rational and irrational forces. This is true also in regard to that capitalistic economics, which socialists love to call anarchistic. Capitalistic economics can be termed anarchistic only in a very conditional and relative sense. The evil of capitalistic economics is bound up with the spiritual life of the people of this era, with their religious and moral downfall, and not with the economic side of capitalism itself per se. This namely is because that economics is an hierarchical system, and not a mechanism, composed of atoms, since at its foundation lies the person with his qualities and capabilities, with his discipline for work. The ascetic discipline of the person has significance for economics, and a certain sort of asceticism is necessary for economic work. Amidst the complete dissipation of the person, economics also is destroyed. Revolutions -- are not favourable for economics. And by revolutionary paths it is impossible to reform and improve the economy. The economic process is not of such a nature. Uprisings and revolts can only have a destructive influence on the economy. The destruction of the discipline of work throws the economy backwards. All the social experiments of revolution tend to abolish the freedom of the person in economic life. The person ceases to be taken into account and answerable, he possesses neither rights, nor obligations. Everything gets relegated to the collectives, coalesced upon the revolutionary path from a chaos of atoms. But with a free economic life, with the free person in economic life, with his free initiative is connected the freedom of man. The asserting of the significance of the person in economic life does not signify an unvaunted economic individualism. Within economic life are possible complex paths and various correlative principles. But the total subordination of the economic person to either the societal collective or the state destroys the economy and enslaves the person. The free existence of the person in the material world presupposes freedom in the economic structure, the free and responsible acts of man in regards to material nature. Here is why "socialism" can only be one of the methods of the organisation of economic life, and it ought to be merely a means for the securing freedom in the economic structure for the person. Each economic person belongs to the economic organism, to the economic hierarchy. But this means also, that the person is free. Organic members of the hierarchy are free. Enslaved however are the members of a collective, which is not an hierarchical organism and possesses a structure one-sided, mechanically mixed together and levelled down, and in which there is only quantity and not quality. Ye however would want to transform human society into such a qualitatively uniform and levelled-down economic collective and ultimately enslave the human person to it. The economy is an organism qualitatively-varied and of hierarchical a structure, not a qualitatively uniform and mechanically levelled-down structure. Against this are impossible any sort of revolutions, such as would seek to replace the organism and the person, created by God, with the substitute of a collective, created by human whim. A deepened approach to the problem of economism ought to link together the economic organism with the cosmic organism. The ideologies of capitalism however have had no desire to see in the economy an organism, and the ideologies of socialism have but continued on with this view of the destruction of the idea of an economic organism. And in this both sorts of ideology are hostile to the human person. An economic universalism has to be opposed alike both to capitalism, and to socialism.

With the principle of the organic hierarchical aspect in economic life is inseparably connected the principle of private property. But the principle of property has long since already has become withered and distorted. The socialists have but brought to a finish this destruction of the spiritual groundings of property, started long since before. The bourgeois capitalistic era long since already has torn the property aspect away from its ontological roots. The transforming of private property into an implement of greed, of gain, and the oppression of those near one spiritually undermines private property and prepares the soil for its socialistic negation. The socialistic attitude also, taken to the limit, is despirited, morally unjustified and exclusively a demand-greedy attitude towards property and towards the objects of the material world. *Socialism tends to collectivise private property and all the objects of the material world, since it does not permit of any sort of spiritual value nor any sort of moral significance in the individual attitude of the human person towards the objects of the material world, towards nature.* For the socialistic mindset all economic acts are totally soulless, unsacred, amoral, they are determined by bare interests and therefore in them cannot be consolidated anything spiritually of value and morally significant. All of you, ye socialists, are insanely caught up in economics and have become slaves to economic activity, but essentially ye despise economics and see in it merely reasons for plunder and redistribution. Ye know nothing of a Divine economism, and have no religious justification of the economic act. For you there does not exist the mysterious side of the economic activity of man upon nature. Here is why ye tend to deny private property with such great ease. In this ye are flesh of flesh and blood from blood of those bourgeois a sort, which long since already have cast down everything sacred, having become occupied with a plundering of nature for a pleasant and well-arranged life. Ye seek to make such a plundering for everyone, to construct for all a pleasant and well-ordered life, free of any anguish or grief over sanctities. An economic attitude towards nature without the rights and responsibilities of property for the human person is a cynical attitude towards economics and towards nature, it represents the transformation of everything material into but a momentary, quick and greedy means and mere tool. This also is a demand-based ideology, the glance upon all the material world as a means for the satisfying of demands.

Property, by its nature, is a principle spiritual, and not material. It presupposes not only the demanding of material goods, but also more stable and emphasised a spiritual life of the person amidst family and kindred. The principle of property is bound up with the metaphysical nature of the person, with its inner right to accomplish acts, surmounting the swift flow of time. Property is born of the struggle of the human person against the elemental forces of nature. The free spirit of man imposes its own will upon elemental nature, and of this act are born inalienable rights and duties. The bond of the person with property inspires its attitude towards material nature, renders it something not exclusively of demands. The principle of property is bound up likewise with the relationship towards ancestors. Property is a fleshly bond of fathers and offspring. The right of fathers to pass on their property to their children, their grandchildren and great-grandchildren, is an obviated act of love and materially significant a connection. A similarly manifest and materially significant connection exists also in the right of passing on property to every near and dear being. The economic acts of man, by his metaphysical nature, spread beyond the bounds of his empirical life, they transcend time. The principle of property is bound up with the immortality of the human person, with his rights over material nature even after his death. Collectivism, denying every right to property, is an enslavement of the person by the elemental forces of nature. It is therefore characteristic to the initial stages of the developement of human society. But even at the summits of this developement it seeks to subordinate the human person to economic life. It denies for the human person the right to work acts, witnessing to his dominion over material nature. Private property upon the earth is moreso inspired an attitude towards the earth, than is a nationalisation and socialisation of the earth. Private property upon the earth makes possible a love for the earth, for field and forest, here perhaps for some particular tree, around which sat grandfathers and great-grandfathers, for some house, for remembrances and traditions, connected with this ground and its former owners, whereby it sustains the bonds of time and generations. Nationalisation and socialisation of the earth evokes an exclusively demand-based attitude of greed towards the earth, coarsely material, bereft of any emotional warmth, it renders impossible any intimate connection with the past, with ancestors, it kills tradition and memories. The attitude towards material objects is rendered impersonal, exclusively utilitarian. This is true also regarding the attitude towards every economic act. More inspired and personal an attitude towards economic activity presupposes private property, a secure perspective, transcending the bounds of the empirical life of people. The Christian transcending of property and all wealth is already however a spiritual phenomenon, and not of economic life. Christ did not deny private property on the material plane, when He proposed dividing one's substance among the poor, He by this even affirmed the existence of property. If property be completely abolished by way of economic coercion, then there will remain no place for the Christian ascetic effort of self-denial, it would become unnecessary and impossible. The cult of poverty of St. Francis was not a denial of property in the objective economic order, and it likewise presupposed the existence of property. In the communistic order, St. Francis would be impossible and impossible also would be any sort of a cult of poverty. But the principle of property has suffered rot and decay. Great abuses are possible in connection with property. And property cannot be admitted as an absolute and utmost principle. It has to be delimited and subordinated to higher principles. The social reformation of society also presupposes such a delimiting of property and its subordination to other principles, connected with cosmic life. The dominance of man over the natural elements ought to possess an ontological strength and basis. The philistine aspect of making a god of property and the abuse of it in economic life distorts this ontological basis, makes man a slave of illusory benefits and makes all the more difficult the approach to the image of man. This is the same temptation, as is the temptation of collectivism, which ultimately is destructive of the image of man. And the attitude of man towards the industrial economic process can assume a false direction in either of two opposite ways: either there is denied the duty of econominisation, the imperative for productivity, or man becomes enslaved to the economy, makes a god of the economy. The spiritual attitude towards the economy presupposes an asceticism, a limiting of the lustings of life. The unlimited growth of demands and the growth of the people's population has created an industrial-capitalistic civilisation, which as impelled great upheavals and catastrophes, and it signifies a waning of spirit in European mankind. And if the peoples intend spiritually to be reborn, then they shall have to enter upon a path of ascetic self-limitation and cultivation of spirit in economic life.

Thirteenth Letter

Concerning Culture

In societal life the spiritual primacy belongs to culture. It is not in politics and not in economics, but in culture that the ends of a society are realised. And high cultural level provides a measure for the value and quality of the societal aspect. The democratic revolution sweeping the world long since already fails to justify itself by any high value and high quality of that culture, which it conveys with it into the world. From its democratisation, culture everywhere declines in its quality and its value. It is rendered cheaper, more accessible, more widely spread, more useful and more comfortable, but also more shallow, lowered in its quality, lacking beauty, and bereft of style. Culture passes over into civilisation. Democratisation inevitably leads to civilisation. The higher expanses of culture belong to the past, and not to our bourgeois-democratic age, which most of all is interested in a levelling process. In this plebian age those of a nature creative and culturally refined tend to sense themself more alone and unacknowledged, than in all the preceeding ages. Never yet has there been such an acute conflict between a select minority and the majority, between the summits of culture and the average level, as in our bourgeois-democratic age. In former ages this conflict tended to weaken the moreso organic aggregate of culture. But in a culture, having lost its "organicity", having reneged its hierarchical structure, in a culture as regards its "critical" structure this conflict has become unbearably tormentive. It evokes the inexpressible sorrow of the best people of our era. For you, ye people of a democratic spirit, unnoticeable is this sorrow and imperceptible is this ominous sense of aloneness in modern culture. For you culture -- is only a means to your politics and economics, only a tool for prospering, merely a matter of culture for the people. Ye lack the ability to surmount your age-old utilitarianism. And insofar as ye have not attempted to embellish yourself with culture, it is quite evident and clear, that no sort of cultural values exist for you. Civilisation is what is needful for you, as a tool of your earthly domain, but culture for you is unnecessary. Culture and civilisation -- are not one and the same thing. Culture is begotten of a cult. Its sources -- are sacral. It was conceived around the setting of temple and in its organic period it was connected with the religious life. Thus it was in the ancient great cultures, in the Greek culture, in the Medieval culture, in the culture of the early Renaissance. Culture -- is of noble origin. The hierarchical character of the cult is bestown it. Culture possesses religious foundations. This mustneeds be regards as established even from a quite positivist-scientific point of view. Culture -- is symbolic by its nature. It received its symbolism from its cultic symbols. In culture is not realistically, but rather symbolically, expressed the spiritual life. All the achievements of culture by their nature are symbolic. Within it obtain not the final achievements of being, but merely its symbolic signs. The nature of the cult is the same, which prefigures the realised Divine mysteries. Civilisation is always characteristic of the parvenue mentality. In it are no connections with the symbols of the cult. Its origin is secular. It is born of the struggle of man against nature, apart from temple and cult. Culture is a phenomenon profoundly individual and unrepeatable. Civilisation however is a phenomenon generalised and everywhere repeated. The transition from barbarism to civilisation has signs in common among all peoples, and the signs are primarily material, as for example, the use of iron etc. The culture however of ancient peoples at their very beginning stages is very unique and unrepeatably individualised, as is the culture of Egypt, of Babylon, of Greece etc. The culture is what possesses a soul. Civilisation however but possesses methods and tools.

The nobility of every true culture is defined by this, that the culture is a cult of ancestors, the veneration of cemeteries and memorials, the connection of sons with fathers. Culture is based upon a sacred tradition. And the more ancient the culture, then the more remarkable and beautiful it is. A culture is always proud of the antiquity of its origin, of its inseparable connection with a great past.

And upon culture rests the grace of a special sort of priesthood. A culture, like a church, esteems most of all its preeminence. In culture there is no boorishness, there is no contemptuous attitude towards the graveyards of the fathers. Whereas a rather new and recent culture, not having a tradition, has this to embarrass its position. But it is impossible to say this for civilisation. Civilisation esteems its own recent origin, it does not seek out the ancient and profound sources. It is proud of its findings of the current day. It has no ancestors. It loves not the graveyards. Civilisation always carries the view, that it arose precisely today or yesterday. All that matters in it is the new, everything is geared towards the conveniences of the present day. Within culture there occurs a great struggle of eternity against time, a great resistance to the destructive grip of time. Culture represents a struggle against death, although powerless to really conquer it. To it is dear the eternal agelessness, the unbroken constancy, the preeminence, the durability of cultural works and monuments. A culture, wherein is a religious depth, always strives towards resurrection. In this regard the grandest model of a religious culture is the culture of ancient Egypt. It was all based upon a thirst for eternity, a thirst for resurrection, it was all a struggle against death. And the Egyptian pyramids survived over long thousands of years and have been preserved down to our own day. Modern civilisation no longer still builds pyramids and nowise holds dear the making of its memorials with a thousand-years durability. Everything is quick paced in modern civilisation. Civilisation, in distinction to culture, does not struggle against death, does not desire eternity. It not only reconciles itself with the death-bearing power of time, but also even upon the death-bearing aspect of the flow of time it bases all its successes and conquests. Civilisation is very receptive and happy to build upon the graveyards, whilst forgetting about the reposed. Civilisation is future oriented. In civilisation is a boorishness involving the parvenue. This boorishness is correlative also to a culture, which desires ultimately to be irreligious.

Within culture are active two principles -- the conservative, oriented towards the past and maintaining predominantly a connection with it, and the creative, oriented towards the future and creating new values. But within culture there cannot act a revolutionary and destructive principle. The revolutionary principle is essentially hostile to culture, is anti-cultural. Culture is unthinkable without an hierarchical preeminence, without a qualitative inequality. The revolutionary principle is hostile however to all hierarchism and is directed at the destruction of qualitative difference. The revolutionary spirit seeks to equip itself with civilisation, to appropriate its utilitarian conquests, but culture it does not desire, culture for it is unnecessary. And it is not by chance that ye revolutionaries love to speak about the bourgeoisness of culture, about the inequity, from which all culture is born, and it is with such pathos that ye declaim against the too dear value of culture, against the inequality and sacrifices, by which it is bought. None of you esteems culture, nor loves it intimately, nor senses it to be for its own value, its own inner wealth. Culture was created by people foreign to you in spirit. Nothing in the great memorials of culture evokes in you a sacred trembling. And with ease ye are ready to destroy all the memorials of the great cultures, all their creative values, in the name of utilitarian ends, in the name of the welfare of the masses of the people. It is time already to unmask your duplicitous attitude towards culture. A new culture ye cannot create, since generally it is impossible to create a new culture lacking any sort of significant connection with past culture, having no sort of tradition, no respect for ancestors. The idea of such a new revolutionary culture is a *contradictio in adjecto*. The new thing, that ye want to create, cannot still be termed culture. Ye speak much about a revolutionary proletarian culture, which your messiah-class will convey into the world. But up to the present time there are not the slightest indications of a proletarian culture arising, there are not even hints at the possibility of such a culture. Insofar as one from the proletariat communes with culture, he wholly borrows it from the bourgeoise. Even his socialism he received from the "bourgeoise". Culture discloses itself from above downwards. The "proletarian" mindset and the "proletarian" consciousness are essentially hostile to culture.

Militantly to regard oneself as "proletarian" -- means to deny every tradition and everything sacred, every connection with the past and its every aspect of preeminence, it means to possess not ancestry, not to know one's origins. In such an inner condition it is impossible to love and to create culture, it is impossible to hold dear any sort of values, as one's very own. The worker can partake of culture, if he does not conceive of himself as "proletarian".

Socialism does not convey with it into the world any sort of new type of culture. And when socialists speak about whatever a new spiritual culture, always there is felt the falsity of their words. The socialists themself even sense the awkwardness amidst discussion on this theme. And those socialists, who sincerely would desire a new culture, do not understand, that they have hopelessly begun their path with this end in mind. Upon these paths culture is not created. It is impossible to make culture an appendage to some essential and basic task, something on the order of a revitalising diversion. One can create culture only then, when it itself is regarded as an essential and basic task. The socialists want to direct the will and consciousness of man exclusively to the material and economic side of life. And then they hold forth with the view, that they are not against culture, that they thirst for a new culture. But from what sort of source will issue this new culture, after all the creative wellsprings in the human soul have dried up, after the spirit is quenched and smothered by social matters? Democracy already has lowered the qualitative level of culture and managed only to spread, not create cultural values. Socialism however has lowered this level even moreso. The dispersion and spreading of culture does not lead to this, that a greater quantity of people begin to live with genuine interests in culture. On the contrary, this dispersion and spreading lessens still more the quantity of people, devoting their life to higher culture. And yet this does not surprise you. The dispersion and spreading that ye make is not in the name of culture itself, not out of creative spiritual motive and impulse, but exclusively out of interests economic and political, out of utilitarian considerations, in the name of mundane benefits. But the higher spiritual life appertains not with those, who wholly direct their energy to the interests of material life. Ye, who teach about culture, as a superstructure obtaining over the material and economic life of society, can only but destroy culture. Your attitude towards culture cannot be deeply serious. The democratisation and socialisation of human societies tends to smother out the upper cultural level. But without the existence of such a level and without esteem for it, culture is impossible. This necessitates being both conscious of and making everywhere all the inevitable conclusions.

By democratic a path there cannot be formed "science" and "art", nor be created philosophy and poetry, nor appear prophets and apostles. The shutting off of the aristocratic wellsprings of culture represents the dessication of all the wellsprings. Spiritually there would have to exist the dead capital of the past, whilst yet denying and hating this past. And the very wellsprings of culture in the past all more and more are being lost, while ripped away from them is everything all ever and more deep. All the European culture of great style was bound up with the traditions of antiquity. Authentic culture is also the ancient Graeco-Roman culture, and no sort of other culture in Europe exists. The era of the Renaissance in Italy also thence was profoundly a cultural era, in distinction from eras of reformation and revolution, in that it not only did not effect a revolutionary split in the traditions of culture, but instead renewed the traditions of ancient culture and upon them set its unprecedented creative upsurge. The spiritual type of the Renaissance is a cultural and creative type. The spiritual type of the Reformation signifies the destruction of churchly and cultural traditions, a principle revolutionary, and not creative. The ancient culture entered into the Christian Church, and the Church was the preserver of the tradition of culture in an era of barbarity and darkness. The Eastern Church received the tradition of ancient culture through Byzantium. The Western Church received the tradition of ancient culture through Rome. The churchly cult is pervaded with culture, and from it and around it was created also the new culture of old Europe. European culture is first of all and most of all a Latin and Catholic culture. There is within it an inseparable connection with antiquity. And by it can be discerned the nature of culture. If we, as Russians, not ultimately be mere barbarians and Scyths, then it is only because that through the Orthodox Church, that through Byzantium we have received the bond with the traditions of antiquity, of Greek culture. All revolutions are directed against the Church and seek to break the bond with the traditions of ancient culture, traditions having come into the Church. And therefore they represent a barbaric uprising against culture. the struggle against noble culture, against cultural symbolics began already with Iconoclasm, with a struggle against the cult. This -- reflects also a spiritual wellspring of culturo-clasm, of struggle against culture.

Every culture has periods of its flourishing, of its high upsurge. At the beginning of a culture -- is barbarism, at the end of this growth -- is decadence. Barbarity and decadence from opposite ends threaten culture. Every culture tends to dissipate itself, to dry up and go into decline. At its summits the culture becomes cut off from its ontological groundings, broken off from its vital wellsprings, becomes refined and begins to wither. The autumn period of a culture -- is a very beautiful and refined season. The late blossoms of a culture -- are a most sought after of its blossoms. A culture at this point attains to a greatest alacrity of knowledge and a greatest complexity. The fragmenting of a declining culture reveals much, hidden earlier for the more flourishing and healthy cultural eras. The epochs of a refined decadence of a culture are not so sterile, as would seem at first glance, -- in them also is its own positive revelation. A flourishing organic wholeness does not yield knowledge of oppositions, it dwells in one aspect and happily does not know the other. Too great a complexity and refinement of culture fractures this wholeness, leads out from this ignorance of oppositions. In art, in philosophic thought, in mystical outlooks become revealed the polar abysses. There is discovered more acutely both the knowledge of good, and of evil. But the will for life, for its ordering and developement fails to have its former wholeness. A refined exhaustedness becomes evident. There is no longer still faith and assuredness of that culture in this world, in the achievement of the perfection and beauty of a flourishing culture. And there grows a dissatisfaction with this world, an anguish for other worlds. The culture inwardly burns itself out. Within it form the materials for a new world, is readied a new revelation, a new advent. Thus it occurred in the period of the decline of the great ancient Graeco-Roman culture. In this decline is opened up something new, unknown to the era of the flourishing of the wholistic and isolated ancient culture. In healthy, flourishing, wholistic eras of the high upsurge of a culture there is also always some sort of delimitedness and self-sufficiency, a satisfaction with this self-contained world. A mystical anguish for other worlds was known down to its depths by the ancient world only during the period of the Hellenistic decadence. Then began the tormentive search for redemptive mysteries, then became manifest such currents, as Neo-Platonism and Neo-Pythagoreanism. Then too in art they discovered a break-through beyond the bounds of the classical perfection of this earthly world, set beneathe the shut-in vault of the heavens. And in answer to this deep anguish, which afflicted culture, there came the Christian revelation from the very depths of life, from its mysteried loins. For the cultured ancient world Christianity had to seem as barbarism. The revelation of its light is not immanent to culture, but rather is transcendent to it and had to be perceived by the shut-in cultural world as a wave of barbarity. This new light extinguishes the waning light of the decrepit culture and at first is perceived by many, as darkness.

The decline tends westward, with the dessication of all the whole of European culture, which has not the wherewithal to endlessly develope. It moves out farther and farther from its creative wellsprings, becomes all more and more abstract, all less and less ontological in its character. The influx of the religious nourishing of European culture is all the more diminishing. At its height, the great Latin culture of Western Europe experienced refinement and decay. In France it gave forth its final blooms and enticed with the charms of an autumnal withering. But the decay and withering of European culture evokes a sense of anguish and sorrow. Ancient culture was saved for eternity by Christianity, by the Christian Church. Yet now even Christianity itself is going old, in it there is not still the creative youthfulness. New religious light is still not apparent. Within history occur periodic waves of barbarity, inward and outward. These waves of barbarity have not only a negative significance, for they indeed tend to renew the decrepit cold blood of the old world. New elements are imparted to culture and give it new vital fluids. Within the character of culture is a danger of ossification, stagnancy and self-smugness. Culture can idolise itself into a god, and then it loses its Divine significance, its connection with the Divine sources of life. The stance of cultural rigour can become transformed into an hypocritical lie. Culture was formed by creative impulses, but in its smugness and tendency to ossification it can become the foe of every creative impulse. Then the arising of barbarity serves as a natural chastisement and can open out to new paths. And at present an impetus of barbarity threatens European culture from both within and without. There was a feeling of this already, when the world war began, and this feeling reached an especial alacrity, when the Russian revolution played itself out. But the whole terrible aspect is in this, that the inward barbarity, which threatens European culture in the revolutionary democratic, socialistic and anarchistic movement, cannot be an influx for culture, eternal in its nature, luminous forces, mighty vital elements from the loins of being, forces and elements, still not spent in their natural vigour and strivings towards the light. The significance of what faces Europe, is altogether different. The inward revolutionary barbarity stormily enters into a cultural world already deeply exhausted by false anti-Christian ideas, by a distorted in judgement semi-enlightenment, with a perverse "proletarian" psychology, with a deadened and paralysed sense of the mystery of life, with pretensions to some sort of a pseudo semi-culture. There is no sort of an immediacy, of a natural integral wholeness, of proximity to naturo-Divine mysteries in this revolutionary barbarity. It transpired through the factories and the industrial revolution, it itself is a product of the godless civilisation, revolting against the higher culture. From the outside is the threat to European Christian culture from the Mongol East, possessed of its own anti-Christian idea, its own civilisation hostile to us and imperceivable for us. And from this barbarity it is impossible to expect an influx of creative forces. European culture approaches a sort of terrible final point.

In culture have acted always two principles -- the classical and the romantic, and in different eras now one prevailed, and then the other principle also created the predominating style of the culture. Greece represented the loftiest model of classical culture. But also in Greece there was already a romantic culture. After Nietzsche it is impossible to deny this. The classical and the romantic interweave, interfold each with the other and interact. Classical culture is an immanent culture, realising a completeness within bounds, a closed-in and accomplished completeness upon the earth. It strives for strict forms, not permitting of impulses, and in it are not realised the boundless distances. Romantic culture is a culture with transcendent impulses, realising completeness within boundlessness, a breaking loose and not allowing of completeness upon the earth. Its forms are not so strict, and in it always there are impulses, always are revealed beyond it the boundless distances. Classical culture does not know of another world beyond its bounds, and says nothing about it. Romantic culture is all about the world beyond the bounds, all with a striving for perfection of completeness in eternity and the immeasurable. Christian culture as regards its principle is romantic, and not classical, although the principle of classicism also acts within it as one of the eternal principles. Classical culture signifies a satisfaction with culture. This satisfaction is impossible in the Christian world. The Christian world has languished with a transcendental anguish. And this langour has imprinted itself upon its culture. A perfection of completeness upon earth, in culture, for this world is impossible. The Gothic bent of soul and the Gothic trend of culture is very characteristic of the Christian world. And never was there possible in the Christian world a fully successful and fully complete Renaissance. The Italian Renaissance was a struggle between pagan and Christian principles. The Christian Church accepted into it the ancient culture and carried on through the darkness. But it transformed it and imparted to it its own symbolism. The Christian Church broke through the pagan vault of the heavens and opened up the upper void. And the relation of the authentic Christian world to culture has always involved a division. The problem of culture for Christian society -- is a tragic problem. The classical pagan world did not know of such a tragedy of culture. The tragedy of culture is a negation of the self-involvedness and self-sufficiency of culture. A perfective culture is just as impossible, as a perfect society is impossible. The perfection is possible only in another world, on another plane, in the graced and not the natural order. Culture possesses religious groundings, it is filled with religious symbolics, and in it are not attained ontologically real results. Science and art, the state and the family, the law and the economy -- are not finalised realities of being, are not ontological attainments of cognition and beauty, of power and of love, of the community of people and of the regulation of nature, but rather merely signs, merely symbols of these real attainments. Both impossible and base would be a completely irreligious culture, but impossible also is an ontologically-religious culture. Culture has appeared by way of a differentiation of the cult, has appeared already as the result of derivation from the temple, of separation from the religious centre. And the process of the secularisation of culture -- is an inevitable and fated process. Secularisation represents also the inward tragedy of culture. Through secularisation, through a distancing from the religious centre and a full autonomy proceed whether be it philosophy, and science, and art, and the state, and the family, and the law, and the economy. Culture is religious by its origin and religious by its task. Yet in its most classical and perfective attainments, in its most strict forms it becomes bereft of its religious character. But the romantic element in culture brings to mind the origins of culture and about its task, and thus readies the crisis of culture, though itself per se be powerless.

At the summits of culture long since already has begun the crisis of culture. In the most refined fruits of culture there is a feeling of the insufficiency of culture, an unsatisfactory aspect of culture, an impaired fracture within it, the search for a path towards trans-cultural being. The crisis of culture and the search for new being, inherent in culture, obtains among that select minority, which has known culture thoroughly and has experienced the paths of culture, at the highest cultural level. This process was known by such people, as Nietzsche and Ibsen, as Huysmans and L. Bloy, as Dostoevsky and Tolstoy. Yet for the enormous majority, no sort of a crisis of culture exists. The enormous majority have yet to commune with culture and travel its paths. The crisis of culture, by its character, is a crisis aristocratic, and not democratic. Ye democrats and socialists, ye revolutionaries, have not experienced any sort of a crisis of culture. And moreover do not even suspect it. Your hostility towards "bourgeois" culture does not signify any sort of a crisis of culture. It signifies merely a lack of culture, merely envy towards culture and the cultural, and not the inward tragedy in it. The adoption of purely economic categories and purely economic outlooks towards culture is an hindrance to involvement with culture and learning its mysterious life. Your question, directed towards culture, is always indeed a very elementary question, in it there is no sort of complexity, no problematics, no depth. The revolutionary dogmatic and socialistic movements throw everything backwards in the sphere of culture, they lower the qualitative level of culture and they weaken interest in the problem of culture. Your "proletkul'turs" ("culture-flights") signify merely this, that culture flies past you and you are on the sidelines to it. What interests you is but the revolutionary "enlightenment" of the masses. But even the more lofty "enlightenment", that of the "Enlightenment" of the XVIII Century transpired alongside genuine culture and readied the collapse of culture. What have you to do with the problems of Nietzsche and Dostoevsky and what have the problems of Nietzsche and Dostoevsky to do with you? For you there exists nothing problematic, ye feel yourself too "enlightened" for this. Your "semi-enlightenment", smug and impudent, nowise trembling nor bowing before any sort of sanctities, is deeply contrary to culture, it demeans culture and corrupts it, but yet is aware of no sort of an inner crisis of culture and hence does not lead to the depths of this crisis, since it leads to no sort of depths. Ye want only, that culture should be popular, accessible, democratic, cheap, and that from it should vanish everything aristocratic, challenging, everything too complex and deep. Ye want simplified correct-writing, simplified language, simplified thought. This is what your "non-bourgeois" culture means. Ye are very modestly unassuming in deeds of culture, ye -- are minimalists, and not maximalists, people of the average. But the crisis of culture is felt and perceived only by those, who are maximalists, and not minimalists in deeds of culture. The crisis of culture in simplified correct-writing is inexpressible. You still know the multiplication tables poorly, at a time when at the heights the multiplication tables have already come into doubt. But it is necessary for you still to learn it. Revolution temporarily weakens the crisis of culture.

Indeed, the crisis of culture happens hierarchically, as does everything, that transpires genuinely, and is not of the merely illusory in the world. This crisis by its nature has nothing in common with what you tend to call "revolutions". This -- is a spiritual and aristocratic revolution, and it transpires on another plane. The crisis of culture transpires at deep a dimension, and not on the surface dimension, where occurs all your deeds and stirrings. What does the crisis of culture signify? This crisis is an acute experiencing at the summits of culture of an inner opposition and an inner incommensurability between culture and existence, between culture and creativity. When culture reaches its ultimate bounds, the ultimate refinements and complexities of its problems, then there begin doubts, that the higher attainments of culture do not really represent new being, new life, that the higher products of culture are incommensurable with the creative impulse, with the creative task.[2] For truly, the task of the creative act should be new being, new life,

---

[2] Vide my book, "The Meaning of the Creative Act".

ontological truth, ontological rightfulness, ontological beauty. But the creative impulse, directed upwards, gets deflected by the gravity of this world and becomes directed downwards. There are thus created values of culture rather than new being, there are created books, pictures, institutions in place of new life, in place of an other world. In culture, in books, in pictures and institutions there transpires as though a diminishing of life itself, a dessication of being. In formal, modern, classical culture, in its sciences and arts, in its state institutions and legal institutes there is revealed a chasm, polarly opposite the chasm of life itself, the chasm of being itself. This is not perhaps perceived in that middle ground, in which lives the mass not only of uncultured people, but also the cultured, this is something that reveals itself only at the limits and the end-points of culture, only at the summits of creative attainment. And a morbid languor of non-being takes hold there, a thirst for genuine being, a thirst for he transfiguration of the world, the thirst for a new heaven and a new earth. A tragic dissatisfaction with culture and all its achievements seizes hold the creators of culture. But it is still something not felt by those demanding culture. Here is why the worldwide crisis of culture transpires not in the democratic movement, not in the mass revolutions, but rather in the aristocratic movement, in the inward revolutions of spirit. The crisis of culture clearly evidences, how pitiful and shallow are all the vulgar oppositions between "revolutionary" and "reactionary", between the "left" and the "right". These oppositions are impressive only at the surface level, in the depths however all the real oppositions -- are otherwise and all this mere husk falls away. In the world there eternally remains the tragic conflict and tragic lack of understanding between the minority, the minority alive to creativity, to spiritual searchings, ideas, the poetry of life, in contrast to the majority, alive to interests, appetites, and the prosaic in life.

The most creative people at the summits of culture can experience a profound dissatisfaction with culture and be conscious of its deep crisis. But people of average culture or altogether uncultured cannot make thereof any sort of inferences against culture, cannot idealise upon this basis a condition non-cultural or pre-cultural. The tragedy of culture and the crisis of culture, the thirst in the finest people to pass over to a condition trans-cultural, to new being, to a new earth and a new heaven, cannot be by way of arguments to the benefit of a Scythian barbarian ideology. With Russians, and indeed the Slavs in general, there is a contemptuous and duplicitous attitude towards culture. We love to speak about the "bourgeois aspect" of culture and very readily consider ourself standing higher than culture. The tendency towards a denial of culture, seeing in it a falling away from the initial wholeness, from the highest vital type, the idealisation of the primordial wholeness in the life of the people, prior to culture, is characteristic also of very remarkable and original Russian thinkers. With Russians there is the temptation to sense ourselves as Scyths and oppose ourself to the Hellenes. The Scythic ideology was born for us in the time of revolution. It assumed the form of an obsession with the revolutionary element in people, enabling a poeticising and mystification of this element. The Scythian ideology -- is one of the masks of Dionysos. In its struggle against the middle ground and moderation for every culture it strives not upwards, towards the utmost upper abyss, but downwards, towards the lower abyss. The modern Scyths sing hymns not to a trans-cultural, but to a pre-cultural condition. And least of all do they aspire towards a new heaven and a new earth, to a transfiguration of the world. They -- are pagans, in them boils the blood of people, not having found the mystery of redemption. The Scythian ideology in Russia is of its own sort a pagan nationalism, passing over into a non-Christian and anti-Christian messianism. The Scyths ought to redeem their sins by a submission to culture and its severe school.

Culture is an unrepeatable path of man and of mankind. It is impossible to avoid it. It is necessary to live out the paths of culture, in order to go beyond the bounds of culture, towards higher creative being. Only at the summits of culture can creative daring break the chains of culture, the fetters to this world. There is still the path of sanctity, a path, existing for the few. But this path is also a path of the higher culture of spirit. It lies within the deepest groundings of Christian culture. Two aspects emerge beyond the bounds of the canonical norms of culture -- sanctity and genius. But sanctity and genius -- are the greatest manifestations of spiritual culture, its true movers. Mankind is fated to have culture. But within it act also forces, hostile to the paths of the achievements of culture, forces nihilistic and anarchistic. The nihilistic and anarchistic revolt against culture never leads to an emergence beyond the bounds of culture, it merely throws things backwards and demarks a new working of culture. Higher culture is needful but for the few. For the average mass of mankind there is needful only an average culture. This also bespeaks the hierarchical structure of culture. The higher ends of world and historical life are bound up with this, that what is conceived of and existent be necessary merely for the few. But this needed and conceived of merely for the few spiritually takes hold of all the world and all history. In culture there is the esoteric and the exoteric. That which is conceived of at the higher steps possesses an essential significance for the lowest steps. Philosophy is needful for technology. The crisis of culture transpires at the highest steps of creative life. But this possesses a worldwide significance. The spiritual wave goes from above down to the very bottom. The revolutionary resolution of the crisis as from below is however a great folly. The ends of the societal aspect inwardly are subordinate to the ends of culture. All you, ye devotees of the societal aspect, are insufficiently aware of this, and therefore for you lie hidden the ends of life, whereas your consciousness is consumed merely with the means of struggle. But even the ends of culture cannot be final ends. Further and deeper lies the search for the Kingdom of God. You, the devotees of culture, are insufficiently aware of this religious distance. Therefore for you also lie hidden the ends of life. Culture is not the final thing, culture -- is before the final. Those creators are aware of this, those who experience the crisis of culture. They stand afront the final task of the transformation of culture into new being. And thus we approach the apocalypsis of culture.

Fourteenth Letter

Concerning the Kingdom of God

All history is filled with the search for the Kingdom of God. This search comprises the hidden soul of history, its holy of holies. All the end purposes of history are but relative in comparison with this absolute end, all other ends are transformed merely into a means. History itself, in its hidden meaning, is but movement towards the Kingdom of God. But the limited human consciousness tends to seek the Kingdom of God within history itself. This also reflects a basic contradiction within the religious philosophy of history. The Kingdom of God -- is the goal of history, the end purpose of history, an emergence out beyond the bounds of history. The Kingdom of God therefore cannot be within history. The seeking of the Kingdom of God within history, within earthly historical activity, is an illusion, an optical illusion. The Kingdom of God is behind history and above history, but not within history. It is always a fourth dimension in comparison with the three dimensional expanse. Thus also it is impossible to seek out the Kingdom of God within history. History possesses absolute a meaning, an absolute source and an absolute end-purpose. But the Absolute per se is not encompassable within it, within history. Historical activity is encompassed within the Absolute, the Divine being, but the Absolute and Divine being cannot be encompassed within it, within historical activity. The relative is a manifestation within the Absolute, but the Absolute cannot dwell fully within the relative. History is but an aspect of the absolute activity. "Everything transitory is but a symbol". History possesses first of all symbolic a significance, it is filled with signs of an other, a Divine activity. The symbolism of history bespeaks the impossibility of the Kingdom of God within history itself, the realm of absolute life upon whatever the stage of historical achievement. The Kingdom of God is an absolute spiritual realm, it cannot be a phenomenon within the material world, it presupposes a victory over the material world and the passing over to an other world. Absolute life is a transition to an other plane, an other dimension of being. Every attainment of absolute life is a breaking through beyond the bounds of the natural and historical order. In the natural and historical order, however, absolute life cannot be encompassed. With the incursion of the Absolute all natural and historical life gives way, becomes fluid, loses its borders, egresses into boundlessness.

The bursting forth of the Absolute into our natural and historical world and the breaking through towards the Absolute from our natural and historical world is indicative of this, that no sort of a shut-in, isolated and self-sufficing "this world" exists. Into "this world" can enter other forces, higher worlds, ontological energies, and the same likewise from "this world" they can go out and break through into other, higher worlds. In our world, in our natural and historical life there is possible the miraculous, there is possible a graced rebirth, there is possible a liberation from the weight of world, from the burden of history, there is possible the breaking asunder the iron chains of the rule of law. Historical activity is not a locked-in activity, is not a prison under iron bars. There exist the breakings through within historical activity into higher a spiritual activity, transfusions of the energy of the three dimensions into the fourth dimension. These breakings through shatter all the rationalistic teachings concerning the historical process, destroy all the legitimacy of the rational sociologies. In the world and in the historical process are active not only spiritual forces immanent to it, but also forces mysterious and mystical, not subject to any sort of accounting: both forces graced, and forces dark. And the higher creative attainments of the historical process represent a breaking through from an other world and into an other world. The incommensurability between the Absolute and the relative, between the Kingdom of God and history cannot be conceived of as a locked-in sphere of the relative, as the isolatedness of history from higher realities. The relative becomes manifest in the Absolute itself, it is aspective for the Absolute itself. Upon this is based the justification of the relative and the rights of the relative. The relative inwardly is needful for a revealing of the plenitude of the Absolute. The relative therefore cannot be split away from the Absolute and be opposed to it. It is impossible to conceive an outside-position of the relative world in relation to the absolute world. At some whatever ineffable depth all the contradictions and all the externalities vanish, all the antinomies disappear. The direction on the outside, however, orienting our consciousness towards the world, always bumps up against a series of insurmountable antinomies. These antinomies, as it were, guard the hidden and mysteried aspects of the vital depths. In the depths of the spiritual (not emotional) life of man is given and revealed the Absolute, we become immersed in absolute activity, we are not slaves of the world, not in the grip of the realm of the relative. Only in the projection of our life onto the outside do we come to present ourself as belonging inseparably to the realm of the relative. In our orientation towards the depths we belong to another actuality, we are co-participants to the Kingdom of God. The mystery of relationship of two worlds in man and mankind is a mystery of Christ, the mystery of His appearance in this world. The appearance of Christ in the world was also a singular and unrepeatable point of the breaking through of God Himself into this natural world. Against this breaking through all other creative break-throughs are incomparable and nowise the same, the break-throughs to which can be applied categories of multiplicity and repeatability. The fullness of Divinity dwells spiritually and corporeally in Christ. But the appearance of Christ was not the appearance of the Kingdom of God upon earth, in the material world. It was but the promise of the Kingdom of God. Christ taught, that His Kingdom is not of this world. And this world cannot encompass His Kingdom, it has to become transfigured, become an other world, emerge out from itself. The seeking of a sensory Kingdom of Christ upon this earth, upon this limited material world is one of the temptations, one of the mirages of the religious consciousness. This is a Jewish temptation, this is a manifestation of a Judaic spirit within Christianity.

The expectation of a tangible Kingdom of God upon earth is a Jewish chiliasm. The Jews awaited the Messiah -- an earthly king, who would fashion upon earth the blest kingdom of Israel. And they spurned the Messiah, Who appeared in the form of a servant and taught, that His Kingdom is not of this world. The Crucified-Messiah is in an eternal contrast to a messiah, such as would realise the Kingdom of God upon earth, bringing an earthly paradise. The utopia of a social earthly paradise is a surviving remnant of Jewish chiliasm. Its materialistic character ought not to obscure for us its old religio-Judaic wellsprings. Christ-Crucified is contrary to the chiliastic utopia, having penetrated into the Christian world, and repudiates it. All the whole world has to pass through crucifixion, through Golgotha, before there ensues the Kingdom of God, the Kingdom of Christ. Without the achieving through to the end of the mystery of the Redemption of mankind and the world there will not transpire the entering into the Kingdom of God. And this means also, that the Kingdom of God in this world, in the material natural order of things -- is impossible. The Kingdom of God is an accomplished transfiguration of this world, the transition over into an other dimension of being. Jewish chiliasm desires the Messiah-King, Who would realise the Kingdom of God upon earth without the Cross and Crucifixion, within the still old nature. And the Judaising Christian chiliasm tends to forget about Christ-Crucified and wants to overleap the Redemption into a sensory thousand-year reign of Christ, upon the still old earth, under the still old sky. Socialism also is a secularised chiliasm, sundered off from its religious roots. The utopia of a social earthly paradise, of an earthly perfection and an earthly bliss, of an earthly absoluteness is also a forgetting of Christ-Crucified, the lack of intent to come to terms with Golgotha, an avoidance of the mystery of the Redemption. At the primal basis of the utopia of an earthly paradise lies a denial of immortality, a lack of belief in immortality, a greediness for this crumb of an earthly life and a lustful attitude for its blessings. The utopia of the Kingdom of God upon earth, within material nature, is a resisting of the Divine world-order. A godless realm comes to substitute for the Kingdom of God.

The transition from the historical plane to the apocalyptic plane represents an irresolvable antinomy for reason. Reason is inclined to conceive of this transition, as transpiring within history itself, as a final, closing end period of history. But this also is an optical illusion. It is possible to speak about the apocalyptic era of world history, about its apocalyptic signs, but this still does not signify a transition from history over into the apocalyptic plane. On the other hand, it is impossible to conceive of the end, transpiring within the apocalyptic plane, as completely transcendent, to relate to it as wholly towards the other world. The apocalyptic plane, to which we relegate the onset of the end of the world, the resolution of world history, cannot be conceived of as completely immanent, nor as completely transcendent, neither exclusively as of this side, nor as exclusively of the other side. This is, for our rational consciousness, also a problem of the relationship of time and eternity. Thus, for example, to think of immortality as a matter for the grave, of other-side life, in distinction to earthly, this-side life, is a rationalistic limitation. Immortality is revealed also in the depths of each moment of earthly life. Thus also within history itself, in its depths is revealed the end, is given an apocalypse, as its other dimension. What transpires in time is however but a projection of that, what has obtained in the depths. The end of history and the surmounting of history will not be within history, the end of time and the surmounting of time will not be within time. But this does not mean, that we are forever doomed to be under the grip of a bad infinity of the historical process, of the temporal flow. For the Christian consciousness there is an all-resolving end, there is a victory over the grip of time. For the Christian consciousness the delimited problem of human society rests upon eschatology. But a Christian eschatology cannot be materialised. Chiliasm always has been also a materialistic eschatology. This does not mean, that the Christian consciousness assumes a spiritualistic eschatology. The Kingdom of Christ will be not only in heaven, but also upon earth, it will be not only spiritual, but also corporeal. But this will be a different, a transfigured earth, and a different, a transfigured body. The descent of the Heavenly

Jerusalem upon earth cannot be thought of as its materialisation. And it never will come forth within the limits of a three dimensional history, it is a fourth dimension of history. The glorified corporeality within the Kingdom of Christ is no longer still a material, physical corporeality. It is sown a soul body, it arises a spiritual body. History within time is a projection upon the surface of what is transpiring within the depths, within eternity. And a resolving of the end within this temporal history is always an irresolvable antinomy, is always an optical illusion for the rational consciousness. The new life, the new world, is the realm of Divine truth, eternal, and not merely something future, opposing itself to what has gone before.

In the Christian dogmatic consciousness, in Christian philosophy the problem of eschatology has not received a clear and generally bearing resolution. Around this problem always have been revealed various possibilities. Within the history of Christianity, the apocalypse has not been dealt with in full and the theme concerning the apocalypse has always been of a theme about a new revelation within Christianity. Thus stood once this matter for Joachim of Flora, thus it stands also for many a religious thinker of our time, prophetically minded. The "Revelation of St. John" was acknowledged a canonical book of Holy Scripture and is included in the New Testament. But the Church has not so recoursed to this sacred book, as it has to the other sacred books. The "Revelation of St. John" did not become a creative wellspring either for churchly dogmatics, nor for churchly practicality for Christians. This book remained mysterious, sealed under the seven seals. Times hitherto it was so and had to be so. And in our time, which mystically sensitive people term an apocalyptic time, the irresponsible misuse of the concept of apocalypse produces disagreeable an impression. The predicting of the end of the world for some definite date in time clearly contradicts the words of Christ, that for the day and hour of this -- no one knows. The awaiting of the end of the world on the morning after tomorrow snatches away from people all sense of responsibility and makes them passive. In these expectations there is always sensed a confusion of various planes, a coarse materialisation of Christian mysteries, a spiritual lack of sight. The inclusion of the Christian absolute into the historical relative begets a whole series of irrational antinomies. An "apocalyptic" mindset can yield very crude and violent resolutions to these antinomies. Within Christianity itself is a very complex clashing and interaction of the absolute and the relative, of the eternal and the historical. Western Papo-caesarism and Eastern Caesaro-papism were both a searching of the absolute within the relative, of the eternal within the historical. And upon this basis was created all the attempts at earthly theocracies, of sacred kingdoms. In them the Kingdom of God obtained only symbolically, and not real-ontologically. The Church is not the Kingdom of God upon earth, and the existence within history of the Church of Christ, against which the gates of hell will not prevail, does not speak about the possibility of the Kingdom of God upon earth. The identifying of the Church with the Kingdom of God, with the City of God was an error, on the part of Bl. Augustine, which influenced the Catholic conception of church. Church is not a theocracy. All the outward theocratic pretensions have been shattered by history. The fateful process of secularisation has not and will not vanquish the sanctities of the Church of Christ, but it is vanquishing the theocratic pretensions, it is shattering the great religious utopias regarding holy empires. The Kingdom of God cometh without notice. It enters unseen into the world and vanquishes the world. From the depths cometh this kingdom and to the depths it is oriented. And too obvious, too visible a kingdom is not still the Kingdom of God. Theocratic illusions were also illusions of a materialised Kingdom of God, of the Kingdom of God in untransfigured a nature, within the three dimensional earthly life. And the Church itself can be taken both in its historical dimension, in its manifestations upon the material plane, and also in the dimension of depth, in its hidden being. There exists the Church exoteric, democratic, guiding the masses of mankind and religiously nourishing them for higher life, and there exists the Church esoteric, hidden, in which for an higher hierarchy are revealed deeper mysteries and deeper communion. There cannot be any sort of opposition between these two understandings of the Church. The singular, integrally whole mystical organism of the Church, hierarchical in its structure, has degrees of manifesting itself, for its core and its periphery. The democratism of historical Christianity safeguards the aristocratism of the hidden Christianity. The illusions of the Kingdom of God upon earth are based upon this, that the hidden aspect be thought of ultimately to become cast out upon the surface, that the esoteric should become completely exoteric, that the spiritual should become fully materialised. But the Kingdom of God belongs to the hidden depths of being, and not its surface, not to its perceptible and visible trappings. The Kingdom of God cometh unnoticed, the Kingdom of God is not of this world. The Kingdom of God is the perfective accomplishing of the transfiguration of the world. The Christian community cannot be that of an external material theocracy. The Christian societal aspect is a mysteried communion in spirit, in the love of Christ. It is incommensurate with any sort of societal aspect set under law. All attempts to juxtapose and align the Christian community in Spirit with democratic and socialistic currents is a religious lie and deception. The freedom of the Christian communion in Spirit has nothing in common with anarchistic "freedom", and the brotherhood of the Christian communion in Spirit has nothing in common with socialistic "brotherhood". The Christian communion -- is a graced community, a communion in the love of Christ. Anarchistic and socialistic community belongs totally to the realm of natural necessity, to the kingdom of Caesar. Suchlike a religious lie is represented by all the connections of the Christian societal aspect with the old pagan state or with the remnant natural economy. The Kingdom of God and the kingdom of Caesar were divided by Christ, and the Kingdom of God cannot be comprised in any sort of kingdom of Caesar, whether old or new, reactionary or revolutionary. Brotherly communion in Christ is already a mysteried entry into the Kingdom of God. And this brotherhood in Christ cometh without observation into the world. In the Kingdom of God there are no sort of collectives, in it is only the person, it consists all of persons of different hierarchical degrees. And in the Kingdom of God will be "a different glory of sun, a different glory of moon, a difference of stars, and star from star will be contrast in glory" [1 Cor. 15: 41].

In the brotherhood in Christ are no sort of outward social distinctions, and there cannot be for it any sort of social criteria for it. In the spirit of St. Francis there was nothing connected with the social realm, in it the Kingdom of God doth enter without observation into the world. Everything social is bound up with the relative means of life, and not with the absolute ends. An absolute social end is unthinkable, the absolute end -- is religious, and not social. Everything outwardly social possesses in itself a material relativeness. And the Kingdom of God recedes, when they consider it a social realm, when they reckon it as realised upon earth, within time. The weight of the world fetters down the spirit, when they absolutise the relative. But the pathos of all social utopias consists in suchlike an absolutisation of the relative. Ye dispute -- whether the Kingdom of God is of the "left" or of the "right". Yet these pitiful measures apply but vilely to the Kingdom of God. Everything of the "right" or of the "left" passes away, when is touched upon the Kingdom of God. One mustneeds assert an healthy pessimism and ascetic severity against social utopias, passing themself off as the Kingdom of God. This pessimism, in regards to the world and everything that is of the world, exists both in the Gospel and the Apocalypse. And ye would do well more frequently to remember. Neither the lesser apocalypses of the Gospel, nor the Apocalypse of St. John, tend to predict the victory and triumph of the love of Christ and the truth of Christ upon earth.

Christian prophecies speak about the coming of the Anti-Christ, about the victory of the prince of this world, about the dessication and drying up of love. And all the utopias of an earthly bliss, of earthly perfection, of an ultimate triumph of truth and justice upon earth are in an incompatible contradiction to the Christian prophecies. That which is spoken of in the Revelation of St. John concerning the thousand year reign of Christ, remains an hidden mystery. And all the attempts to discern this mystery, conveying it over into the rational language of earthly utopias, -- is not religious, in such attempts is stronger the searchings for the kingdom of this world than are the searchings for the Kingdom of God. The apocalyptic thousand year reign of Christ is likewise a miraculous surmounting of the antinomy of time and eternity, of the earthly and the heavenly, of the this-sidely and the other-sidely, of the immanent and the transcendent. And therefore this reign is inexpressible in the language of the poles of this antinomy, it is inconveyable into the flatness of the temporal, the earthly and the this-sidely. The mysterious aspect of the Apocalypse is bound up with this, that the language of this book -- is not of our language. Therefore it can be posited only symbolically. Symbol -- is of time and eternity, of the world earthly and the world heavenly. The Kingdom of God is revealed to us symbolically. This comprises also a radical objection against all attempts to transform the Kingdom of God into an earthly utopia. Entering into apocalyptic an atmosphere, we become subject to the danger of substitutes and ambiguity. All the mysteriousness, the riddled antinomic aspect, the irrationality of the Apocalypse is bound up with this possibility of substitutes and ambiguity, presupposed by the freedom of man. In the Apocalypse cannot be the Gospel clarity and simplicity. Within it is revealed a spiritual splitting apart taken to the limit, in it appears the utmost lie, a likeness the reverse to Christ. In the Gospel everything transpires in an atmosphere of solar clarity, of Divine simplicity, the Logos is manifest in the flesh, and His blindingly bright rays penetrate down into the souls of people. In the Apocalypse everything transpires in an atmosphere convoluted and complex, -- in this atmosphere everything becomes divided, in it everything is pervaded by wrath and the clash of polarly opposite principles. The solar light of the Person of Christ falls already not upon the virginal soil of the soul's simplicity and wholeness, but upon souls terribly complex, divided, plunged and lacerated by a long history, having to face posited entirely new problems. We have emerged already out of the Gospel atmosphere and entered into an atmosphere apocalyptic. Our spiritual atmosphere does not resemble the atmosphere of the early Christians. The visage of Christ ceases clearly to be distinguished, and people are wont to confuse Him with the reverse image. The visage of Christ becomes twofold for modern man. Terribly unsteady is the modern soul, twofold for it has become good, twofold for it has become evil. Evil is appropriated by it in deceptive images of good. The spirit of the Anti-Christ is also a spirit of the lie and the substitute, a spirit of ambiguity, ungraspable in its inner essence, since this essence -- consists in non-being.

The utopia of a social paradise upon earth is one of the Anti-Christ's substitutes and deceptions, in an obverse likeness to the Kingdom of God. The unlimited social dreaminess of untethered souls, having lost all the ascetic discipline of self-abnegation, torn away from the spiritual centre of life -- is a felicitous soil for the temptations of the Anti-Christ. The Anti-Christ seduces by suggestion of the realisation of the Kingdom of God upon earth, of social bliss. He promises to realise that which was not realised by Christ-Crucified. After the coming of Christ into the world, that truth and right have not proven victorious upon the earth. And this tempts many. This was a temptation for the Jewish people. This enters into the temptation also of modern searchings for earthly truth and right. Higher than Christ would seem to be that one, who should realise truth and right upon earth, or else that one would be the Coming Christ, who would realise this truth and right, and end the human torment and sufferings. But Christ not only did not realise truth and right and bliss upon the earth, He also did not promise this realisation. He called for the taking up of one's cross and then to follow Him. He taught, that the life upon earth, in this world, is a cross, and that the path of the Kingdom of God lies through Golgotha. And thus all the more seductive would have to be that one, who should instead promise the Kingdom of God upon earth without Golgotha and redemption.

The socialistic and anarchistic movement in the world possesses enormous a religious significance, since this movement renders acute the problem of the Anti-Christ for the Christian consciousness. This movement takes things to the limit, it already passes over into the emotional atmosphere of the Apocalypse. The modern consciousness has ceased to clearly see evil and distinguish it from the good. There transpires a sort of decrystalisation. The spiritual life is become murky, already in it are no clear crystals, there is not that gem-like glistening, for which a man is prepared to surrender all the goods of the world. The aspect of person within modern man disintegrates and decrystalises, loses the clarity of features, the firmness of edges. This soil is very propitious for all sorts of impulses of the dark powers. The person is situated under the grip of whatever a sort of powers, imperceptible to it. It is not the person per se that acts, but rather the "nothing" acts within it. All the Anti-Christ's substitutes and deceptions are based upon the negation of the person, upon the destruction of the person. The person, preserving its integrity, its image, its boundaries, can fall, can sin, can do evil, but it is not subject to the temptations and seductions of the twofold images proffered by the spirit of the Anti-Christ. And resistance to the spirit of the Anti-Christ means first of all a strengthening of the person, the spiritual discipline of the person, the safeguarding within the human person of the image and likeness of God against the elements of the "this world" besetting it.

Elemental raging whirlwinds seek to tear apart the person and prepare the soil for the earthly kingdom of the Anti-Christ. And the person has to fortify itself in Christ, in order to oppose these whirlwinds, to resist these forces. In our era, evil appears ever newly adorned. It is not an elementary evil that tempts, but an evil complex and convoluted. Murkiness and lack of clarity interweave, push towards the shattering of all the boundaries, of everything between, of all the distinctions. This is true for the intimate life of man, but true also for societal life. And in societal life man seeks to hurl himself into the abyss, to surrender himself to the elements in the hope, that he will find a new earth, that he will attain the Kingdom of God. Upon this path man loses his aspect of person, but hopes to discover bliss. Modern people live by illusions moreso, than the people of former eras, they are less so realists in the true sense of this word, more torn off from the realities and more at the mercy of the wisps of the winds. The illusions of progress, of an all-liberating revolution, of a socialistic earthly felicity etc. are infinitely distant from an ontological realism. Revolutionary illusions ideologically start with rationalism and end up with irrationalism. The human reason rises up against history, it believes, that by its powers it can arrange human life upon earth, to rationalise it entirely without a remnant trace, not leaving place for the acting of powers mysterious and supra-rational. But the rationalistic revolution tends to end up by this, that chaos is unleashed and powers irrational and dark begin to prevail. Both the revolutionary rationalism, and the revolutionary irrationalism alike dislodge all the ontological realities, alike both deny the meaning of history, and its mysterious irrationality. Within history act occult forces, both the organised, and the not organised. And those, who are under the grip of these forces, often themself do not know about their existence. The acting of forces completely irrational tends to be the product of a completely rational consciousness. This is one of the paradoxical contradictions of societal and historical life.

When people of a religious consciousness strive for the Kingdom of God, they have the presentiment, that the coming of the Kingdom of God into the world represents a new revelation. Within Christianity from its beginnings there was a prophetic side, there was an aspiration for an ensuing unknown, as yet only in symbols and signs revealed in the sacred writings. But is there possible the admitting of a new revelation for those, who remain faithful to the eternal Christian revelation? This -- is one of the antinomies of the Christian religious consciousness. Christianity is not only revelation, but also concealed veiling. The Kingdom of the Spirit remains veiled, it opens itself in the creative life of spirit, in free propheticism. The creativity of man is not something that can be disclosed in the sacred scriptures, it is something to be freely discerned by man himself. But an authentic religious creativity is possible only for a man, fulfilling the truth of the law and the truth of redemption, strengthening his spirit through Christ and in Christ. A creativity against Christ, a creativity, rising up against the law and redemption, is a creativity of non-being, an illusory and phantasmic creativity. Within it there is no coming nigh to the Kingdom of God. The creativity of secular culture from a religious point of view is better, than a sectarian religious creativity, such as would destroy the eternal sanctities of the Church. Leonardo, in a certain sense, and from a religious point of view, is better than Luther, and Goethe better than L. Tolstoy. Luther and Tolstoy -- are religious destroyers. Leonardo and Goethe -- are creators of new values. They are like each other and in regard to each other. Least of all possible is to see the conceivings of a new revelation and a new creativity in sectarianism and Protestantism. These conceivings are moreso in the secular creative culture, in the surfeit of genius. The religious creativity of man can only be as a revelation of human love for God, in responding to the revelation of God's love for man. In such however a creativity there is approach to the Kingdom of God, which is a Kingdom of God-manhood. The dynamism of religious life determines the search for the Kingdom of God. Indeed, truly, never ought we to be bereft of the sense of evil and the improper aspect of this world and life in it. We ought to have the wherewithal to struggle for everything of value in the world and have also the wherewithal to be renunciatory of everything in the name of the Kingdom of God. The religious creativity of man is not a right and a pretension, but rather a religious duty of man, a duty of his exuberant love. The Apocalypse can be understood both passively and actively. The apocalyptic consciousness in Russia in a majority of cases is a mystical passivity, an awaiting, an experiencing of terror, and not as activeness and creativity. An active attitude towards the Apocalypse was found there only in N. F. Fedorov. An apocalyptic consciousness -- is perilous a consciousness. It can falsely diminish man and falsely exalt him. The apocalyptic consciousness -- is something mysterious. The Kingdom of God cannot be the result either of evolution, nor of revolution, -- it is a miraculous transfiguration. Within Orthodoxy has been a great awaiting and a great endurance. But there ensues the hour of the revealing of the prophetic-apocalyptic side of Christianity for the struggle against the powers of the spirit of the Anti-Christ, growing in the world. It is impossible to ultimately relegate this world to the evil powers. Wholeness within the coming earthly community is already impossible, and division inevitable. And therefore impossible is an earthly theocracy. But there ought to be a concentration and unification of the powers of the Kingdom of God. Seek ye first the Kingdom of God, and all else shalt be added unto. For Christianity this remains the ultimate religious truth, before which fade all remaining truths. All is unenduring and all is uncertain, except for the Kingdom of God, all however for it has to be fulfilled and completed. To the Kingdom of God ought to give way whether be it the state, the economy, and a culture, and all the world. In eternity, and not in time, is possible the conquering of time and possible the ensuing of the Kingdom of God. But the will for the onset of the Kingdom of God in eternity can be revealed in each instant of our life, in its depths. Thy Kingdom come!

Postscript

My book, "The Philosophy of Inequality", was written in the Summer of 1918 in the atmosphere of a passionate spiritual resistance against the triumphant Communist revolution. In this book, perhaps, feelings rather too negative are reflected, which at present do not still grip me. Back then for me there still had not ensued a spiritual catharsis, I had not then yet lived through to the depths the spiritual experiencing of revolution and had not thought it out to the end in its religious light. As of 1923 also I have parted ways with basic hierarchical social-philosophic thoughts, as expressed in the year 1918, but my outlook is more freed and cleansed from the grip of the negative feelings, from all the hostility, even though it had blazed up in the name of a true idea and rightful faith. Revolution, godless and satanic in its nature, mustneeds be survived in experience, spiritually deepened and religiously enlightened. And one who has not spiritually and not religiously experienced the revolution, is one who has carried off from it only a feeling of malice and hate and who thirsts only for the restoration of the revolution-begetting old life with all its falsity. One has not spiritually-religiously experienced it, who experienced it greedily. Not having spiritually experienced the revolution is that land-owner or factory-owner, who first of all thirsts for the return to him of the snatched-away estates and factories and for revenge against those, who have taken them away from him. Also not having spiritually experienced the revolution is that politician, who first of all is malevolent against those, who are not of his political party and have not brought victory for his political ideology, and who awaits the hour, when he will come to power and deal with those, which in place of him have triumphed in the revolution. Not having spiritually experienced the revolution is also that ideologue and thinker, who is filled with malice over the fact, that his ideas are attacked, and he stands ready to unite with any power, such as would avenge his non-acceptance and this shattering of his idea. Not having spiritually experienced the revolution is also that man on the street, who sees in the revolution only the destruction of his interests and the structured manner of life customary for him, and who daily awaits the restoration of these his interests and this lost lifestyle structure. Spiritually having experienced the revolution is only the one, who has seen in it his own hapless fate and the hapless fate of his people, one who has sensed in it a requital for the sins of the past, who has undergone repentance, having gone through the unmasking not only of the revolutionary, but also of the pre-revolutionary falsity, who has become conscious of the enlightening and transfiguring of life. Such an one is become already neither revolutionary nor pre-revolutionary, but rather a *trans-revolutionary man*, the man of a new era. Our counter-revolutionariness has to be trans-revolutionary, and not pre-revolutionary, affirming principles, dissimilar to those, who have triumphed during the time of the revolution, and dissimilar also to those, who triumphed prior to the revolution and led to it. A spiritual experiencing of the revolution cannot lead to a thirst for restoration, i.e. a restoring of the old world with all its untruth. The untruth of the old world led to the untruth of the revolution, and a return to it is folly, a dooming of the life of the people to an inescapable circle. It is necessary to get out of the inescapable vicious circle of revolution and reaction, to some sort of a new life, to pass over to creativity. It is impossible to oppose a "bourgeois" truth against the Anti-Christ's untruth in Communism, since in "bourgeoisness" there is no Christ, just the same as in Communism also, and the one godlessness begets the other godlessness. Communism is only the consequential deduction taken to the limit of the godless untruth of the bourgeois world.

Revolution is not an event external for me, it is but the imaging-out of something in me and transpiring within me, of my guilt, of my spiritual incapacity. If I, if each I, were sufficiently spiritually strong and had possessed a genuine might of faith, then the revolution would not have occurred, there would have rather occurred the enlightening and transfiguration of life. Granted that I -- am a "reactionary", within me is a reaction, a deep spiritual reaction against the untruth and lies, against the inhumanness and godlessness of the revolution. But it is necessary to understand the sense of this aspect of "reaction". My "reaction" aspect is not "pre-revolutionary", but rather "trans-revolutionary". This -- is a reaction against revolution, with those spiritual insights, attained as a result of an inner thinking out of the experience of the revolution, of an inner plunging the depths of this experience. This "reaction" leads indeed not to a restoration of the pre-revolutionary order of life, of the pre-revolutionary condition of spirit. The revolution has happened, it was horrible the same, as is every revolution, but it is necessary to move on towards that, what is possible after it, and not towards that, what was before it. Before it was also that, which led to it. We shall strive towards that, which will not lead to it. Revolution itself per se has to be survived in experience and dealt with, and it is impossible for it to be dealt with from the outside.

Am I on the "left" or on the "right"? It is a question, which can interest only those, imbued with an external and superficial perspective on life, those who do not have to avow a dimension of depth. Indeed, "rightness" and "leftness" derive from shiftings about on the surface. Every motion towards the heights or into the depths cannot be something either "right" or "left". External motion along the surface of life, a falling away from the depths, has led peoples already to bloody dissension and to unprecedented catastrophe. I however desire, that there should begin movement into the depths and into the heights. This is why I am totally not of the "right" and totally not of the "left". It is impossible to squeeze my thoughts into these old and inadequate categories. The difference and oppositions between "rightness" and "leftness" only but deepen the divisions in mankind and fan malevolent feelings. It is necessary to seek truths and what is rightfully just, to seek God, and not "rightness" nor "leftness", not for "rightist" and not for "leftist" interests. Truth does not know the categories of "rightness" and "leftness", it is not amenable with those wicked instincts, which blaze round "rightness" and "leftness". In the world has to occur a great spiritual reaction against the grip and dominance of politics, against the lust for political power, against the raging of political passions. Politics ought to occupy its own subordinate, second-stage place, ought to cease to define the criteria of good and evil, ought to give way to spirit and spiritual aims. The dominance of politics, just like the dominance of economics, is a distortion of the hierarchical ordering of life. People become good or evil, devoted to God's truth or fallen away from it, not because they are monarchists or republicans, aristocrats or democrats, adherents of a bourgeois order or of a socialistic order. At the surface level of life is ignited the struggle of passions and interests, and therein is situated the lust for political dominance amidst the establishing of external criteria and values. But, indeed, deeper and more spiritual criteria of values ought to hold the predominant place and subjoin for itself, ought to overshadow onto the secondary plane the prevailing political criteria of values, there ought to be surmounted in the world the dictate of politics, from which the world is smothering and shedding blood. Truly, unification ought to occur in the world along a different principle, a different criterion. Spiritual life anew ought to occupy its proper hierarchically predominant place. People ought to unite first of all along spiritual, and not political tokens and principles. And then only in the world will occur a spiritual renewal. The grip of the external societal aspect over the human soul ought to have limits set to it.

All these thoughts have tormented me over these years, and I considered it necessary to formulate them within this postscript, in order that the ideas of my book should be comprehended in true a light. It is impossible that these ideas should serve to benefit any sort of wicked political aims. Human society possesses eternal foundations, and these foundations speak to the eternal, and not merely temporal and transitory of the past and present. The spiritual consideration of events, transpiring in the world over the last years, affirms the truth of an historical pessimism, which has firm groundings in Christian propheticism and which I long since already confess. This austhere historical pessimism frees us from all the earthly utopias and illusions of the modern societal outlook. But it does not free us from the duty to realise with all our powers the truth of Christ. It is not easy to conquer the radical evil of human nature and the nature of the world, and the ultimate victory over evil represents a transfiguration of the world, "a new heaven" and "a new earth". But consequently it does not mean, that we have to consent to the power of evil and to evil power, nor that our will should not be directed to the maximum of truth in life.

29 March 1923

Berlin

Spirits of the Russian Revolution:

Gogol/Dostoevsky/L. Tolstoy

(1918, Moscow-Peterburg,"Russkaya mysl'")

Klepinina # 299.

We are lost. What are we to do?
Into the field the devil evidently doth take us,
Spinning us round and round every which way.
Pushkin (*Besy/Devils*)

Introduction

A terrible catastrophe has happened with Russia. It has fallen into a dark abyss. And for many it begins to seem, that the unified and great Russia was merely a phantasm, that in it was not an authentic reality. Not easily is detected the connection of our present with our past. The expression of face for Russian people has quite changed, in some few months it has been rendered unrecognisable. At superficial a glance it would seem, that in Russia has happened a turnabout unprecedented in its radicalism. But deeper and more pervasive a perception would tend to discern in Russia the revolutionary spirit of old Russia, of spirits, long since detected within the creativity of our great writers, of devils, long since already having taken hold within Russian people. Much of the old, the long since familiar appears merely under a new guise. The lengthy historical path leads to revolutions, and in them are discernable national particulars even then, when they inflict a grievous blow to the national might and the national dignity. Each people has its own style of revolution, just as it has its own conservative style. The English Revolution was national, just the same as the French Revolution was national. In them can be recognised the past of England and of France. Each people makes its revolution with that spiritual baggage, which accumulated in its past, it carries over into the revolution its own sins and vices, but likewise also its own capacity for sacrifice and for enthusiasm. The Russian Revolution is anti-national as regards its character, it has turned Russia into a breathless corpse. But in this also its anti-national character is reflected national particulars of the Russian people, and the style of our unhappy and ruinous revolution -- is Russian a style.

Our old national ills and sins have led to revolution and have defined its character. The spirits of the Russian Revolution -- are Russian spirits, though used also by our enemy to our doom. Its phantasmic aspect -- is characteristically Russian an obsession. Revolutions, transpiring upon the surface plane of life, never essentially change nor alter anything, they merely uncover the ills, hidden within the organism of the people, and anew they rearrange all the same elements, and the old images appear in new dressings. Revolution to a remarkable degree is always a masquerade, and if the masks be stripped off, one can then meet up with the old recognisable faces. New souls are begotten only later, after a profound regeneration and pondering of the experience of the revolution. On the surface everything seems new in the Russian Revolution -- new expressions of face, new gestures, new costumes, new formulas dominate life; those, who were below, have come out on top, and those who were on top, have fallen below; holding power are those, who were the persecuted, and persecuted are those, who held power; slaves have become boundlessly free, and the free in spirit are subjected to violence. But try to penetrate beneathe the surface coverings of revolutionary Russia into the depths. There you will recognise the old Russia, you will meet with the old, the familiar faces. The immortal images of Khlestakov [Gogol's "Revizor", alt. "Inspector General"], Peter Verkhovensky [Dostoevsky's "Besy" -- "The Possessed", alt. "The Devils"] and Smerdyakov [Dostoevsky's "Brothers Karamazov"] at every step are to be met with in revolutionary Russia and in it they play no small a role, they have vaulted to the very heights of power. The metaphysical dialectics of Dostoevsky and the moral reflection of Tolstoy define the inner course of the revolution. If one look deep into Russia, then behind the revolutionary struggle and the revolutionary phraseology it is not difficult to discern the Gogolesque snouts and mugs. Every people at whatever the moment of its existence is still living in various times and in various centuries. But there is no people, in which have been brought together such different ages, which have so combined the XX Century with the XIV Century, as has the Russian people. And this contrast of differing ages is the source of the unhealthiness and hindrance to wholeness in our national life.

To great writers are always revealed images of national life, images having significance both essential and non-transitory. Russia, as discerned by its great writers, the Russia of Gogol and Dostoevsky can be found also in the Russian Revolution, and in it you run afoul of basic values, as foreordained by L. Tolstoy. In the images from Gogol and Dostoevsky, in the moral evaluations of Tolstoy it is possible to seek for the enigmas of those calamities and misfortunes, which revolution has brought to our native land, the knowledge of the spirits, possessive within the revolution. With Gogol and Dostoevsky there were literary perspicacious insights, ahead of their time. Russia revealed itself variously to them, their literary efforts differed, but both with the one and with the other there was something truly prophetic for Russia. Something pervasive in its very essence, in the very innermost nature of Russian man. Tolstoy as artist is for our purposes not of interest. Russia, as revealed in his great artistic ability, tends within the Russian Revolution to decompose and die. He was a literary artist of the static aspects of the Russian lifestyle, that of the nobility and the peasantry, whereas the eternal however revealed itself to him, as an artist, only in the elementary national aspects. Tolstoy was more cosmic, than anthropogenic. But in the Russian Revolution there was revealed, and in its own way there triumphed, another Tolstoy -- the Tolstoy of moral values, with Tolstoyism as characteristic for Russian world-concepts and world-views. Many are the Russian devils, which revealed themself to Russian writers or obsessed them, -- the demon of lies and substitution, the demon of equality, the demon of disgrace, the demon of denial, the demon of non-resistance and many many another. All these -- these nihilistic devils, have long since been tearing at and lacerating Russia. At the centre for me stand the perspicacious insights of Dostoevsky, who prophetically revealed all the spiritual groundings and moving principles of the Russian Revolution. I begin however with Gogol, whose significance in this regard is less clear.

I. Gogol in the Russian Revolution

Gogol belongs to the most enigmatic of Russian writers, and still little has been done for an understanding of him. He is more enigmatic than Dostoevsky. Dostoevsky himself did much by way of revealing all the contraries and all the abysses of his spirit. It is apparent, how the devil is at war with God in his soul and in his creativity. Gogol however hid himself and took to the grave with him the whatever unsolved secret. There truly in him is something vexing. Gogol -- is the sole Russian writer, in whom there was a taste for the magical, -- he artistically bestows credence to the active workings of the dark and evil magical powers. This, actually, came to him from the West, from Catholic Poland. A "Terrible Vengeance" is replete with suchlike magical an aspect. But in more subtle forms this magicism is there also within "Dead Souls" and "Revizor". Gogol was quite exceptional in his powerful sensing of evil. And he did not find the consolations, that Dostoevsky found in the image of Zosima and in the attachment to Mother-Earth. With him there is not at all those glued leaflets, nowhere a salvation from all the demonic grimaces surrounding him about. The old school of Russian critics failed totally to sense the horrid aspect in Gogol's artistry. And indeed where could they have gotten a feel for Gogol! Their rationalistic enlightenment guarded them from perceiving and understanding such horrid aspects. Our critics were too "progressive" of an image of thought, they did not believe in the unclean spirits of evil. They wanted to utilise Gogol only for their own utilitarian-societal aims. They indeed always utilised the creativity of the great writers for utilitarian-societal preaching. The first to have sensed the frightful aspect of Gogol was a writer of different a school, of different sources and of different a spirit -- V. V. Rozanov. He is not fond of Gogol and writes about him with evil a feeling, but he understood, that Gogol was an artist of evil. And here is what first of all mustneeds be ascertained -- the creativity of Gogol is a literary artistic revelation of evil as a principle both metaphysical and inward, not of evil societal and outward, such as might be ascribed to political backwardness and lack of enlightenment. Gogol was not given to see images of good and artistically render them. In this was his tragedy. And he himself was frightened by his exclusive seeing of images of evil and the monstrous. But that which derived from his spiritual crippling tended to issue forth in the acute aspect of his artistry of evil.

The problem of Gogol was addressed only by that religio-philosophic and artistic current, which assumed significance among us at the beginning of the XX Century. It had been the accepted thing to read Gogol as the founder of the realist trend in Russian literature. The strangeness of Gogol's creativity was explained away exclusively, in that he was being satirical and that he depicted the falseness of the old Russia under serfdom. They tended to look at everything extraordinary in Gogol's artistic mannerisms. And yet in Gogol's creativity they saw nothing problematic, because in general they tended to see nothing as problematic. To the Russian critics all seemed clear and easy to explain, all was rendered simple and cramped down towards an elementary utilitarian aim. It truly can be said, that the critical school of Belinsky, Chernyshevsky, Dobroliubov and their successors had in view the inner meaning of Russian great literature and they lacked the ability to evaluate its artistic revelations. There had to happen a spiritual crisis, there had to be shaken all the foundations of the traditional intelligentsia world-view, in order for the creativity of the Russian great writers to be revealed anew. Then only was there rendered possible an approach to Gogol. The old view on Gogol as a realist and satiricist demands a radical review. Now already, after all the complexifying of our psyches and our thought, it is quite clear, that the view of the literary old-believers on Gogol fails to get atop the Gogol problem. To us it seems monstrous, how they could see realism within "Dead Souls", a work incredible and unprecedented. The strange and enigmatic creativity of Gogol cannot be relegated away as a social satire, exposing the times and transient vices and sins of pre-Reform Russian society. Dead souls do not have an obligatory and inseparable connection with the serf-era way of life, not the Revizor Inspector General -- with pre-Reform officialdom. And now at present, after all the reforms and revolutions, Russia is full of dead souls and inspectors general, and the Gogolesque images have not died, have not faded away into the past, as have the images from Turgenev and Goncharov. The artistic modes of Gogol, which least of all can be termed realistic, and which represent unique an experiment, dismembering and distorting apart the organic wholeness of actuality, reveal something very essential for reforms and revolutions. That inhuman boorishness, which Gogol espied, is not merely a product of the old order. not explicable by reasons social and political, on the contrary, -- it tended rather to beget everything, that was vile in the old order, it imprinted itself upon the political and social forms.

Gogol as an artist was ahead of his time in anticipating the modern analytic trends in art, evidenced in connection with the crisis in art. He was a predecessor to the art of A. Bely and Picasso. In him were already those perceptions of actuality, which led to Cubism. In his artistry is already the Cubist dismembering of the living being. Gogol already saw those monstrosities, which Picasso artistically later caught sight of. But Gogol introduced a deception, since he veiled over his demonic content with a laugh. Of the newer Russian literary artists after Gogol, a most gifted one of them -- is Andrei Bely, for whom ultimately the murkiness of the image of man has become submerged in the cosmic whirlwind. A. Bely does not see an organic beauty within man, just as Gogol does not see it. In much he tends to follow upon the literary artistic methods of Gogol, but he does tend also to make quite new achievements in the area of forms. Gogol had already subjected to analytic dismemberment the organically whole image of man. With Gogol there are no human images, there is only snouts and grimaces, only the monstrosities, similar to the habitual monstrosities of Cubism. In his creativity there is a killing off of man. Gogol had not the ability to provide positive human images and he suffered much over this. He tormentedly sought for the image of man and he did not find it. On all sides formless and unhuman monstrosities surrounded him. In this was his tragedy. He believed in man, he sought for the beauty of man and he did not find it in Russia. In this was something unspeakably tormentive, this could lead to madness. In Gogol himself there was a sort of spiritual disjointedness, and he bore within himself some sort of unsolved secret. But it is impossible to fault him for this, that in place of the image of man he instead saw in Russia Chichikov, Nozdrev, Sobakovich, Khlestakov, Skvoznik-Dmukhanovsky and suchlike monstrosities. His great and implausible gift was to reveal the negative sides of the Russian people, its dark spirits, all that which in it was inhuman, distortive of the image and likeness of God. He was terrified and wounded by this unrevealedness of the human person in Russia, this abundance of the elemental spirits of nature, in place of people. Gogol -- was infernal the literary artist. Gogol's images -- are shredded bits of people, and not people, they are the grimaces of people. It is not his fault, that in Russia there were so few images human, genuine persons, so many lies and pseudo-images, false substitutes, so much ugliness and more ugliness. Gogol suffered terribly from this. His gift of insight into the spirit of triteness -- was woesome a gift, and he fell victim to this gift. He discerned the intolerable evil of triteness, and this haunted him. With A. Bely the image of man is also lacking. But he belongs already to a different era, in which faith in the image of man has become uncertain. This faith was still there in Gogol. Russian people, intent upon revolution and putting great hopes in it, tended to believe, that the monstrous images from Gogol's Russia would disappear, when the revolutionary storm would cleanse us from every defilement. In Khlestakov and Skvoznik-Dmukhanovsky, in Chichikov and Nozdrev they saw only images of old Russia, the results of autocracy and serfdom. In this was an error of the revolutionary consciousness, incapable of penetrating into the depths of life. In the revolution has been revealed all that selfsame old, eternally-Gogolesque Russia, the unhuman, semi-beastly Russia of vile mugs and snouts. In the insufferable revolutionary triteness there is an eternally Gogolesque aspect. In vain have proven the hopes, that the revolution would reveal in

Russia the human image, that the human person would rise up to his full stature, with the collapse of the autocracy. Among us they were too accustomed to put the blame on the autocracy, all the evil and darkness of our life they wanted to impute to this. But by this they cast off from themself as Russian people the burden of responsibility, and inclined themself to irresponsibility. There is no longer the autocracy, but the Russian darkness and the Russian evil have remained. The darkness and evil are lodged down deeper, not in the social externals of the people, but in its spiritual core. There is no longer the old autocracy, but autocracy as before rules in Russia, as before there is no respect for man, for human dignity, for human rights. There is no longer the old autocracy, the old officialdom, the old police, but bribery as before is a basis of Russian life, its underlying constitution. Bribery has become more widespread, than ever. A grandiose profit is to be made off the revolution. The scenes from Gogol are being played out at every step in revolutionary Russia. There is no longer the autocracy, but as before Khlestakov pawns himself off as an important official, and as before all tremble before him. There is no longer the autocracy, but Russia as before is full of dead souls, and as before there is a marketing with them. Khlestakov's audacity at every step that he takes is to be felt in the Russian revolution. But now Khlestakov has risen to the very summit of power and has far more a basis, than of old, to say: "the minister of foreign affairs, the French ambassador, the English, the German ambassador and I", or: "and curious a thing how they happen to be looking for me in the vestibule, when I am not yet even awake: counts and princes jostle and flutter about there, like bumblebees". The revolutionary Khlestakovs with great plausibility could say: "who's in charge of this place? Many of the general sort appear to be volunteers just starting out, but it depends, it could be, -- no, just consider... There's no other way -- it's up to me. And at this very moment down on the streets are couriers, couriers, couriers... imagine it for yourself, thirty-five thousand couriers!" And the revolutionary Ivan Aleksandrovich then takes over the managing of the department. And when he passes by, "tis simply an earthquake, all tremble and shake, like leaves". The revolutionary Ivan Aleksandrovich grows irritated and shouts: "I have no love for joking, and I'm warning all in the back about it... I mean it! There's no one I won't see... I'm everywhere, everywhere". We hear these Khlestakov tantrums every day and at every step. All tremble and shake. But, knowing the history of the old and eternal Khlestakov, in the depths of their souls they expect, that the gendarme will come in and say: "On orders just arrived from the Peterburg official, he demands to see you at once". The fear of counter-revolution, pervading the Russian revolution, also bestows the Khlestakov character a revolutionary impertinence. This constant expecting of the gendarme exposes the illusory and fraudulent aspect of the revolutionary attainments. But there is no mistaking the externals. The revolutionary Khlestakov appears but in a new costume and calls himself otherwise by different a name. But he essentially remains the same. The thirty-five thousand couriers can be the representatives of the "Soviet of Workers and Soldiers Deputies". And this changes nothing. At its core rests the old Russian lie and deception, long since espied by Gogol. Estrangement from the depths renders all movements too facile. In the presently prevailing and ruling powers there is little, just the same of the ontological, of the genuinely existing, as there was in Gogol's Khlestakov. Nozdrev says: "This is the boundary! Everything, that you see along this side, -- all this is mine, and even along the other side, all that forest out there of bluish a tint, and everything that is beyond the forest, -- is all mine" ["Dead Souls", Ch. 4]. In large part the adaption to the revolution has something of Nozdrev to it. The mask replaces the person. Everywhere are the masks and the two-facedness, the grimaces and the scraps of a man. An incorrigible falseness of being rules the revolution. All is illusory. Phantasmic are all the parties, phantasmic all the authorities, phantasmic all the heroes of the revolution.

Nowhere is it possible to sense a firm footing, nowhere is it possible to catch sight of clear an human face. This phantasmic aspect, this non-ontological aspect is begotten of falsehood. Gogol revealed it within the Russian element.

Chichikov as before rides the Russian land and deals in dead souls. But he rides along not slowly in the carriage, instead, he dashes about in courier rail-cars and everywhere dispatches telegrams. The selfsame element operates a new a tempo. The revolutionary Chichikovs buy up and resell non-existent riches, they operate with fictions and not realities, they transform into a fiction all the whole economic life of Russia. Many of the degrees of the revolutionary authority are totally Gogolesque in their nature, and in the enormous masses of ordinary people they meet with Gogolesque a response. In the revolutionary element is detected a colossal swindling knavery, dishonesty as a sickness of the Russian soul. Our whole revolution seems to represent an haggling over the people's soul and the people's dignity. All our revolutionary agrarian reform, the SR and the Bolshevistic, represents an official meddling and hindrance. It operates with dead souls, it derives the people's wealth upon an illusory, unreal basis. Within it is the Chichikov audacity. In our heroic summertime of an agrarian revolution there was something truly Gogolesque. There was likewise no little of a Manilovschina [from character Manilov, cf. "Dead souls", Ch. 2] during the first period of the revolution and during the revolutionary provisional government. But "Dead Souls" possesses also a profound symbolic meaning. All the ugly mugs and grimaces along the Gogol line are manifest basically of a deadening numbness of Russian souls. The deadening numbness of souls makes possible the Chichikov resemblances and encounters. This prolonged and lengthy numbed deadening of souls is sensed also in the Russian revolution. And therefore possible within it becomes this shameless haggling, this naked deception. The revolution itself per se did not create this. The revolution -- is a great manifestor, and it manifested merely that, which lay concealed in the depths of Russia. The form of the old order held in check the manifestation of many Russian traits, kept them within the limits of restraint. The downfall of these old time-worn forms has led to this, that Russian man is ultimately proven to be unruly and stark nakedly shown to be so. The evil spirits, which Gogol caught sight of in their static form, have broken free and are having an orgy. Their grimaces evoke a shuddering in the body of suffering Russia. For the Khlestakovs and Chichikovs there is now an even greater scope of opportunity, than there was in the time of the autocracy. And a becoming free of them presupposes a spiritual regeneration of the people, a turnabout within it. The revolution has not produced such a turnabout. A true spiritual revolution in Russia would involve a liberation from that deceitful lying, which Gogol saw within the Russian people, would involve a victory over that illusory and substitutive aspect, begotten of the deceitful lie. Within the lie there is a facile irresponsibility, it is not connected with anything substantial, and upon lies can be constructed very bold revolutions. Gogol revealed dishonesty as an age-old Russian trait. This dishonesty is connected with the failure of the developing and revealing of the person within Russia, with the stifling of the image of man. With this also is connected the inhuman triteness, with which Gogol overwhelms and smothers us and with which he himself was overwhelmed. Gogol saw into Russia more deeply than did the Slavophils. He had a strange sensing of evil, which the Slavophils lacked. In the eternally Gogolesque Russia the tragic and the comic are interwoven and intermixed. The comic appears as a result of confusion and substitution. This confusion and interweaving of the tragic and the comic is there also in the Russian revolution. It is all based upon confusion and substitution, and much in it therefore assumes the nature of a comedy. The Russian revolution is a tragi-comedy. This -- is the finale of the Gogol legacy. And, perhaps, the most gloomy and hopeless thing in the Russian revolution -- is the Gogolesque aspect in it. What there is in it from Dostoevsky bears more glimmerings of hope. But Russia mustneeds get free from the grip of the Gogolesque ghoulishness.

II. Dostoevsky in the Russian Revolution

If Gogol, set within the context of the Russian revolution, is not at once directly apparent and the very positing of this theme possibly evokes doubts, then in Dostoevsky nevertheless it is impossible not to see a prophet of the Russian revolution. The Russian revolution is impelled by those themes, which Dostoevsky had a premonition of and which with genius he put in sharp contrast. Dostoevsky had the ability to reveal in depth the dialectics of Russian revolutionary thought and to derive from it its final conclusions. He did not stay merely at the surface level with the socio-political ideas and constructs, he penetrated down into the depths and uncovered the metaphysics underlying the Russian revolutionary aspect. Dostoevsky discovered, that the Russian revolutionary aspect is a phenomenon both metaphysical and religious, not merely political and social. And thus religiously he succeeded to grasp the nature of Russian socialism. Russian socialism involves the question, does God exist or not. And Dostoevsky foresaw, how bitter would be the fruits of Russian socialism. He laid bare the element of Russian nihilism and Russian atheism, a thing quite unique, and dissimilar to that of the West. There was with Dostoevsky a gift of genius in revealing the depths and discerning the final limits. He never remains at the middle, never halts merely dwelling upon the transitory conditions, but instead always pushes towards the finalative and the ultimate. His creative artistic act is apocalyptic, and in this he is -- truly a Russian national genius. The method of Dostoevsky is different, from that of Gogol. Gogol was more perfected the literary artist. Dostoevsky was first of all a great psychologist and metaphysician. He reveals the evil and the evil spirits inwardly within the soul-emotive life of man and inwardly within his dialectics of thought. The whole entire creativity of Dostoevsky is an anthropological revelation -- the revelation of the human depths, not only the soul-emotive, but also the spiritual depths. To him are revealed those human thoughts and those human passions, which represent not merely the psychology, but rather the ontology of human nature. In Dostoevsky, as distinct from Gogol, there remains always the image of man and there is revealed the inward fate of man. Evil does not ultimately destroy the human image. Dostoevsky believes, that by way of inner catastrophe, evil can make the transition over to good. And therefore his creativity is less frightful, than the creativity of Gogol, which leaves almost no kind of hope.

In Dostoevsky, the greatest Russian genius, it is possible to study the nature of human thinking, its positive and its negative polarities. The French -- are dogmatists or sceptics, dogmatists at the positive polarity of their thought and sceptics at the negative pole. The Germans -- are mystics or criticists, mystics at the positive pole and criticists at the negative. *The Russians however -- are apocalyptic or nihilistic, apocalyptic at the positive pole and nihilist at the negative polarity.* The Russian instance -- is very extreme and very difficult. The French and the Germans can create culture, since culture can be created both dogmatically and sceptically; it is possible to create it also mystically and critically. But it is difficult, very difficult apocalyptically and nihilistically to create culture. Culture can have at its depths the dogmatic and the mystical, but it presupposes, that beyond the median vital process is admitted something of value, that it possesses a significance not only absolute, but also relative. The apocalyptic and nihilistic self-derived feeling casts aside all the average median vital process, all the historical steps, has no wish to know of any sort of values of culture, it aspires towards the end, the limit. These two opposites readily transfer each into the other. The apocalyptic easily transitions into nihilism, can prove nihilistic in regard to the greatest values of earthly historical life, to all culture. Nihilism however can undetectedly take on an apocalyptic hue, can appear as a demanding of the end. And with Russian man, so shifting back and forth and entangled are the apocalyptic and the nihilistic, that it becomes difficult to distinguish these polarly opposed principles. It is not easy to determine, why Russian man is wont to negate the state, culture, native land, normative morals, science and art, why he demands an absolute impoverishment: whether from his apocalyptic or his nihilistic aspect. Russian man can wage a nihilistic pogrom like an apocalyptic pogrom; he can lay himself bare, tear away all the veilings and stand naked as it were, since he is a nihilist and denies everything, and since also, because he is filled with apocalyptic presentiments and anticipates the end of the world. In Russian sectarians the apocalyptic is interwoven and compounded with nihilism. The same thing occurs with the Russian intelligentsia. The Russian searchings for the truths of life always assumes an apocalyptic or nihilistic character. This -- is a profoundly national trait. This creates the grounds for confusion and substitutes, for pseudo-religion. Within Russian atheism itself there is something of the spirit of the apocalyptic, totally dissimilar to Western atheism. And in Russian nihilism there are pseudo-religious features, a sort of religion in reverse. This tempts and leads many into error. Dostoevsky revealed down deep the apocalypticism and nihilism within the Russian soul. And therefore he also guessed, what sort of character the Russian revolution would assume. He perceived, that revolution would not at all signify for us, what it does in the West, and therefore it would be more terrible and more extreme than Western revolutions. The Russian revolution -- is a phenomenon on religious a basis, it is a deciding of the question about God. And this mustneeds be understood in more profound a sense, than is conceived in the anti-religious character of the French revolution or the religious character of the English revolution.

For Dostoevsky, the problem of the Russian revolution, of Russian nihilism and socialism, as a religious problem essentially -- involves the question about God and about immortality. "Socialism is not only the workers question, or of the so-called fourth estate, but is predominantly an atheistic question, the question of the modern embodiment of atheism, the question of the Babylonian Tower, constructed not in the name of God, not for reaching heaven from earth, but rather for the contraction of heaven onto earth" (Brothers Karamazov"). It can even possibly be said, that the question on Russian socialism and nihilism -- is a question apocalyptic, oriented towards the all-destroying end. Russian revolutionary socialism has never thought of itself as transitional a condition, as a temporary and relative form in the building up of society, it has always thought of itself as ultimate a condition, as the kingdom of God upon earth, as the solving of the question of the fates of mankind. This -- is not an economic and not political a question, but rather a question of spirit, a religious question. "And indeed the Russian boys up til now, what about them? Here, for example, in a local wretched tavern, here they tend to come, seated off in a corner...What are they deciding? The issues of the world, no less: is there a God, is there immortality? And for those not believing in God, well, these talk about socialism and about anarchism, about the redoing of the whole of mankind along new a form, all indeed the same result, all the same questions, only with different a conclusion". These Russian boys never have been capable of politics, of constructing and building up societal life. Everything has gotten jumbled up in their heads, and having repudiated God, they refashioned God out of socialism and anarchism, they wanted to rework the whole of mankind into new a form and in this have seen not relative, but rather absolute a task. Russian boys have been nihilistic-apocalyptic. They started it, having the endless conversations in the wretched taverns. And it would have been difficult to believe, that these conversations about replacing God by socialism and anarchism and the reworking of the whole of mankind into new a form could become a defining power in Russian history to shatter apart Great Russia. The Russian boys long since already have proclaimed, that everything is permitted, if there is no God and no immortality. Bliss upon earth would remain then as the goal. Upon this basis also has emerged Russian nihilism, which to many naive and well-intentioned people has seemed innocent and cute a phenomenon. Many even saw in it a moral truth, though distorted by mental error. Even Vl. Solov'ev did not understand the dangers of Russian nihilism, when he jokingly formulated the credo of the Russian boys in suchlike a manner: "Man is descended from the ape, therefore, let us love one another". Dostoevsky tended to penetrate deeper into the secret corners of Russian nihilism and he sensed the danger. He revealed the dialectics of Russian nihilism, its hidden metaphysics.

Ivan Karamazov shews himself a philosopher of Russian nihilism and atheism. He proclaims a revolt against God and against God's world out of very lofty motives -- he cannot reconcile himself with the tears of a tormented innocent child. Ivan puts Alyosha a question very acute and radically so: "Tell me straight out, I implore thee, answer: imagine, that thou art building up the edifice of human fate with the aim at the final end to bring happiness to people, to finally give them peace and tranquility, but for this it would have to be needful and inevitable to torment of all only one tiny creature, this child here beating itself with tiny fist upon the breast, and upon its unavenged tears set the foundation of this edifice; would thou consent to be the architect upon these conditions?" Ivan posits here the age-old problem as regards the price of history, about the acceptability of those sacrifices and sufferings, by which are bought the creation of states and cultures. This is preeminently a Russian question, an accursed question, which Russian boys have brought out against world history. In this question has been lodged all the Russian moral pathos, sundered off from its religious sources. Upon this question has morally been based the Russian revolutionary-nihilistic revolt, which Ivan also proclaims: "In the final result this world of God's -- I do not accept, and though also I know, that it exists, I do not accept it at all. It is not God that I do not accept, it is the world created by Him, God's world that I do not accept and cannot consent to accept". "For what purpose is it to recognise this devilish good and evil, when it involves so much? Indeed the whole world of knowledge cannot then stand up to those tears of a child to dear-God". "I renounce entirely the higher harmony. It is not worth the tiny tears of that one tortured child, beating its breast with its little fist and praying in its fetid hovel with its unexpiated tears to dear-God... I don't want, that they should suffer more. And if the suffering of children goes towards the filling up of that sum of sufferings, which be necessary as the price for truth, then I declare beforehand, that all the truth be not worth such a price... I don't want the harmony, out of love for mankind I do not want it... And indeed they have valued the harmony too dearly, we cannot at all afford the price of entry. And therefore I hasten to return back my ticket for entry... It is not God that I do not accept, but rather only the ticket to Him that I most respectfully return back". The theme, presented by Ivan Karamazov, is complex, and within it are interwoven several motifs. Dostoevsky from the lips of Ivan Karamazov pronounces judgement upon the positivist theories of progress and upon the utopias of a coming harmony, erected upon the sufferings and tears of prior generations. All the progress of mankind and all its perfect arrangement stand for nothing as regards the unhappy fate of each man, his final death. In this is a Christian truth. But the acute question, posited by Ivan, nowise consists in this. He presents his question not as a Christian, believing in a Divine meaning to life, but rather as an atheist and nihilist, denying a Divine meaning to life, seeing only absurdity and untruth from limited an human perspective. This -- is a revolt against the Divine world-order, a non-acceptance of human fate, as determined by the design of God. This -- is a dispute of man with God, a refusal to accept suffering and sacrifice, to grasp the meaning of our life as atonement. The whole course of revolt in the thoughts of Ivan Karamazov is a manifestation of extreme rationalism, is a denial of the mystery of human fate, inscrutable within the bounds and limits of the estrangement within this earthly empirical life. To rationally grasp within the limits of earthly life, why an innocent child should be tormented, is impossible. The very positing of such a question -- is atheistic and godless. Faith in God and in the Divine world-order is a faith in the deep and hidden meaning of all the sufferings and tribulations, having fallen to the lot of every being in its earthly wanderings. To wipe away the tiny tears of the child and ease its sufferings is a deed of love. Yet the pathos of Ivan is not in love, but in revolt. In him there is a false sentimentality, but not love. He is in revolt, because he does not believe in immortality, because for him all consists in this meaningless empirical life, full of suffering and grief. A typical Russian boy, he has mistaken the negative Western hypotheses for axioms and has put his trust in atheism.

Ivan Karamazov -- is a thinker, a metaphysician and psychologist, and he provides a deep philosophic grounding to the troubled experiences of an innumerable number of Russian boys, the Russian nihilists and atheists, socialists and anarchists. At the core of the question of Ivan Karamazov lies a sort of false Russian sensitivity and sentimentality, a false sort of sympathy for mankind, leading to an hatred towards God and the Divine purpose of worldly life. Russians all too readily become nihilistic rebels out of a false moralism. The Russian takes God to task over history because of the tears of the child, returns back the ticket, denies all values and sanctities, he will not tolerate the sufferings, wants not the sacrifices. Yet he however does nothing really, in order to lessen the tears, he adds to the quantity of flowing tears, he makes a revolution, which is all grounded upon uncountable tears and sufferings. Within the nihilistic moralism of Russian man there is no moral forging of character, no moral austerity in the face of the terrors of life, no capacity for sacrifice nor disavowing of the arbitrary. The Russian nihilistic moralist thinks, that he loves man and sympathises for man, moreso than does God, that he will straighten out God's design for man and the world. An incredible pretentiousness is characteristic of this emotional type of soul. From the history, over which the Russian boys have taken God to task as a result of the tears of the child and the tears of the people, and out of their excited conversations in the taverns was born the ideology of the Russian revolution. At its core lies atheism and a disbelief in immortality. The disbelief in immortality begets a false sensitivity and sense of sympathy. The endless declamations about the sufferings of the people, about the evil of the state and culture, grounded upon these sufferings, issued forth from this God-contending source. The desire itself to ease the suffering of the people was proper, and in it can be discovered the spirit of Christian love. But this also led many into error. They failed to notice the confusions and substitutions, situated at the core of Russian revolutionary morals, with the Anti-Christ temptations set within the revolutionary morals for the Russian intelligentsia. Dostoevsky did take note of this, he revealed the spiritual substrate of the nihilism, preoccupied with the welfare of the people, and he predicted, to what the triumph of this spirit would lead. Dostoevsky understood, that the great question concerning the individual fate of each man is decided completely otherwise in the light of religious awareness, and that in the darkness of the revolutionary consciousness, is a pretension to become a pseudo-religion.

Dostoevsky revealed, that the nature of Russian man is favourable a soil for the Anti-Christ temptations. And this was a genuine revelation, which also made of Dostoevsky a seer and prophet of the Russian revolution. To him was given an inner vision of the spiritual essence of the Russian revolution and Russian revolutionaries. The Russian revolutionaries, the apocalypticists and nihilists by their nature have succumbed to the temptations of the Anti-Christ, who wants to make people happy, and they thus had to lead the people tempted by them to that revolution, which has inflicted a terrible wound upon Russia and has transformed Russian life into a living hell. The Russian revolutionaries wanted a worldwide turnabout, in which would be burnt away all the old world with its evil and darkness with its sanctities and values, and upon the ash-heap would be substituted a new and graceful life for all the people and for all peoples. Upon lesser than worldwide an happiness, the Russian revolutionary could not reconcile himself. His mindset is apocalyptic, he wants the end, he wants the finishing off of history and the inception of a supra-historical process, in which will be realised a realm of equality, freedom and bliss upon earth. And this allows for nothing transitional nor relative, no sort of steps of developement of awareness. Russian revolutionary maximalism is also an unique, and distorted apocalyptics. Its reverse side always manifests itself as nihilism. The nihilistic destroying of all the manifold and relative historical world inevitably spreads also to the absolute spiritual foundations of history. Russian nihilism does not admit of the very source of the historical process, which is lodged within the Divine actuality, it rebels against the Divine world-order, in which history takes shape with its steps, with its unavoidable hierarchical aspect. In Dostoevsky himself there were temptations of Russian maximalism and Russian religious populism. But in him there was also a positive religious power, a power prophetic, helping him to reveal the Russian temptations and unmask them. The "Legend of the Grand Inquisitor", as related by the Russian atheist Ivan Karamazov, is in its power and depth comparable only with sacred writings, and it reveals the inner dialectics of the Anti-Christ temptations. The fact, that Dostoevsky gave Catholic a guise to the Anti-Christ temptations, is inessential and has to be ascribed to its defects and weaknesses. The spirit of the Grand Inquisitor can appear and can act in various guises and forms, is capable to utmost a degree of re-embodiment. And Dostoevsky distinctly understood, that within revolutionary socialism the spirit of the Grand Inquisitor is active. Revolutionary socialism is not an economic and political teaching, is not a system of social reforms, -- it has pretension to be a religion, it is a faith, in opposition to the Christian faith.

The religion of socialism in its following after the Grand Inquisitor consents to all the three temptations, rejected by Christ in the wilderness, rejected in the name of the freedom of the human spirit. The religion of socialism consents to the temptation to turn stones into bread, the temptation of the social miracle, the temptation of the kingdom of this world. The religion of socialism is not the religion of the free sons of God, it renounces the birthright of man, it is a religion of the slaves of necessity, of the children of dust. The religion of socialism speaks with the words of the Grand Inquisitor: "All will be rendered happy, all the millions of people". "We shall compel them to work, but in the hours free from toil we will arrange their life like child's play, with childish songs, a chorus, with innocent dances. We shall absolve also the sin, for they are weak and lacking in strength". "We shall give them the happiness of the weak-powered beings, as also they were fashioned". The religion of socialism says to the religion of Christ: "Thou art proud of Thine select ones, but Thou hast only the select, but we will comfort all... With us all will be happy... We shall convince them, that only then also wilt they become free, when they renounce their freedom". The religion of socialism, just like the Grand Inquisitor, reproaches the religion of Christ for having insufficient love for people. In the name of love for people and a sympathy for people, in the name of the happiness and bliss of people upon earth, this religion rejects the free, the God-imaged nature of man. The religion of heavenly bread -- is an aristocratic religion, -- is a religion of the select, the religion of "the tens of thousands of the great and strong". The religion, though, of "the remaining millions, numerous like the sands of the sea, the weak" -- is a religion of earthly bread. This religion has inscribed upon its banners: "feed them, and then ask virtues of them". Dostoevsky with genius foresaw the spiritual foundations of the socialistic anthill. He religiously perceived, that the socialistic collectivism is a pseudo-sobornost', a pseudo-communality, a pseudo-church, which conveys with it the death of the human person, such as involves the image and likeness of God in man, and is thus a killing of the freedom of the human spirit. Dostoevsky spoke very powerful and fiery words against the religion of socialism. And he also sensed, that for Russians socialism is a religion, not politics, not a matter of social reforms and upbuilding. That the dialectics of the Grand Inquisitor can be applied to the religion of socialism, and were applied by Dostoevsky himself, is evident from this, that many of the revolutionaries of his tend to repeat the train of the thoughts of the Grand Inquisitor. The same was said also by Peter Verkhovensky, and on the same basis was constructed the Shigalev aspect. These thoughts were there already with the hero of "Notes from the Underground", when he spoke about "the gentleman with a derisive and retrograde physiognomy", who would topple over all the coming social felicity, all the well-constructed anthill of the future. And the hero of "Notes from the Underground" sets in opposition to this socialistic anthill rather instead the freedom of the human spirit. Dostoevsky -- is a religious foe of socialism, he exposes the religious lie and the religious danger of socialism. He is one of the first to have sensed within socialism the spirit of the Anti-Christ. He understood, that in socialism the spirit of the Anti-Christ seduces man under the guise of good and of love for mankind. And he understood, however, that it is easier for Russian man, than for Western man, to succumb to this temptation, to be seduced by the twofold image of the Anti-Christ as regards the apocalyptic aspect of its nature. The hostility of Dostoevsky towards socialism nowise signifies, that he was an adherent and defender of whatever a "bourgeois" order. He further on uniquely confessed an Orthodox socialism. But the spirit of this Orthodox socialism has nothing in common with the spirit of revolutionary socialism, is the opposite to it in everything. Grounded in the soil and unique as a Slavophil, Dostoevsky saw in the Russian people an antidote against the temptations of the revolutionary and atheistic socialism. He confessed a religious populism. I tend to think, that all this religious-populistic, soil-Slavophil ideology of Dostoevsky was part of his weak, rather than powerful side, and was in contradiction to his foresights of genius as an artist and metaphysician. At present it can straight out be said, that Dostoevsky was mistaken, that in the Russian people there has not proven an antidote against the Anti-Christ temptations in that religion of socialism, which the intelligentsia has imparted to it. The Russian revolution has ultimately shattered all the illusions of a religious populism, as well as of every populism. But the illusions of Dostoevsky himself did not hinder him from revealing the spiritual nature of Russian religious socialism and predicting the consequences, to which it would lead. Within "The Brothers Karamazov" is provided the inner dialectics, the metaphysics of the Russian revolution. In "The Possessed" is provided an image of the realisation of this dialectics.

Dostoevsky revealed the obsessiveness, the element of demonic possession in the Russian revolutionaries. He perceived, that within the revolutionary element what was active was not man himself, that what impelled it was not human spirits. In these days with the revolution having been realised, when one happens to read through "The Possessed" ("Besy"), one then tends to shudder. It is almost incredible, how it could have been possible to have foreseen and predicted all so much. In a smallish city, on outwardly small a scale long since already the Russian revolution was played out and had its spiritual primal-foundations revealed, its spiritual primal-images presented. The Nechaev affair served as a source for the plot in "The Possessed". Our leftist circles have tended to see in "The Possessed" a caricature, almost a lampoon on the revolutionary movement and revolutionary figures. "The Possessed" was included on an index of [forbidden] books, condemned by the "progressive" mindset. To grasp all the depth and truth in "The Possessed" was possible only in the light of a different mindset, that of a religious consciousness; this depth and this truth tend to elude the positivistic consciousness. If this novel be viewed as realistic, then much in it is inaccurate and does not correspond to the activity of that time. But all the novels of Dostoevsky are inaccurate, they were all written via a depth, which it is impossible to catch sight of at the surface level of actuality, they were all prophetic. And they mistook the prophetic for a lampoon. At present, after the experiencing of the Russian revolution, even the foes of Dostoevsky have to admit, that "The Possessed" -- was prophetic a book. Dostoevsky perceived with spiritual a sight, that the Russian revolution would namely be such and could not be otherwise. He foresaw the inevitability of the demonic-possession within the revolution. The Russian nihilism, active within the Russian Khlysty element, could not but be a devil-possession, a frenzied and circular whirling. This frenzied circular whirling is also described in "The Possessed". There it occurs in a small town. Now it occurs throughout all the vast Russian land. And there has begun this frenzied circular whirling from the same spirit, from these same principles, from which it came into that same small town. Now the purveyors of the Russian revolution have declared to the world a Russian revolutionary messianism, that they will bring to the peoples of the West, dwelling in a "bourgeois" darkness, light from the East. This Russian revolutionary messianism was discerned by Dostoevsky and perceived by him as a negative variant of the positive, as a distorted apocalyptics, as an upside-down and turned around variant of a positive Russian messianism, not actually revolutionary, but religious rather. All the heroes of "The Possessed" in this or another form preach a Russian revolutionary messianism, all of them are obsessed with this idea. With the vacillating and equivocating Shatov are shiftings about between a Slavophil consciousness and a revolutionary consciousness. And the Russian revolution is full of such Shatovs. All of them, just like the Shatov of Dostoevsky, are deliriously ready to cry out, that the Russian revolutionary people -- is a *God-bearing* people, but in God they do not believe. Certain of them would want to believe in God -- and cannot; for the majority however it would suffice, that they believe in a God-bearing revolutionary people. In Shatov as the typical populist there transposes revolutionary elements with reactionary "Black Hundredist" elements. And this is characteristic. Shatov can be both an extreme leftist and an extreme rightist, but both in one and the other instance he remains a lover of the people, a democrat, believing first of all in the people. The Russian revolution is full of such Shatovs; in all of them one cannot figure out, where their extreme leftist and revolutionary aspect ends and where begins their extreme rightist and reactionary aspect. They are always enemies of culture, and always they destroy the freedom of the person. This however they assert, that Russia is higher than civilisation and that no sort of law need be written for it. These people are ready to destroy Russia in the name of Russian messianism. Dostoevsky had a weak spot for Shatov, he sensed within himself the Shatov temptations. But by the power of his artistic foresight he rendered the image of Shatov repulsive and negative.

At the centre of the revolutionary demon-possession stands the image of Peter Verkhovensky. This also is a chief demon of the Russian revolution. Dostoevsky in the image of Peter Verkhovensky uncovers a still deeper level of revolutionary devil-possession, actually veiled over and invisible. Peter Verkhovensky could have had more noble a look. But Dostoevsky tore away from him the veils and laid bare his soul. And thereupon the image of revolutionary devil-possession was presented in all its ugliness. He is all atremble in shuddering from demonic possession, which draws all into a frenzy of circular whirling. He is everywhere at the centre, behind all and everything. He -- is a devil, pushing everything and with his hand in everything. But he is also himself devil-possessed. Peter Verkhovensky is first of all a man totally empty, in him there is no sort of content. The demons ultimately have taken hold in him and have rendered him their obedient tool. He ceases to be in the image and likeness of God, in him is lost already the human visage. His obsession with a false idea has made of Peter Verkhovensky a moral idiot. He has become obsessed with the idea of a worldwide restructuring, of a worldwide revolution, he has fallen for a tempting lie, has allowed the demons to take hold his soul and has lost the elementary distinction between good and evil, has become bereft of spiritual a centre. In the figure of Peter Verkhovensky we meet with a person already disintegrated, in which it is no longer possible to discern anything ontological. He is all lie and deception, and he leads all into deception, wrought into a realm of falsehood. Evil is a lying fraudulence of being, pseudo-being, non-being. Dostoevsky showed, how a false idea, seizing hold the entire man and driving him into demonic-possession, leads to non-being, to the disintegration of person. Dostoevsky was a great master in exposing the ontological consequences of false ideas, when they have taken complete hold upon a man. What sort of an idea is it that has completely taken hold of Peter Verkhovensky and brought him to the disintegration of person, transforming him into a liar and sower of lies? This is all the selfsame basic idea of Russian nihilism, of Russian socialism, of Russian maximalism, all the selfsame infernal passion for a worldwide leveling, all the selfsame revolt against God in the name of a worldwide love for people, all the selfsame replacement of the Kingdom of Christ by the kingdom of the Anti-Christ. There are many suchlike demoniac Verkhovenskys in the Russian revolution, they everywhere attempt to pull things into the demonic whirling motion, they feed the Russian people on lies and drag it toward non-being. Not always do these Verkhovenskys get recognised, not everyone has the ability to see at depth, behind the veilings. The Khlestakov revolutions are more easy to distinguish, than the

Verkhovensky ones, but these too not everyone does distinguish, amidst the throngs exalting and crowning them with glory.

Dostoevsky foresaw, that the revolution in Russia would be joyless, frightening and gloomy a thing, that there would be in it no rebirth for the people. He knew, that Fedka the convict would play no small role within it and that the *Shigalevschina, the Shigalev aspect*, would win out in it. Peter Verkhovensky has long since already revealed the value of Fedka the convict for the doings of the Russian revolution. And the whole triumphant ideology of the Russian revolution is the ideology of the Shigalevschina. It gets frightful our days to reread the words of Verkhovensky: "Our teaching in essence is a negation of honour, and the revelation of his right to be dishonourable is the easiest of all ways to win over a Russian man". And the reply of Stavrogin: "The right to be dishonourable -- yes, this will have everyone come running to us, none will hold back!" And the Russian revolution has proclaimed "the right to be dishonourable", and all everyone has gone running after it. And here no less important are the words: "Socialism among us is spread primarily by means of sentimentality". Dishonour and sentimentality -- are the fundamental principles of Russian socialism. These principles, discerned by Dostoevsky, are also triumphant in the revolution. Peter Verkhovensky saw, what sort of role in the revolution would be played by "pure swindlers". "Well, perhaps, this is a fine bunch of people, at times very profitable, but on them much time gets wasted, and demands a vigilant eye". And further on P. Verkhovensky ponders on the factours of the Russian revolution: "The chiefmost force -- the cement, binding it all together, is shame at having an opinion of one's own. How powerful this is! And this is with one who has worked, this is one who is the "dear chap" so given to toil away, that he has not a single idea of his own in his head! Aught else they would consider shameful". This was a very profound and penetrating insight into revolutionary Russia. In Russian revolutionary thought there was always "a shame at having one's own opinion". This shame among us was imputed to the collective consciousness, a consciousness regarded higher, than the personal. In the Russian revolution there has been ultimately extinguished every individual attempt at thinking, the thinking was rendered completely impersonal, relegated to the masses. Read the revolutionary newspapers, listen to the revolutionary speeches, and you will receive a confirmation of the words of Peter Verkhovensky. Regarding someone who has so toiled away over it, that "not a single idea remains in their head". Russian revolutionary messianism leaves it to the bourgeois West to have one's own ideas and opinions. In Russia all has to be collective, of the masses, impersonal. Russian revolutionary messianism, is Shigalevschina. The Shigalev aspect impels and directs the Russian revolution.

"Shigalev looked, as though he expected the destruction of the world, and not at some indefinite when according to prophecies, but quite definitely, say the morning after tomorrow, at exactly ten twenty-five". All the Russian revolutionary Marxists tend to look, as Shigalev looked, all await the destruction of the old world the day after tomorrow, in the morning. And that new world, which will arise upon the ruins of the old world, is a world of Shigalevschina. "Starting from unlimited freedom, -- says Shigalev, -- I conclude with a limited despotism. I adduce, moreover, that except for my decisive societal formula, there can be no other". All the revolutionary Shigalevs speak thus and act thus. Peter Verkhovensky formulates the essence of the Shigalevschina to Stavrogin: "To level the mountains -- is a fine thought, not ludicrous. Education is not the needed thing, enough of science! Even without science there is enough material for a thousand years, but the needed thing is to build obedience... The thirst for learning is already an aristocratic thirst. Just a bit of having a family or love, and here already is a wishing of private property. We will kill off that desire; we will allow drunkenness, slander, denunciation; we will permit unheard of depravity; we will extinguish all genius in its infancy. All to a single denominator, total equality... Only necessary is the necessary -- herein is the catchword of the earthly globe henceforth. But necessary is a knuckling under; about this we shall concern ourselves, as rulers. With slaves there have to be rulers. Total obedience, total lack of person, but once in thirty years Shigalev allows also for a convulsion, and all suddenly will begin to devour each other, up to a certain point, naturally, so that things not become boring. Boredom is an aristocratic sensation". With these stunning and prophetically forceful words Dostoevsky through the lips of P. Verkhovensky reduces it all down to the course of thought of the Grand Inquisitor. This demonstrates, that in "The Legend of the Grand Inquisitor" Dostoevsky to a remarkable degree had socialism in view. Dostoevsky uncovers all the phantasmic aspect of democracy within the revolution. No sort of a democracy exists, there rules instead a tyrannical minority. But this tyranny, unprecedented in the history of the world, will be based upon an overall compulsory leveling. Shigalevschina is also a frenzied passion for equality, pushed to its end, to its limit, to non-being. Unchecked social dreaming leads to a destruction of being with all its riches, in its fanatics it degenerates into evil. Social dreaminess is nowise innocent a thing. Dostoevsky understood this. The Russian revolutionary socialistic dreaming is also Shigalevschina. In the name of equality, this dreaming would seek to destroy God and God's world. In this tyranny and this absolute leveling, which will be the crowning point of "the developing and deepening" of the Russian revolution, will be realised the golden dreams and visions of the Russian revolutionary intelligentsia. These were dreams and visions about a Shigalevschina realm, much prettier to imagine, than has proven in actuality. Many naive and simple of soul Russian socialists, in dreaming about a social revolution, tend to get befuddled by the triumphant shouts: "Each belongs to all, and all to each. All are slaves and equal in slavery... The first step is a lowering of the level of education, of science and talents. The high level of science and talents is permitted only to the higher in aptitude, and unnecessary are the higher in aptitude!" Dostoevsky was more perspicacious, than were the acknowledged teachers of the Russian intelligentsia, he knew, that the Russian revolutionism, the Russian socialism in the hour of its triumph would have to end with these Shigalev outbursts.

Dostoevsky foresaw not only the triumph of the Shigalev aspect, but also of the Smerdyakovschina, the Smerdyakov aspect. He knew, that there would arise in Russia the lackey who in the hour of great danger for our native land would say: "I detest all of Russia", "I not only have no wish to be a military hussar, but I wish, on the contrary, the abolition of all the soldiery". To the question: "And when the hostiles arrive, who will defend us?", the revolting lackey replied: "In 1812 there was the great invasion of Russia by the French emperor Napoleon I, and a good thing if then these same French had subdued us: an intelligent nation would have subdued an extremely stupid one and annexed it to itself. There would even have been an altogether different order of things". Defeatism during wartime is also a manifestation of Smerdyakovschina. The Smerdyakov effect has led also to this, that the "intelligent nation" of the Germans is subduing the now "stupid" nation of the Russians. The lackey Smerdyakov among us was one of the first internationalists, and all our internationalism has received a Smerdyakov engrafting. Smerdyakov declared a right to be dishonourable, and behind him have flocked many. How profound of Dostoevsky this was, that Smerdyakov should be the other half of Ivan Karamazov, his reverse image. Ivan Karamazov and Smerdyakov -- are two manifestations of Russian nihilism, two sides of one and the same essence. Ivan Karamazov -- is the lofty, philosophic aspect of the nihilism; Smerdyakov -- is the lowly, its lackey aspect. Ivan Karamazov at the summits of intellectual life had to go and beget Smerdyakov at the base levels of life. Smerdyakov also brings to realisation all the atheistic dialectics of Ivan Karamazov. Smerdyakov -- reflects the inner core of Ivan. In all the masses of mankind, the masses of the people, there are more Smerdyakovs, than Ivans. There triumphs in the revolution the atheistic dialectics of Ivan Karamazov, but Smerdyakov brings it to realisation. This he did through a practical conclusion, that "all is permissible". Ivan sins in his thought, in spirit, Smerdyakov accomplishes it in deed, he embodies the idea of Ivan. Ivan commits parricide in his thoughts. Smerdyakov commits the parricide physically, in actual fact. An atheistic revolution always commits parricide, always denies the fatherly bond, always breaks the connection of son with father. And it justifies this transgression on the basis, that the father was very bad and sinful. Such a murderous attitude towards a father is always Smerdyakovschina. The Smerdyakov aspect is always a final manifestation of boorishness. Having committed in fact, that which Ivan committed in thought, Smerdyakov asks Ivan: "You yourself all the time then said, that everything is permissible, so why are you now so anxious?" This question by Smerdyakov to Ivan gets repeated in the Russian revolution. The Smerdyakovs of the revolution, having realised in deed the principle of Ivan that "all is permissible", have the basis to ask the Ivans of the revolution: "Now why are you so anxious?" Dostoevsky foresaw, that Smerdyakov bears an hatred towards Ivan, while educated in his atheism and nihilism. And this is playing itself out in our own day between the "people" and the "intelligentsia". The whole tragedy between Ivan and Smerdyakov was unique as a symbol in revealing the tragedy of the Russian revolution. The problem over the issue, whether everything be permissible for the triumph of the good of mankind, stood already before Raskol'nikov. The elder, starets Zosima, says: "Truly they have more of a dreamy fantasy about them, than do we. They think justice will be set up, but having spurned Christ, it will end with this, that the world will be drenched in blood, for blood calls for blood, and he that taketh up the sword doth perish by the sword. And were it not for the promise of Christ, they would then destroy each other even right down to the last two men on earth". These words -- are prophetic.

"People will join together, in order to take from life all, that it can give, but assuredly for the joy and happiness of this one only present world. Man will exalt himself in a spirit of a would-be godly and titanic pride and there will appear the man-god... Everyone will recognise, that he is entirely mortal, without resurrection, and he will accept death proudly and calmly, like a god. From pride he will understand, that it does him no good to complain over this, that life is but a moment, and he will love his brother without need of any reward. Love will suffice only for the moment of life, but already the consciousness alone of its momentary aspect will stoke up the fire of it such, as before previously it was spread on hopes beyond the grave and endless". It is the devil speaking these words to Ivan, and in these words is revealed Dostoevsky's tormented thought, that love for people can be godless and of the Anti-Christ. This love lies at the basis of revolutionary socialism. An image of this godless socialism, grounded upon the Anti-Christ type of love, is put forth by Versilov ["Podrostok"]: "I imagined for myself, that the fighting will have ended and the struggling wound down. After the cursings, the mud-slinging and jeers there will have settled in a calm, and people will have been left alone, like they wanted: the great former idea has forsaken them; the great source of strength, up til then having nourished and warmed them, has departed, but this was already as though the final day of mankind. And people suddenly will have realised, that they have been left altogether alone, and at once they will feel a great sense of being left orphaned... The people thus orphaned will at once nestle closer and more fondly together; they will as it were grasp hands, understanding, that now they alone only comprise all each for another! There will have vanished the great idea of immortality, having to be replaced... They will have become fond of the earth and life unrestrainedly and in that measure, in which gradually they will have become aware of their own temporary and finite aspect, and already with an especial, already not with the former love... They will awaken and hasten to kiss greeting each other, in haste to love, conscious, that the days are short, that this -- is all, that remains for them. They would work each for the other, and each would bestow his goods to all and by this alone be made happy". In this fantasy is revealed the metaphysics and psychology of a godless socialism. Dostoevsky depicts the manifestation of the Anti-Christ love. He understood, better than anyone, that the spiritual basis of socialism -- is a denial of immortality, that the pathos of socialism -- is the desire to set up the kingdom of God upon earth without God, to bring about love between people without Christ -- the source of love. And he thus reveals the religious lie of humanism in its limited forms. Humanistic socialism leads to a destroying of man in the image and likeness of God. It is directed against the freedom of the human spirit, does not tolerate the testing of freedom. Dostoevsky with an as yet unprecedented acuteness posited the religious question concerning man and posited alongside it the question concerning socialism, as regards the earthly unification and arrangement of people. He discerned this as an encounter and a confusing of Christ and the Anti-Christ within the soul of Russian man, of the Russian people. The apocalyptic aspect of the Russian people also renders this encounter and this confusion particularly acrid and tragic. Dostoevsky had presentiment, that were a revolution to happen in Russia, it would then occur via the Anti-Christ dialectic. Russian socialism would prove apocalyptic, and contrary to Christianity. Dostoevsky foresaw it farther and more profoundly than anyone. But he himself was not free from the Russian populist illusions. In his Russian Christianity there were sides, which provided a basis for K. Leont'ev to term his Christianity as rosy. This rosy Christianity and rosy populism was most of all bespoken in the images of Zosima and Alyosha, images impossible to be termed as fully successful. The great positive revelations of Dostoevsky obtain by negative a path, by way of negative an artistic dialectic. The truth, expressed by him concerning Russia, is not the sweet and rosy truth of a love and worship of the people, this -- is instead a tragic truth, a truth concerning the Anti-Christ seductions of an apocalyptic people in its spirit. Dostoevsky himself was tempted by a churchly nationalism, which impeded the Russian people from emerging out onto the world stage. Dostoevsky's worship of the people suffered its crash within the Russian revolution. His positive prophecies did not transpire. But there do transpire his prophetic foresights of the Russian temptations.

III. L. Tolstoy within the Russian Revolution

In Tolstoy there was nothing prophetic, he had presentiment of nothing and he predicted nothing. As an artist, he was oriented towards a crystalised past. Within him there was not that delicacy of perception for the dynamism of human nature, which to a supreme degree Dostoevsky had. In the Russian revolution there triumph not the literary insights of Tolstoy, but rather his moral values. L. Tolstoy, as a seeker after the truth of life, as a moralist and religious teacher, is very characteristic of Russia and of Russians. The Tolstoyans, in the narrow sense of the word, following the doctrine of Tolstoy, are few, and they represent insignificant a phenomenon. But Tolstoyism in a broader, non-doctrinal sense of the word, are very characteristic of Russian man, and determinative of Russian moral valuations. Tolstoy was not a direct teacher of the Russian leftist intelligentsia, his religious teaching was foreign to it. But Tolstoy reflected and expressed a peculiarity of the moral habits of a large part of the Russian intelligentsia, perhaps too, even of Russian man in general. Yet the Russian revolution tends to manifest its own unique triumph of Tolstoyism. Imprinted upon it is both a Tolstoy Russian moralism, and Russian amorality. This Russian moralism and Russian amorality are interconnected and are two sides of one and the same impairment of the moral consciousness. This impairment of the Russian moral consciousness I view first of all as a denial of personal moral responsibility and personal moral discipline, in a weak developement of the sense of duty and the sense of honour, in the absence of awareness of the moral value of the selection of personal qualities. Russian man does not sense himself to a sufficient degree morally involvable, and he little esteems the qualitative aspect of person. This finds its expression, in that the person senses himself submerged within the collective, the person remains as yet insufficiently developed and conscious. Such a condition of moral consciousness gives rise to a whole series of pretensions, in the orientation towards fate, towards history, the rule of authority, cultural values, unadmissible for the given person. The moral outlook of Russian man is characterised not by an healthy involvement, but rather by sick pretension. Russian man fails to sense an inseparable connection between rights and obligations, obscured for him is both the consciousness of rights, and the consciousness of obligations, he flounders within an irresponsible collectivism, in the pretension for all. For Russian man the most difficult thing of all is to sense, that he himself -- is the blacksmith forging his own fate. He has no love for qualities, uplifting the life of the person, and does not love power. Every sort of power, uplifting of life, represents for Russian man something morally suspicious, moreso evil, than good. With these peculiarities of the moral consciousness is connected also, that Russian man views the values of culture as morally suspicious. Towards the entirety of higher culture he puts forth a whole series of moral pretensions and fails to sense a moral obligation to create culture. All these peculiarities and impediments of the Russian moral consciousness present a favourable ground for the arising of the teachings of Tolstoy.

Tolstoy -- was an individualist, and very extreme an individualist. He was quite anti-societal, and for him societal problems do not exist. Tolstoy's morality is also individualistic. But from this it would be a mistake to conclude, that Tolstoy's morals rest upon a clear and firm consciousness of the person. Tolstoy's individualism is decisively hostile to the concept of the person, just as always transpires with individualism. Tolstoy fails to see the human countenance, knows not its visage, he is all submerged within the natural collectivism, which presents itself to him as life divine. The life of the person does not seem to him to be the true and divine life, this -- is the false life of this world. A true and divine life is a life impersonal, general life, in which have vanished all qualitative distinctions, all hierarchical scales. The moral consciousness of Tolstoy demands, that there should be nothing greater than man as an autonomous and qualitative being, and there should be only an all-common unqualitative divinity, equalising all and everything in the impersonal divinity. Only the total annihilating of every personal and diversely-qualitative being into an impersonal unqualitative all-commonness represents for Tolstoy a fulfilling of the law of the Master of life. The person, the qualitative is already sin and evil. And Tolstoy ultimately would want to destroy all, everything that is connected with the person and the qualitative. In him this was an Eastern and Buddhist sort of outlook, hostile to that of the Christian West. Tolstoy renders himself a nihilist out of moral zeal. His moralism is truly demonic and is destructive of all the richness of being. The egalitarian and nihilistic passion in Tolstoy impels him to the destruction of all the spiritual realities, of everything authentically ontological. The unrestrained moral pretentiousness of Tolstoy renders everything illusory, it casts under suspicion and subverts the reality of history, the reality of church, the reality of state, the reality of nationality, the reality of the person and the reality of all supra-personal values, the reality of all of spiritual life. Everything seems to Tolstoy as morally reprehensible and impermissible, everything based upon sacrifices and sufferings, towards which he exhibits a purely animal-like fear. I know of no other genius within world history, to whom was so foreign the totality of spiritual life. He is totally immersed in the corporeal -- the emotive, animate life. And the whole religion of Tolstoy is a demand for suchlike an all-common mild beastliness, free from suffering and of contentment. I know of no one in the Christian world, to whom was so foreign the very idea of redemption, so uncomprehending of the mystery of Golgotha, as was Tolstoy. In the name of happy animal-like a life he repudiated the person and repudiated every supra-personal value. Truly however, the person and supra-personal value are inseparably connected. The person only therefore also exists, because that in it is the supra-personal content of value, in that it belongs to hierarchical a world, in which exist distinctions and a scale of the qualitative. The nature of the person cannot put up with a jumbled confusion and unqualitative leveling. And the love for people in Christ is least of all a matter of suchlike a jumbled confusion and unqualitative leveling, it is infinitely deeper an affirmation of every human countenance in God. Tolstoy failed to know this, and his morality was of a lower sort morality, the pretentious morality of a nihilist. Nietzsche stands infinitely higher, has more spiritual a morality than Tolstoy. The alleged loftiness of Tolstoy's morality is a great misconception, which has to be exposed. Tolstoy in Russia hindered the engendering and developing of the morally responsible person, he impeded the selection of personal qualities, and therefore he proved an evil genius for Russia, a seducer of it. In him occurred a fatal encounter of Russian moralism with Russian nihilism and there obtained a religio-moral justification of Russian nihilism, which seduced many. In him the Russian populism, so fateful for the destiny of Russia, received a religious expression and moral justification. Almost all the Russian intelligentsia have admitted Tolstoy's moral values as very lofty, to the far extent of which a man might ascend. They have further reckoned these moral values as even too lofty and therefore they reckoned themself unworthy of them and incapable to ascend to their lofty height. There are but few who call into doubt the loftiness of Tolstoy's moral consciousness. And simultaneously with the acceptance of this Tolstoy moral consciousness, it leads by it to pogroms and the destruction of the greatest sanctities and values, of the greatest spiritual realities, the death of the person and the death of God, inverted and converted into an impersonal deity of the average sort. There has with us not yet been scrutinised with sufficient seriousness and depth the tempting falsity of Tolstoyan morals. The antidote against it would have to be the prophetic insights of Dostoevsky. The Tolstoyan morals have emerged triumphant within the Russian revolution, but not by those idyllic and love-abundant paths, proposed by Tolstoy himself. And Tolstoy himself, actually, would have been horrified by this embodiment of his moral values. But he was desirous of much, too much of that, which is happening now. He conjured up those spirits, which rule the revolution, and was himself obsessed by them.

Tolstoy was a maximalist. He repudiated every historical precedent, he did not want to allow for any sort of stages within historical developement. This Tolstoyan maximalism exists within the Russian revolution -- it is impelled by the destructive morals of maximalism, it breathes hatred towards everything historical, and in a spirit of Tolstoyan maximalism the Russian revolution has wanted as though to rip each man out of the world historical wholeness, to which he organically belongs, to transform him into an atom, so as to plunge him abruptly into the impersonal collective. Tolstoy repudiated history and historical tasks, he renounced the great historical past and did not want a great historical future. The Russian revolution has been faithful to him in this, it represents a cutting off from the historical legacies of the past and the historical tasks of the future, seemingly intent, that the Russian people not live historical a life. And just the same as with Tolstoy, in the Russian revolution this maximalist repudiation of the historical world is begotten of a frenzied egalitarian passion. Let there be an absolute leveling, even if it be a leveling right down to nothingness! The historical world -- is hierarchical, in it -- are distinctions and distances, in it -- are qualitative variances and differentiation. All this is so odious for the Russian revolution, just as it was for Tolstoy. It has wanted as though to create a world dull and grey, all-alike, simplified, bereft of all qualities and all beauties. And Tolstoy taught this as an higher truth. The historical world is disintegrating into its atoms, and the atoms compulsively unite into an impersonal collective. "Without annexations and indemnities" is also an abstract negative of all positive historical tasks. Yet truly indeed all historical tasks presuppose "annexations and indemnities", they presuppose the struggle of concrete historical individualities, they presuppose the composing and dissolution of historical entities, the flourishing and decay of historical bodies.

Tolstoy managed to engraft into the Russian revolution an hatred towards everything historically individual and historically manifold. He was an expression of that side of the Russian nature, which sustained an abhorrence towards historical power and historical glory. In an elementary and simplistic manner regarding this, he was accustomed to moralise about history and to transpose upon historical life the moral categories of individual life. By this he morally subverted the possibility for the Russian people to live historical a life, to fulfill its historical destiny and historical mission. He morally prepared the historical suicide of the Russian people. He clipped the wings of the Russian people as regards being historical a people, he morally poisoned the wellsprings of every impulse towards historical creativity. The world war played itself out lost for Russia, because in it took hold the Tolstoyan moral attitude towards war. Tolstoy's morals disarmed Russia and betrayed it into the hands of the enemy. And this Tolstoyan non-resistance, this Tolstoyan passivity enchants and attracts those, who sing hymns to the accomplishing by revolution of the historical suicide of the Russian people. Tolstoy was also an expresser of the non-resisting and passive side in the character of the Russian people. The Tolstoyan morals has debilitated the Russian people, deprived it of valour within a severe historical conflict, but also has left it remaining with an untransfigured animal-like nature of man with merely the most elemental of instincts. It has killed in the Russian brood the instinct for power and glory, but has left remaining the instinct for egoism, envy and malice. This morality is powerless to transform human nature, but it can weaken human nature, bring it into decline, sap it of the creative instincts.

Tolstoy was an extreme anarchist, an enemy of anything to do with the state on moral-idealist grounds. He repudiated the state, as based upon sacrifices and sufferings, and he saw in it a source of evil, which for him led to coercive force. The Tolstoyan anarchism, the Tolstoyan hostility towards the state likewise has prevailed among the Russian people. Tolstoy proved an expresser of the anti-state, anarchistic instincts of the Russian people. He provided those instincts with a moral-religious sanction. And he is one of the culprits in the destruction of the Russian state. Tolstoy likewise was hostile to all culture. Culture for him was based upon untruth and violence, in it the source of all evils in our life. Man by his nature is essentially good and decent and is inclined to live according to the law of the Master of life. The arising of culture, just like the state, was a downfall, a falling away from the natural divine order, and hence a start of evil, of violence. Totally foreign to Tolstoy was a sense of Original Sin, of radical evil for human nature, and therefore he felt unneeded was a religion of redemption, and he did not understand it. He was lacking in a sense of evil, since he was also lacking in a sense of freedom and the autonomy of human nature, he lacked a sense of the significance of the person. He was immersed in an impersonal and non-human nature and within it he sought for the sources of Divine truth. And in this Tolstoy proved to be a wellspring source for all the philosophy of the Russian revolution. The Russian revolution is hostile to culture, it seeks to revert the life of the people back to a natural condition, in which it sees an unmediated truth and bliss. The Russian revolution seeks as it were to destroy the whole of our cultural segment, to drown it within the natural darkness of the people. And Tolstoy is one of the culprits in the destruction of Russian culture. He has morally subverted the possibility for cultural creativity, has poisoned the wellsprings of creativity. He poisoned Russian man by a moral reflection, which has rendered him powerless and incapable for historical and cultural activity. Tolstoy -- is a genuine poisoner of the wellsprings of life. The Tolstoyan moral reflection is a genuine poison, toxic, destructive to every creative energy, and undermining as regards life. This moral reflection has nothing in common with the Christian sense of sin and the Christian demand for repentance. For Tolstoy there is neither sin, nor repentance, for the regenerating of human nature. For him there is only a debilitating and graceless reflection, which is an obverse side of the revolt against the Divine world-order. Tolstoy idealised the common people, saw therein the source of truth and he deified physical toil, in which he sought salvation from the meaninglessness of life. But in him there was a disdainful and contemptuous attitude towards all spiritual toil and creativity. All the acrid Tolstoyan criticism was always directed against the cultural segment. These Tolstoyan values likewise have won out in the Russian revolution, which extols to the heights the representatives of physical toil and disdains representatives of spiritual a toiling. The Tolstoyan populism, Tolstoy's denial of a division of labour is posited as a basis of the moral judgements of the revolution, if one can speak about its moral judgements. Tolstoy has indeed no less a significance for the

Russian revolution, than Rousseau had for the French revolution. True, the violence and bloodshed would have horrified Tolstoy, he presented the realisation of his ideas by other paths. But Rousseau also indeed would have been horrified by the doings of Robespierre and the revolutionary terror. But Rousseau nevertheless bears responsibility for the French revolution, as does Tolstoy for the Russian revolution. I even tend to think, that the teachings of Tolstoy were more destructive, than were the teachings of Rousseau. Tolstoy did this by rendering morally impossible the existence of Great Russia. He caused much in the destroying of Russia. But in this suicidal deed he was a Russian, in him was expressed fatal and woesome Russian features. Tolstoy was one of the Russian seductions.

Tolstoyanism in the broad sense of the word -- is an inward Russian danger, assuming the guise of a lofty good. Only but inwardly destructive of Russian strength can be this seductive and false good, a pseudo-good, this idea of a graceless sanctity, a pseudo-holiness. The tempting aspect in the Tolstoyan teaching is a radical impulse for perfection, for a perfect fulfilling of the law of the good. But this Tolstoyan perfection is so thus destructive, so nihilistic, so hostile to all values, so incompatible with whatever the creativity, because this perfection -- is graceless. In the sanctity, to which Tolstoy aspired, there was a terrible gracelessness, a God-forsakenness, and therefore this -- is a false, an evil holiness. A grace-endowed sanctity cannot commit such acts of destruction, cannot be nihilistic. In genuine saints there was a blessed aspect of life, there was mercy. This blessed aspect of life and this mercy were there first of all in Christ. In the spirit of Tolstoy, however, there was nothing of the spirit of Christ. Tolstoy demands an instantaneous and total realisation of the absolute, of the absolute good in this earthly life, subject as it is to the laws of sinful nature, and it fails to take into account the relative, is destructive of everything relative. He thus sought to tear away every human being from the world totality and plunge it into the void, into the nothingness of a negative absolute. And absolute life is rendered into but an elementary beast-like life, transpiring in physical toil and the satisfying of the most simple needs. In such a negative absolute, desolate and nihilistic, the Russian revolution also seeks to plunge all Russia and all the Russian people. The ideal of a graceless perfection leads to nihilism. The denial of the rights of the relative, i.e. of all the manifold aspects of life, of all the steps of history, causes in the final end a separation from the sources of absolute life, from the absolute spirit. As a religious genius, the Apostle Paul once perceived the whole danger of allowing Christianity to become transformed into an apocalyptic Jewish sect and he instead led Christianity into the currents of world history, having acknowledged and religiously sanctioned the right of relative steps. Tolstoy first of all was in revolt against the work of the Apostle Paul. All the falsity and phantasmic aspect of Tolstoyanism tended with an inevitable dialectic to unfold within the Russian revolution. In the revolution, the people is living out its seduction, its errors, its false values. This is much instructive, but this instruction is bought at too dear a price. It is necessary to get free from Tolstoy as moral an instructor. The overcoming of Tolstoyism as such represents a recovery of spiritual health for Russia, its return from death to life, to the possibility of creativity, the possibility of fulfilling its mission in the world.

IV. Conclusion

Russian man is inclined to experience everything transcendentally, and not immanently. And this can easily become slave-like a condition of spirit. But in any event, this -- is an indicator of insufficient spiritual courage. The Russian intelligentsia in its enormous masses never conceived for itself as immanent -- the state, the church, the fatherland, the higher spiritual life. All these values seemed to it transcendentally remote and evoked in it hostile a feeling, as something foreign and threatening. The Russian intelligentsia never experienced history and historical destiny as immanent to itself, as its own particular affair and therefore it led the process against history as against an act of violence being committed upon it. The transcendent experiences in the masses of the people was accompanied by a feeling of religious blessing and submissiveness. And thereupon was possible the existence of Great Russia. But this transcendent experiencing has not passed over into an immanent experiencing of sanctity and value. All has remained transcendent, but it evokes towards itself no longer a reverent and submissive attitude, rather instead an attitude nihilistic and rebellious. The revolution is also a debilitatingly catastrophic transition from a reverent veneration of the transcendent, over to a nihilistic revolt against the transcendent. An immanent spiritual maturity and liberation via the revolution is not attained. Too many have tended to see in the immanent morals and the immanent religion of L. Tolstoy the onset of a spiritual maturity. But this has been a terrible error. In actuality, the immanent mindset of Tolstoy was a nihilistic negation of all those sanctities and values, which earlier had been venerated as transcendent. But this is merely a return to the initial slavery. Suchlike a revolt is always a slave's revolt, in it is no freedom nor sonship to God. Russian nihilism is also an incapacity immanently and freely to experience all the riches and values of God's world, an inability to sense oneself in a filial relationship to God and possessing all the legacy of world history and of kindred history. The Russian apocalyptic aspect frequently involves the fervent expectation of a miracle, which somehow should halt life of this alienation from all the riches and surmount the debilitating transcendent rift. Whereof the creative immanent developement becomes so difficult for Russians, since their sense of historical succession is so weak. There is a sort of inner sickness to the Russian soul. This sickness has terrible negative consequences, but in it is revealed also something positive, inaccessible to Western peoples of more immanent a tendency. To Russian great writers were revealed abysses and limits, the likes of which remain hidden for Western people, moreso restricted and restrained by their immanent emotive discipline of soul. The Russian soul is more delicately sensitive to mystical wisps, it meets up with spirits, which stay hidden from the staid Western soul. And the Russian soul succumbs to temptations, readily falls into confusion and gets taken in by substitutes. It is no accident that the forebodings of the Anti-Christ -- is a Russian foreboding chiefly. A feel of the Anti-Christ and the terror over the Anti-Christ has been there in the Russian people, down at the bottom and with Russian writers, at the very summit of spiritual life. And the spirit of the Anti-Christ has tempted Russians such, as never it has tended to tempt Western peoples. In Catholicism there has always been a strong sensing of evil, of the devil, but almost no sensing of the Anti-Christ. The Catholic soul has tended to represent a sort of fortification, defending against the Anti-Christ waftings and seductions. Orthodoxy has not transformed its soul into such a sort of fortification, it has left it more openly vulnerable. But the apocalyptic aspect is experienced by the Russian soul passively, and not actively. Active weapons for struggle against the spirits of the Anti-Christ there are not, these weapons have not been made ready. There has been no armour, no shield and sword, no knight's forging of the soul. The Russian struggle against the Anti-Christ is always a withdrawal, an experience of terror. And too many, not having withdrawn from the seductions, have instead succumbed to the seductions, have gotten mixed up, have been taken in by the substitute. Russian man is situated in the grip of a false morals, a false ideal of the righteous, perfect and holy life, which has weakened him in the struggle with temptations. Dostoevsky revealed this false morality and false sanctity and predicted their consequences. Tolstoy however preached them.

Russian revolutionary morals represents quite unique a phenomenon. It was formed and crystalised among the leftist Russian intelligentsia over the course of a series of decades and happened to gain prestige and allure among broad circles of Russian society. The average man of the Russian intelligentsia was accustomed to bow before the moral image of the revolutionaries and their revolutionary morals. He was ready to admit himself unworthy of the moral heights of this revolutionary type. In Russia there took form a special cult of revolutionary sanctity. This cult has its saints, its sacred tradition, its dogmas. And for a long time every doubting of this sacred tradition, every criticism of these dogmas, every non-reverential attitude towards these saints led to an excommunication, as exclusion not only on the part of the revolutionary societal opinion, but also from the side of the radical and liberal societal opinion. Dostoevsky fell victim to this ostracisation, since he first saw into the lie and substitution in revolutionary sanctity. He perceived, that revolutionary moralism has as its reverse side a revolutionary amoralism and that the seeming semblance of revolutionary sanctity with that of the Christian is a deceptive resemblance of the Anti-Christ to Christ. The moral degeneracy, with which the 1905 revolution ended, inflicted somewhat a blow to the prestige of revolutionary morals, and the halo of revolutionary sanctity became tarnished. But the actual healing, on which some had hoped, did not occur. The sickness of the Russian moral consciousness was too prolonged and serious. The healing can ensue only after the terrible crisis, when the whole organism of the Russian people will come close to death. We live during days of this almost mortal crisis. Now even for people half-blind much is more apparent, than after 1905. Now "Vekhi" would not be met with in so hostile a manner in the broad circles of the Russian intelligentsia, as happened in the time, when it appeared. Now even those begin to admit the truth of

"Vekhi", those who formerly reviled it. After the demonic coursing of the revolution, the sanctity of the Russian revolutionary intelligentsia does not come off so canonically indisputable. The spiritual recovery of Russia mustneeds be sought in an inward exposing of this revolutionary pseudo-sanctity and getting free of its bewitchment. Revolutionary sanctity is not a genuine sanctity, this -- is a fraudulent sanctity, a deceptive semblance of sanctity, a mere substitute. The outward persecutions, instigated by the old powers against the revolutionaries, the outward sufferings, which they happened to undergo, much enabled this deceptive and seeming appearance of sanctity. But in the revolutionary sanctity there has never occurred a true transformation of human nature, a second spiritual rebirth, a victory over inward evil and sin; never within it have been set tasks of the transformation of human nature. Human nature has remained the same old thing, it has dwelt in slavery to sin and wicked passions and has sought to attain to a new and higher life purely by external and material means. But a man, deluded with a false idea, is capable of enduring outward deprivations, want and sufferings, he can be ascetic in this not because, that by the power of his spirit he overcomes his sinful and servile nature, but rather because, that obsessed with a single idea and a single purpose it crowds out for him all the richness and multiplicity of existence and renders him impoverished in nature. This -- is a graceless asceticism and a graceless poverty, a nihilistic asceticism and a nihilistic poverty. The traditional revolutionary sanctity -- is a godless sanctity. It is a godless pretension to attain sanctity via the human alone and in the name of the human alone. Upon this path becomes crippled and stumbles the image of man, since the image of man -- is the image and likeness of God. The revolutionary morality, the revolutionary sanctity -- is profoundly the opposite of Christianity. This morality and this sanctity make pretense to substitute in for and to replace Christianity, a Christianity having its faith in the filial sonship of man to God and in graced gifts, gotten for man through Christ the Redeemer. Revolutionary morality is hostile to Christianity the same, just like the Tolstoyan morality, -- one and the same lie and switching poisons and saps the strength in both. The deceptive externals of the revolutionary guise of sanctity has been sent the Russian people as a temptation and a testing of its spiritual powers. And Russian people herein have not held up under this testing. Honestly attracted by the revolutionary spirit, they do not see the realities, they fail to discern the spirits. The deceptive, fraudulent and twofold images tempt and entice. The Anti-Christ allures, the Anti-Christ morals, the Anti-Christ sanctity all influences and entices Russian man. For Russian people, spiritually captivated by the revolutionary maximalism, there are peculiar experiences, very akin to Jewish apocalypticism, that apocalyptic aspect which was surmounted and overcome by the Apostle Paul and the Christian Church. The victory over this Judaic apocalyptic aspect also rendered Christianity a world historical force. Russian apocalypticism includes within it the greatest of dangers and temptations, it can direct all the energy of the Russian people onto a false path, it can hinder the Russian people from fulfilling its vocation in the world, it can render the Russian people into a people non-historical. The revolutionary apocalyptics sidetracks Russian people from the realities and precipitates them into a realm of phantasms. Getting free from this false and unhealthy apocalyptics does not mean the destroying of all the apocalyptic consciousness. In Russian apocalyptics lie concealed also positive possibilities. In the Russian revolution are being extirpated the Russian sins and the Russian temptations, things discerned by the Russian great writers. But great sins and great temptations can only be with a people great in its possibilities. The negative is a caricature of the positive. The Russian people has fallen low, but in it lie concealed great possibilities and to it can be revealed great distances. The idea of a people, the intent of God concerning it remains there even after the failing and fall of the people, having betrayed its aims and subjecting its national and state dignity to utmost humiliations. A minority can remain faithful to the positive and creative idea of the people, and from it can begin a renewal. But the path to renewal lies through repentance, through an awareness of sins, through a cleansing of the spirit of the people from spirits demonic. And the thing first of all necessary is to begin to discern spirits. Old Russia, in which there was much evil and ugliness, but likewise also much good and beauty, is dying away. The new Russia, born of its death pangs, is still enigmatic. It will not be such, as the figures and the ideologues of the revolution imagine it to themself. It will not be uniform in its spiritual visage. In it will be more harshly divided and opposed the Christian and the anti-Christian principles. The Anti-Christ spirits of the revolution will beget their dark domain. But the Christian spirit of Russia also has to manifest its strength. The power of this spirit can operate in the minority even if the majority falls away from it.

N. A. Berdyaev, 1918

Bibliographic and Translator Comments

The 1978 edition of the "*Nicolas Berdiaev: Bibliographie*", by Tamara Klepinina, (YMCA Press, Paris), remains the "authoritative" bibliographic sourcebook regarding Berdyaev's published writings: books, journal articles, collective anthologies (sborniki), etc., -- nearly 500 items total! Klepinina catalogued the 1st edition bibliographic data not only of Berdyaev's works published in Russian, but also of translations published in a surprising number of other languages. Under the classification schemata of the several types of works, Klepinina assigned an unique number to each work, whether Russian or otherwise. This has been of immense benefit!

Translation of Berdyaev primary materials into English largely ceased in the early 1950's, with the demise of Berdyaev's generation. We have since attempted to rectify this situation via the Internet with our own translations of the hitherto untranslated primary works, roughly 150+ items to date, as well as "Online Indices". In doing so, for codification purposes we have referred to each work by its "Klepinina#", or "Kl.#" for short, along with year and language. The Internet, however, is very fluid a medium, with possible duration and durability for a posted work likely only but ephemeral, given the rapid changes in technological formats. Quite mindful of Berdyaev's "New Middle Ages" theme, formally printed books offer greater chances of longevity for the long term survival of serious works, -- hence our present volume, and others in future...

Berdyaev's present tome, "*The Philosophy of Inequality*" [Kl.#20], was initially published in 1923 in Berlin, Obelisk Press, under the Russian title/subtitle: "*Filosofia Neravenstva. Pis'ma ko nedrugam po sotsial'noi filosofia*". Berdyaev's "*Postscript*", itself written in 1923, indicates that he began writing this work in the Spring/Summer of 1918, some mere few months after the onset of the Communist/Bol'shevik "October Revolution" [N.S. 7 November 1917]. A 2nd Russian language edition was published by YMCA Press Paris in 1970. This was subsequently included by the Paris

YMCA Press within the year 1990 Volume #4 of Berdyaev's "Collected Works", p. 253-592, from which the present English translation has been made. Also it should be noted, -- in 1976 a French language translation by Constantin & Anne Andronikof was published under the title, "*La Philosophie de l'Inegalite*", Lausanne, l'Age d'Homme.

Berdyaev's incisive essay, "*Spirits of the Russian Revolution*" [Kl.#299], was of course not part of his book, "The Philosophy of Inequality". We include it, as quite pertinent, and also as an example of Russian republishing of the post 1990's repatriated Berdyaev, -- volumes that contained several works all in one, under but one title... Bibliographic details of Berdyaev's essay, "*Spirits of the Russian Revolution*" (Russian title "*Dukhi russkoi revoliutsii*") are as follows: Article was originally published in the periodical "Russkaya mysl'", jul. 1918, p. 39-73 (Berdyaev's last article in this Moscow-Peterburg journal); (Klep.# 299). Simultaneously it was included the same year in an anthology by various authors of articles concerning the Russian Revolution, entitled "*Iz glubiny. De profundis*", Moscow-Peterburg, Russkaya mysl', 1918, 273 p.; text was subsequently reprinted by YMCA Press, Paris, 1967, 333 p.; (Klep. # 57,1). The article was also recently republished in the Berdyaev anthology tome of articles entitled, "*Padenie svyaschennogo russkogo tsarstva: publitsistika 1914-1922*", Astrel', Moscow, 2007, c. 775-807.

Finally, through an oversight, we neglected to provide the Klepinina#, -- Kl.#4, in our 2014 Vilnius Press publication of Berdyaev's 1910 "*The Spiritual Crisis of the Intelligentsia*" -- the first as such translation of the work into English.

***

Some further comments and observations on both this book, and Berdyaev's subsequent thought, seem in order. The "*Philosophy of Inequality*" was composed in the literary format of "Open Letters", akin in theme to public lectures, as adapted from historical models. During this period and in preceeding years Berdyaev had a tendency to "recycle" his published journal articles into a sbornik/collection subsequently published together in a book. But "The Philosophy of Inequality" was a book written in entirety as such, written as one long, passionately fiery outburst.

If one were searching for a simple slogan to express the theme and gist of Berdyaev's "Philosophy of Inequality" -- there comes to mind the title of one of Nietzsche's books: "Twilight of the Idols" (though the "idols" that Nietzsche assailed were somewhat different). Berdyaev assails the "idols" of ideas and ideologies that have sapped and weakened Russia from within, resulting in the miserable state of conditions that beset Russia by early-mid 1918: the Communist-Bolshevik "1917 Oktyabr Revolution" [N.S. November 7th] and the beginnings of the social-political upheavals that followed, with Russia dropping out of World War I, widespread misery and uncertainty rampant everywhere amidst heightened passions and distrust, hatred and brutality, such as resulted in the Bolshevik's vicious execution of the tsar and his family in July 1918, and the tragic reality of the Russian Civil War. Mindful of Carlyle, revolutions do tend to devour their makers (a college primer from a long generation ago used to be Crane Brinton's "The Anatomy of Revolution", tracking the common patterns in 4 different revolutions). The Russian Revolution would continue on to consume the liberal Cadet Party, the Socialist Revolutionaries Party, the various anarchists, the Bolshevik-kindred "Menshevik" Social Democrats, and Trotsky too, and in time followed by the 1939 "show-trial" purges of the "Old Communists" by Stalin... not to mention along the way deliberate famines and the efficiently bloody legacy of Derzhinsky and his ilk.

One can well imagine that Berdyaev initially penned "The Philosophy of Inequality" as a sort of private journal, of thoughts as it were "against the current", not knowing, whether either he or this book would survive the turbulent times. Fortunately, Berdyaev was expelled from Russia in 1922 by the Bolsheviks. From the book's "Postscript", penned in 1923 in Berlin, we learn that Berdyaev began writing "The Philosophy of Inequality" in the Spring-Summer of "early" 1918. Why would Berdyaev append a brief "Postscript" summation to "this very emotional book", a "Postscript" written 5 years later abroad in exile, rather than opening the book instead with an "Introduction"? And why, many years later, somewhat unhappy with it, did he not set about revising it, as he did with some other other articles? Why, in a sense, did he stand back with a certain sense of awe at what he had once written, nowise daring to to touch it anew? For the very reason that the text, bursting forth in all its passionate intensity must first speak for itself, all the acute feelings of utmost repugnance, revulsion and disgust experienced within the actual revolutionary atmosphere -- must first be experienced in the pathos of the reader, himself/herself. Only then, hopefully, can begin the "spiritual catharsis", which as Berdyaev notes, "back then for me... still had not ensued".[1]

---

[1] Berdyaev many years later reminisces in his [posthumously published] autobiography, "Samopoznanie": "During the early beginning of the year [19]18 I wrote a book, "The Philosophy of Inequality", which I am not happy with, I consider it in much to be unjust and not genuinely expressive of my thought.... But it mustneeds be said, that in this very emotional book, reflecting a stormy reaction against those days, I remained true to my love for freedom. I likewise also at present think, that equality is a metaphysically empty idea and that social sense of truth ought to be based upon the dignity of each person, and not upon equality". Samopoznanie, YMCA Press, Paris, 2nd ed. 1983, p. 264-265.

There is something to be said for textual fidelity in matters of translation. And in this regard, the 1949 English translation of Berdyaev's autobiography by K. Lampert, under the title "Dream and Reality", has over the years come under correctly strong criticism by the noted scholar and specialist, Dr. George Kline, as a "dramatically revised and abridged version" of the Russian original. And indeed, in our "Samopoznanie" passage just given, there is a certain degree of literary license in K. Lampert's rendering of the original Russian "которую не люблю" into "which I dislike most among all those I have written" ["Dream and Reality", MacMillan, New York, 1951, p. 227]. More accurate a rendering certainly would read: "which I am not fond of / not happy with".

Berdyaev's 1922 banishment from Russia represents a transition point both in his literary work and in his thought, from as it were his "formative period" into his "mature phase". Nearly all of his books written abroad have long since been translated into English, and indeed many another language. But many of his books, written while still in Russia, have for long a while remained inaccessible both in Russia and in the West. This changed in the 1990's, when Berdyaev and other "forbidden" Russian emigre authors were "repatriated" to Russia. A delightful deluge of Berdyaev's hitherto inaccessible texts in Russian became available both in Russia and in the West, indeed, often with several books compressed together under single an original title. But in the English speaking West, these "formative early period" Berdyaev texts have remained untranslated, -- which the current translator is attempting to rectify. Furthermore, we find an evidence of the "transition point" in Berdyaev's thought, when he states in our present text's "Postscript", that: "As of 1923 also I have parted ways with basic hierarchical social-philosophic thoughts, as expressed in the year 1918,...". This represents a departure from many of the traditional assumptions and approaches, -- those of the hierarchical degrees of reality inherent to Neo-Platonism, and the emphasis of the Hegelian Absolute in the German Idealist tradition, both which heavily influenced various currents of Russian aesthetic and religious thought, such as Sophiology. And somewhere, in one of his many books, Berdyaev describes his reorientation as a sort of "Copernican Revolution". It is a reorientation away from the "moribundly-perfect" stasis of the Platonic Realm of Ideas and the Neo-Platonic semi-pantheistic "One" (το ‛εν), as well as from the Hegelian Absolute, the whole for which its component elements become secondary or even less in significance. Berdyaev's reorientation is towards the concrete individual, the existing living person, its integrality (tselost'), indeed its integrity and dignity. Only from this starting point, amidst the striving towards a "Christian anthropology", can there be an active perception of man as both micro-cosmos and micro-theos within his existential situation. And thus, Berdyaev is very much a Christian existentialist philosopher.[2]

---

[2] But what are the structural beliefs underlying Berdyaev's thought, as an Orthodox Christian? Very significant is the heritage deriving from the IV OEcumenical Council at Chalcedon in 451 A.D. In the Christology of the Orthodox Church, Jesus Christ is the 2nd Person of the MostHoly Trinity, in a mysteried "hypostatic union" of 2 natures: perfect "by nature" God and perfect "by nature" Man. "Hypostasis" (ʽυποστασις) is a Greek theological term for "person". Jesus is consubstantial, of "same nature" [homo-ousios] with God the Father, not of "similar nature" [homoi-ousios] or less so Divine than the Father (as asserted by Arianism, reflecting the influence of pagan Neo-Platonism). Jesus is authentically "by nature" human also, since "what is not assumed and taken upon, is not saved" (St. John Damascene), -- whence Christ would have suffered and died in vain. The mysteried "hypostatic union" of the Divine and the human in Christ preserves the uniqueness and integrity of each nature, without instead having the Divine nature in all its might and consummate glory annihilating and consuming the human nature (as occurs in the subliminal death-wish typical to pantheism). The Divine as it were thus preserves the integrity of the human, rather than supplanting and destroying it: this transpires both as regards the God-Man [Bogochelovek] Jesus Christ, and God-manhood [Bogochelovechestvo]. To ignore, deliberately or otherwise, this primally basic Chalcedon Christological perception, and instead to loosely translate "богочеловечество" as "Divine humanity", as is the wont of some currently, is to potentially confuse by admixture the Divine and the human natures, and thus render the "pan-entheism" of Vl. Solov'ev into merely another variant of pantheism. In the religious process of appropinquity to the Divine, there transpires the divinisation or theosis of the human person, who does not cease "by nature" to be human, but is the rather illumined or becomes transfigured by the Light of Mt. Tabor.

It is of verymost significance, nowise mere coincidence nor caprice, that Christ should have chosen the appelation "Our Father" to open the most famous prayer in all Christendom, whilst preaching the Sermon on the Mount [Mt. V-VII]. The Sermon on the Mount duly bears reading amidst its recurrent reference to God the Father. Christ calls for an altered relationship with the Divine, of filiation or "sonship to the Father". A conscientious son or daughter will far more likely be zealous in preserving

One of the most intriguing challenges in translating Berdyaev's "Philosophy of Inequality" consists in an accurate rendering of the cryptic wording of the subtitle: "*Pis'ma k nedrugam po sotsial'noi filosofii*". Nuance is everything, especially when conveying a tone of invective irony. The Russian word "*drug*" (друг) in neutral a setting means "*friend*", and the word "*nedrug*" (недруг) means literally a "*non-friend*". There is certainly a wide range of possible terms for someone, -- a "non-friend". What better choice might there be of appropriately nuanced word, considering the extreme underlying ironic tone?[3] "Opponents" seems too hollow, and "enemies" is too polite; however, "despisers" would seem to fit, as well as the more archaic term, "contemners". Indeed, there is perhaps an echo of indignation as was expressed in Berdyaev's notoriously effective 1913 article, "Quenchers of the Spirit", which needlessly neglects to provide proper attribution of source for that title.[4]

The subtitle evokes some several further mental associations, whether valid or not. Berdyaev adopted the format of "literary open letters", in ways suggestive of Friedrich Schleiermacher's 1799 book, "On Religion: Speeches to its Cultured Despisers".[5] Schleiermacher's book marked a significant cultural "event", which forced a major

---

the dignity, the integrity and "good name" of their paternal legacy handed down from their fore-fathers, even amidst adversity, in comparison to mere "contractual" hired hands, often inconstant mercenaries. Sorry to so belabour the obvious, a clergyman failuing perchance, but the obvious has much dimmed in our time...

[3] The 1976 C. Andronikof "L'Inegalite" translation from Russian into French of Berdyaev's "Philosophy of Inequality" renders the subtitle as: "*Lettres sur la philosophie sociale a des gens qui ne m'aiment pas*". What extent of nuance this conveys is for a reader fluent in French to discern.

[4] 1 Thess. 5: 19. The very next verse, 1 Thess. 5: 20, exhorts: "Prophetias nolite spernere" ("Contemn not prophesyings").

[5] "Über die Religion: Reden an die Gebildeten unter ihren Verachtern".

reevaluation of religion, in an age under the influences of the Enlightenment and materialist thought which regarded religion as "out-moded" and antiquated. Berdyaev's "Philosophy of Inequality" is a similar digging in of the heels, "against the current".

And the subtitle evokes yet more, in conjunction with the text. Generally, the propriety of normal literary form avoids useage of the word "you", the 2nd person singular/plural. However, cast in the format of literary "open letters", this hindrance is bypassed. And in "The Philosophy of Inequality" there is an invective torrent of "you" again and again, brimming with loathing and disgust. To break the monotonous flow of this reproachful "you", we have interspersed the somewhat archaic form of "ye", evoking as it does both a suggestive hint and a subliminal stance in spirit of Nietzsche's Zarathustra. Zarathustra, that solitary of the rarified mountain air, sensitive to soaring aspirations towards the heights, and the murky depths of existence, so remote and disdainful towards the narrowly focused "flat-landers" perspective of horizon. Nietzsche's thought was refracted rather differently in Russia, perhaps less superficially so than in the West.

And then, too, Berdyaev has given this book the provocative title, "The Philosophy of Inequality". How can any sensible person stand up for and defend "inequality", how can one not but assail the ignoble bastions of inequality, be they social or political, economic or otherwise? And yet, alas, the grey stifling uniformity of mass culture and totalitarian collectives under the banner of "equality", all those demagogues and their cronies with the egalitarian slogans, who become drunken with power and lucre, while sowing hate in the name of love and an intolerant "tolerance" as the pathways towards the "brotherhood of humankind", -- all this gives truth to the deceptive lie enshrined in George Orwell's "Animal Farm" fable: "All are equal, but some are more equal than others..." In response, some might seek to castigate Berdyaev, for being both a defender of aristocratism [Sixth Letter], and himself born an aristocrat. But important here is to be mindful of the century-long course of the social movement in Russia, -- Berdyaev is merely one member of a long series of figures from the nobility with a "societal conscience", a tradition that was initiated by the instigators of the 1825 Decembrist Revolt. This is perhaps an oversimplification, but in part it represents also the fracturing and stratification of the organic wholeness of Russia, consequent over long duration from the reforms of Peter the Great. For Berdyaev, the important and relevant aspect is not some chance aristocratism "by birth" (which often is given to decay), but rather that aristocratism "by spirit" -- a noble and high-minded sense of purpose, of character, of integrity, of honour and of values to be upheld, of a "great-souled" magnanimity of bearing. Berdyaev throughout his writings tends to draw a contrast between the *qualitative* and the *quantitative*. The *qualitative* is of course aristocratic a perceiving, -- it concerns itself with the dignity and integrity of the concrete individual human person, not with social classes nor collectives nor abstract groupings. In the *quantitative*, however, as characterised by modern culture and life, the individual human visage dissolves its clarity of form amidst the levelling egality of a faceless mob, where in the name of conformity all are rendered into but an economic/statistical number, a depersonalised and dispensible cog in the wheel of societal progress, in our modern "use, abuse and throw away" view on life.

This qualitative aristocratism "in spirit", rather than "in pedigree", also finds expression in Berdyaev's writings in reference to a sense of "*rytsarstvo*" ("knightly code of chivalry"), which he considered more weakly developed historically in Russia than in the West. Berdyaev tends to criticise the "Russian Soul" as being too passively feminine, seeking the colective warmth of the hearth, and he challenges it instead towards greater a forging of individual masculinity. At the opposite extreme, of course, is Germany, which Berdyaev during the war years (WWI) metaphorically tends to describe as a ponderously masculine "clumsy suitor" attempting to force itself upon the passive-hearted feminine Russia. But even farther afield, at least a long generation ago, we had the inspiring myth of the "American Cowboy", -- that lonely self-reliant figure, a solitary fighting some chanced-upon injustice, often against daunting odds and considerable risk to himself, and amidst this he was an "unmercenary" hero, at the finish riding off into the sunset amidst the grateful faint sobs of the heroine (in the films and novels of a now bygone era). And this individualised aspiration has parallels also for Berdyaev in the Renaissance, that period of great human creativity. There may be a bit of the romantic idealist to Berdyaev, -- but what innocent lad is there who has not dreamt of winning glory in the eye of some fair maiden, and conversely, what sweet maiden perchance has not dreamt of some noble hero to champion her honour. And yes, all this nowadays seems so out of vogue. The crude cynicism of our age will prove to its demise! This "unmercenary" existential posture has antecedents also in religious hagiography, as commemorated in the Orthodox Liturgy.[6]

In reading Berdyaev, and indeed in understanding Berdyaev's thought, it is important always to consider the "context" of what he is addressing, the "from whence" and "thence" of the train of his thought, rather than taking "convenient quotations" at random, as some are wont to do. He is nowise systematic a philosopher, a fact he readily admits. The scope of his inquiries is vast, and far-flung. And yet there is an integral unity to his thought, wherein the inter-connecting whole is greater than its composite parts, -- as in any

---

[6] A priest-craft insight, not overly apparent even to Orthodox laity: In the Orthodox Pre-Liturgy, or Prokomedia, 5 prosphora-loaves of bread (in the Russian tradition) are used, deriving from the symbolism of Christ's miracle with 5 loaves [Mt. 14:14ff.]. The 1st loaf becomes the Agnets or Lamb; the 2nd loaf has a particle taken for the Mother of God; the 3rd loaf has particles taken for the 9 Ranks of Saints (the 7th such particle is in prayerful commemoration of "Unmercenaries" ["Bezebreniki"]; the 4th loaf has particles taken for the Living; the 5th loaf particles for the Dead. In the formalism of Orthodox Christianity there are certainly more than 9 Ranks of Saints. But the "Bezebreniki-Unmercenaries" were typically "Unmercenary Physician/Healers", who ply their craft "gratis", for free, not out of any love for money, but rather out of love for God and their fellow-man. And certainly, even still, many initially pursue this noble vocation out of similarly lofty motives.

living organism, as distinct from its corpse. Berdyaev is an unabashedly Christian philosopher, and the innate virtue of his thought is in this, that it transcends any restrictive confines of Christianity, avoiding the pitfalls of narrow sectarian interests, by its universal scope of significance. To ignore this aspect is to ignore the primal basis of Berdyaev's integral intuition. Each of the unique thematic aspects of Berdyaev's thought inter-relate and are inter-dependent, each with the other; to analyse each aspect separately can lead to distortion and misunderstandings of his philosophy. Yet because of his universal scope, those outside any Russian Orthodox background, even those from different religious or even non-religious traditions, find him beneficial in addressing matters of concern to them. In his own generation Berdyaev assumed a great prominence beyond the emigre community, causing him some degree of consternation, in being viewed as an "authoritative voice" on Russian Orthodox Christianity...

In commenting further, we shall attempt to elucidate some aspects and sources of Berdyaev's thought, some aspects not especially profound on our part, but perhaps readily overlooked. Some of the central unique themes for Berdyaev are certainly: *creativity*, *freedom*, *spirit*, *person*. The sweep of Berdyaev's thought beyond this, though, is quite broad. History, meta-history, the teleological coursings of time and history, as a consciousness unique to the Judaeo-Christian civilisation. Culture and aesthetics: the Medieval, the Renaissance, antiquity, the "New Middle Ages", Picasso, Cubism and Futurism in art, Polish messianists, poets, significant but obscure European figures (read and ruminated upon by Berdyaev) whose works largely remain still inaccessible to the English reader (e.g. Franz Baader). The societal: Berdyaev's wrtings against Soviet Communism, his deep disdain towards Fascism and Anti-Semitism, towards any sort of totalitarianism, towards the crushing collective conformity leading to depersonalisation and dehumanisation and disbasement, -- the dynamic already operative within the structures of a bourgeois "Philistinism" (Russ. "Meschanstvo"). Berdyaev was a significant participant in what later became known as the "Russian Religious Renaissance of the XX Century" during the Russian cultural "Silver Age". During the opening decades of the century, the members of this current re-evaluated inherited trends, largely of German Philosophy (Kant, Hegel, Schelling, Neo-Kantianism, Marxism, Nietzsche, etc.) and rescued from otherwise oblivion such names as "Russia's First National Philosopher" Vl. Solov'ev, along with A. S. Khomyakov and related Slavophil figures, and then too such eccentric challenging voices as K. Leont'ev and N. F. Fedorov, whilst engaging the profound themes of Dostoevsky's literary genius. The enterprising reader can further research all this on his own...

Russian religious philosophy in its ponderings has tended variously to take a fresh look at matters religious, from within rather than from outside the context of the religious tradition, and in doing so it has uncovered some profound insights, the overlooked obvious as it were, in historically long "dead dogmas" and formalised terms. Religious philosophy is, however, not the same thing as theology. Literally, the word "philosophy" means "love of wisdom". Berdyaev makes the distinction that theology proper is the scientia of Divine Revelation, whereas religious philosophy is man's creatively-active intellectual and spiritual response to the profundities of wisdom embedded within Revelation. Some examples: what is "wisdom"?[7] Russian thought sought to answer this question -- via Vl. Solov'ev's "Three Encounters" and various "Silver Age" poets and finally, the

---

[7] The word for "wisdom" in Greek is "sophia" (σοφια), in Slavonic "premudrost'" (премудрость). Churchly attentive Orthodox several times during the Liturgy hear the refrain: "Sophia orthoi!"/"Premudrost', prosti!"/"Wisdom, let us attend!". And then too, familiar to them at certain festal Vespers is a passage that begins: "Wisdom hath built herself an house, and set up seven pillars...[Prov. 9:1ff]. It may well be that "The fear of the Lord is the *beginning* of wisdom" [Prov. 9:10], but what is it that follows this *beginning step*, the equivalent of a first page in a big fat Russian novel over which one is wont to drowse, eh? Perchance a transcendence of fear amidst a deepening of wisdom, of its love...

massively complex Sophiology of the eminent emigre theologian-philosopher, Fr. S. Bulgakov, who perchance was too caught up in Neo-Platonic modalities, thereby hypostasising what more properly should be considered a Divine attribute. Berdyaev, however, tends to interpret Sophia quite differently, in context with the German theosophist, Jakob Boehme.[8]

Another example: "God-manhood" (богочеловечество). What is Christ? And in consequence of this, what is man -- in his individual concrete existential situation, what is humankind/humanity, what is the cosmic significance of Christ the Logos? The early Christian centuries, especially in the Greek-speaking East -- with its greater linguistic subtlety of nuance and Platonic profunity, devoted much energy towards precision in defining *what* Christ is.[9]

---

[8] Vide the (Kl.#351) 1930 Berdyaev article in Journal Put', "The Teaching about Sophia and the Androgyne. J. Boehme and the Russian Sophiological Current".

[9] Several important points mustneeds be made. Greek was the "lingua franca" throughout the Roman Empire during the earliest times for Christians; literate Latins studied and spoke also Greek, and this together with the "Pax Romana" ("Roman Peace") facilitated the spread of Christianity both East and West. Thus St. Paul, for example (reading between the lines), on his many journeys likely started at the Greek-speaking Disapora local Jewish communities, splitting them both for/against St. Paul's message. Another example, -- St. Ireneius of Lugdunum (modern city of Lyon in France), hailed from the city of Smyrna in the East, the city of the "Apostolic father" St. Polykarp, who himself as a youth sat learning at the feet of St. John the Evangelist/Theologian, who likewise learned directly sitting at the feet of Jesus.

St. Ireneius (†202) wrote a still extant book, "Against Heresies" ("Adversus Haereses", "Κατὰ αἱρέσεων"), detailing the occult pseudo-Christian teachings of a mishmash of the many Gnostic syncretic sects of the time, in ways reminiscent of our modern syncretistic religious "New Age" trends; moreover, St. Ireneius revealed *gratis* for free the Gnostic "secret mysteries" that these seeming gurus of old were wont handsomely to charge for, as one "advanced"... But even in the time of Christ, Judaism

Briefly, as regards Christology, from the (year 381) Constantinople/Nicene Creed generally used at Liturgy, we learn -- that Christ as the "one [only] Lord" is likewise the "only-begotten [μονογενῆ] son of God", "begotten not made [i.e. not created] before all ages [i.e. in eternity not in time]", "true God of true God,... consubstantial [i.e. same essence, ὁμοούσιον] with the Father"... "and was incarnated [incarnatus est, σαρκωθέντα]"..."and became man [i.e. human, καὶ ἐνανθρωπήσαντα]". All which is to say, -- that Christ is authentically as much Divine as is the Father, and not some lesser magnitude of divinity as is Plato's Demiourgos, the purported

---

was no homogenous monolithic religion, with its various Pharisees, Saducees, Zealots, Essenes, etc. And similarly the influx of converts to Christianity from the "pagan Roman" world reflected a process of assimilation from a multiplicity of competing religious sources, as might becloud one's understanding. At this point the classical "Graeco-Roman paganism" in its cultus had become ossified and diluted of vigour, whether with the formalised apotheosis of the Emperor, and the political expediency of including the gods of defeated peoples, or the Persian Zoroastrian-influenced cults such as Mithraic bull-worship and "Sol Invictus" sun-worship, the Egyptian cults, the Asiastic Dionysian and Orphic Mysteries from Greece, etc., all this along with the philosophic perspectives of Stoicism, Epicurianism, Cynicism, and significantly the mystical trends within the Neo-Platonic philosophers of the time, such as Plotinos.

Reminiscent perhaps of India, Plotinos teaches of a mystical union or "henosis" (ἕνωσις) with "the One" (τὸ ἕν), and "emanation" or lesser a state of being in the descending degrees of evil materiality. Plotinos, it should be noted, also makes the significant distinction between apophatic or negative knowing and kataphatic positive rational knowledge (apophatic knowing underlies the symbolism of St. Paul's sole convert in Athens, St. Dionysios the Areopagite (Patron Saint of France), at the "altar to the Unknown God" [Acts 17: 23-24]. Emanation is also part of the system of the Christian apologist, Origen of Alexandria, in his tome, "On First Principles" (Περί αρχών - De principiis). If the general reader finds all this lengthy digression confusing, the confusing complexity involved was even moreso.

Artificer or Fashioner of this world, nor is Christ merely one in a long series of semi-divine avatars/sages in syncretic New Age a perspective. There was an early heresy, Docetism [i.e. "seeming"], suggesting that Christ was "by nature" Divine only, but not human, and thus on the Cross Christ only "seemed" to painlessly suffer and die, for mere appearances sake. The late Patristic father, St. John Damascene, in countering a later Monophysitism coined the phrase, "what is not assumed [i.e. taken upon] is not saved", which is to say, that if Christ be Divine only and not also truly human by nature, then His death on the Cross would have been "in vain", and nowise to the salvation of humankind. But if Christ be both God and Man "by nature", -- then what is the relationship between these two natures, the Divine and the human? To avoid the confusion of one into the other, Nestorianism preserves both distinct, yet connected in a schizophrenia-type union of a Divine Person and nature with an human person and nature, potentially in tension and in conflict each with the other. To counter this diminished and destabilising view of Christ, Monophysitism arose, declaring that the magnificence of the Divine nature in Christ overwhelms and annihilates the human nature (much like the self is annihilated by Nirvana in Buddhism).[10]

So what is the solution? Basically, to admit that this is the stuff of profoundest mystery, of the realm of apophatic/negative knowing that transcends the limits of kataphatic/positive rational knowledge. This

---

[10] A variant of these mindsets exists among a portion of the semi-literate Orthodox of the English speaking world, who appropriate the exotic Greek title of "theotokos" for Mary, whilst declaring that it is improper to term Her in English as "the Mother of God". Indeed, the title "Theotokos/Birthgiver of God" arose to counter the Nestorian distinction and title of "Christotokos/Birthgiver of Christ". To deflect our modern scolds, one has only to point to any of the innumerable Russian or Greek proper icons of Mary, atop which in abbreviated Greek letters is the title "MP ΘY", i.e. "Mother of God"! Thankfully, no seminary professor has yet seized upon the concept of "surrogate motherhood" from modern science, to further muddy the waters of confusion...

is what transpired in the year 451 at Chalcedon at the IV OEcumenical Council, with its famous definition of the mystical union of the Divine and the human natures in Christ, -- all couched in four negative terms.[11] There exists not two persons in Christ (even within the realm of the human, dual or multiple personalities are a mark of radical abnormality, of schizophrenia or worse); -- there exists only one, as unique Divine Person, the Son of God. Why is the Chalcedon negative definition important? In this apophatic mystical union of the two natures, the Divine and the human do not become admixed or confuse together to produce something altogether neither Divine nor human; rather, the integrity of each nature is preserved. The Divine, in its dazzling magnificance and power, does not burn away and annihilate the human nature; rather, the Divine as it were respectfully steps back and affirms the unique integrity of the human nature. Similarly, God as it were steps back and respects the oft-times capricious freedom of each human person, a freedom that for Berdyaev exists within the confines of natural necessity. And herewith Christological concerns largely slowed historically, without addressing its consequences within humankind, until that pioneer of Russian religious philosophy, Vl. Solov'ev, shook off the centuries-long dust from this Chalcedon seemingly "dead dogma". All which has spurred renewed discussion and insights of significant aspects latent in Christ's preachings in the Gospel, such as "filiation" or "sonship to God", and "theosis" or "divinisation", -- the spiritual rendering of the individual human image (Grk. "ikon", Slav. "obraz") into "God-likeness" ("Bogopodobnost'" "богоподобность")[12]

---

[11] "ἐν δύο φύσεσιν ἀσυγχύτως, ἀτρέπτως, ἀδιαιρέτως, ἀχωρίστως" / "in duabus naturis inconfuse, immutabiliter, indivise, inseparabilite" / "in two natures, non-confused, immutable, indivisible, inseparable".

[12] Man was created "in the image and likeness of God" [Gen.1:26]. Several centuries after Chalcedon, the Church in the East became embroiled in the Iconoclast Controversy -- stemming from the Biblical prohibition against "worshipping graven images", i.e. "idololatreia" or "idolatry". The Iconoclasts (Slav. "ikonobortsi"), whose adherents at times included the

through the mystical process associated with the hesukhiast practise of the Jesus Prayer.

As mentioned before, some scholars nowadays tend loosely to translate "bogochelovechestvo" as "Divine humanity", ignoring its Christological source, and instead emphasise a Divine pan-entheism, the sophianic presence of the Divine underlying all reality. Berdyaev, as an existentialist, is in contrast, concerned with the tragic fate of the unrepeatably unique individual human person, the dignity and worth of the indiviual against all assaults, all the allures to slavery, manifest in the crushing forces of dehumanisation and depersonalisation and the conformity demanded by collectivism, by pretensive ideologies political, societal, economic, scientific -- all reducing the individual nameless into the "collateral damage" of a blind statistic, a mere "thing", to be used and abused and then thrown away. "Crocodile tears" amidst a bourgeois righteousness notwithstanding. Berdyaev, in describing the infinite dignity and worth of each concrete

---

heavy thumb of the Byzantine civil authorities, viewed as idolatrous the churchly reverence of holy icons by the icon-venerators (Grk. "ikonodouloi", Slav. "ikonopoklonitsi"). The icon or image is a visual "symbol", literally a representational window through to the reality imaged, much as, to use simple an example, one might hold precious and bestow a tearful kiss to a photo or painting of a long dead dear grandmother, or a far-afield dear sweetheart in pre-Internet days. One might almost be tempted to suggest that the iconoclast mentality evidences a sort of taboo akin to primitives that refuse to have their photo taken, lest it "snatch their soul away" [i.e. their mana-power]. Religiously, iconography, the "writing" of sacred images, is an highly formalised and symbolic discipline. And Orthodox Christianity subtly engages all the five human senses in its worship. The aforementioned St. John Damascene likewise wrote a treatise in defense of holy images. For a Christian, however, the most compelling argument for religious holy images is precisely this, -- the Incarnation, that Christ as God was born in the flesh, He was seen and touched and heard by others, and by tradition permitted His image to be imprinted to a veil. This seeming digression on the symbolic aspect of the image is quite relevant to Berdyaev's understanding of "person".

individual human person in the eyes of God, often employs the Russian word, "nepovtorimaya lichnost'" (*неповторимая* личность), "unrepeatably unique person". It is all too possible to "love mankind" while loathing our individual fellow man.[13] In this is Berdyaev's

---

[13] It is very difficult to love one's enemies [Mt.5: 44], when not only do they merely hate you, but physically threaten both life and limb in demonic a frenzy. Berdyaev in his book, "*The Destiny of Man*", makes the point, that the good themself often become evil, in their struggle against evil, a strange dynamic and paradox. Berdyaev begins this book with an enigmatic epigramme by N. Gogol', "The sad part of this, is that thou see no good in goodness" ("Грусть от того, что не видиш добра в добре"). And indeed, the "*Jenseits von Böse und Gut*" ("*Beyond Good and Evil*") book-title by that great "bogoborets/God-struggler" Nietzsche, directly echoes the Mt.5:43-48 Gospel passage, which exhorts not mere goodness in reaction to evil, but rather, -- "*perfection*", such as is shewn by God the Father (in making rains to rain on both the good and the wicked). It seems impossible enough even merely to be "good", let alone "perfect"...

Christ's "Sermon on the Mount" [Mt.5:1-7:29] is paradoxical and radically challenging, when examined closely. There is, as it were, an unified vision threading throughout it, a glimpse of the dynamics of the Kingdom of Heaven which is not of "this world", a transcending "absolute moral intuition" largely in opposition to the relative moral stances, operative in the realm of this world. It reflects the dynamic intersection of two planes, of two concurrent realms of which we find ourself, at times torn between their seemingly incompatible demands. In the Sermon on the Mount, there is so much that resonates to the very depths of the soul, but there is also that which is of strictest austerity [Mt.5:19ff]. The Mt.5:38 command, "non resistere malo" ("resist not evil"), once widely significant and known, seems largely nowadays out of vogue, and unknown. Again, how to "not resist evil" without becoming evil, becoming complicit in evil in the process... (Was Dostoevsky's "Grand Inquisitor" evil, or not??).

The middle path is nowise the "strait gate"... There is a tendency to pick and choose quotes from the Sermon, such as are convenient for the moment: "Love your enemies", "Judge not, lest ye be judged withal by the measure by which ye judge"... But if Christ's Sermon on the Mount be as it were woven of whole cloth in its inner vision and teaching, and not merely for picking out convenient quotes, what then are we to say of Mt.5:28-29?

vindication of Chalcedon, in preserving the autonomy and integrity of the concrete human person.

Another contribution of Russian religious philosophy is the concept of Sobornost' (Соборность), a term which has come into broader useage within Orthodox Christianity. In context, sobornost' can be translated as either "catholicity" or "communality", or the less accurate "conciliarity". In Russian, the word "sobor'" is cognate with "sobiranie", a "gathering" or "assemblage". "Sobor'" is also the term for a "cathedral" church ("cathedral" derives from the Latin word, "cathedra" meaning "chair", -- literally, the "bishop's chair" from which he presides, and which in Orthodox practise sits symbolically in other churches for when the bishop visits). In the context of an "assemblage", it relates not only to churchly convocations, but also gatherings in the civil sphere, such as the traditional All-Russian Zemsky Sobor', and other regional and local representative gatherings.

But sobornost' also conveys the concept of "catholicity", -- issuing from its use in adjective form in the Nicene Creed in the Liturgy. The relevant Slavonic, transliterated is: "Veruiu... vo edinu svyatuiu *sobornuiu* i apostol'skuiu tserkov" ("I believe... in One, Holy, Catholic and Apostolic Church").[14] The awareness of the significance of sobornost' as "catholicity" arose in the Slavophil circle centred round A.S. Khomyakov, and later gained currency in general religious discussion through the efforts of the rebirth of Russian religious thought in the early 1900's, which re-discovered and re-evaluated the thought of earlier conservative writers. (Berdyaev actually wrote a 1912 book on Khomyakov, never yet translated into English, which we expect soon to remedy).

One might well ask, -- how many, self-inflicted at that, "one-eyed" "one-armed" and likely "one-legged" Christians have there likely been, hopping on their way up to Heaven?? Things are nowise as simple as they might seem at first glance...

[14] Actually, each of these aspects inter-relate and depend each upon the other.

Investigating more deeply the concept of "catholicity", Khomyakov and others sought to rebut the demands of Romanist papal pretensions. The word "catholic" derives from the Greek, "καθ ῾ολον" -- "regarding the whole/entirety". But "regarding the whole" implies *what* comprises it, i.e. the unity securing the "oneness". For Khomyakov, "catholicity" represented an "unity within multiplicity", wherein the fullness of the faith resides in each "mestnoe"/local church, each churchly community, and ultimately each authentic "believer". This position would seem to echo Protestantism. But the "sola scriptura" Protestantism shatters the connecting bond of the living Tradition of churchly apostolicity and hence "oneness", in negating the experience of the many generations stretching back through the Apostolic Fathers to Christ Himself. Against Romanist papal pretensions, the Orthodox argue that St. Peter was not the "only apostle"; he was but one of the twelve in "the dignity of apostle", the "foremost among equals" ("primus inter pares", a term deriving from Octavian Caesar). Even today, the Orthodox accord St. Peter the title "foremost/*pervoverkhovnyi*". But as a result of the 1054 "Great Schism", St. Peter's ancient see is considered to have abdicated its proper position and stature, increasingly over the passage of centuries. The "Great Schism" is but one tragic aspect of the fracturing apart and increased stratification of the Latin West and the Greek Byzantine East.

Sobornost' thus has come to signify the "unanimity of consensus" and agreement, arrived at representative councils and assemblages, both civil and religious, and hence -- sobornost' also translates as "conciliarity", a nuance of "catholicity". This superficially defines the relationships involved, to satisfy polemic needs. But is there some deeper dynamic involved, some rather more profound process transpiring at depth? The Orthodox Liturgy provides subtle hints, building as it does in an increasing crescendo dynamic, reached at the climax point of the Epiklesis and subsequent Communion. In the Liturgy we find such relevant flash-words as "*edinomyslie*" (единомыслие, "oneness of mind"), and "*dazhd' nam edinemi ousty i edinem serdtsem*" ("grant us oneness of mouth and oneness of heart"). It involves a mystical dynamic of Christ-invoking Presence of the Holy Spirit (Mt.18:20), -- "where two or three are gathered together in My Name, there I am in the midst of them". In the Orthodox Church, a priest cannot consecrate the sacred elements by himself alone, the laypeople not only are not optional, but essential! Indeed, the very root of the word "liturgy" derives from the Greek "leit-ourgos", meaning "work of the people". It is the effect of a gathering, a sobiranie, hence a sobor', which in Greek is conveyed by the word "ekklesia", i.e. the church as a liturgically religious ecclessia.

But is there an even more profound aspect to sobornost', than the aspects just covered? Yes, indeed! Consider the MostHoly Trinity, that Tri-Unity of Persons, those three unrepeatably unique and non-interchangeable Persons, and that relationship of tri-unitary communality which obtains amongst Them -- this is a relationship eternally abiding in harmonia, nowise inconstant. But it is not a static relationship, not stasis (that death symbol of a corpse). Stasis is a category that derives from our fallen world, whereas the plane of eternity is of an altogether other realm, variously intersecting ours. What transpires within the Trinity is something dynamically constant, in perfectmost harmony, -- since the God of the Christians is a "Living God"[15] (cf. the "Athens and Jerusalem" motif of Tertullian and L. Shestov). To speak of the realm of eternity and the perfect TriUnity of the Trinity is already to venture beyond the rational categories of thought into the trans-rational, the apophatic symbolic apperception. The abiding and constant accord that transpires amongst the Persons of the Trinity would thus seem to indicate a

---

[15] This is radically significant a point, ignored by various theological and philosophical systems, which relegate the Divine into a semi-mechanical modality of forces and precesses. In contrast to this is St. Peter's inspired declaration: "Thou art the Christ, Thou art the Son of *the Living God*" [Mt.16:16]. And Christ Himself declares: "God is not the God of the dead, but of the living" [Mt.22:32]. And thus a profound paradoxical significance of the Resurrection: if the dead be not alive for us in Christ, then we ourself are but dead in Christ...

most perfect manifestation of sobornost', of communality, of abiding communion each with the other.

In the philosophy of both M. Buber and Berdyaev, the "I" finds its affirmation in the "thou", a dynamic which is significant for other existentialist philosophers also. The "thou" is radically different from an individual "you" or "it", which are from the realm of objectification and alienation. The "I" in affirming the "thou" as an other "I" authentically, -- is itself authenticised as an "I", not an "it" or "object-thing". Such a relationship might be described as a true communing, a true communion with an other. This also further involves clarifying Berdyaev's concept of "person" (Russ. "lichnost'"). M. Buber's famous book, "*I and Thou*" (German original "*Ich und Du*") discusses the "I-Thou" relationship primarily in terms of the individual man relative to God, and how this relation is inconstant, as it were fading in and out, even if once achieved. There is a great deal of truth to this, as anyone persuing spiritual a life can attest. This is something that is often overlooked by those who employ the term sobornost' in facile and superficial a manner. The sobornost' that obtains within the churchly community is not something constant and unfading, rather it is religiously fragile, atained only in those intense moments when man as it were meets God face to face, in oneness of mind and heart and spirit. And then subsequently acting together with God in a co-working, a co-operation with God, -- in what the Orthodox theology terms "synergia". Sobornost' seems in ways inter-connected with the concept of God-manhood.

What is "*person*" and what is the "*human person*"? What is the foundational core basis (Russ. "*osnova*"), the grounding to "person"? A different perception, perhaps radically so, exists between West and East, based on linguistic differences between the Latin and the Greek derivations for "person", -- an important point to be explored later in this essay. Granted, the Divine Persons of the MostHoly Trinty are a matter of unfathomable mystery. But then, too, is not the human person also a matter of utmost unfathomable mystery, analogously after a manner, to answer which has ever been the quest of philosophy?

Sometimes, of course, it is needful to begin at the beginning, and in a sense, Berdyaev did so. In the year 1912 was published his remarkable and noteworthy book, "The Meaning of Creativity" (Engl. title "*The Meaning of the Creative Act*"). The book speaks of man's creative endeavours across a broad spectrum of life: religious, social, artistic, intellectual. What is the source to Berdyaev's assertion that man is a "creator"? Berdyaev indeed begins "at the begining", with the Bible Genesis (Slav. "Bytie") account of the Creation,[16] -- from which Berdyaev draws the obvious and logical conclusion: that if man is created, is indeed created in "the image and likeness" of his Creator, then man too is a "creator". This is an aspect of "man" long overlooked or perhaps ignored within the Judaeo-Christian tradition. Whereas God the Creator of course by the creative fiat of His mere Word alone creates "ex nihilo", man as a "creator" in contrast creates "the new" from some material at hand, much as a sculptor might from a block of stone, or composer or painter similarly. And part of the tragedy of the human creative act is that the finished product, howsoever excellent, fails to measure up to the crystaline perfection of the initial creative intuition in the "mind's eye" of the creator. In his book, of course, Berdyaev had the then shocking audacity to

---

[16] For Berdyaev, to use the term "myth" in describing the Genesis Creation account is not to imply that it is merely an empty fable or fairytale, devoid or distortive of facts, which is a common connotation of the word "myth". A creation account explaining the genesis (i.e. beginning) of things seems to be a common element among the primitive stages of various peoples, and is often deeply symbolic and highly formalised. Thus, in the Bible it is accurate even if inaccurate (by positivist a "scientific mindset") -- hence an antinomy. As in any highly symbolic creative work, such as a deep poem or painting, it becomes a matter of discerning and attempting to interpret the significant meanings embedded therein. Berdyaev and his fellow philosopher, L. Shestov, spent long hours in "friendly" heated argument over their differing insights concerning the Genesis Creation account.

equate as exemplars of creative genius, each in their own way, Pushkin and St. Seraphim of Sarov (Ch. VII).[17] The philosophic issue of authentic "newness" involving man's creative vocation remained a motif throughout Berdyaev's later thought, -- a sort of synergistic cooperation of man with God in a sort of "continuing creation" dynamic.This motif finds echoes within trends of Orthodox Christian thought on a "transfiguration of the cosmos" (i.e. the enlightening of the primieval darkness, the rendering of "cosmos" from out of formless chaos).

Assuming that, from within the context of a Christian perspective, there obtains the element of Providential revelation underlying the Holy Scripture Creation account, -- two passages regarding "man" from the book of Genesis are extremely significant: "*And God said: let Us make man in our own image and likeness*" (Gen. 1:26), "*And God created man, created him in the image of God: male and female He created them*" (Gen. 1:27). The most obvious point here is that "man", the human male and female, is created in the "image of God", the idiomatic "*imagio dei*". In each human person there exists the image/obraz/eikon (i.e. icon) of God, the image of the eternally All-Sacred, and thus in effect each human person, albeit distorted by the effects of sin,[18] is a symbolic "living icon" of the All-Holy, though only the greatest of saints with profoundest spiritual perspicacity might perceive such. The image of God in man has been grievously wounded and distorted, of course, by the effects of the Fall, the Sin-Fall (Slav. "*Grekhopadenie*"), but not ultimately abolished. From the "imagio dei" within man derives the

---

[17] As an existentialist, a creative response to God and to life ought to be seen as a matter faced by everyone each in their own way within their own situation, and not the perogative of an "elite few".

[18] What is "sin"? On simple a level, sin is an act of violence, abuse, a violation, a sacrilege against God directed towards the image of God within oneself. And sin against our neighbour is an act of violence, a violation, a sacrilege against God, of God as imaged within our neighbour.

perception of the eternal foundation of the utmost dignity and worth of each human person, a dignity more primal upon its eternal basis than all the totalitarian demands of conformity, be such demands those of the state, economics, society, etc. Without this solid foundation for asserting the dignity of the human person, all the other lofty attempts -- the "Declaration of the Rights of Man and Citizen", of constitutions, social concordats, "inalienable rights", etc (beset by legions of lawyers and the politically unscrupulous), -- at best prove to be relative constructs all too like the proverbial "houses foundationed upon sand", as evidenced by the torrents of brutality and blood in the not so distant past and present. Upon the inviolable dignity of the image of God in man is grounded the freedom of the human conscience (Russ. "*sovest'*"), the final redoubt against every tyranny and despotism.

Returning to the Genesis account. Is what constitutes the human person the same thing as the "icon of God" in man, or is it somewhat different? Generally, in the work of creating, God acts through the mere fiat of His Word: "Let there be... firmament, day, dry land, etc". But the creation of man obtains differently: "And God said, Let *Us* make man in *our* own Image and likeness' (Gen. 1:26). What is this "*Us*" and "*Our*"? Generally, this is interpreted merely as the Lord God speaking the the "majestic plural", as might a king or some other august personage. But what if it is indicative of something far more, far more significantly profound? Indeed, might not this "*Let Us*" suggest instead some sort of synergistic dynamic transpiring amongst the Persons of the Holy Trinity in the act of the creation of "man"? Echoing this perspective is the "Logos" theology as expressed in the opening of the Prologue of St. John's Gospel: "*In principio erat verbum, et verbum apud Deum, et Deus erat verbum... Omnia per ipsum facta sunt: et sine ipso factum est nihil, quod factum est*".[19] If the "image of God" in man represents a creative dynamic involving

[19] "In the beginning was the Word, and the Word was with God, and the Word was God... All things were made through Him, and apart from Him was naught else made..." (Jn.1:1-3).

the Persons within the Holy Trinity, then this provides absolute a grounding to the human person, as person, as regards "inalenable rights", innate dignity etc., notwithstanding the effects of the Fall.

The Gen.1:27 refrain on Gen.1:26, expressing God's intent to create "man", is interesting on several points, both the spoken and the unspoken. Firstly as regards the spoken: "...in the image of God: male and female He created them". By Divine intent, the "imagio dei" is manifest in humankind in twofold, in binary, a form -- male and female, man and woman. Both within them authentically and equally in dignity bear the "image of God". As such, each has its own unique peculiar traits, its own strengths and weaknesses, those unique to its sex, beyond the mere physical aspects of sexuality. Rather than denying or negating the uniquely dual aspects of human sexuality, it would seem far more proper to appreciate their interacting significance: for men to properly cultivate their masculinity, not brutishly, and for women to cultivate their femininity, not crudely. A very curious fact, as others have already noted elsewhere, is that the Russian root word "pol" (пол) is indicative of both "sex" and "half" -- the linguistic derivation of which from of old would require a right proper philologist to trace. But in the context of an existentialist philosophy, with a personalist approach sensitive to the fragility of the "I-Thou" dynamic, this is of extreme significance. The innate consciousness of "half-ness", of "incompleteness", of a deep longing and yearning for completeness, to become "whole", underlies the existentialist sense of angst/anxiety, of aloneness in an hostile and threatening world, a world of the pervasive and dehumanising forces of alienation and atomisation. "Alone, always ever alone" is a foretaste of hell, experienced by many. This passionate subliminal desire to find one's "soul-mate", a passionate quest, provides impetus to the search for the meaning of life, of life in an apparently meaningless world, of a world bereft of meaning and filled with antinomies, -- (sic) "the end (i.e. telos end-purpose) of life is death", its annihilation and negation. The yearned "soul-mate" is one with whom we can put off the protective armour constantly worn against fickle strangers, one with whom it is possible to trustingly bare one's inmost soul in an abiding communion, a sobornost'-type togetherness, a mutual authenticating of each the other as an "I", and not an "it", not an "object-thing". Such an oneness of mind and heart and soul is at best rare, and even more rarely constant and abiding. The physical act of sex is an attempt to transcend this "half-ness" of the human person symbolically by a brief conjugal uniting of bodies which, while fleetingly satisfactory as an emotional sexual release, still fails to achieve an abidingly constant level of profoundest intimacy; rather, each retreats into their own self and is rendered again a "stranger" to the other, as Berdyaev notes. And tragically, couples even that start out on terms of great intimacy and compatibility still all too often, after the passage of long years, tend to wither increasingly into a pair of married "strangers" -- a societal problem. Healthy marriages require serious work to keep them healthy. But the significant thing is this, that the "imagio dei" is twofold dual an aspect, that of an incomplete "half-ness" in each. Plato likewise introduced this concept in philosophy with his mythos of the "androgyne", the sexually complete "male-female". And Jakob Boehme likewise makes use of the "androgyne", as the Sophia which has flown off heavenward in consequence of the Fall, the *Грехопадение*.[20] The "image of God" would thus ultimately transcend the incomplete "half-ness" of sexuality.

There is yet another exegetical nuance of difference between Gen.1:26 and Gen.1:27. The Lord God sets about the creation of humankind by saying: "Let Us create man in our own image and

---

[20] It is of interest that the Sin-Fall narrative occurs separately and later, as though appended into the primal archaic intuition of "ab origine" beginnings. As such, it would indicate a coalescing of concepts and meshing together or oral traditions,, -- something scholars suggest, as an example, is evidenced also in the unsatisfactory ending to the Book of Job. Similarly, even the concept of the immortality of the soul is something that only gradually coalesced and evolved in the consciousness of the ancient Greeks, -- a process superbly investigated by that colleague of Nietzsche, Erwin Rhode, in Rhode's classically erudite book, "*Psyche*" (available in English translation).

likeness". But what results is this, that "God created man, created him in the image of God: male and female...". What has become of God's intended "God-likeness / Bogopodobnost'" (Богоподобность)? For man, what is it that is immediately missing from the result? Berdyaev would likely suggest that this is deliberate an omission, involving the inscrutable ways of Divine Providence, that God awaits man's free creative response in striving towards God-likeness, both religiously and trans-religiously. Consider for a moment, with no scurrilous blasphemy intended, how God's two acts of creation turned out: the first, the angelic realm, saw half the angels go bad; the second, this world, the whole edifice came crashing down in result of the Fall. Downright pathetic results, no? Many religious people are all too content if not happy that the devil should finally walk off with the "devil's share", leaving God only with small a remnant. This echoes the taunt of Dostoevsky's "Grand Inquisitor", who "improves" matters... But the saying is: "God ultimately is not to be mocked". The inscrutable paths traversed by Providence are beyond human kenning. Both in Dostoevsky and in Berdyaev one can perceive a very subtle sense of tragic optimism, as regards the finalative end, however tragic the paths traversed, as seen in Dostoevsky's great novels. Within the "Brothers Karamazov" there is the figure of the starets-elder, Fr Zosima, that soothing ray of warmth[21] in a moribund world. Any proper student of Russian thought is certainly familiar with Ivan Karamazov's famous refusal and repudiation of "the tiny tear of one tormented innocent child as the required ticket price for heaven/world harmony". Not just heaven, but "world harmony" -- at whose pagan altars of rational utopianism so terribly many innocents over the course of history have been, and continue to be tormented. In this is to be heard the anguished lament of "Rachel weeping for her children, and she would not be comforted, because they are no

---

[21] So akin to the comforting and welcoming warmth in the voice of Jesus, with Face yet unseen, in many of the great miracles of healing -- this hearing of the beckoning Voice of the Unseen Son of God is actually a spiritual dynamic.

longer" (Mt.2:18). Eh, and what does Christ say concerning "whoso doth scandalise one of these little ones" and the proverbial "millstone about the neck" (Mt.18:5)? Not to be affected by this is indicative of a coarseness and insensitivity of heart, not to mention dullness of mind, and deadening of soul; sadly so, as with the adopting of the modern euphemism of "collateral damage". Various forms of jesuitry may momentarily calm the mind, but not the heart. Through Ivan Karamazov, Dostoevsky presents the poignant religio-philosophic problem of theodicy: how if at all possible to justify an omnipotent omniscient God in the face of all the horrors and cruelty and unmerited sufferings throughout all the ages? On the face of it, the all-powerful God, if one assumes such exists, proves instead impotent, or worse still -- uncaring; this indeed is one of the strongest arguments for atheism -- both as regards religious utopianism and secular utopianism (i.e. "man-godhood"). Ivan Karamazov's statement of the problem is quite penetrating and indeed quite radical, but his brother Alyosha's implied reply, something commentators often miss, is even more radical, to wit -- "somehow or other in the final end God will, God must resolve this", i.e. if not, then God is not God, or does not exist. It is a matter of a radical deep faith in the inscrutable paths of Providence, inaccessible to the purely Euclidian mind. But it is also the provenance of the thoughts with which the Russian philosopher L. Shestov wrestled. Yet what does "God-likeness" (Богоподобность) have to do with any of this? Perhaps, everything. That it did not result initially at the creation of man is perchance deliberate, providential, of Divine Providence. How so?

In the mix of what comprises man is "freedom", an authentic not merely formal freedom or "free will", but rather something primordial and primal. It often seems that God desires man's freedom moreso than does man, who seeks to escape the existential anguish of his freedom, either through the narcotic effects of "demon rum", eroticism, consumerism, utopian ideologies etc. God-likeness is a possibility *only because man is free*, just as God is free. Had God initially created man to include "God-likeness", then the "imagio dei" within man would not be a true authentic eikon/obraz/image, but rather a "false idol", a sort of "graven image". The lonely paths of introspection bring us face to face with ourself and our innermost freedom, a frightening moment fraught with existential angst. It is there that we forge who and what we are, it is there through the trials and tribulations of the experiences in life that we temper into strength our character, as steel is tempered in fire and gold is purified of its dross. It is man's active, not passive, but rather active creative response to God, paternally indeed expected of us by God, that results in some semblance of "Bogopodobnost'/God-likeness".

What is the source of man's freedom? Freedom is a central core tenet of Berdyaev's thought, not some mere liberal utilitarian convenient slogan, but rather a passionate primal intuition threading its way throughtout his musings. This passion for freedom inspired the writer, Michel Alexander Vallon, to title his 1960 book on Berdyaev, "*An Apostle of Freedom*" -- evidenced moreover by its inscribed "dedication". Indeed, already back in the year 1911 Berdyaev published his book, entitled "*The Philosophy of Freedom*" (as yet untranslated into English). But available to English a reader, and well worth perusal, is Berdyaev's book, "*Slavery and Freedom*",[22] originally published 1939 in Russian. "Slavery and Freedom" is a product of Berdyaev's matured thoughts, and quite powerful writing. In the book is a very important chapter on "person" (lichnost'), which we shall address later. Another chapter discusses man's all too willing self-enslavement in context of the well known Hegelian "Bad Faith" aspect such as obtains in the dynamics of the "master-slave" relationship: in the act of enslaving the master himself becomes enslaved to his slave -- be it alive or some inanimate object/thing. Strange at first sight, but true. In the traditions of

[22] The English version bears abridged a title, bereft also of the significant subtitle. The full Russian title, rendered into English, would be: "*Concerning the Slavery and Freedom of Man: an etude on Personalist a Philosophy*".

German philosophy, the subject as a noumenal "I" becomes alienated from its own "self", betrays its self-autonomy (i.e. freedom) by becoming objectified as an "it" or "object/thing" into a world of things, a world of phenomena. This results from the self-betrayal of what is noumenal into the surface realm of phenomena, or of a "congealed materiality" (a Neo-Platonic term). There is all a world of difference between a corpse and the live being that it formerly was -- the corpse is indeed an ultimate ossified form of "congealed materiality", in finalative a sense. A long generation ago, readers were well aware of Sartre's emphasis on the "bad faith" involved in the existential posture of "*role-playing*", wherein *being-in-itself* becomes immersed in the superficial level of *being-for-itself.* And Berdyaev likewise notes: "In his social life, while acting parts that in no way reflect his true self, man... invariably impersonates some personage, be it a king, an aristocrat, a bourgeois, a man of the world, a father of a family, a civil servant, a revolutionary, an artist... Thus man's 'theatrical' ego is but another form of objectification".[23] Priest, lawyer, professor, whatever, we all too often become merely identical and identified with the roles that we act within life, too often rendering us but two-dimensional, superficial, shallow, lacking for depth, living by rote actions and words. All which fits in well with the demands of mass culture, that levelling mob-like demand for conformity in the name of blandly original non-conformity, that innate desire to "belong" to the collective's warmth of massed bodies, that terror of solitude and loneliness.

In the successive chapters of "Slavery and Freedom" , Berdyaev lists and discusses various allurements that seduce man into enslavement. Some are obvious, such as the constraints of dealing with natural necessity. Others are less so. Thus, man's servile mentality in relationship to God, and man's slavery to self under the lure of individualism. There are any number of subliminal societal and social allures beckoning a betrayal of one's innate freedom -- the

---

[23] p. 98, "Solitude and Society", Geoffrey Bles, London, 1938. Russian title: "I and the World of Objects" (1934).

state, family, civilisation and culture, class, nation, war, economic, the ideologies of collectivism and revolution, eroticism, aestheticism. Yes, a text well worth perusal.

But again the question, -- what is the source of man's freedom? If God created the freedom that constitutes the composite of what comprises man, then the omniscient God is somewise complicit in responsibility for the results that obtain (like putting a loaded pistol into the hands of a mentally or morally unstable person). This is an issue that has bedeviled any satisfactory attempts at theodicy, has bedeviled the omniscient omnipotent God's two seemingly flawed efforts at creation, -- both which issued forth with evil, with endless torrents of wanton torments, anguished tears amidst pain and suffering, ending in the spasms of the sting of death. Death indeed is the utmost sacrilegious blasphemy against the Living God (Mt.22:32). Man's existential freedom is far deeper and more profound a matter than "free will", a religiously convenient forensic device to shift any complicit blame for evil away from God. Dostoevsky's Grand Inquisitor of course seeks to "correct" God's "error", by eliminating the troublesome nuisance of freedom and in its place substituting "obedience"; this unshoulders the blame for evil not only from God but also from the obedient masses -- it is a seemingly "small price" to pay for a miracle of "changing stones into bread". And yet Christ in the 1st of the Three Temptations refused. Indeed, *why?*[24] The Grand Inquisitor has had many an adept student

---

[24] "Not by bread alone doth man live..." (cf. Mt.4:4; Dt.8:3). There is a shocking aspect to the Three Temptations of Christ, when one first clearly perceives what is transpiring: *It is a Scripture-quoting contest between the devil and Christ*. And what it dramatically shows is this, that the devil is able to twist and to quote Holy Scripture more adeptly and more excellently than any mere mortal, but out of context, and indeed to the devil's own nefarious ends. It is frightening to realise that the devil himself can wield the Bible as a weapon. One often chances upon the sort of Christian with a convenient "scriptural quotation for any occasion". The appeal of the sloganeering art is of course not limited to Christians. True critical discernment is important. Every scoundrel and his cousin, when

not only religiously, but also secularly, and among the ideologues of both modern and past times, demanding this "small price" in exchange for the felicitude of a rosy utiopian secularised humanism[25] the gradual surrendering of freedom.

An authentic, and not merely nominal, human freedom would seem to require that it be truly indeterminate, that its volitional paths not be pre-ordained nor pre-destined by God, lest God again be complicit in the emergence of evil. Berdyaev thus suggests that human freedom is "primeval, pre-cosmic, pre-existent" an aspect to man, it was there already prior to God's creation of man (evidenced by man's freedom in Eden prior to the Fall), and is hence "uncreated" a freedom. In addressing this, Berdyaev resorts to J. Boehme, to Boehme's mythopaeic concept of the *Ungrund*, the initial Ungroundedness, reflecting as such the Nothingness of the "*ex nihilo*", the "from out of nothing" that God created the Creation through the Divine fiat of His Logos, the Divine Word ("Omnia per ipsum facta sunt: et sine ipso factum est nihil, quod factum est", (sic) the "logical" structure underlying science and knowledge). Innate to this "pre-beginning" nothingness of the Ungrund is freedom, an uncreated freedom, an indeterminate element fraught with and

---

caught red-handed, knows how to quote the Gospel adage, "Judge not, lest ye be judged" [Mt.7:1]. But few seem to know its corollary, a seemingly contrary quote [Jn.7:24]: "Judge not by appearances, but rather judge righteous judgement" ("Nolite iudicare secundum faciem, sed iustum iudicium iudicate"). And in the corresponding Greek, "krisis" (κρισις) is the word for "judgement", as in discernment, and the marginalia suggest Jn.8:15 as a key to unlocking this "crisis of judgement".

[25] Dostoevsky with genius provides a surreal expression of this future "felicitude" of mankind, finally at last unshackled from ideas of religion and immortality, as voiced by Versilov's Dream-outlook in the novel "*Podrostok*" (Engl. title: "The Adolescent", alt. "Raw Youth". Cf. Berdyaev's quote of this in the final paragraph of the Dostoevsky segment of "Spirits of the Russian Revolution", included in our above translation.

allowing for potentiality, the possibility of newness, and of becoming. It is a "*meonic freedom*". Greek thought makes the distinction between the barrenness of an absolute nothingness (ουκ ον), and the potentiality inherent to meonic (μη ον) a nothingness.[26] As such, this meonic freedom is itself neither good nor evil, but bears within it the possibility of leading to good or evil. Likewise, this meonic nothingness is quite different from the apophatic Divine Nothingness as expressed in mystical experience.[27]

---

[26] cf. Berdyaev, "The Destiny of Man", p. 127. The concept of the Ungrund and meonic freedom is woven throughout Berdyaev's writings; moreover, "The Destiny of Man" is well worth reading in toto. On a specific discussion of the Ungrund within Boehme's thought, vide Berdyaev's 1930 Journal Put' article, "Boehme: Etude I: the Ungrund and Freedom". (Kl.#349).

[27] This Greek distinction of "ουκ ον" and "μη ον" as regarding nothingness is noted also on p. 92 of Vladimir Lossky's 1944 work, "*The Mystical Theology of the Eastern Church*" (perhaps the best of his several books translated into English). Vl. Lossky was, of course, a noted Orthodox emigre theologian (son of the Russian philosopher, Nicholas Lossky). Vl. Lossky's line of approach is rather more strictly theological, derived from the Patristic tradition; indeed, while he makes no mention specifically of Berdyaev, there are striking confluences of thought with Berdyaev. One such is a detailed discussion of apophaticism, the *via negativa* or trans-rational negative knowing, in contrast to kataphatic/positive rational knowledge. Thus, in positive kataphatic terms, one can say, that God as source of goodness is hence "good". Indeed, to superlative a degree, God is "verymost good". And yet, in over-simplified apophatic a sense, God is beyond superlative a degree of any superlative that may be said concerning Him, (sic) God as transcendent beyond all human rational constructs transcends mere "goodness", and thus, in a sense, God is "not good", as beyond all goodness. This is another example of "God, Who in revealing Himself conceals Himself", -- herein upon the rational plane. An echo of apophaticism might even help explain the strange dynamic of the Sermon on the Mount, where we are commanded to be, not merely good, but the rather to be "perfect" on the example of "Our Father", Who makes the rains

In his 1928 Journal Put' article, "The Metaphysical Problem of Freedom" (Kl.#329), Berdyaev makes very profound an observation: "Freedom lies at the basis of God's design concerning the world and man. Freedom begets evil, but without freedom there is also no good. Compulsory goodness would not be good. In this is the fundamental contradiction of freedom. The freedom for evil is, evidently, a condition for the freedom for good. Forcefully abolish evil without a trace and there remains nothing of a freedom for good. Here is why God tolerates the existence of evil".

And such perchance is the source and purpose for human freedom. But that leaves still the issue of the use of freedom in the hands of man, in his existential situation. Berdyaev distinguishes two possible paths of freedom, the positive and the negative. In the positive, man grows into a greater stature of his being, in a creative response and enrichment, whether inwardly through deepened introspection or outwardly in response to the challenges of life, amid the manifold aspects of one's "vocation" in life. Suchlike a "vocation" transcends distinctions of the narrowly religious or purely secular spheres. It involves a process of forging the human "person", much as in a fiery forge gold is purged of its dross, and steel rendered strong. Such trials and tribulations and vicissitudes of life that we survive, and tragically not all actually do, can render us stronger and finer a person. In religious a context, one might say that God awaits a free creative response from man, so as to bring the "imagio dei", innate in man, into a clearer focus and clarity of "God-likeness" ("Bogopodobnost'). This image of a fiery forging of the human person into its strengthened integrity is a recurrent thread throughout Berdyaev's writings. It is the "*gornilo somnenii*" (горнило сомнений), the crushing "*crucible of doubt*" (and "self-doubts"), that Berdyaev's colleague, (St.) Mother Maria Skobtsova, also voices in a

---

to rain on both the good and the wicked. Nietzsche, in his own wounded way, was sensitive to this, with his "Beyond Good and Evil" and "Transvaluation of All Values" concepts.

quote from somewhere in Dostovsky in her 1929 booklet, "Dostoevsky and the Present".[28] The existential angst of this "crucible of doubt" becomes at times further intensified by devastative periods of "God-forsakenness" wherein we inwardly cry out and echo the words from its most dramatic and extreme example, those uttered by Our Lord on the Cross: "My God, my God, wherefore hath Thou forsaken Me?" [Mt.27:46].[29] Mother Maria Skobtsova uttered her final "hosanna" at Ravensbrück in 1945, an example of what Orthodox hagiography tends to term as a "*strasnoterptsa*/passion-sharer".

So what of this? What sense to make of it? Anyone long married and truly caring knows well the myriad non-verbal ways that husband and wife probingly test each the other with the poignant question: "*Lovest thou me*?". It is a crucial test of the veracity and vitality of the personal bond between them. Similarly, God puts us to the test, and we in turn put God to the test with the pervasive personal question: "*Lovest thou me*?". Authentic love involves respecting the integrity of the other as an other "I", neither perceiving nor seeking to possess the other person as an "it", an object, let alone a "sex object"; in the eyes of the other one finds mirrored the affirmation of oneself as an "I", rather than as an "it/thing". Nor is this a "bad faith" betrayal of one's self, of existentially casting oneself onto the surface in playing out a "role". There are, of course, elements of "role-playing" that happen in

---

[28] "Через горнило сомнений моя осанна прошла" ["Through the crucible of doubt my hosanna has passed"], c. 6, "Достоевский и Современность", YMCA Press, Paris, 1929.

[29] "Боже мой, боже мой, вскую мя еси оставилъ". And then too, the incident, when the fickle celebrity-mongering crowd, along for the joyride of seeing the next miracle, abandon and forsake Christ, as He tearfully turns to the remaining 12 and asks, "Desire ye also to go?" [Jn.6:67] -- a rebuke stinging us to the quick, mindful of our own failings. There is the old expression: "To hell and back", the challenging path of spiritual experience trod initially by Christ via the Resurrection and beyond, indeed challenging us to "Come, follow Me!"("Гради по Мне!")... *Quo vadis*?

any healthy relationship, but these occur on the plane of the superficial. Rather, what importantly transpires is on deep a level, the proverbial meeting of souls upon the pervasive basis, the grounding of freedom. Grounded in freedom, it requires "risk", the personal openness to the risk of "hurt", upon the basis of "mutual trust". It involves a transcending of the alienation that obtains normally amongst isolated "I's", that residual sense of loneliness set amidst a crowd of "arm's-length" acquaintances nowise of the true bosom-buddy sort... In contrast to this crowd of acquaintance-strangers with whom perchance we daily rub elbows, -- stands Berdyaev and M. Buber's "I and Thou" concept, of an intimate connectivity with an other "I" as a "*thou*", rather than as the normally obtaining "*you*" in the singular case (a concept indeed archaically embedded linguistically in our Indo-Aryan and perchance other tongues).[30]

---

[30] In former times, in quite many cultures, there existed the distinction between a "literary language" (which set the sophistication of tone and mind of the culture), in contrast to the "vernacular language" of the everyday streets. And indeed historically, religion has stood at the vanguard in leading cultural creativity, whereas nowadays generally it has become an irrelvant laggard barely able or even interested in matters cultural or creative. Sadly, it devolves increasingly into the self-centred sectarian, and seems not to care... The great churches of Europe, and increasingly America also, soaring to the heights heavenward in their aspirations, now stand all too often as but tombs, mausuleums to the souls of the past; whereas modernly, churchy structures now squat earthward in their avant-gaarde efforts, dully bland and boring and insipid of taste and spirit.

In modern times, religion has suffered a "crisis of consciousness", as regards "relevance". In its facile attempts to be "relevant", it tends to render itself "irrelevant". Under the guise of "relevance", the sense of the "sacral presence", of "the sacred" approached in joyful fear and trembling and tremulation, has become dulled and lost. There is a subtle nuance of difference in the Russian words for "church", -- "tserkov'" (*церковь*) and "khram" (*храм*), the latter term more specifically rendered as "*temple*". This significant nuance finds antecedents in the Judaism of antiquity in the time of Christ: in Jewish worship of God, there was *one only* Jerusalem

In this real transcending of subjective isolation, the "I-Thou" becomes an authentic "We", i.e. a freely and inwardly impelled

---

Temple, in which a distinct priesthood "offered sacrifice" on behalf of the gathered people. Other places of Jewish worship were/are "synagogues" (literally from Grk. "gatherings-together") presided over by rabbis/teachers in "non-sacrificial" services devoted to the Scriptural. Similarly, in the Reformation splintering of Christianity in the West, Roman Catholicism has continued with the tradition of of a distinct priesthood "offering of Sacrifice", whereas Protestantism at its extremes has diminished or eliminated such, becoming as it were, a Christian sort of "synagogue" gathering. Traditionally, an unique space was reserved in the "temple" for the symbolic hence real presence of the Holy -- be it the altar area, the tabernacle, the "Holy Place" or "Holy of Holies" -- to be approached in utmost reverence. If this no longer exists, then a "temple" reverts merely into being a "church"...

Linguistically, this is also relevant. In the modern English egalitarian vernacular, "you" has supplanted the 2nd person singular use of "thou", which has come to seem quaint and archaic. Even in English historically, complex grammatical conventions governed when to address someone in the "intimate thou" in contrast to "formal you", just as the German "Du" in contrast to "Sie", and Russian "Ты" in contrast to "Вы". In historical useage, "thou" addressed someone intimately close, whereas "you" addressed strangers or mere acquaintances, someone at "arm's length". This subtle linguistic nuance is at the very core of Berdyaev and M. Buber's "I and Thou" personalist insights. More broadly, it involves liturgical useage and the language of prayer: "you" has become the general norm for addressing God, Christ, or a singular saint., even when translating prayers from languages where "thou" has been the general norm. But overlooked modernly is the *linguistic dynamic* that transpires therein: during fervent prayer where formerly we addressed whatever the saint as "thou", inviting intimate a closeness to hearken, we now tend to address that saint as "you", i.e. someone to kept at "arm's length". In effect, a gesture to be content to leave the saint remote in its statue or icon on high its pedestal, an "imploring but shoving-away". It is all part of the thoughtless egalitarian levelling of the lofty that Berdyaev deplores, as in his mocking of the radical contrast between "brother" and tovarisch"...

human sobornost'/communality, in contrast to the artificial forms of community coercively imposed by the dictate of society. This free and inwardly impelled striving for human communality, preached by even if oft poorly practiced by Christianity, is the only true basis for an authentic brotherhood of mankind, of humankind, of truly free men and women rather than cringing slaves. Berdyaev in various places mocks the Soviet proletarian innovation of addressing others as "tovarisch, "comrade", a purely utilitarian and capriciously artifical arrangement, subject to ideological whims, as Trotsky among so many others was wont to learn. Externally coerced and forcibly imposed "brotherhood", even that by legal dictates of societal collectives and states, is not authentic "brotherhood"; rather, it but masks various sorts of the "conventional lie" agendas and power ploys. Indeed, in 1939 Berdyaev penned an interesting article in the Journal "*Sovremennye zapiski*" entitled, "The Paradox of the Lie". And for Berdyaev, socialism is the progeny of capitalism, the inherited poison of its sins. In our own time, the modern state via technology has become increasingly totalitarian, irregardless of ideology, spreading a virtual spider-web of laws and regulations, stifling personal freedoms. Dostoevsky's Grand Inquistor might now indeed blush with utmost envy. The Sophists of ancient Greece were adept at twisting the basic societal needs for law to their own pecuniary profit; how little things have changed. Is it not telling then, that when Christ chose the 12 Apostles, -- none of them was a zakonik/lawyer, let alone a churchly "canon lawyer"; one of the Twelve was a repentant tax-collector (publican) and the rest were mere fishermen, even one of which turned out to be a bum...

Granting that human existential freedom actually exists within the constraints of natural necessity, that it is not merely some sort of determinist self-delusion of consciousness, resulting from chemical imbalances, -- one might ask, -- to what purpose? Is freedom some vanity plaything to indulge the human experience, in a reality fraught without meaning in any authentic validity? Our modern world would seem increasingly indicative of such. Yet, from religious a perspective, one might ask, -- why did Christ curse the barren fig tree? [Mt.21:19]. Why too the Parable of the Talents [Mt.25:14-30], with the accursed wicked sevant burying his one talent in the ground, to return it in effect "pure and inviolate", the same as when given, to the returned "Dread Master"?[31] In contrast to this hapless servant are the other servants [Mt.25:21,23] who risked and grew the talents they had been given. Sometimes in life it seems, that one must risk all, to gain all. As with the fig tree, barrenness, sterility, bears its own curse. In contrast to this, though often shoddily translated, in the Orthodox Liturgy we find the word, "*plodotvorennyi*", i.e. "*fruitful*". And similarly, in former times, sons in following out their own differing independent paths in life, sought to win glory and respect in the eyes of their father, to prove that they were indeed "their father's son". This is quite transparent in the mindset of the Russian thinker, N. F. Fedorov. But on an even more profound level, we find this echoed in the tropar for Theophany: "...for the Voice of the Father bare witness to Thee, and called Thee His Beloved Son" [cf.Mt.3:17]. A son, growing into the maturity of his powers and talents and potential, represents a positive manifestation of human freedom, a positive potentiality of fruition. For the human person, both male and female, this is the striving to bring into clearer focus for oneself what it means to be a "person", imaged of God, to bring the "imagio dei" into greater clarity of "Bogopodobnost'", as reflected in the dynamic of Persons within the MostHoly Trinity. It is for God alone to truly judge the measure of our efforts. For Berdyaev, such is freedom in positive a sense, a fruitful freedom, freedom as an actively creative response to life and to God.

But freedom can also be negative, can also lead to hatred masking as love, and to self-hatred, to viciously wanton destruction, to profoundest depths of evil. What it does therein, what it can do to the

---

[31] Strangely, this Parable of the Talents serves a a prelude to the Parable of the Dread Last Judgement, which immediately follows [Mt.25:31ff]. Sadly, certain of the Orthodox would seem to echo the duplicity of the wicked servant as regards the verymost precious "talent" of our Faith, proclaiming to "preserve it pure and inviolate, as was given" by burying it in the ground for safekeeping...

human person, is downright frightening. We are modernly bombarded with images of raging mobs, in the frenzied and hysterical grip of passions. It is quite startling, quite unsettling, to view the individual human faces, transfixed with a blinding rage and hatred. The individual human face, the human visage, the human countenance -- becomes somehow distorted, becomes tranformed into something barely to be recognised as human, of human semblance. In this distortion is something demonic, a raging demonic blood-lust. This distortion of the human visage is vividly noted also by Berdyaev, in his Gogol' section of the "Spirits of the Russian Revolution" article, which we have appended to the "Philosophy of Inequality" offering. We know all too well the increasingly pervasive cynicism and nihilism threaded throughout modern life, throughout the modern world and modern culture. And yet this is nothing new -- we remember still from our highschool Latin days of long ago the phrase, "*nihil sancti, nihil veri*" ("nothing sacred, nothing true"), spoken by Livy of that ancient scourge of Rome, Hannibal. The devil weaves a clever web of lies, under the guise of a sneering cynicism and nihilism, masked by a "progressive" positivist approach, along with utopianism. Dostoevsky was profoundly aware of this. At the very core of a nihilism run amuck lurks the demonic suggestion: "If there is no God, all is permissible!", -- a motif Dostoevsky grapples with through all his major novels. Indeed, one such novel is even entitled "*Besy*" ("Бесы", Engl. title "Devils", alt. "The Possessed"). *Besnovanie* -- under the grip of demonic delusions. "If there is no God, everything ultimately is permissible!", -- societal concordats notwithstanding, as Orwell's "Newspeak" tends to evidence.[32] A

---

[32] A verymost strange question, then, that never seems to get addressed -- is even the devil himself an "agnostic" as regards God? Both Dostoevsky's "Brothers Karamazov" and the 2nd Temptation of Christ hint at this, that even the devil is unsure whether God exists! A God Who in revealing Himself conceals Himself, Who eludes all "proofs" of His existence, both rational and otherwise, even from the devil. But then too, among modern sophisticates, even the devil has his doubters. Perhaps then this is all some

vivid example of the demonic is provided to churchly Orthodox in the Sunday Gospel passage of the "Gadara Demoniac" [Lk.8:26-40], which curiously falls closely to Halloween or shortly thereafter. In this passage, Christ has come to shore and is trodding up a desolate path, one of those kinds of places that seize upon us with an unseen sense of dread foreboding. And here before us appears this fellow, ferocious, menacing, dressed but in tatters and his limbs sporting broken fetters, a fellow veritably haunting the abandoned graveyards -- appropriate to Halloween, this is the "real McCoy", a frightful spook's spook, no mere pretend. We learn that he calls himself "Legion", from the host of demons infesting him. In torment before Christ, the demons beseech Christ not to return them to the abyss, but rather to go into the herd of swine feeding some distance off, which Christ then bade. Wherefore, seized with a mad frenzy, the whole herd of swine rush off a steep cliff to plunge over, perishing in the waters beneathe. Even swine, with their malicious beady eyes, cannot put up with being infested with demons. Picture the scene of frenzied panic, the herd of swine momentarily in mid-air, their limbs thrashing and flailing about, amidst horrid squeals. (Somewhere there exists an old woodcut of this scene, this frozen image of panic, which Schopenhauer would have criticised as improper art, for the same reasons of his criticism of the Laocoon sculpture). Truly dramatic a Gospel passage. And strange too the realisation, that Christ-God shews pity even upon the demonic; paradoxically, these same demons seem still to range raving and raging across the earth, in ever increasing fury of blood-lust and madness. Such be the depressing negative consequences of freedom...

Central to Berdyaev's thought as an existentialist philosopher is *Personalism*, the concrete unrepeatably unique individual human person. Mention of this concept of "person" has been made throughout this essay, even suggesting some aspect of analogy with the Divine Persons of the Holy Trinity. All well and good as regards

---

peculiar form of "schizophrenia", as the powerful novel "Master and Margarita", by the Russian writer, Mikhail Bulgakov, would suggest...

the realm of religious speculation. But that still leaves everything mired down in the grist and the grey uncertainties of actual life in this world, which is nowise simple a matter, especially when dealing with the complex minutiae of interpersonal relationships and challenges in the human realm. In facing this, one assumes and adopts an "axiological posture" existentially in the concrete instances, with the stance of values that one actually dons in response towards life. Berdyaev sees this personal value-positing, the choosing of the values by which one lives life, as an *active choice* (hence a true moral grounding for culpability, etc), inwardly appropriated. This stands in sharp contrast to the commonly held view of a passive response in choice, a passive obedience, to external codes of moral laws and norms.

In adopting an active "axiological posture" existentially, an active positing of the values in life by which one lives, one assumes and takes on one's shoulders actual responsibility,[33] that pang of conscience, for one's thoughts and deeds, initiated "from within" rather than "from outside". Of course, "if there is no God, then everything ultimately is permissible" -- everything thence is relative and subject to compromise. But even amongst most atheists and agnostics, in whom there has not obtained a deadening of the inner conscience, there exists some semblance of a personal moral code. But for the Smerdyakov-type scoundrel, for whom the conscience has become deadened, the only pertinent rule is, -- "Don't get caught!" Berdyaev in his later years quite often, in addressing the issues regarding the human person, resorted to the term "tselost'" (целость), the need for integrality or whole, of "having it all together", in face of the swirling forces of fragmentation and disintegration. But a preliminary step in pursuit of the integrality of person, its preliminary

[33] The Russian word for "responsibility" is "otvetstvennost'" (ответственность) deriving from the root word "otvet" (ответ) meaning "answer", -- hence, the innate intuition that "responsibility" implies "answerability", "being answerable" in one's approach to life...

foundation, would seem to be -- "integrity", howsoever antiquated the notion.

But personalism, however, and the concept of what actually constitutes "person" is a subject investigated by various disciplines with various interpretations. Our approach here, though, is in the context of Berdyaev's religio-philosophic thought. Clarity and accuracy with the terms we use is important, as are the quality of his tools for any true craftsman. Hence the initial question, -- what is the linguistic derivation of our English word "person", its historical antecedents from other tongues, from other languages that contributed to its formation in modern English? Early on in our essay we made mention of Prof. George Kline (who just recently reposed: † 21 October 2014) and his rigorous approach regarding textual translation. Many years back, in private conversation concerning the many tomes of Berdyaev's works already translated into English during Berdyaev's lifetime or shortly thereafter, Prof. Kline noted a significant flaw in this, that the English translators had haplessly translated the Russian word "lichnost'" (личность) as "personality" rather than "person". In this, Prof. Kline was eminently correct, although he did not explain why. And at first glance, it might seem like trivial a matter, but it is not. (In deference to that former generation of translators, the word "person" tends at times to be unwieldy to transpose into English within a sentence).

The Russian word for "person", "lichnost'", appears to be cognate with the Russian word "litso" (лицо), meaning face, one's visage or countenance. In this connection seems to be an echo of the Gospel image "of the eyes as the window to the soul". Reading the face of an other person is an attempt to discern the disposition concealed within. In conversing, direct and sustained eye-contact is generally difficult and awkward a proposition; for even if "to look someone in the eye" is considered the mark of an honest man, scoundrels obviously are adept at adopting this "false face" technique, necessitating some degree of perspicacity of discernment.

Our English word, "*person*", derives of course from the Latin word "*persona*", which in its meaning derives from the Greek word, "*prosopon*". But what did these terms denote in classical antiquity? Perhaps surprisingly, -- it was a "mask"! That selfsame "happy/sad face" mask that has become the symbol of the thespian art, of theatre. These were the suggestive masks used by actors anciently. Even without these prop-masks, the very art of acting involves what is but an "act", in which an actor assumes a "persona", assumes and plays out a "role", and if effective becomes consciously immersed in it. But in the final end, it is still only an "act", a "role-playing" mask, though sometimes it becomes rather more.[34] And in actual life, does being a "person" imply nothing more than living out some mere act, being but an actor, playing various roles in life to greater or lesser effect, projecting the "persona-mask" happy-faced personality, whilst inwardly lying to oneself and to others, as to the actual inner disposition of our heart and soul? The pathos evoked in the dramatic "persona" projected by, for example, Aleksandr Vertinsky's clown-visage captures this dichotomy to great effect. The "personality" that one projects is nowise necessarily the same thing as the "person" that one is. Somehow this seems apparent.

Grappling with the varied issues that arose in Christology, Greek Patristic thought provided greater clarity in terminology regarding "person". It is a terminology deriving from the mysteried Chalcedon "hypostatic union" of the two natures in the Person of Christ, couched in fourfold negative terms (Berdyaev in various of his writings laments that these were "negative terms", somewhat ignoring his own penchant for apophaticism in such regards). "Prosopon" (πρόσωπον) was still used in a general sense for "person", but the more precise and significant technical term adopted was "ὑπόστασις" ("hupostasis", modern Grk. "hypostasis"), which as

[34] St. Ardalion (14 April, 27 Apr. O.S.) was a Roman actor of pagan times, in a play meant to mock Christians as breaking under torture; St. Ardalion became so immersed in his "role" that he instead refused to renounce Christ and was thus subsequently martyred for real. Another was the actor, St. Porphyrios (15 Sept., 28 Sept. O.S.), who met similar a fate.

"hypo-stasis" means "the underlying, the *sub-stantial*, that which abidingly is set standing beneathe". Which is to say, -- that hypostasis residue which "unrepeatably" remains when all else ephemeral, the epi-phenomenal, has been stripped away. In more modern philosophic terminology, -- "*person*" is of the realm of *noumema*, whereas the ephemeral surface aspect "*personality*" is essentially of value only as a number, a statistic, a "thing" to be used and abused and thrown away as appropriate... on a par with little children dancing blithely on the graves of their forebearers [Mt.11:16-17ff.][35]...

---

[35] Concerning an astute rendering in translation, perhaps true is the Gospel adage, "qui fidelis est in minimo" [Lk.16:10], with the corollary in fecklessness to details reflecting a fecklessness to the large, the total aspect. Please note that the present writer, and ernstwhile Berdyaev translator, makes no pretense at being a Biblical scholar of any breadth; he is merely a simple priest, with a smattering of classical Greek and Latin and Slavonic, attempting to accurately convey the Gospel passage dealt with. And yes, there do exist delicate nuances of style and meaning, such that one who is an adept of only English, will perchance fail to grasp both nuance and implied meaning.

Consider, for example, the profound Mark 8:34-9:1 Gospel passage, which churchly Orthodox hear twice a year: on the 3rd Sunday of Great Lent and on the GreatFeast of the Exaltation of the Cross [14/27 September]. The Latin reads: "*Qui enim voluerit animam suam salvam facere, perdet eam...*"; i.e. "Whosoever doth will to save their soul, doth perish/lose it". How strange, since Christians are all about "saving one's soul". But the Gospel passage continues: "*qui autem perdiderit animam suam propter me, et Evangelium, salvam faciet eam*", i.e. "whoso however doth perish/lose their soul on account of Me, and the Gospel, doth save it". Yet in their rendering of this passage, almost all "authorised" English Gospel translations tend willy-nilly one after the other substitute the word "*life*" in place of "*soul*", willy-nilly unanimous, almost like shifty-eyed students glancing about during an exam over the shoulders of their fellows for the "answer". It should be noted, however, that "*psukhe, anima, dusha*" (i.e. "soul") is the actual word found in the Greek/Latin/Slavonic texts, -- not "*zoe, vita, zhizn'*" (i.e. "life"). And yet the actual original significance is

Christ or Xerxes? What again is our effectual concept of the "human person"? Is "person" nothing more than the ephemeral epiphenomena that comprise the "persona", the surface "personality", or is there some deeper and abiding durable core "constant amidst change" as the Greek inspired "hypostasis" concept would suggest? Early on in the Christian West, reflecting the Latin mindset of "persona", there arose the heresy of Sabellianism, or Modalism. Sabellianism in essence viewed the Divine Persons of the Trinity as mere fluidly transitory "modalities", three inter-changeable "personae-masks", such that each could "fill in" and substitute for the other as occasion warranted, e.g. the Son could "fill in" and peer out through the "persona-mask" of the Father, perchance grown weary and in need of a long Sabbath rest after heavy a bout of creating... Sabellianism reflects possibly the early syncretic Gnostic influences widespread in antiquity at the time, and early on it was repudiated by both Christian East and West. But its mental legacy has lived on in, for example, the "filioque" issue. But even in the "New Age" syncretic mindset, Christ, in His human manifestation, ceases to be "unrepeatably unique" (as does also each "human person"), and becomes instead repeatably only one in a long series for mankind of avatar "wise-men" sages, along with Sokrates, Buddha, etc. Psychological "negative reinforcement" can sap a person's initiative, and ultimately convince him that he is insignificant and of no consequence, with results impacting both himself and his fellow man.

---

not all that enigmatic, when connected with the image of the proverbial "Grain of Wheat" (зерно пшенично, Jn.12:24): "If a grain of wheat fallen to earth die not, then it abideth alone, but if it die, it will bring forth much fruit". Again, the concept of "fruitfulness", so unlike the accursed barren fig tree, or the wicked servant burying his talent away to safeguard and save it -- a "growth-stunted" soul. Discrepancies, such as with our example noted above, would seem moreso problematic for those whose traditio is "sola scriptura"...

Somewhat related to this displacive a perspective, Berdyaev penned a rather insightful 1927 article in Journal Put', (rather weakly) entitled: "*The Scientific Discipline of Religion and Christian Apologetics*" [Kl.#318].

Again, Christ or Xerxes? The Hellenic language of antiquity denoted anyone non-Greek as a "barbaros", which has negative a connotation in modern English. Berdyaev's "New Middle Ages" theme has affinities to Spengler, both reflecting postwar currents in the cultural milieu. Christ or Xerxes, the Greek West versus the Asiatic hordes of Xerxes, the light of civilisation versus the darkness that threatens, the noble impulses versus the dark impulses besetting indeed every society. Russia, historically a great East-West entity, itself historically the seismic boundary line between West and East, between Europe and Asia, has long faced this "crisis of consciousness". But now indeed the modern world has become smaller, has now itself become faced with the Christ-Xerxes contention of values, has now itself become faced with an existential and critical "crisis of consciousness". Despite its historical shortcomings and currently foppish decadence, even non-religious a person can recognise the unique contribution of the Judaeo-Christian legacy both to civilisation, and to humankind.

Christianity, Berdyaev suggests, exhausted its speculative genius in dealing with Christological issues, and was subsequently faced with pressing mundane matters both internal and external, and thus has been largely remiss in developing a coherent "Christian anthropology". Various of Berdyaev's journal articles address this issue, which the enterprising reader will find worthwhile to peruse directly. Four such articles by way of suggestion: 1936 "*The Problem of Man (Concerning the Construction of a Christian Anthropology)*" [Kl.#408]; 1918 "*The Revelation about Man in the Creativity of Dostoevsky*" [Kl.#294]; 1926 "*Salvation and Creativity*" [Kl.#308]; 1932 "T*he Two Concepts of Christianity*" [Kl.379].

Another central motif within Berdyaev's thought is that of "Spirit". What is *Spirit*? The realm of spirit represents a plane of reality differing from that of the physically experienced materiality, variously underlying or intersecting with, or "an other world" at times independent of, the physical plane. The realm of spirit is a realm of the unseen, of that which cannot be physically touched, cannot even be proved by any empirical proofs in positivist an approach; it is grasped only by intuition, a "primal intuition" archaic in its sources. Philosophy, as a distinct discipline, emerged in somewhat now blurred a process from the religious apperception of the ancient Greeks. The pre-Sokratic philosopher, Parmenides of Elea, spoke of two distinct paths of knowing: the "Way of Aletheia" ("Truth") and the "Way of Doxa" ("Appearances, Seeming or Opinion").[36]

---

[36] "Doxa" is obviously part of the Greek derived word, "orthodox". But, as regards linguistic derived a meaning, one might ask the seemingly absurd question: is Orthodox Christianity "orthodox"? In general English useage, the word "orthodox" in literal translation, means "right beliefs" or "correct opinions", sometimes rigidly so. The Russian tongue, however, has two distinct words for "orthodox". The first, "*ortodoks*" (ортодокс), is the generic meaning, often negative or perjorative in tone, suggesting rigid narrow-mindedness. Thus, one can even be an "orthodox" militant atheist or not, a Stalinist "orthodox" Marxist-Leninist, or not (Kautsky, Trotsky). The second Russian word, "*pravoslavnoe*" (православное) uniquely refers to the Eastern Orthodox Church. "Pravoslavnoe", literally translated, means "rightful glory". At first glance, this would seem to evidence an unimaginable shoddy translation from Greek into Church Slavonic. "*Pravoverie*" (правоверие) is the proper Russian word for "right belief". But this involved no shoddy translation: over the centuries of Greek thought spanning the time separating Parmenides from that of Christ, the Greek word "doxa" shifted meaning, -- where formerly it meant "opinion/belief", in New Testament times it came to mean "glory". Hence also our Latin derived word "doxology", meaning literally "words of glory" (Slav. "*slavoslovie*"), the glory rendered by words of praise.

Moreover, for those who would reduce Orthodox Christianity to merely a "right-belief", a "correct doxa", -- Parmenides himself provides curious a twist. For Parmenides indeed, the "Way of Doxa", the "Way of Appearances/Beliefs", -- no matter howsoever "correct" or "right", -- still is nowise the selfsame path with that of the "Way of Aletheia", the "Way of Truth", which is the important choice. Somehow still very relevant an observation.

For clarity in his translations, the present writer has tended to capitalise "Orthodox" when it refers religiously to Orthodox Christianity ("pravoslavnoe"), and to leave in lower case the generic "orthodox",

Parmenides "Way of Truth" is a path to the knowledge of reality as it really is, in contrast to how it is seemingly manifest in appearances, in believed opinions based upon appearances. (Indeed, by way of example, we know that a *mirage* can trick our senses). This insight of Parmenides, of a path to truth grounded not in appearances, finds echo later in Plato's famous metaphor of the Cave of Shadows, in contrast to the dazzling light of actual reality, in the Platonic Realm of Ideas, of Ideal Forms. Centuries later, NeoPlatonists such as Plotinos and Origen carried this perception still further, with their teaching about "Emanation", a lessening of reality the further down one descended into the varied degrees of the muck of materiality. This "other world", this Platonic Realm of Ideas, of Ideal Forms, is an eternally abiding and constant realm, in perfect unchanging stasis, albeit perchance with the seemingly contrary insights of the pre-Sokratic Herakleitos. An interesting question arises concurrently, regarding gnosseology, where if the ideational be the only authentically real, -- where stands the apprehending "centre of consciousness" in relation to this? In some ways, Parmenides seems to have anticipated Kant's noumenon/phenomenon distinction by several millenia. For Kant, the noumenon, the thing-in-itself is unknowable by reason alone and by rational thought; we know only phenomena, the manifest thing-as-appearance. In effect, this becomes an intensely scrutinised approach to even the very possibility of Parmenides "Way of Truth" via any rational faculty, in effect, a major hurdle if not opposite a conclusion from Parmenides. The scope and dynamic of German philosophy rather differs from that of ancient Greek philosophy. Berdyaev attributes this in part to the addition of a "volitional element", the aspect of *Will* so characterisitic of German thought, in Schelling, Schopenhauer, Hegel, Nietzsche et al. And Berdyaev further traces the introduction of this volitional element of the *Will* back to the influence of the German theosophist J. Boehme upon German thought. Transparent in title, Hegel's phenomenology is

---

sometimes also using instead the transliterated "*ortodoks*", as perjorative intensity might warrant.

the "Phenomenology of Spirit (Geist)". Furthermore, much of the uniquely autonomous Russian philosophy has had its initial schooling in the wellsprings of German philosophy. Kant, in a sense, frees us from an unknowable "noumenon" and leaves us adrift amidst the currents of "phenomena". The phenomenological currents in German Idealism, as with Hegel, involve an intuitional type aspect of "transcendence" (Aufgehoben) in dealing with this. The realm of the spiritual plane of reality, which for Platonism most authentically is a static realm frozen into a congealed stasis of ossified perefection, -- under German philosophy becomes "infused" with a dynamic principle, is rendered fluid with the volitional element of the *Will*. Perfection becomes subsumed to teleology. Existentialist philosophy arose in reaction to the tyranny of the Hegelian Absolute within the legacy of German Idealism, doing so in defense of the plight of the concrete individual. For Berdyaev, the spiritual plane both intersects and coheres with the natural plane "in depth", and "at depth" represents a fluid and dynamic "subterranean" realm where varied and contending underground forces interact and at times violently "erupt" onto the surface in the Zeitgeist currents of the time. Man is the focal point between time and eternity, his consciousness and apperception the intersecting point between the natural and the spiritual planes. And for philosophy in general, it is this intersection point of conscious apperception that gives rise to the myriad questions within philosophy. Furthermore, man was classically seen as threefold, comprised of body, soul and spirit, wherein the nuances of distinction between soul and spirit are also relevant of consideration.

"Spirit" is an integral aspect of Berdyaev's thought. Metaphorically, one might say that spirit is the aether through which Berdyaev's philosophy courses its way. Nor is spirit religiously neutral, autonomous from the religious aspect, as occurs with various other thinkers. Regarding this, one has but to consider the titles of some of Berdyaev's major books: "*Freedom and the Spirit*" (1927); "*Spirit and Reality*" (1937); "*The Divine and the Human*" (1947);

"*The Realm of Spirit and the Realm of Caesar*" (1949); "*Truth and Revelation*" (1953).

Mindful of Parmenides, one might ask, -- "What has spirit to do with truth?", since truth itself would seem to stand at the very heart and soul of philosophy, in its quest for wisdom. Christ or Xerxes, Christ or Caesar, Christ or the tyrannous *mirage* woven by the father of lies in his vicious rending of "this world". What has truth to do with spirit, assuming that truth actually exists, assuming that the spiritual plane of "an other world" at the deep foundational basis of "this world" actually exists... Hence the radically significant existential question, resonating to the very fibre of our being, long ago expressed in great tremulation and vexed irritation by Pontius Pilate: "*What is truth*?" ("*Что есть истина;*") [Jn.18:38]. Significant for Berdyaev, likely early on in the formation of his religious consciousness, was the penetrating insight from a post-Paschal Gospel passage, -- that spoken by Christ to the Samaritan woman at the well of Jacob in Sykhar: "*God is spirit, and they that worship Him, worship in spirit and in truth*" [Jn.4:24]. And then too, in connection with J. Boehme, Berdyaev in one of his many books evokes the profound Gospel passage: "*Spirit spirits whence it will, and its voice thou will hear, but not know from whither it doth come, nor whereof it lead: thus are all, who are born of spirit*" [Jn.3:8].[37]

---

[37] The Latin reads: "*Spiritus ubi vult spirat: et vocem eius audis, sed nescis unde veniat, aut quo vadat: sic est omnis, qui natus est ex spiritu*". The Greek word for "spirit", "*pneuma*", also connotes in meaning a "breath of wind", and hence the rendering of this passage appears in some English language lyrical renderings as, "the wind listeth as it wilt"...

Regarding Pontius Pilate again. For long centuries theologians and philosophers have constructed elaborate rational arguments and "proofs" for the existence of God, -- all which on the whole have proven rather unpersuasive, and in all honesty ultimately unconvincing. Symbolically, Pontius Pilate in standing literally face to face with truth, still failed to recognise it... Why? Perhaps because, that he was asking the *wrong question*. Perhaps instead of asking "*What* is truth?", the real question he should have asked is, "*Who* is truth?". It is a question especially quite

Finally, in summation, some closing thoughts, assuming that any reader has persevered this far. Perchance even, the thoughts expressed here may prove to be of benefit, in opening obscure paths to meaningful ideas nowise commonplace. Little effort here has been devoted to any direct analysis of the textual content of Berdyaev's "Philosophy of Inequality". Although Berdyaev in his final years revised some of his early articles, yet in a sort of vexed awe at this "period piece", he refrained from retouching "The Philosophy of Inequality". The book mustneeds speak for itself, as the *primary* text. The title itself, chosen by Berdyaev, is intentially provocative. And thus, our bias is to follow Berdyaev on this, and "let the text speak for itself". It is indelicate a matter, and perhaps a transgression against polite civility, to proffer thoughts to general an audience on the elements of Berdyaev's religious formation, under the guise and approach of a Kantian "*als ob*" ("as if") validity. It is indelicate nowadays to openly dicuss religious ideas as having "validity", rather than treating such with "objective" a distance. And indeed readers finding affinity with Berdyaev come from a wide variety of religious backgrounds, or non-backgrounds even, -- be they Christian, Jewish, agnostic or other, even Moslem or Hindu. Moreover, each person has their own derivatively unique conceptual "religious formation", originating from whatever the faith-confession or lack thereof, a factour affecting their own particular cognitive perceptions and understanding. Then too, religious education nowadays is nowise in depth the same, as it was a long generation ago, as it was under the guise of a "classical education". Our age is an age of great sophistication in one's own professional discipline, yet having lost cross-disciplinal an agility. Thus, many an English speaking Orthodox Christian, with typically erratic a religious formation, will but poorly grasp what is religiously and theologically basic in Berdyaev's thought. And thus also, other Berdyaev readers will

---

pertinent, in light of Berdyaev's existentialist personalist philosophy, with its signification relating to "person", in both the Divine and the human regard.

variously interpret his religious thoughts and sources through the refracting prism of their own faith-confessions and personal paths. The religious aspect underlying Berdyaev's thought is not something of no consequence, to be merely ignored or discarded, rather instead, it constitutes an essential core element regarding freedom, person and creativity. Berdyaev's thought, however, is not parochially sectarian but rather universal in its scope and significance, in its *qualitative aristocratism* (i.e. the qualitative "best", most truly noble), a Christian perception of both God and man, freed of any philistine element of opportunism. Insofar as theological ideas are concerned, Berdyaev's religious insights can be considered as "theologoumena", i.e. theological opinions. Our views here, in accord with Berdyaev's important distinction between theology proper and religious philosophy, constitute an effort in "religious philosophy". Berdyaev's view on man, as inherently "dignified" enough, indeed also expected by God, to offer a creatively active response both to God and to life, is critically important, and constitutes a justification of religio-philosophic thought. Here in the West currently, religion seems to have fallen under a Neo-Jannsenist and Quietist spell of passivity, of defeatist exhaustion, amidst a self-induced deep slumber of societal irrelevance, punctuated only by an occasional loud snoring on secondary matters. And if religion does not take itself seriously, why then should people, even the nominally believing, take it seriously. Christ three times commanded Peter to "Feed My sheep!", and certainly not with "stones for bread, nor vipers for fish"... A deficient diet leads to malnutrition of body, and an exclusive diet heavy on ascetic literature absent a Gospel balance, can lead to "dessicated souls" in yet living bodies, nigh close to the cultic sectarian. The convenient conceit has arisen, that Berdyaev is not truly and authentically Orthodox, that his ideas and views are at best only on the periphery of what is properly Orthodox, not "ortodoks" enough, and therefore he is not worthy of actual reading or consideration. And this dismissive view nowadays sadly seems to have extended to the legacy of Russian religious philosophy in general. One is left then to be a "*vox clamantis in deserto*". To this vacuous conceit that

Berdyaev's thought does not represent authentic an Orthodox Christianity, one might offer quite contrary an argument. Berdyaev is not some typical philosopher whose national and religious legacy is purely of irrelevant chance and circumstance, for Berdyaev rather, it reflects an important aspect in the creative synthesis of his thought. One might validly argue that Berdyaev is a Christian philosopher, and indeed verymost Christian a philosopher. Why? Precisely because of his existential personalist philosophy, in his refocusing attention to the concept of "person", to the "*who*" that constitutes the concrete individual living person, rather than the "*what*" that constitutes an abstract mankind in general ("abstract" just like that of the Marist "proletariat"). In general philosophy there exists the principle of "*commensurabilty*", of "common measure", whereby "like can only be known by like", which also forms the basis of the "Logos" gnosseology. It is on the spiritual plane of reality, since "God is spirit", that we encounter God on the commensurable basis of "person", upon the dynamics of the "I-Thou" immediacy involved, with each a living presence respecting the integrity of the other as a "thou", not an "it" held afar distant at arm's length. Respecting the integrity of the other demands freedom. Without freedom, "person" does not exist, becomes only hollow a myth. "Person" is an unfathomable mystery that each of us grapples to make sense of, in the concrete individuality of our life. It is only by plumbing the profound mystery of the human person, that there opens the primordial mystery of encountering the Living God as "person", which already is of the realm of mysticism. The mystery of the MostHoly Trinity, of the unrepeatably unique Three Divine Persons, is considered to be the penultimate mystery within Christianity. In light of this, the personalist emphasis within Berdyaev's existentialism renders him indeed verymost a Christian philosopher. The whole scope of Berdyaev's ideas, of which religious a personalism forms integral a part, remains critically important today. The title of his book, "The Philosophy of Inequality", was intended to be provocative, just as Berdyaev's philosophy tends to be provocative. Just as the long meandering thread of thought in our present essay is likely provocative, intentionally. Wherefore, it seems fitting to conclude with a provocative quote from Pontius Pilate: "*Quod scripsi, scripsi!*" [Jn.19:22].

Fr. Stephen Janos, translator

28 February 2015